DIGNITY AND LIBERTY

Constitutional Visions in Germany and the United States

Edward J. Eberle
Foreword by Donald P. Kommers

Issues in Comparative Public Law

Westport, Connecticut
London

Library of Congress Cataloging-in-Publication Data

Eberle, Edward J., 1955–
    Dignity and liberty : constitutional visions in Germany and the United States / Edward
J. Eberle ; foreword by Donald P. Kommers.
        p.   cm.
    Includes bibliographical references and index.
    ISBN 0–275–97249–6 (alk. paper) — ISBN 0–275–97491–X (pbk. : alk. paper)
    1. Personality (Law)—Germany. 2. Personality (Law)—United States. 3. Human
rights—Germany. 4. Human rights—United States. 5. Constitutional law—Germany. 6.
Constitutional law—United States. 7. Liberty. 8. Dignity. I. Title.
    K627.E238   2002
    342.43′085—dc21   2001034586

British Library Cataloguing in Publication Data is available.

Library of Congress Catalog Card Number: 2001034586
ISBN: 0–27597249–6
        0–275–97491-X (pbk.)

First published in 2002

Praeger Publishers, 88 Post Road West, Westport, CT 06881
An imprint of Greenwood Publishing Group, Inc.
www.praeger.com

10   9   8   7   6   5   4   3   2   1

Copyright Acknowledgments

The author and publisher gratefully acknowledge permission for use of the following materials:

Excerpts from Donald P. Kimmers, *The Constitutional Jurisprudence of the Federal Republic of Germany*, 1st ed. Copyright 1989, Duke University Press. All rights reserved. Reprinted with permission.

Excerpts from Edward J. Eberle, "Hate Speech, Offensive Speech, and Public Discourse in America," 29 *Wake Forest Law Review* 1135 (1994).

Excerpts from Edward J. Eberle, "Public Discourse in Contemporary Germany," 47 *Case Western Reserve Law Review* 797 (1997).

Excerpts from Edward J. Eberle, "Practical Reason: The Commercial Speech Paradigm," 42 *Case Western Reserve Law Review* 411 (1992).

Excerpts from Edward J. Eberle, "Human Dignity, Privacy and Personality in German and American Constitutional Law," *Utah Law Review* 963 (1997).

To Jane
Always My Love

Experience is the oracle of truth; and where its responses are unequivocal, they ought to be conclusive and sacred.

James Madison
Federalist Number 20

Contents

Foreword

Donald P. Kommers

Edward Eberle's book constitutes a significant addition to the literature of comparative constitutional law and interpretation. This captivating study compares selected decisions of the United States Supreme Court with equivalent cases handed down by Germany's Federal Constitutional Court. Singled out for comparison are leading German and American cases on abortion, privacy rights, and freedom of speech. (The speech cases focus mainly on the review of laws that regulate defamatory, offensive, and hateful utterances.) Controversial in both countries, these cases are important because they attempt to define the core of what the author calls "modern human personhood."

What makes these cases such marvelous candidates for comparative study and analysis is their differing perspectives on the human personality. The American cases tend to view personhood through the lens of liberty, whereas the German cases tend to view personhood through the lens of dignity. There is a textual basis for the difference. The U.S. Constitution celebrates the general value of liberty in no fewer than three crucial places (Preamble, Fifth and Fourteenth Amendments). Germany's Basic Law, by contrast, establishes dignity as its controlling value; it proclaims the "inviolability" of "human dignity" in its opening paragraph and envisions persons as the subjects of both rights and duties.

Liberty and dignity are of course converging values, and they blend together in the constitutional jurisprudence of both Germany and the United States. Claims to liberty are usually rooted in respect for dignity, just as the realization of dignity requires the exercise of liberty. But liberty often trumps dignitarian values in one system, whereas dignity often trumps libertarian values in the other. Liberty as interpreted by the Supreme Court exalts individual choice and expression, often at the expense of social values—such as reputation and civility—that any good society would revere. But as interpreted by the Federal Constitutional Court, rights such as choice and expression are subject to the scrutiny of dignity whose components include those social values—and the principle of social solidarity—deemed fundamental to human flourishing.

A major premise of this book is that Germans and Americans have a great deal to learn from each other's jurisprudence in the subject-areas under study. Professor Eberle does more than compare constitutional doctrine. He holds each country's constitutional case law up to the light of the other in a self-critical quest to define what is the best and most philosophical convincing in both bodies of law. The author's project prompts the reader to do nothing less than to wonder whether a synthesis of liberty-based and dignity-based liberalism would produce a public philosophy more worthy of our respect and admiration than one provided by any single tradition of constitutional governance.

Finally, good reasons support the comparison of Germany and the United States. First, the two countries are among the world's strongest constitutional democracies. Second, their constitutions command worldwide respect; both documents have substantially influenced the process of democratic constitution-making around the world. Third, and relatedly, their highest tribunals are arguably among the world's most powerful and prestigious courts of constitutional review. They have created sophisticated bodies of case law cited with increasing frequency by other national courts charged with the interpretation of their respective constitutions. So what they have to say about the meaning of liberty and personhood in our time truly matters.

Preface

This is a book about human personality. By human personality I mean the essential traits or characteristics that constitute us as human beings. Now certainly the idea of human personality is a complicated one, studied through the ages, and one studied from innumerable perspectives: philosophical, psychological, social, or artistic. Each of these perspectives, and others too numerous to mention, illuminates something vital about the human condition. Any complete study of human personhood would have to encompass these dimensions.

This book addresses one of these perspectives—constitutionalism—a dominant force of modern times. Constitutionalism—the fixing of principles and values as society's highest law—reflects important dimensions of human personality, dimensions that for the most part have not been extensively explored. One aim of this book is to shed light on this important perspective. Constitutionalism as a force is a fairly recent phenomenon. It can be traceable to the English experience in the 1600s, or, through philosophic speculation, even earlier. But the main experiment in constitutionalism—in the sense of running a country by a constitution—is the American one, starting in 1787.

Constitutionalism does not offer a complete view of the human person. But it does offer unique perspectives. Constitutionalism reflects those traits of human personality valued especially highly in the constitutional order, such as freedom of expression, freedom of conscience, or equality. Traits such as these evidence society's judgment that they are indispensable to the human condition. Thus, an examination of human personality as situated within a constitutional setting is a rich field of study. This is especially the case because constitutionalism, in one form or another, is a dominant force today. Countries newly formed or newly constituted in the post–World War II era and after the Cold War search for new meanings and values on which to base and organize society.

The book draws upon the perspective and experiences of two countries, the United States and Germany. Today, both these countries are highly developed constitutional orders. Each provides well-tested and alternative strategies for achieving the proper balance between human freedom and social order. In our interdependent global world, it makes sense to step outside our native culture and assess ideas from a cross-cultural view. Comparative study is especially valuable in illuminating deeper perspectives about the nature of human personhood. Often we learn best by comparing our lives to others. We can then get better perspectives on ourselves. This is certainly the intention of this book. As concerns this study, the comparative perspective helps identify human traits or values that are transcendent, resonating across borders, and not dependent on a specific culture.

I have settled on a study directed at uncovering a core of human personhood within society. This core comprises human dignity; freedom to act; freedom to develop within, including along a more spiritual sphere; freedom of identity, autonomy, and self-determination; and freedom of expression. These traits comprise a core component of modern human personhood as conceived in a constitutional setting in Western culture.

A broader study could easily have included additional traits. Religious belief and exercise, freedom of conscience, family, and equality would have been worthy of study as well. Likewise, for the traits examined, a more comprehensive evaluation could have been undertaken. For example, worthy topics of freedom of expression beyond those surveyed would be pornography and obscenity, violence, and new technologies, such as the Internet. Moreover, because Germany is a signatory to the European Convention for the Protection of Human Rights and Fundamental Freedoms and is a member of the European Union, examination of these European dimensions of German constitutionalism would have been fruitful as well. However, pursuit of these matters would have substantially increased the scope of this study. My main aim was less a comprehensive study and more a search for an essence of human personality and freedom in modern society. This book, thus, has as its focus the distillation of a silhouette of human personality and, in addition, an assessment of the force of modern constitutionalism in this endeavor in the two societies under review, Germany and the United States.

Acknowledgments

I conceived this book over the past several years and owe its existence to work done in earlier articles that explored and developed these themes. The book relies, in certain respects, on these earlier articles of mine: "Hate Speech, Offensive Speech, and Public Discourse in America," 29 *Wake Forest Law Review* 1135 (1994); "Public Discourse in Contemporary Germany," 47 *Case Western Reserve Law Review* 797 (1997); "Practical Reason: The Commercial Speech Paradigm," 42 *Case Western Reserve Law Review* 411 (1992); and "Human Dignity, Privacy, and Personality in German and American Constitutional Law," 1997 *Utah Law Review* 963. These articles served as a foundation for the book. The translations are mine unless otherwise noted.

I owe a debt of gratitude to many people who read and commented on these earlier articles. Another round of thanks is due them: Jay Conison, David Day, Dan Farber, Mary Shacklett, David Currie, Donald Kommers, and Bodo Pieroth. My valued friend, Dick Huber, read the whole manuscript. I owe Dick special gratitude for his sage advice and support, for this project and over the years. Also reading and commenting on the whole manuscript were Werner F. Ebke, Donald Kommers, and Cliff Larsen. Special thanks and gratitude to all of them.

Thanks are also in order to a number of persons and institutions that encouraged and supported this project. Special thanks go to Bernhard Grossfeld of the Universität Münster, who arranged my visit at the university's Institute on International Business Law and Comparative Law in the summer of 1995. I would also like to thank the German Marshall Fund, which underwrote my travel and scholarship for that period. Special thanks also go to Werner F. Ebke of the Universität Konstanz, who arranged for my visit as a visiting professor at that university in the summer of 1998. These stays in Germany were instrumental in providing me with the time and opportunity to develop the project. Versions of portions of this book were presented at the Universities of Erlangen, Konstanz, and Münster in Germany, and Roger Williams in the United States. I thank the many colleagues at these institutions who commented on the presentations. I also want to thank Winfried Brugger of the Universität Heidelberg, who read the manuscript and provided invaluable support. And I want to thank my editor, Michael Hermann.

Thanks also go to Deans John Ryan, Bruce Kogan, Matt Harrington, and Harvey Rishikoff, who supported my travel and scholarship, especially by giving me the time to bring the project to completion. A number of research assistants researched points and collected materials. Thanks are thus in order to Debra Noll, Eric Schweibenz, Christine Fraser, Jennifer St. Laurent, and Patricia Holmes. The librarians at Roger Williams also provided valuable support. Thanks especially go to Gail Winson, Stephanie Edwards, Nan Balliot, and Donna Miller. My secretary, Theresa Kruczek, provided excellent support, and I am grateful to her.

Finally, I wish to thank my wife, Jane, to whom this book is dedicated, and my children, Sarah and Ben, for their love and support. And I also wish to thank my parents, Edward and Elfriede Eberle, for their love and support.

Introduction

The quest for human dignity in modern society is a noble but elusive goal. Difficult to define and difficult to realize, personally or socially, dignity nevertheless remains a defining trait of human character, and a preeminent ideal of any civilized society.[1] From the perspective of an individual, dignity might be thought of as the ability to pursue one's rights, claims, or interests in daily life so that one can attain full realization of one's talents, ambitions, or abilities, as one would like. That is one path to satisfaction, social recognition, and stature, certainly attributes of dignity. This might be thought of as self-realization, although that is not the only conception of dignity. What matters here is that each person should be free to develop his or her own personality to the fullest, subject only to restrictions arising from others' pursuit of the same.

Of course, there must be some limit to individual freedom if society is to function in a reasonably orderly manner. Thus, from the standpoint of society, individual aspiration must be measured against the demand for order, peace, and social harmony. The balance between the aspiration of individual freedom and the demands of organized society has been a central quest of modern constitutional law.[2]

Today this balance is harder than ever to achieve. Social demands have escalated, placing elevated pressures on the integrity of human personhood. We live in the global economy, a world where business is transacted and ideas are exchanged instantaneously, through telephone, computers, e-mail, and fax, and where distances are bridged almost completely. One can buy stocks in the morning on the New York Stock Exchange and wake up the next day to see their value affected by developments in Japan, Russia, or South Africa. Countries and people are linked together as never before, economically, communicatively, and by methods of transportation. The global economy has produced unprecedented wealth, as countries, companies, and individuals have found their niche. The lessons of David Ricardo's "comparative advantage," by which nations would produce goods in which they have an advantage, has perhaps never been put to practice so diligently. There is, indeed, a "wealth of nations."

But it is less obvious whether globalization brings a wealth of human happiness and fulfillment as well. There are, in fact, human costs to globalization, costs that often are underappreciated in the pursuit of material wealth. Costs include pressures to choose the right job, be adaptable, learn to learn new skills, and live in cyberspace as well as normal space. If left unchecked, these pressures have a propensity to contort human character, as decision makers and economic planners tend to measure value, including human worth, in terms of what, economically, is added to the unit of production. This has resulted in severe pressure to conform to the dynamics of globalization. For many, the choice is conform, exit, or wither. The market exacts a toll on people and society. The twenty-first century thus poses severe challenges to human freedom and happiness. These are the challenges for our generation.

With globalization goes increased internationalization, which poses its own challenges to human freedom. Both in the United States and in the countries of Europe, government is downsizing at a national level and upsizing at an international level. In the countries of Europe, the harmonization process of the European Union has a deep and pervasive effect on the daily life of Europeans. European Union regulations dictate the size, quality, and character of wine, beer, sausage, and spirits; requirements for cars, construction, and professions; and rules for product liability, consumer protection, insurance, and banking, among other matters. There is a sense of loss of control over one's destiny. In France, truck drivers blockaded the nation's highways, bringing traffic to a standstill, in protest over stagnating wages due to the country's rush to meet the economic criteria for the European currency union. The common currency itself, the euro, marks a loss of national control, as monetary policy has now shifted to a European Central Bank. In national polls, Germans overwhelmingly expressed anxiety about their loss of the deutsche mark for the unproven euro. Denmark rejected participation in the monetary experiment. National referenda on approval of the 1992 Maastrict Treaty on European Union resulted in some defeats, and also narrow approvals, including in Denmark and France. In December 2000 the heads of state of European Union members agreed to enlarge the European Union by admitting Central and Eastern European countries. The broadening of the European Union will help end the division on the European continent caused by the Cold War.

The trend is similar in America. There is increasing convergence in the economies and societies of North America, through the fountainhead of the North American Free Trade Agreement (NAFTA) and its coming expansion. Planners project a wide free market in the Americas, from Canada to Chile. In America today a person can buy fresh fruit year round, supplied by South America as well as traditional sources such as California and Florida. Despite such benefits, politicians frequently decry the transfer of sovereignty to the World Trade Organization (WTO) and commitment to the International Monetary Fund (IMF), as such economic organizations increasingly penetrate national economies, forming a web of interlocking arrangements among the countries of the world. The summer of 1998 financial crisis in Asia rippled from market to market across national borders, causing, in part, the near collapse of Russia and a steep, simultaneous correction in the stock markets of the world. Such interlinkage in economies vividly demonstrates that most national developments have worldwide implications. On both sides of the Atlantic, layers of government intensify at international levels. What remains to be seen is whether increased bureaucratization will enhance and ennoble the human race, or stifle it.

There are other challenges to human satisfaction. Technology now develops so rapidly and pervasively that it risks overwhelming individuality. The average life of a generation of computers is from six to twelve months. Computers can gather, store, and transmit information so capably that they can access and even mimic human functions. Ideas once foreseen only in the movies (such as Hal, the all-knowing but ultimately paranoid computer in *2001: A Space Odyssey*) are becoming everyday realities. IBM recently constructed a computer, Deep Blue, that capably challenged Garry Kasparov, the reigning world champion, in a game of chess. Deep Blue, which never tired, frustrated Kasparov and triumphed. Gene technology, cloning, artificial insemination, and the ability to prolong and, indeed, end life pose troubling existential questions. How are we coping in this world, in isolation or in comparison to others?

This book takes up these themes by exploring the concept of human dignity, as reflected in the legal order of two comparable modern Western societies: Germany and America. We live in the global economy, where one country is no longer isolated from another. Americans, once "kindly separated by nature and a wide ocean," as Thomas Jefferson famously observed, are no longer insulated.[3] Ideas, as well as goods and services, speed across national borders, and thus it seems appropriate, as global citizens, to consider new ideas and new perspectives beyond national borders as we search for a better understanding of ourselves and the human condition, one that is perhaps better equipped to deal with the constant change of our world, including the ubiquity of globalization. This book proposes to do just that by examing the conceptions of human liberty and personality in the two societies. The book contrasts the countries' alternative visions of human dignity, autonomy or self-determination, and freedom of expression—central traits of Western man—as developed within the constitutional orders of the two societies.

Germany and America are a good choice for the comparison. They are the two economic giants of the Western world. The U.S. economy is the largest in the world. Germany's is the fourth largest, behind Japan and China, producing over one-quarter of the gross economic product of the European Union. Germany is the world's second-biggest trading nation after the United States. Both Germany and America share similar European intellectual and cultural influences. Gottfried Leibnitz (who contemporaneously with Isaac Newton invented calculus, among other accomplishments), Alexander and Wilhelm von Humboldt, and Johann Wolfgang von Goethe were leading figures of the Enlightenment and its aftermath that decisively influenced the young United States. From Germany, the United States inherited the research university (modeled on Wilhelm von Humboldt's ideas); from the United States, Germany learned high constitutionalism. Both countries are highly developed, advanced industrial societies, coping with change and technological revolution. Both countries strive to meet the aspiration of individual freedom within a stable social construct. And both countries are liberal democracies committed to the idea of human liberty and human satisfaction. In short, there is much that the two countries have in common.

Human dignity is, of course, an elusive concept to define. One might consult the wealth of philosophic speculation through the ages, perusing the work of Plato, Aristotle, Thomas Aquinas, or Kant. The musings of poets might also reveal truth. Or, in contemporary culture, psychological perspectives would add insight. For our purposes, however, we will concentrate on the constitutional law of both countries. It makes sense to focus on the constitutional law of the countries because recording in a constitution a culture's highest values is a defining attribute of Western society. Western society, in particular, is a culture organized by law, stating its fundamental structural principles in written law. Written law is a mark of our age, as oral traditions were of ancient Greece or Native American culture. Commitment to written law is the case in both the United States and Germany. In Germany, the Basic Law (the country's fundamental charter), as interpreted by the Constitutional Court (the highest court in constitutional matters), guides and organizes society. In the United States, the Supreme Court has long secured the role of declaring out of the fabric of the Constitution the most fundamental values for the social order. Both countries are thus heavily committed to the idea of constitutionalism.

In particular, we will explore how persons are free to develop their personalities. A person might choose, for example, to be let alone as master of his or her realm. Or one might vigorously engage in the affairs of the day. Or a person might choose to do both, sometimes seeking solitude, sometimes engaging in activity. In Germany, these matters are covered in the right to the free unfolding of personality; in the United States, this is the topic of privacy rights, including the zone of personal autonomy that emanates therefrom.

By exploring this concept of human dignity in each constitutional order, insight can be derived as to the quality of the human condition, the reach of individual freedom, and the makeup of the social order. The particular traits, activities, or essences sought to be realized by each country reveal something important about human personality as it relates to society. We can thus discern a silhouette of human character as it develops and functions in modern society. Likewise, the limitations on freedom articulated are instructive of the social structure sought to be created. In short, the balance struck between individual freedom and the social order illuminates the legal culture. We can then see, perhaps, what vision or visions of human nature best suit the challenges of our day.

It makes particular sense to focus on these concepts from a cross-cultural perspective. First, it is important to realize that there are other visions of humanity beyond our own that may be ennobling or enriching or both. Second, it is worthwhile to explore the similarities and differences in constitutional vision and doctrine, in itself and as a basis for assessing the transplantation of legal norms. Third, this comparison may yield a set of higher principles of constitutional order or a sounder public law philosophy than what is customary for the country. Fourth, the foreign legal regime may serve as an alternative standard by which to measure the work of the native court. Fifth, in an increasingly interdependent world, realization of a mutual cultural influence may prove beneficial.[4] This is particularly important to the United States, whose Constitution has been an inspiration to many in the world, but yet remains insular in relation to outside ideas. Only recently has there been a desire, by some, to examine thoughts in other countries.[5] Sixth, through study of other cultures, we learn, by comparison, something important about ourselves. "For only by making comparison can we distinguish ourselves from others and discover who we are, in order to become all that we are meant to be."[6] So understanding ourselves by comparing is perhaps the main mission of comparative law.

While Germany and the United States share many features in their constitutional structures, such as separation of powers, federalism, and an independent court committed to judicial review, each country ultimately has a different constitutional strategy to realize the objective of securing liberty and human happiness. Americans believe in individual liberty more than any other value. For Americans, this means freedom to do what you choose. From a legal standpoint, such freedom actually means freedom from government and official control. But ideas of the American Constitution, and the legal order, take on a meaning in the hearts and minds of citizens different than the strict legal interpretation. The Supreme Court, through its rulings and language, plays an important role in the building of culture. The rhetoric of the Supreme Court resonates in the American mind, and helps set the tone of society. Thus, Americans internalize the idea of freedom—regardless of technical legal usage—so that it takes on the additional meanings of cultural and social liberty. In this sense, freedom means the ability to do what you like. Left to one's own devices, a person may pursue his or her own vision of liberty and happiness. In this way, freedom or autonomy is the central aim of the American constitutional order, as developed by the Supreme Court and believed by most Americans. Americans thereby place tremendous faith in individual merit and ability. Americans believe individuals can best discern their own best interests and, collectively, the path of society.

No American principle of law demonstrates this concept of individual liberty better than the idea of free speech. Free speech represents freedom, freedom to think as one likes, say what one feels or believes, and imagine or recreate oneself as one would like. Free speech thus becomes a zone of near absolute freedom, a freedom striving to transcend oneself and the social order in an ethereal search for truth or one's place. Free speech functions legally, as well as symbolically, in promoting this vision of individuality. In this sense, free speech is the embodiment of the preeminent value of American society: liberty. As reflected in American constitutional law and filtered into American society, free speech is indeed the archetypal American freedom.

Germany has a different constitutional strategy. Arising from the horrors of the Nazi time, the founders of the Federal Republic drew deep upon German tradition to found the legal order on moral and rational idealism, particularly that of Kant and Hegel. The framers of the basic charter, the Basic Law, thus designed a legal system around objectively ordered principles, rooted in justice and equality, that restore the centrality of humanity to the social order, and thereby secure a democratic society on this basis. These principles are not to be sacrificed for the exigencies of the day, as had been the case during the Nazi era.

At the top of this value structure is human dignity, which "shall be inviolable."[7] By human dignity Germans mean that each person must always be treated as an end in himself or herself, and that the intrinsic dignity of each person consists of realizing and acknowledging that person as an independent personality. For example, violence in film or literature may be restricted in its access to youth if it portrays people as inhumane, depraved, or as mere objects. Capital punishment is prohibited by the Basic Law, as is life imprisonment without possibility of parole, because no person is so depraved that he or she can entirely be beyond rehabilitation. In this sense, human dignity is the central value of the German social order, as liberty—especially its cognate, free speech—is of American society.

As the essence of each legal order, human dignity and freedom of expression (as the embodiment of liberty) form a natural point of comparison over the nature of freedom and individuality in each society. We can speak of a German constitution of dignity as compared to an American constitution of liberty, as Donald Kommers observes.[8] I have also chosen to examine the idea of personality, and its cognates, privacy and autonomy, which radiate in both legal systems. The idea of personality thus provides a nice bridge between the two cultures. These three values coalesce to form an insightful portrait of human character in each society. Other values might also profitably be examined, such as religion, freedom of conscience, or equality. But I have chosen to focus on the human composite of dignity, personality, and expression because these are,

I believe, the central reflections of the two legal orders. Through this comparison, we can then discover how the two societies converge and diverge over the idea of human freedom.

To further the aims of the book, some grounding in German and United States constitutional law is first necessary, particularly their protection of human dignity. This is the subject of Chapter 1. In particular, we need to see how German law contrasts with American law. For example, the Basic Law comprises a set of objectively ordered principles, enumerating both individual rights and duties, whereas the U.S. Constitution is value-neutral pursuant to a scheme of negative liberties, specifically enumerating rights or principles that government may not infringe, but not stating comparable duties citizens must assume or values government must realize. Thus, there is a difference in the nature of the constitutional polity and the idea of personal freedom. In Germany, freedom is defined within the social community; one exercises individual rights with an eye toward social responsibilities. In the United States, freedom is the right to do what one wants; rights do not ordinarily carry corresponding duties, except those that society might reasonably impose.

Chapter 2 examines the idea of human dignity in the constitutional orders of Germany and the United States. The German constitutional order centers upon human dignity and the free unfolding of human personality within the social community. This determination reflects the conscious intention to elevate modern Germany beyond the inhumanity of Nazism, signaling a new constitutional order. As the central value of the Basic Law, human dignity infuses the whole legal order, obligating the state to both protect it and realize it. Human dignity thus requires, for example, respect for human life, which has resulted in the Constitutional Court's circumscription of abortion and prohibition of capital punishment.

By contrast, American constitutional law has never really sought to define or invigorate human dignity as an animating idea. No idea of human dignity outlaws capital punishment or limits life imprisonment. Rather than helping society's most wretched, Americans are prone to seek retribution. The focus in the United States has been, instead, on outlining the limits of government and preserving individual spheres of autonomy—a private liberty—more than commitment to any substantive value structure, like human dignity, or establishing minimum conditions of human subsistence. Self-sufficiency, independence, and personal responsibility is the language of America, not community, human solidarity, or *fraternité*.

The book then turns to an elaboration of human dignity as developed in German and American personality rights, and evaluates personality law from three components. Freedom of action, elaborated in Chapter 3, is outward in focus. It empowers one to do fundamentally what one desires insofar as such actions do not interfere with others or the constraints of the social order. German law has developed this concept of freedom comprehensively, protecting activities like freedom to travel or pursuit of a sport or occupation. In the United States, by comparison, there is no comprehensive constitutional concept of a general freedom of action, entitling persons to do what they like within the constraints of the social order. The concept is more likely to be handled under general private law concepts, like tort, contract, or property.

A second component of personality law is inward in orientation, a contrasting opposite of freedom of action. In German law this covers such matters as privacy, informational self-determination (control over personal information), and rights to control presentation of oneself in society, including control over one's words, images, portrait, and reputation. These matters are covered in Chapter 4. The personal sphere delimits an essential core of privacy in which one can fundamentally determine who one is and how one should relate to the world, if at all. German law is more highly developed on these points than American law.

Chapter 5 explores a third component of personality, constitutional issues central to personal identity, self-determination, and autonomy. This area provides the greatest overlap between German and American law. In German law, this has entailed a search for biological parenthood, sexual identity, and rights to one's name, among other matters. In American law, self-determination has encompassed control over procreation, conception, marriage, and child rearing, to name a few of the human affairs captured. The American approach has been more selective than the German, concentrating on identifying those personal freedoms thought to be "fundamental" or "implicit in the concept of ordered liberty."[9] As American law is grounded in privacy, not personality, it resonates more with the idea of a right to be let alone than any concern for well-being, as with the Germans. These three components—outer freedom, inner freedom, and self-determination—form a composite of some central characteristics of human personality as developed in the constitutional order.

Chapter 6 continues this discussion of human personality by evaluating the growing convergence in German and American law over abortion, a searing issue of our time meriting separate treatment. Starting from different constitutional premises and different original judicial precedents, both courts appear to have had their eyes on one another in structuring a similar solution to this vexing problem of modern society. In addition to capturing this trait of human personality, examination of abortion allows us to focus carefully on the balance struck, in modern society, between liberty and order. Abortion, as much as any issue, tests the ability to maintain social harmony amidst partisan forces.

Chapter 7 discusses freedom of expression as a final freedom illuminative of the nature of personality in both cultures. Free speech is the central value of the American constitutional order, as made evident through the work of the Supreme Court, which has privileged extraordinarily the right to engage in free speech. Justice Cardozo captured this sense of American law well when he observed that free speech is "the matrix, the indispensable condition of nearly every other form of freedom."[10] The American romance with free speech is emblematic of Americans' search for personal liberty. German law will be assessed against the more absolute nature of American law. German expression freedoms are more circumscribed, notwithstanding a recent pronounced emphasis on the right to say what one likes.

The final chapter of the book explores the contrasting visions of human personality, freedom, and community in the two countries in order to achieve a better understanding of the quality of the human condition and the reach of individual freedom, and a better sense, enriched from a transnational perspective, of the appropriate balance to be struck between liberty and society. We can then assess more perceptively the countries' contrasting views of human dignity and the comparative strength of their constitutional visions. Maybe then we can start down the path of becoming global citizens, part of a global community, and not just traders in the world.

NOTES

1. In Western thought the most definitive elaboration of the concept of human dignity is in the work of Immanuel Kant, especially his seminal FOUNDATIONS OF THE METAPHYSICS OF MORALS 39 (L.W. Beck trans., 2d ed. 1959) ("Act so that you treat humanity, whether in your own person or in that of another, always as an end and never as a means only"). The ideas expressed in this introduction are developed in Edward J. Eberle, *Human Dignity, Privacy, and Personality in German and American Constitutional Law*, 1997 Utah Law Review 963.

2. A fine expression of this idea exists, by Justice John Harlan, in the Supreme Court case of Poe v. Ullman, 367 U.S. 497, 542 (1961) (Harlan, J. dissenting) ("Due process has not been reduced to any formula; its content cannot be determined by reference to any code. The best that can be said is that through the course of this Court's decisions it has represented the balance which our Nation, built upon postulates of respect for the liberty of the individual, has struck between that liberty and the demands of organized society").

3. THOMAS JEFFERSON, *Inaugural Address, in* THE LIFE AND SELECTED WRITINGS OF THOMAS JEFFERSON 323, edited by Adrienne Koch and William Peden (New York, Modern Library 1944).

4. These points are noted in Edward J. Eberle, *Public Discourse in Contemporary Germany*, 47 CASE W. RES. L. REV. 797, 804 (1997). *See also* Donald P. Kommers, *The Jurisprudence of Free Speech in the United States and the Federal Republic of Germany*, 53 S. CALI. L. REV. 657, 658–59 (1980); Bodo Pieroth, *An Essay on an Export from the United States: Constitutional Doctrine and Ideas*, 9 ST. LOUIS U. PUB. L. REV. 311, 322 (1990).

5. For example, Chief Justice Rehnquist remarked, on the forty-fifth anniversary of the Basic Law, before a conference of German and American lawyers, that "it is time that United States courts begin looking to the decisions of other constitutional courts to aid them in their own deliberative process." Chief Justice Rehnquist's remarks are cited by Professor Donald P. Kommers in a speech, "Can German Constitutionalism Serve as a Model for the United States?" presented July 24, 1998, at the University of Heidelberg, Germany. Likewise, Justice Breyer recently encouraged pursuit of comparative constitutionalism, at a November 1998 conference in New York City. Both Chief Justice Rehnquist and Justice Breyer seem to be following their advice, in deed as well as words. In Washington v. Glucksberg, 521 U.S. 702, 734 (1997), the Court, in an opinion by Chief Justice Rehnquist, reviewed other countries' treatment of assisted suicide, especially the Dutch experience, in rejecting a constitutional right to die. In Printz v. United States, 521 U.S. 898, 976–77 (1997), Justice Breyer, in his dissent, undertook an extensive inventory of comparable federal systems, including those of Switzerland, Germany, and the European Union, in seeking illumination of the proper relationship between the federal and state governments in the United States. These developments, coming in 1997, are encouraging and, perhaps, portend the twenty-first century as the one for comparative constitutionalism. Yet they must be tempered by the common skepticism about such endeavors. Note, for example, Justice Scalia's view, also in *Printz*, 521 U.S. at 921 n. 11: "We think such comparative analysis inappropriate to the task of interpreting a constitution, though it was of course quite relevant to the task of writing one."

6. Thomas Mann, *Joseph in Egypt, translated in* David P. Currie, THE CONSTITUTION OF THE FEDERAL REPUBLIC OF GERMANY (1994) (1933).

7. GRUNDGESETZ [GG] art. 1(1).

8. Kommers, *supra* note 5.

9. Palko v. Connecticut, 302 U.S. 319, 325 (1937).

10. *Id.* at 327.

1

The Constitutions of America and Germany

AMERICA

In 1787, Americans wrote a Constitution, forming one of the great experiments in government: the idea of a society ruled by written, ultimate law. Law forms the basis by which society is to be brought under the control of reason.[1] As first declared in the 1780 Massachusetts Constitution, in Article XXX, and later reaffirmed in the famous 1803 case of *Marbury v. Madison*, American democracy is to be "a government of laws and not of men." Early Americans had experienced the perils of rule by men, first under King George III of England, and then under the Articles of Confederation (1781–1788), with the human passion, factionalism, and self-interest engendered by the initial experiment in democracy. Thus, the Constitutional Convention, during 1787, served as the fulcrum by which to reconceive the notion of republicanism. Out of the Convention, held behind closed doors, came the Constitution, the oldest and shortest written charter of its type in the world. The Constitution has been a great success in taming the passions of men and women and channeling human impulse along carefully chosen principles, such as separation of powers, equality, and freedom of conscience. Commitment to ideals like these—over and above human desire—is what we commonly call our "higher law"; that is, the fundamental principles that guide and limit human conduct. Higher law is the paramount organizing principle of society, binding all, playing the role of past kings and queens in the Old World. It is perhaps the greatest accomplishment of the American experiment in government. The goal of rule by law has been substantially realized. Today, the American Constitution is the most enduring continuous written charter in the world, for which Americans can be justly proud.

The American Constitution arose from Enlightenment thought on the science and theory of government. American Framers, such as Jefferson and Madison, studied the history and science of government carefully, especially turning to the thought and practice of ancient Rome, England, France, and Switzerland. From Rome, they took the original idea of republicanism, dividing representation into two houses, a Senate, modeled on the Roman Senate, and a chamber for citizen representation, the House of Representatives. From the practices of English mixed government (a government shared by monarch and Parliament), they devised a sharing-of-power arrangement. From Swiss experience, they took the modern idea of republicanism and confederation of sovereign cantons, transforming it into a new version of federalism. And from the great French thinker Montesquieu they devised their own separation-of-powers strategy.[2] From these European sources, Americans fashioned a new version of republicanism. The American version featured balanced government, the spreading of government power among three coordinate branches of the legislature, executive, and judiciary, and the additional division of power among federal departments and sovereign state governments.

This separation of power reflected the great insight of Madison over human nature. People, when in power, could not be trusted over the long term to rule with wisdom and disinterest for the common good of all. So Madison added three prominent innovations to republican theory. First, each of the federal branches was vested with power to resist encroachments of the other branches. Officials exercising power unwisely could best be checked by other officials with the power to resist them. "Ambition must be made to counteract ambition," Madison observed in Federalist No. 51. "The interest of the man must be connected with the constitutional rights of the place." After all, as Madison continued, "What is government itself, but the greatest of all reflections on human nature? If men were angels, no government would be necessary. If angels were to govern men, neither external nor internal controls on government would be necessary." So, for Madison, the problem lay in how government could "control itself." "A dependence on the people is, no doubt, the primary control on the government; but experience has taught mankind the necessity of auxiliary precautions."

The second "auxiliary precaution" was the elevation of the judicial branch as a third, coordinate, coequal branch of government. No society previously entrusted control of the government, even in part, to judges. Thus, elevation of the judiciary to the levers of power was a very notable innovation to republican theory.

The courts were designed to be an intermediate body between the people and the legislature, in order, among other things, to keep the latter within the limits assigned to their authority. The interpretation of the laws is the proper and peculiar province of the courts. A constitution is, in fact, and must be regarded by the judges, as a fundamental law. . . . If there should be an irreconcilable variance between [the constitution and the legislature] . . . that which has the superior obligation and validity ought, of course, to be preferred; or, in other words, the Constitution ought to be preferred to the statute, the intention of the people to the intention of their agents.[3]

Elevation of the courts to the forefront of society set the stage for the creation of American "higher law," a republic governed by the written word of the Constitution as interpreted by the court. Such cogoverning of society by the courts was a radical innovation in the science of government, constituting the world's first experiment in judicial control of the levers of power. Today the role of the Supreme Court in relation to democracy is a controversial and unresolved question, known as the "counter-majoritarian difficulty."[4] By counter-majoritarian difficulty, scholars mean a rule by unelected judges, which poses a quandary in a democracy of elected officials. Each generation tries to come to terms with the place of the courts in society.

A third innovation was the designation of the people—not a monarch or parliament—as the ultimate sovereign. This was a revolutionary idea, announcing a clean break from Europe, where government ruled over people. "The government of the Union . . . is, emphatically and truly, a government of the people. In form, and substance, it emanates from them."[5] All forms of American government are ultimately beholden to the people, their ultimate ruler. "The power of the people is superior to [the legislature and judiciary]; and that where the will of the legislature, declared in its statute, stands in opposition to that of the people, declared in the Constitution, the judges ought to be governed by the latter rather than the former."[6] That is what Americans mean by the idea "We the people."[7] Through the idea of people as ultimate sovereign, the Court was able to cement the principle that the federal government, acting through "the legislature of the Union alone, [where] all [are] represented,"[8] possesses the peoples' necessary confidence so that only it can truly govern on behalf of the nation. In this manner, the federal government, representing all the people, was made supreme over the states.

Other important ideas animated the American Constitution as well. Among the most notable were the social contract theories of Locke and Hobbes and, especially, Locke's theory of natural rights. Americans transformed Locke's idea that men formed society primarily to secure their natural rights of life, liberty, and property into a more basic demand of "inalienable liberty" for individuals within society. The cry for inalienable liberty seemed, in eighteenth-century America, the proper response to perceived foreign oppression and the desire for human satisfaction.

At the root of this American vision is the clear premise that the pursuit of happiness is best secured by careful delineation and limitation of the power of government. The main preoccupation of the Framers was, in fact, defining the proper role of government. With government properly assigned to its own sphere, people could be left alone to determine their best interests.

In the original scheme, an appeal to and inculcation of civic virtue was thought by some, especially those known as Antifederalists, sufficient to contain human impulse. For the framing generation, civic virtue depended on a willingness of citizens to subordinate their private interests to the general good.[9] Natural leaders within communities, such as ministers, educators, or lawyers, would inculcate virtue, proper values, and right patterns of conduct and behavior, by example and exhortation, so that communities as a whole could discern the true common good, selecting the values that would control public and private life. This "civic republicanism" lay at the heart of the American experiment, and was envisioned as one of the main constraints on excessive individualism. America depended on the good character of its citizens more than other countries, as Madison observed in his *Federalist* No. 55: "As there is a degree of depravity in mankind which requires a certain degree of circumspection and distrust, so there are other qualities in human nature which justify a certain portion of esteem and confidence. Republican government presupposes the existence of these qualities in a higher degree than any other form." Sadly, too little of that vision remains today.

Churches, learned societies, Freemason groups, and other associations were also primary institutions for the formation of good character and the transmission of community values. As George Washington observed in his farewell address, religion and morality are "indispensable supports" for republican government, being the "firmest props of the duties of men and citizens."

As we observe the American Constitution from the perspective of the generation entering the twenty-first century, it is quite remarkable how well it still functions over matters of government structure. Indeed, the basic structure of government remains intact today, over 200 years later. In the interim, the Constitution has survived civil war, two great world wars, a great depression, and significant industrial and technological change. It has also adjusted to a radical influx of new, diverse, and numerous citizenry, far beyond the small agrarian communities envisioned by Jefferson.

Yet the Constitution too is a product of its time, reflecting the eighteenth-century Enlightenment in which it was framed. As such, the Constitution speaks mainly to government and its limitation—the core concern of the Framers—and not people. Outside the official sphere, human conduct is mainly a private affair, left to the people within, of course, the fabric of the law. Limitation of government endows Americans with tremendous freedom. The nature of this freedom is essentially unchanneled or guided, left to the vagaries of community spirit or the legislative process.

Once shorn of its civic republicanism roots and without any other clear animating vision, such as the substantial consensus on religion and morality that existed in the eighteenth century, the American Constitution, as viewed today, exists somewhat as bare text, limiting official power but not educating citizens or imparting values seminal to the building of culture, as is common to European legal culture. In this context, individual pursuit of liberty and happiness has become the main preoccupation, sometimes resulting in excessive individualism, sometimes resulting in innovative change. The spirit of the people controls more than any set vision. That is one reason why free speech, with its ability to capture expression and human spirit and facilitate personal creation and recreation, has become the preeminent value of American society, at least as seen through the eyes of the Supreme Court and the souls of Americans. In these ways we can see that the Constitution posits a private realm of freedom for citizens to enjoy beyond government power. It is for this reason that we can speak of a "constitution of liberty."

GERMANY

Germany also adopted a written constitution, called the Basic Law, in 1949, following a crisis, the debacle of World War II. The Basic Law was influenced by the American success with constitutionalism, just as the American Constitution had been influenced by ideas about government from Europeans 200 years before. In particular, the Basic Law incorporated American ideas about separation of powers, federalism, an independent court exercising judicial review with the power to declare unconstitutional acts of the legislature, and an independent national central bank, insulated from politics, to control the money supply. Indeed, these particular ideas, and the general idea of a constitution, are American influences that resonate universally, inspiring the worldwide movement toward constitutionalism that flowered after World War II and, after the fall of the Berlin Wall, in the countries behind the former Iron Curtain.

As a modern, post–World War II constitution, the Basic Law arose from different historical experiences and a different cultural milieu. Two decisive events shaped modern German constitutionalism: the horror of the Nazi time and the preceding failure of the Weimar experiment in democracy, particularly the political maneuvering that led to stalemate and eventual exploitation by the Nazis, facilitating their rise.

Post–World War II Germans assimilated the lessons of these experiences. They sought distance from the horrors of Nazism. Accordingly, they designed the Basic Law so that it would make a sharp break from this immediate past, signaling a new constitutional order for Germany. Germans intentionally delved deeply into law in order to refound their society and instill a sense of hope. Law had been put to mischief and abuse in the preceding time, sometimes with the support of parts of the judiciary. Yet Germans, especially their guardians of the law—the scholars—had always distinguished between law in its pure or natural state and the law that lawyers, judges, or politicians applied.[10] So, as Professor Bernhard Schlink observes, "rather than being shattered by the Third Reich, the German belief in law over politics motivated a return to law as it originally and naturally was—a legal renaissance as a natural law renaissance."[11] Natural law served as the soil for the new society, replacing positive made law (positivism), the law of the sovereign.

In this way, Germans drew the same lesson as Madison had before. Human passion and impulse, left unchecked, can create great mischief. Indeed, Germans observed how unbridled human will, when imbued with the power of the sovereign, can cause horrific destruction. Human behavior is never wholly predictable or controllable. However, one "auxiliary precaution," according to the Madisonian design, is to channel human will through preordained fundamental principles of law. Society must follow a rule of law, and not that of men and women. Like the Americans of 200 years before, Germans went outside of society and its rules to refound the social compact on the fundamentals of law in its more natural state. To secure this refashioned rule of law, the Germans instituted judicial review as a check on the operation of democracy. Today Germany and the United States are the world's two great experiments in a judicially reviewed constitutional order. In both Germany and America we can speak of a *Justizstaat, le government des juges*, or a "counter-majoritarian" difficulty. In this regard, the American influence is quite prominent. Today, the German influence is also quite prominent, especially in the newly constituted states of Central and Eastern Europe. "In recent decades . . . Germany's Basic Law has replaced the American Constitution as the world's leading model of democratic constitutionalism."[12]

The German version of the rule of law is different, in some respects, than the American one. Germans drew deeply upon their own tradition to found the legal order on moral and rational idealism, particularly that of Kant, and also Hegel.[13] For Germans, Kant is the source to draw upon in order to check human passion. In a sense, the Basic Law is the natural successor to the German classical philosophic tradition, moving high thoughts from the drawing room to society. Thus, we can conceive of the Basic Law as a value-oriented constitution that obligates the state to realize a set of objectively ordered principles, rooted in justice and equality, that are designed to restore the centrality of humanity to the social order and thereby secure a stable democratic society on this basis. In particular, human values are to be served and nourished through the anchoring of society to the concept of the inviolability of human dignity. These values are not to be sacrificed for the exigencies of the day, as had been the case during the Nazi time.[14] Thus, the Basic Law provides a new avenue of substantive moral vision to check human passion and self-interest, in contrast to the limitation of government and accompanying neutral value choice of the American scheme.

The *Rechtsstaat* principle, for example, obligates society to adhere to a rule of law, requiring that legal measures have a legal basis and discernible content, provide fair notice, and be necessary and proportional to the ends they seek to accomplish (Proportionality Principle). By *Rechtsstaat*, Germans mean a state based on reason and the rule of law. Under the concept, state power must be exercised pursuant to previously established principles that are themselves rational, as a guard against the arbitrary exercise of power. The *Rechtsstaat* principle further restricts official power by requiring that any limitation on liberty have a sufficient legal basis, such as a statute.[15] For this reason, most basic rights provisions contain a reservation of authority to the Bundestag, the German parliament. The legislative preserve in article 2(2) is typical: "Intrusion on these rights may only be made pursuant to a statute."[16] From the standpoint of a *Rechtsstaat*, legislative oversight assures that restrictions on liberty be openly justified as a matter of democratic deliberation. The concept of *Rechtsstaat* can also be said to embody the concept of meaningful judicial review of official action.[17] The return to the *Rechtstaat* marks the continuation of a long German tradition, begun systematically during the era of Frederick the Great, of the tempering of state power with the rule of law. The idea is expressed in article 20(3) of the Basic Law, which provides, "The legislature shall be bound by the constitutional order, the executive and the judiciary by law and justice."

The principle of the Social State (*Sozialstaatsprinzip*) continues the European idea that the state is obligated to take necessary social-welfare measures so that all citizens will have a dignified existence.[18] In Germany, the modern idea of a social state is traceable to Prussia and its 1794 Civil Code expressing the idea that the purpose of law is to provide for the welfare of the commonwealth and its people. Thus, the state is obligated to provide food, work, and wages for those who cannot support themselves.[19] This affirmative vision of government runs deep in Europe, but is mainly foreign to America. The uniting of the *Rechtstaat* with the *Sozialstaat* is a great innovation in thought, combining Western liberalism with social solidarity.

In the United States, it took the catastrophe of the Great Depression in the 1930s to motivate proactive government action. Responding to social crisis, President Franklin D. Roosevelt proclaimed the New Deal for American citizens, helping assure basic conditions of human decency, such as provision of food, housing, jobs, and social security. In the 150 years prior to FDR, the idea and reality of government was a limited one. What FDR really proposed, therefore, was a radical new vision for American government. He went so far as to propose a Second Bill of Rights, providing for economic and social security, such as a right to a job and the ability to earn a decent wage and to provide adequate food, clothing, and recreation.[20] While this proactive vision of government animated American society for about fifty years after FDR, reaching its apex in the Great Society of President Lyndon Johnson, the United States now rings with the declaration of President Bill Clinton that "the era of Big Government is over." The defeat of President Clinton's health care plan in 1993, intended to complete FDR's original idea of providing decent health care for all Americans, led him to announce a new era of limited government. In comparison to Germany, and Europe generally, American government is not proactive.

Another distinguishing trait of modern Germany is the concept of a "militant democracy" (*streitbare Demokratie*), which obligates the state to resist any threats to the basic democratic order, thereby better assuring the flourishing of democracy. The idea is a direct response to the Weimar experience, as the Federal Republic strives not to repeat that regime's mistakes. As the Constitutional Court has stated,

It is especially significant that the Constitution . . . has decided in favor of "militant democracy" that does not submit to abuse of basic rights or an attack on the liberal order of the state. Enemies of the Constitution must not be allowed to endanger, impair, or destroy the existence of the state while claiming protection of rights granted by the Basic Law.[21]

Accordingly, all basic rights are subject to forfeiture when used to "combat the free democratic basic order" under Article 18. Under article 20(4) of the Basic Law, "All Germans shall have the right to resist any person seeking to abolish this constitutional order." These provisions are unique to constitutions. With the outbreak of neo-Nazi violence in Germany that followed reunification, political, church, and community leaders acted to safeguard democracy, calling on the government to clamp down on right-wing activities, not allowing the problem to fester as under Weimar.[22]

Political parties must also conform to democratic principles. Parties that seek to impair or abolish the free democratic order may be declared unconstitutional under Article 21(2). The Constitutional Court has twice outlawed political parties under this article: the Socialist Reich Party, successor to the Nazi party, in 1952 and the Communist Party in 1956.[23] Moreover, under Article 79(3), basic principles like human dignity, federalism, and popular sovereignty are inviolable, secure against future amendment, as a further guard to preserve democracy. Finally, there is tight restriction on the use of emergency powers, the ruse Hitler used to take power.

COMPARISON

As a matter of comparative law today, these two constitutions, the American and German, and the courts that interpret them, constitute the two charters that have the deepest impact on their respective societies. In this sense, the Constitution and the Basic Law are the two leading charter documents in the world, and a worthy subject for comparison over ideas such as human liberty and satisfaction. Let us now look more carefully at the similarities and differences in the countries' conceptions of human rights and approaches to constitutionalism.

Both the German and American social orders are committed to human rights, which are set forth in the basic charters. The German Basic Law enumerates a comprehensive catalogue of basic rights that includes protections of free conscience, faith and creed, freedom of expression, equality, and occupational freedom. There is a clear American influence over the idea of individual liberty, although other influences, most prominently that of France, especially the fervor of its 1789 Revolution, were important too. In keeping with the developments of modern, post–World War II constitutions, the Basic Law is very specific and comprehensive in its listing of basic freedoms, enumerating at least twenty specific individual liberties. The detail of the Basic Law compares to the relatively sparse enumeration of liberties in the American Constitution. Apart from criminal due process protections, which is the primary focus of the Bill of Rights, American rights consist mainly of freedom of expression, freedom of conscience, due process, and equality.

The difference in enumeration of basic rights is, upon reflection, not so surprising. The American Bill of Rights dates from 1791. Germany's Basic Law is a 1949 document. The difference in time, 150 years, reflects different philosophies and different motivations. Following the horrors of World War II, the Western world as a whole sought protection of humanity through the securing of basic dignity, resulting in the great movement toward human rights that still marks our era. International conventions, such as the 1948 Universal Declaration of Human Rights and the 1950 European Convention for the Protection of Human Rights and Fundamental Freedoms, are products of this ferment. The 1949 Basic Law is a product of this cultural milieu as well. Like those international charters and national charters of the modern era, the Basic Law details its treatment of individual freedom.

The American Constitution lacks this comprehensive enumeration of rights, as the American Framers most acutely focused on outlining the limits of govenment. The idea of freedom was simpler in 1791, compared to 1949. Yet despite the relatively skeletal framework of rights set forth in the Constitution, the Supreme Court has, through elaboration, devised a system of basic rights that has proved quite influential. The Court has used eighteenth-century ideas as a base for a twenty-first-century society.[24] Many foreign national and international courts look to the American Bill of Rights for inspiration. As observed by the Canadian Supreme Court, "The courts in the United States have had almost two hundred years experience at this task and it is of more than passing interest to those concerned with these developments in Canada to study the experience of the United States courts."[25] The Bill of Rights resonates deeply in the American pysche. Mary Ann Glendon observes the phenomenon of "rights talk," Americans' propensity to turn all great questions of social policy into a rights claim.[26]

Ironically, despite America's 200 years of experience with judicial review, the movement toward judicially enumerated human rights has been a recent one, occurring mostly in the post–World War II era, primarily through the efforts of the Warren Court, the name given to the Supreme Court under the leadership of Chief Justice Earl Warren. Prior to the Warren Court and its immediate predecessors, the Court's experience with judicial review had been mixed. In the first 100 years of the republic, the Court declared only two acts of Congress unconstitutional, the 1803 case of *Marbury v. Madison*,[27] where the Court fashioned the idea of judicial review out of the skeletal text of the Constitution, and the infamous 1857 *Dred Scott* case, where the Court found slaves to be "property" within the meaning of the Due Process Clause, and thus subject to the control of their masters.[28] In the eyes of the Court, *Dred Scott* was to be another of the great compromises resolving the dispute among the northern and southern states over slavery. In the judgment of history, *Dred Scott* is a major cause of the American Civil War (1861–1865). In the first century of the country, judicial activism was not, from the standpoint of human welfare, an especially positive force.

The Court's next significant experience with judicial review was over economic rights, in the period of the late nineteenth century and early twentieth century known as the *Lochner* era.[29] This experience was likewise not an especially positive one. In this era, the Court became known, perjoratively, as a "super-legislature" for its second-guessing of the social policy judgments of the majoritarian process. Imbued with the ideals of laissez-faire capitalism and social Darwinism, the Court rendered invalid attempts by the legislatures to limit the workweek of bakers to sixty hours or ten hours a day;[30] regulate child labor by prohibiting work in factories of children under age fourteen;[31] and establish a minimum wage for women.[32] While the Court followed its vision of correct economic or social policy, the country struggled in the 1930s to escape the clutches of despair, economic depression, and social malaise. Rule by men seemed to many, in the grips of crisis, to be superior to rule by law, if by law one meant the fiats of the Court. Chastened by this experience, the Court withdrew from serious review of social legislation until recently.[33]

In fact, even today the Supreme Court, comparatively speaking, is not an especially activist institution in relation to the decisions of coordinate branches of government. According to one 1988 study, the Supreme Court declared a federal law unconstitutional about 100 times in two centuries. By comparison, the German Constitutional Court rendered invalid 160 federal laws from 1951 to 1980, the Austrian Constitutional Court 357 laws from 1946 to 1980, and the Italian Constitutional Court 600 decisions in a comparable period.[34]

The modern idea of judicial activism in the United States begins prominently with the Warren Court, the Supreme Court active between 1953 and 1969. The Warren Court built on a new conception of the judicial role, formulated by influential justices such as Black, Douglas, and Stone, that advocated judicial deference to legislative policy judgments but heightened scrutiny of violations of the Bill of Rights. The Warren Court started the rights revolution in the famous 1954 *Brown v. Board of Education* case and its search for equality through its declaration that "in the field of public education the doctrine of 'separate but equal' has no place."[35] Through such pronouncements, the Warren Court taught Americans the meaning and value of the Bill of Rights through the 1950s and 1960s.

Like the Constitutional Court, the Warren Court responded to changed social conditions in the mid-twentieth century. These changes included the New Deal society of Franklin Roosevelt and its reconception of the role of government. With the apparent failure of the old common law regime to adequately handle the social problems resulting from the Great Depression, FDR set up a new administrative governmental apparatus to help fashion a more positive approach to human welfare. In response, the New Deal Court, with some tension, reconceived its role away from enforcement of contract and property rights and toward deference to legislative powers over these matters. This left the legislature in control of much of society, outside significant constitutional protection or guidance. The vagaries of the legislative process control more than constitutional norms.[36] These adjustments gave rise to Big Government in a way never previously seen in the republic, including the rise of the administrative state. Responding to this, the Warren Court and its predecessors sought ways to check the new power. One strategy was a return to a purer, more natural form of law, one in keeping with the original search for human freedom. Thus, the Court devised a human rights strategy, an outgrowth of natural law, as a means of better keeping government in check. These human rights, such as those over free expression, conscience, and autonomy, replaced the older regime of contract and property freedoms. Citizens could now exercise a fuller panoply of rights to mark out a sphere of personal freedom beyond government's reach. So human rights became the higher law of the twentieth century, as limitation of government had performed this role in the eighteenth century. In this way, both American and German rights grew in the same soil.

There are differences in the countries' conceptions of basic rights. Fundamental to the German conception is the principle of objective and subjective rights, or positive and negative liberties. By objective rights Germans mean society's most fundamental values, which the state is obligated to achieve proactively. The objective dimension of rights is the most fundamental difference between the German and American constitutions. Objectification of rights results in "maxims according to which social relationships, as well as the relationship between state and society, are to be ordered."[37] Rights are thus fundamental values, or "value-determining norms."[38] So conceived, rights obligate government to create the proper conditions in society so that rights might be realized as basic norms. The effect of this empowerment is to bestow duties on the state, calling for state activism along these lines. For example, the concept of human dignity protected in article 1 of the Basic Law obligates the state to provide a basic minimal existence for citizens. Human dignity provides the foundation for the social welfare state, anchored in article 20(1) of the Basic Law, that distinguishes Germany from the United States. Through this theory of objectification, the state becomes a partner with citizens in the realization of justice, including with respect to fundamental rights and fundamental needs. In this way, Germany posits a public or social dimension to freedom. Theoretically, positive liberty is designed to emancipate human potential.[39] Unfortunately, such proactive state power has too often in the twentieth century ended up in the hands of despots, like Hitler or Stalin, where it became a coercive power for evil.[40] Thus, while it possesses great potential for achieving benefit, positive liberty has risks as well.

The objective dimension of basic rights is tied to the value-ordered nature of the German constitutional scheme, obligating government to realize in society the set of objective values embodied in the Basic Law. "This value-system, which centers upon human dignity and the free unfolding of the human personality within the social community, must be looked upon as a fundamental constitutional decision affecting all areas of law, public and private."[41] By interpreting basic rights as establishing an "objective" ordering of values centered around human dignity, the Constitutional Court transformed those values into principles so important that they must exist "objectively," as an independent force, separate from their specific manifestation in a concrete legal relationship. So conceived, objective rights form part of the fundamental legal order, the *ordre public*, thereby becoming part of the governing principles of German society.[42] Objective rights thus become a measure by which to gauge society's commitment to justice. In this way, the

Basic Law acts as a blueprint for society, setting forth the values to be realized, pressing for a close fit between its text and society. Germany is striving to make positive liberty a source for good in society.

The reasons for this rather stunning development lie again in the German reaction to the debacle of World War II and the preceding Nazism. In adopting the Basic Law as a new legal order for Germany, the country was determined to make a clean break with the past. So too was the Constitutional Court. Thus, when presented with the opportunity to define the meaning of basic rights in the famous *Lüth* case of 1958,[43] the Constitutional Court seized the moment to free law from the ideological baggage of the time of the Nazis and the Empire.[44] The Court reconceived the traditional idea of rights into this objective dimension in order to anchor society to fundamental norms grounded in the core idea of human dignity. Objective rights thus became the core governing principles of society. In creating this opportunity, the Constitutional Court became the legal locomotive for change, in this direction, in society. As a new court, the Constitutional Court was well positioned to assume this role. Unlike its predecessors, the highest civil and criminal law courts, the Constitutional Court was not discredited by its association with the Nazis.[45]

By contrast, there is no such objective aspect to the American constitution. Nor does the Supreme Court act as proactively to realize a substantive set of values as the Constitutional Court. The American Constitution, in its original design, mainly provides the outline for government, concentrating on limiting official power. Americans are by nature skeptical about the existence and use of government power. Thus, it seems appropriate that the American conception of rights lacks any claim to government action.[46] In this way, again, we can see that the American model of freedom posits a sphere of private freedom in which citizens can act free from government action. Whatever proactive role government is to play is the subject of normal politics, not constitutionalism.

These points were made quite starkly by the Supreme Court in the *DeShaney v. Winnebago County Department of Social Services* case, infamous for finding that no constitutional duty could be imposed on a state even when the state supervised the welfare of a young child known to be abused and beaten by his father.[47] Sadly, the father eventually beat his child so severely that the child was rendered incapacitated, permanently brain damaged, necessitating his commitment to an institution. In the case, the Supreme Court declared the noninterventionist role of the state as follows:

[Nothing] in the language of the Due Process Clause itself requires the State to protect the life, liberty, and property of its citizens against invasion by private actors. The Clause is phrased as a limitation on the State's power to act, not as a guarantee of certain minimal levels of safety and security.[48]

The conception of a very limited governmental role, at the root of *DeShaney*, is diametrically opposite to the German idea of government–citizen cooperation over the idea of freedom.

The second aspect of German basic rights is their subjective or negative dimension. In German law, subjective rights denote a set of rights exercisable by individuals. Each person may exercise his or her rights as a sword to ward off unwarranted government intrusion. In this manner, rights play a defensive role, delimiting a sphere of personal liberty beyond governmental control. The exercise of rights by individuals, in turn, facilitates their participation in the constitutional order.[49] Indeed, as people exercise rights and their claims are adjudicated, the constitutional order acquires the new meaning achieved in the adjudication. The exercise of rights, accordingly, is very influential in creating new dimensions to society. The essential character of this subjective dimension corresponds to the American conception of fundamental constitutional rights. For example, this was the interpretation intended by the Supreme Court in the *DeShaney* case, and also the one that animates rights cases generally, such as those involving free speech. Again, this is the private sphere of freedom, the liberty that results from citizen initiative in the face of limiting official power.

A second contrast to the American Constitution involves the German theory of third-party effect (*Drittwirkung*), under which the constitutional order affects private legal relationships as well as public ones. The theory of third-party effect follows from the objective theory of rights and was also developed in the famous 1958 *Lüth* case, involving freedom of expression. In the case, Erich Lüth, a Hamburg press official, called for a boycott of a new film by Veit Harlan, who had produced notoriously anti-Semitic films during the Nazi period.[50] Harlan had worked under the general direction of Nazi propaganda minister Josef Goebbels, producing Nazi propaganda and anti-Semitic films. After the war, a criminal court convicted Harlan of a crime against humanity by making a film, the notorious *Sweet Jew* (*Jud Süss*), that contributed to the persecution of Jews during the Nazi period. He was subsequently acquitted of the crime because the war tribunal could not disprove his assertion that he worked under "compulsion." He was also later "exonerated" in de-Nazification proceedings.[51]

Lüth was active in a group seeking to repair relations between Christians and Jews. Incensed by Harlan's reemergence on the German film scene, Lüth's call for a boycott was motivated by his desire to demonstrate to the world that the new German cinema was free from the darkness of the Nazi period.[52] He believed Harlan's Nazi past would bring moral condemnation to Germany, inside and outside the country.[53] Suing in the civil courts, the producer and distributor of Harlan's film were able to obtain an injunction against Lüth that prohibited him from continuing the call for a boycott on the theory that this caused injury to their business interests under Section 826 of the German Civil Code (BGB), one of the famous general clauses of the Code.[54] Under Section 826, a person who contrary to "good morals" (*gute Sitten*) intentionally causes harm to another person is liable to pay damages to the other person.

Since the legal relationship between Lüth and Harlan sounded in tort, under the BGB, it would be characterized as one involving private parties, and thus ordinarily beyond the reach of public law. Instead, however, the Constitutional Court used the case to reconceive the relationship between public and private law. Because basic rights are essential to the public good as part of the objective order of fundamental principles that rule society, the Court reasoned, it follows that basic rights must affect private as well as public actors. "This value-system, which centers upon human dignity and the free unfolding of the human personality within the social community, must be looked upon as a fundamental constitutional decision affecting all areas of law, public and private. . . . Thus, basic rights obviously influence civil law too."[55]

In this way, the Constitutional Court interpreted the Basic Law as marking a fundamental change in the German legal order, one free from the ideological baggage of the Weimar era. Basic rights are a constituent part of the "objective" order of fundamental principles that govern German society. Insofar as they are tangible radiations of human dignity, basic rights, together with certain other basic principles, might even be viewed as "permanent ends of the state," not changeable "even by constitutional amendment" through their anchoring in article 79.[56] The role of article 79 as a firewall in braking the excesses of democratic passion is unique to constitutions. The permanence of these fundamental values contrasts with what became "the legal relativism of the Weimar Constitution, in which basic principles could be easily altered by constitutional amendment."[57]

Since basic rights form part of the "objective" legal order, they must apply generally in society, against both state and private actors that would act to curtail them. Thus, basic rights must effect private individuals too, insofar as they seek enforcement of their claims and interests through the rules of private law. In this way, German law safeguards the integrity of basic rights against impairment from private actors as well as public ones. Exactly what effect basic rights have on private law is a complicated question that the Constitutional Court, necessarily, shortly took up as well.

The Basic Law's influence on civil law is a notable contrast to American law. In American law, the Constitution applies when government acts. In the absence of official action, the Constitution does not apply, subject to the contours of the state action doctrine under which some private actors are held to be acting as "public" officials, thereby triggering application of the Constitution. The state may also "act" when the rule enforced by the court has been formulated by government, even if the parties in dispute are private. The rules of libel at issue in cases following *New York Times v. Sullivan* fit this category.[58] Since the business law claim at issue in *Lüth* was formulated by government, *Lüth* might likewise make out state action under this doctrine of American law. However, in comparison to the Basic Law's "objective" ordering of society, the American Constitution withdraws from the important private sector of society. For example, except as already noted, the American Constitution ordinarily has only a minimal impact on private law relations, such as those governed by contract, tort, or trusts and estates. In this way, the reach of the German Basic Law is broader than its American counterpart. This also demonstrates, again, how the American model of freedom posits private liberty, whereas Germany envisions a public, social dimension to freedom as well. In Germany, as compared to the United States, the state is a more ready participant in individuals' achievement of freedom.

Lüth presented the Constitutional Court with the first opportunity to clarify the nature of the relationship between basic rights and the private law. Given its conclusion that basic rights are fundamental to the legal order, this question now became all important. The Constitutional Court opted for an intermediate but creative solution to this relationship. Between the extremes of the Basic Law being limited to government action (as in the United States) and its application to any action, public or private, which curtails rights, the Court split the difference, deciding that the Basic Law should apply "indirectly," not directly, to private law. By "indirect" application, the Constitutional Court meant that constitutional norms "influence" rather than govern private law norms.[59] "A certain intellectual content 'flows' or 'radiates' from the constitutional law and into the civil law and affects the interpretation of existing civil law rules."[60]

Constitutional norms are to be emphasized, especially in construing and applying the general clauses of the Civil Code, such as the "good morals" term of section 826. General clauses are to take into account the prevailing concerns and values of society, including constitutional values. They form part of the objective legal order as well. Thus, when private law claims involve general clauses of the Civil Code, as in *Lüth*, ordinary courts must give especially strong effect to constitutional norms. In this way, constitutional norms seep into the texture of the private law.[61]

When faced with article 5(1) claims, therefore, ordinary courts must look to the article 5(2) "general law" textual constraint not as a one-sided limitation on communication freedoms.[62] Rather, article 5(1) freedoms and general law norms have a mutual effect on one another. It is as much the case, if not more so, that article 5(1) expression freedoms can influence interpretation of the article 5(2) general law textual constraint as that constraint can limit those expression freedoms. Under the theory of objective values, general laws "must be interpreted in light of the value-establishing significance of the basic right in a free democratic state, and so any limiting effect on the basic right must itself be restricted."[63] In German law, this mutual reciprocal effect that basic rights and the general law have on each other is known as the reciprocal effect theory (*Wechselwirkung*).[64]

The Court's conclusion is somewhat startling when one considers that it, in essence, implied a fundamental limitation on the reach of the express general law limitations on communication rights. This illustrates the profound effect of the objective theory on German constitutionalism. The constitutional order is certainly the premiere organizing principle for all of German society, public and private. It also illustrates the high regard the Court placed on the value of free expression in a democratic society. Last, the result shows the Court's dynamic, creative interpretation of the Basic Law to accomplish these goals.

Within this framework of the reciprocal effect theory, it is the job of the Constitutional Court to assure that private law courts adequately take into account the "objective" order of values.[65] Exactly what this entails has varied over time, as the Court has taken both rights-protective and rights-restrictive approaches. Today, the Court applies an exacting standard of review. Still, the dispute "remains substantively and procedurally a dispute of civil law."[66] Thus, the civil law courts will have the last word, subject to the Court's control of constitutional principles. The interpretations of the ordinary courts must be harmonious with the objective system of values. In these ways, German constitutional law connects to private law in a more seamless way than in American law.

A third contrast to the American Constitution is that the German Basic Law also sets forth certain duties incumbent upon citizens or government to perform. The idea of coupling rights with duties is a European one, going back to the first continental rights declaration, the 1789 French Declaration of the Rights of Man and the Citizen. The idea, in fact, has deep roots in European culture, traceable to the classical period of Plato and Aristotle and the Biblical tradition of concern for the poor and downtrodden. Rousseau, more than any other thinker, kept this tradition alive with his mediation of individual claims with concern for the common good.[67] European law has maintained this tradition of exercising rights within a communal context, expressed as duties and responsibilities.

The Basic Law continues this tradition. For example, article 6(2) provides that "the care and upbringing of children is the natural right of parents and a duty primarily incumbent upon them. The state shall watch over them in the performance of this duty." Article 14, which guarantees property, provides, in subsection 2, that "property entails obligations. Its use shall also serve the public good." Yet in comparison to other European constitutions and the former Weimar constitution, the Basic Law is actually quite sparse in spelling out duties. Rather than textual enumeration, the main idea of "duties" comes from internalization of cultural norms, of how one ought to exercise rights. Here the Constitutional Court plays a key role. In working out the objective value order, the Court calibrates the relationships between rights and among rights and duties. Through such interpretation, the Court instructs citizens and society as to the meaning and function of rights. The rhetorical use of language to educate the public, as practiced by the Constitutional Court, has deep roots in European law as well, harking back to Montesquieu and Rousseau and their concern for development of virtue and civic responsibility. European law continues to draw inspiration from the classical period of Plato and Aristotle, and the idea that the purpose of law is to lead citizens to virtue, and to be noble and wise.[68] In sum, German citizens have claims to both subjective rights, which they may exercise, and objective rights, which they can call on government to perform and which cement the social order. In addition, they must assume certain duties as to how to act on such rights.

We can thus see that the contrast between the text and nature of the two constitutions is striking in these ways. Certainly there are numerous commonalities between the two constitutions, including over ideas like separation of powers, federalism, human rights, and an independent court. Yet the Basic Law revolves around three ideas quite foreign to American law. These are, by way of summation, that rights have an objective dimension that animates the value structure of society, as well as a subjective dimension. Second, therefore, the Basic Law effects all legal relationships in society, public and private, through the judicially invented concept of third-party effect (*Drittwirkung*). Third, duties, as well as rights, comprise part of the constitutional order. The interrelationship between these three core ideas is a distinguishing trait of the Federal Republic.

And thus, we can observe, again by contrast, that the German Basic Law is value oriented and sets forth both rights and duties, whereas the U.S. Constitution attempts to be value neutral pursuant to a scheme of negative liberties, specifically enumerating rights government may not infringe but not stating comparable duties citizens must assume or values government must realize. In the United States the content of duties and values, and their fulfillment, is left primarily to citizens and community initiative, consistent with the original aim of limiting government power. The decisions and statutes of the legislatures perform this role as well. In America, thus, people rely on basic republicanism, and not constitutionalism, to carry out this program. This would seem to reflect Americans' basic faith in political process and democracy as the preferred way to solve fundamental social problems. And Americans' essential success at this, over a period of 200 years and through a number of serious crises, including the Civil War and the Great Depression, attests to the political maturity of the country, and that the faith may be well placed.

By contrast, the details of the Basic Law, and fundamental function it performs in steering society, may reflect the relative political immaturity of the German constitutional polity.[69] In fairness, there have only been 50 years of the Federal Republic, as compared to over 200 years of American democracy. And, as important, German constitutional democracy (certainly successful to date) has not yet suffered a crisis comparable to those the American republic has survived. In some sense, the test for any polity is how it responds to crisis. As Justice Holmes observed, "It has taken a century and has cost . . . [us] much sweat and blood to prove . . . [we] created a nation."[70] Thus, there are sound grounds for Germans' skepticism about the performance of their political democracy.[71] Accordingly, safeguarding the society through a detailed charter spelling out and steering the way seems a sound precaution.

A final constitutional difference is worth noting. There is a difference in the techniques of constitutional interpretation that the two courts use. Under American canon, one must consult, in order of importance, constitutional text (including structure and purpose), precedent, Framers' intent, and then, perhaps, social, economic, or philosophic perspectives prior to reaching a plausible result. By contrast, German law places a premium on the text of the Basic Law and its applicability to social and economic conditions. In this way, German constitutional interpretation can be a dynamic process, one that aims more truly to keep the charter "in tune with the times."[72] One reason Germans focus on text is that they utilize formal constitutional amendments to accomplish constitutional change more frequently than Americans. Given the infrequency of formal constitutional change in the United States, the Supreme Court has mainly performed the role of adjusting the constitution to changed social conditions.

Beyond textual and structural exegesis, German interpreters employ historical and teleological (a search for the purpose or goals served by the language) analysis, before integrating the whole through techniques of harmonization (*praktische Konkordanz*) and integration.[73] Such harmonization (or concordance) consists of bringing some unity to the overall interpretation. The technique reflects the lessons of German legal science, with its emphasis on unity, systematization, and logic in striving to build an internally consistent, complete system of law. It also follows from the aims and methods of German philosophy, a main motivation of German law, especially classical idealism, such as that of Kant or Hegel, where unity and harmony are sought in presenting an integrated, whole system of thought. From the standpoint of today, concordance is desired for the mediating influence it can exert on conflicting claims, helping achieve some peace in society. Symbolically, thus, the technique has value quite apart from the tangible results reached in a case. In practice, harmonization is marked by a sense of balance and equilibrium as the Court tries to resolve tensions between potentially conflicting rights, such as, for example, the claims of liberty and life in abortion cases. In these ways, the technique of concordance is distinctive to Germany. In sum, both courts employ a variety of reasoning techniques, including arguments based on text, structure, history, and natural law, although the reasoning process of the courts is not the same.[74]

Functionally, German case law operates like American decisions, setting forth fundamental principles and legal determinations that guide other courts and people in society.[75] In Germany, however, there is no formal stare decisis system, as in the United States. The idea of stare decisis is an inheritance of the English common law system. The German doctrine follows from civil law premises that judicial decisions serve only as a gloss on the open development of the law, which is to be found in the rules and principles of the governing text. However, in practice, German courts strive to be consistent with principles and rulings determined by prior court decisions out of concern that the law be applied equally. In this way, German courts function in a manner somewhat akin to American courts. Moreover, decisions of the Constitutional Court have the force of law. The ability of the Constitutional Court to declare the law is an innovation in German law, consistent with the idea that the Constitutional Court is a new court for a new legal order.

The biggest difference between the two laws relates to Framers' intent. In Germany, the Constitutional Court treats history as an auxiliary source of interpretation. While the Court is free to consult Framers' intent, such history generally lends support to a result reached through other interpretative methods, such as the textual, structural, or teleological analysis already noted. Framers' intent is not an independent source of authority.[76] For example, the Constitutional Court has commented that "the original history of a particular provision of the Basic Law has no decisive importance" in constitutional interpretation.[77] Instead, the Court mainly interprets constitutional text in relationship to the conditions of modern society. This dynamic is perhaps most pronounced in relation to the article 1 concept of human dignity, where the Court has stated, "Any decision defining human dignity in concrete terms must be based on our present understanding of it and not on any claim to a conception of timeless validity."[78] There is thus a freeness and creativity to the Constitutional Court's interpretation, as the Court tries to capture the essence of the norm embodied in the language and then apply it to the social and economic conditions presented by the case.

The techniques of the Constitutional Court are a far cry from those of the Supreme Court, which ordinarily employs text, structure, history, and Framers' intent to achieve decisions in order to bring predictability and stability to the law. Some, like former Judge Bork and Justice Scalia, even argue, forcefully, that this guards against judicial activism. The conservative reaction to the Warren Court has sought limitation of judicial review through a search for originalism.[79] Moreover, in the area of unenumerated rights (those rights denoting a range of freedom beyond the explicit ones set forth in the first eight amendments to the Constitution), the Supreme Court has sought to anchor its decisions in timeless concepts, like justice or natural law, to avoid the appearance of judicial bias or result orientation.[80] More recently, the Supreme Court has scoured history and tradition to defuse claims for unenumerated rights.[81] These differences show, almost by definition, that the Constitutional Court is to be a more activist body than the Supreme Court. This again accords with the special role of the Constitutional Court as a new court invested with the mission of helping erect a new constitutional order. It also points out, in a sense, how the Constitutional Court is forward looking, whereas the Supreme Court, especially under Chief Justice Rehnquist, is backward in focus.[82]

NOTES

1. MARY ANN GLENDON, ABORTION AND DIVORCE IN WESTERN LAW 127 (1987).

2. CHARLES MONTESQUIEU, THE SPIRIT OF THE LAWS (1748), trans. and edited by Anne M. Cohler, Basia Carolyn Miller, and Harold Samuel Stone (1989).

3. THE FEDERALIST No. 78 (Alexander Hamilton).

4. ALEXANDER BICKEL, THE LEAST DANGEROUS BRANCH 16 (1962).

5. McCulloch v. Maryland, 17 U.S. (4Wheat.) 316, 404 (1819).

6. THE FEDERALIST No. 78 (Alexander Hamilton).

7. U.S. CONST. pmbl.

8. *McCulloch*, 17 U.S. at 431.

9. GEOFFREY R. STONE ET AL., CONSTITUTIONAL LAW 5 (3d ed. 1996).

10. Bernhard Schlink, *German Constitutional Culture in Transition*, 14 CARDOZO L. REV. 711, 724 (1993).

11. *Id.* at 724.

12. Winfried Brugger, *Der moderne Verfassungsstaat. Rechtsvergleichunge Bemerkungen aus Sicht der amerikanischen und der deutschen Verfassung* (1999) (manuscript on file with author) *citing* Donald P. Kommers, *Can German Constitutionalism Serve as a Model for the United States?* 58 ZaöRV 1, 2 (1998).

13. 1 INGO VON MUENCH, GRUNDESETZ, KOMMENTAR, 72–73 (2d ed. 1981) [hereinafter MUENCH COMMENTARY]; DONALD P. KOMMERS, THE CONSTITUTIONAL JURISPRUDENCE OF THE FEDERAL REPUBLIC OF GERMANY 47 (1989); Peter Badura, *Generalprävention und Würde des Menschen*, 19 JURISTENZEITUNG 337, 339–40 (1964).

14. George P. Fletcher, *Human Dignity as a Constitutional Value*, 22 U. W. ONTARIO L. REV. 171, 178–79 (1984).

15. DAVID P. CURRIE, THE CONSTITUTION OF THE FEDERAL REPUBLIC OF GERMANY 318 (1994).

16. *See also* GG art. 19(1) ("statutes [restricting rights] shall apply generally and not solely to an individual case . . . [and] name the basic right").

17. CURRIE, *supra* note 15, at 19.

18. *See* Basic Law GG art. 20(1).

19. MARY ANN GLENDON, RIGHTS TALK: THE IMPOVERISHMENT OF POLITICAL DISCOURSE 36 (1991).

20. Available to all "regardless of station, race or creed," FDR's second Bill of Rights included:

The right to a useful and remunerative job in the industries or shops or farms or mines of the Nation;

The right to earn enough to provide adequate food and clothing and recreation;

The right of every farmer to raise and sell his products at a return which will give him and his family a decent living;

The right of every businessman, large and small, to trade in an atmosphere of freedom from unfair competition and domination by monopolies at home or abroad;

The right of every family to a decent home;

The right to adequate medical care and the opportunity to achieve and enjoy good health;

The right to adequate protection from economic fears of old age, sickness, accident, and unemployment;

The right to a good education.

F. D. ROOSEVELT, Message to the Congress on the State of Union (Jan. 11, 1944), *reprinted in* 13 THE PUBLIC PAPERS AND ADDRESSES OF FRANKLIN D. ROOSEVELT, VICTORY AND THE THRESHOLD OF PEACE, 1944–45, at 41 (1950), *cited in* Cass R. Sunstein, *Constitutionalism After the New Deal*, 101 HARV. L. REV. 421, 423 (1987).

21. *See, e.g., Klass Case*, 30 BVerfGE 1, 19–20 (1970), *translated in* Kommers, *supra* note 13, at 230.

22. Stephen Kinzer, *The Neo-Nazis: How Quickly They Remember*, N.Y. TIMES, November 17, 1991, at sec. 4, p. 1.

23. 2 BVerfGE 1 (1952); 5 BVerfGE 85 (1956). The Constitutional Court has not reviewed the constitutionality of a political party since the Communist Party case. The old communist party (KPD) reorganized itself in 1968 in West Germany as the German Communist Party (DKP). The government failed to move against the DKP, even though it resembled the old KPD. Similarly, the government did not initiate proceedings to have declared unconstitutional an extremist right-wing party, the National Democratic Party of Germany (NPD). However, the government could monitor the organization and publicize its findings, including its conclusion that the NPD was a "party engaged in anti-constitutional goals and activity," and was "radical right and an enemy of freedom" and "a danger to the free democratic basic order." *See* 40 BVerfGE 287 (1975); Kommers, *supra* note 13, at 231. The toleration of these extremist parties would seem to evidence the heightened sense of toleration and security of modern Germany. With the reunification of Germany, the Party of Democratic Socialism (PDS), successor to the old controlling East German Socialist Unity Party (SED), is active. Yet in view of recent outbreaks of neo-Nazi violence, there have been efforts to ban extreme right parties. At present, the Constitutional Court is considering whether to take this step in a case before it.

24. Letter from Professor Richard Huber to Edward Eberle (November 10, 1997).

25. Law Society of Upper Canada v. Skapinker [1984] 1 S.C.R. 357, 366–67 (Estey, J.).

26. GLENDON, *supra* note 19.

27. 5 U.S. (1 Cranch) 137 (1803).

28. Dred Scott v. Sanford, 60 U.S. (19 How.) 393 (1857).

29. Lochner v. New York, 198 U.S. 45 (1905).

30. *Id.*

31. Hammer v. Dagenhart, 247 U.S. 251 (1918).

32. Adkins v. Children's Hospital, 261 U.S. 525 (1923).

33. The case of New York v. United States, 505 U.S. 144 (1992), where the Court invalidated a Congressional plan, at states' urging, to store nuclear waste, marked the Court's return, in limited guise, to serious review of Congressional legislation.

34. Louis Favoreu, *The Constitutional Council and Parliament in France, in* CONSTITUTIONAL REVIEW AND LEGISLATION: AN INTERNATIONAL COMPARISON 81–108 (C. Landfried ed., 1988).

35. 347 U.S. 483, 495 (1954).

36. Huber, *supra* note 24.

37. Schlink, *supra* note 10, at 713.

38. *Id.* at 717–18.

39. Richard Bernstein, *Foxes, Hedgehogs and the Defense of Freedom,* N.Y. TIMES, November 25, 1998, at B17 (reviewing *Isaiah Berlin, A Life*).

40. *Id.*

41. *Lüth*, 7 BVerfGE 198, 205 (1958).

42. Edward J. Eberle, *Public Discourse in Contemporary Germany*, 47 CASE W. RES. L. REV. 797, 811 (1997); Peter E. Quint, *Free Speech and Private Law in German Constitutional Theory*, 48 MD. L. REV. 247, 261 (1989) (noting GG art. 79(3)).

43. 7 BVerfGE at 198.

44. Schlink, *supra* note 10, at 722.

45. *Id.* at 725.

46. The most that might be said is that, under certain circumstances, American government cannot totally deny a right or a benefit. Usually, such cases are decided under the Equal Protection Clause. *See, e.g.,* Plyer v. Doe, 457 U.S. 202 (1982) (state may not deny free public education to illegal aliens); Shapiro v. Thompson, 394 U.S. 618 (1969) (state may not condition receipt of welfare benefits on one-year residency requirement because this violates right to travel and equal protection).

47. 489 U.S. 189 (1989).

48. *Id.* at 195.

49. Schlink, *supra* note 10, at 713.

50. 7 BVerfGE at 199–200.

51. *Id.* at 219, 222–26.

52. *Id.* at 199–200.

53. *Id.*

54. *Id.* at 200–02. The court found Lüth's action to be an incitement contrary to Section 826 of the German Civil Code, which reads, "Whoever causes damage to another person intentionally and in a manner offensive to good morals is obligated to compensate the other person for the damage." Kommers, *supra* note 13, at 368 (trans.). The "general clauses" of the German Civil Code constitute an important exception to the prevailing view that European codes are so specific that they allow for the rote application of cases to enumerated language. Instead, the general clauses allow for significant judicial creativity. Quint, *supra* note 42, at 253 n. 18.

55. *Lüth*, 7 BVerfGE at 205.

56. Quint, *supra* note 42, at 261. Article 79(3) provides, "Amendments to this Basic Law affecting the division of the Federation into Länder, their participation on principle in the legislative process, or the principles laid down in Articles 1 and 20 shall be inadmissible."

57. Quint, *supra* note 42, at 261–62.

58. 376 U.S. 254 (1964).

59. *Lüth*, 7 BVerfGE at 205 (the Basic Law "influences obviously also civil law; no civil law provision may contradict the Basic Law; all (legal provisions) must be interpreted consistent with its spirit").

60. *Id.* at 205 (from the Basic Law "flows a certain constitutional content"); Quint, *supra* note 42, at 263.

61. *Lüth*, 7 BVerfGE at 205–207; Quint, *supra* note 42, at 262–65. The relationship of the Basic Law to the private law is a very complicated one. Professor Quint provides an excellent description of this complicated relationship. *See id.*

62. Article 5 of the Basic Law provides,

(1) Every person shall have the right freely to express and disseminate his opinions in speech, writing, and pictures and to inform himself without hindrance from generally accessible sources. Freedom of the press and freedom of reporting by means of broadcasts and films shall be guaranteed. There shall be no censorship.

(2) These rights shall find their limits in the provisions of general laws, in provisions for the protection of young persons, and in the right to personal honor.

(3) Art and scholarship, research, and teaching shall be free. The freedom of teaching shall not release any person from allegiance to the constitution.

63. *Lüth*, 7 BverfGE at 209.

64. *Id.* at 208–209 ("The relationship between basic rights and the private legal order must be calibrated as follows: general statutes must be interpreted in light of the important limiting effect of basic rights, so that a specific content of the basic rights carries over into all areas of law out of recognition of the fundamental importance of free discussion to a free democratic order. This leads to a presumption that free discussion is protected, and must be preserved especially concerning matters of public life. The mutual relationship between basic rights and general statutes is thus not a one-sided limitation of the effect of basic rights through 'general statutes' but must be interpreted in light of recognition of the value-establishing significance of basic rights for a free democratic state so that the basic right itself establishes a limitation on general statutes").

65. *Lüth*, 7 BVerfGE at 207 ("The Constitutional Court must test to see whether the ordinary courts have adequately taken into account the scope and impact of basic rights on civil law").

66. *Id.* at 205.

67. GLENDON, *supra* note 19, at 33–34.

68. GLENDON, *supra* note 1, at 6–7.

69. Winfried Brugger, *Der moderne Verfassungsstaat. Rechtsvergleichunge Bemerkungen aus Sicht der amerikanischen und der deutschen Verfassung* (1999) (manuscript on file with author).

70. Missouri v. Holland, 252 U.S. 416, 433 (1920).

71. Brugger, *supra* note 69.

72. Griswold v. Connecticut, 381 U.S. 479, 522 (1965) (Black, J., dissenting).

73. These four schools of interpretation constitute the classic catalog of statutory interpretation in Germany, and also the core of constitutional interpretation. With the exception of teleological interpretation, they were also the classic methods of interpretation in Germany established in the classic 1840 treatise on Roman law by FRIEDRICH CARL VON SAVIGNY, SYSTEM OF MODERN ROMAN LAW (Scientia Verlag 1981) (1840–1851) (8 vols.). *See* Winfried Brugger, *Legal Interpretation, Schools of Jurisprudence, and Anthropology: Some Remarks from a German Point of View*, 41 AM. J. COMP. L. 395, 396–98 (1994). *See also* KOMMERS, *supra* note 13, at 48–49. One can thus see that there is some overlap between American and German methods of textual interpretation.

74. KOMMERS, *supra* note 13, at 48–49.

75. *Id.* at 48.

76. Brugger, *supra* note 73, at 401; KOMMERS, *supra* note 13, at 49. Of course, numerous decisions of the Constitutional Court rely more heavily on history.

77. *Homosexuality Case*, 6 BVerfGE 389, 431 (1957), *translated in* KOMMERS, *supra* note 13, at 49.

78. *Life Imprisonment Case*, 45 BVerfGE 187, 229 (1977), *translated in* DAVID P. CURRIE, THE CONSTITUTION OF THE FEDERAL REPUBLIC OF GERMANY 315 (1994).

79. *See, e.g.,* ROBERT BORK, THE TEMPTATION OF AMERICA (1990); Robert Bork, *Neutral Principles and Some First Amendment Problems*, 47 IND. L.J. 1 (1971).

80. *See, e.g., Griswold* 381 U.S. at 486 ("We deal with a right of privacy older than the Bill of Rights"); Skinner v. Oklahoma, 316 U.S. 535, 541 (1942) ("We are dealing here with legislation which involves one of the basic civil rights of man").

81. *See, e.g.,* Troxel v. Granville, 530 U.S. 57 (2000) (Court refused to recognize right of grandparents to assist raising of grandchild); Washington v. Glucksberg, 521 U.S. 702 (1997) (nonrecognition of right to die).

82. *Compare*, especially, *Transsexual Case*, 49 BVerfGE 286 (1978) (as matter of fundamental human dignity, person has right to live according to sex of choice) *with* Bowers v. Hardwick, 478 U.S. 186 (1986) (no right to engage in homosexual activity since it is not noted in traditions of country), discussed in Chapter 5.

2

Human Dignity

Human dignity is the central value of the Basic Law. This determination reflects the conscious intention to elevate modern Germany beyond the inhumanity of Nazism, signaling a new constitutional order. Article 1(1) of the Basic Law therefore states, "Human dignity shall be inviolable." The second paragraph of article one reinforces the centrality of human rights to the concept of human dignity, listing it in first place in the text of the Basic Law: "The German people therefore acknowledge inviolable and inalienable human rights as the basis of every community, of peace and of justice in the world."[1] Indeed, the specific enumeration of basic rights in the Basic Law is itself a tangible manifestation of human dignity. The catalogue of basic rights is systematically ordered, making up a central aspect of the objectively determined set of values that govern German society. In this way, dignity and basic rights have a mutually nourishing effect on one another.[2]

But human dignity means more than the specific catalog of basic rights. Dignity is not merely a focus on individuality. As the central value of the constitution, dignity infuses throughout the whole constitutional order, obligating the state both to protect and to realize it. Consequently, dignity radiates throughout society, animating the whole public legal system of Germany. Thus, dignitarian considerations influence education, health care, land use, and immigration, among other topics. Dignity includes a communitarian dimension as well; by requiring respect for others' claims to dignity, vindication for the human dignity of all is better assured, and a community of mutual cooperation and solidarity is fostered. One prime example of this is the Social Welfare Principle, enshrined in article 20(1) of the Basic Law, by which society is obligated to provide everyone with adequate economic and social conditions to ensure a minimal level of existence. Only with some guarantee of life's essentials can a person have a chance to thrive. Another example is the field of criminal justice. The German focus lies in rehabilitating felons and then restoring them to a place in society, as part of a community. The focus on rehabilitation contrasts with the pronounced American concern with retribution.

The first draft of the charter, arising from the constitutional convention, the Herrenchiemsee conference, stated, "The dignity of man is founded upon eternal rights with which every person is endowed by nature." Christian Democrats (a Christian-inspired and generally conservative party) sought to link the language "eternal rights" with "God-given rights." But this effort was resisted by Social Democrats (a social-welfare democratic party) and Free Democrats (a nineteenth-century liberal party), more secular and liberal parties. The result was the more neutral language reflected in article 1(1) of the Basic Law. There is general consensus that this language means that the guarantee of human dignity is inalienable, being both prior to and a constituent part of the social contract.[3] The drafters of the Basic Law consciously sought to anchor the social order to the ideal of human dignity as society's transcendent principle. The American Declaration of Independence—with its ringing pronouncement that "We hold these truths to be self-evident, that they are endowed by their Creator with certain inalienable rights, that among these are Life, Liberty, and the Pursuit of Happiness—That to secure these Rights, Governments are instituted among Men"— seems the closest reflection of this understanding. Human dignity is thus a constituent part of humanity in the German view, and its guarantee is the essence of the German social order. In this sense, dignity is the highest legal value in Germany.

The concept of human dignity in the Basic Law reflects the influence of three main schools of thought, although it was not intended to be strictly associated with any one of them. The three influences are Christian natural law, Kantian moral philosophy, and more individualistic, or existential, theories of personal autonomy and self-determination.[4] Under Christian natural law theories, dignity is a gift of God and, therefore, an inalienable aspect of humanity, beyond human tampering. Under Kantian philosophy, dignity is an indispensable part of human nature. For Kant, the concepts of freedom, development of moral personality, reverance of the moral law, and treating people as the final end are interlinked. Under a more individualistic theory of self-realization, the decisive aspect of human dignity is self-realization of one's identity through exercise of one's talents and abilities. This last theory seems the one most in accord with American views, notably present in free-speech law. The deep linkage to natural law and Kantian thought reflects a yearning to distinguish modern German law from its discredited past.

In the dignitarian jurisprudence of the Constitutional Court, the Court has mainly followed Kant's theory of moral autonomy. This is evident, for example, in the leading *Life Imprisonment Case*, where the Court attempted to capture the essence of human dignity: "It is contrary to human dignity to make the individual the mere tool [*blosses Objekt*] of the state. The principle that 'each person must always be an end in himself' applies unreservedly to all areas of the law; the intrinsic dignity of the person consists in acknowledging him as an independent personality."[5]

Still, human dignity is essentially an abstract, normative concept, albeit with a philosophical framework, and the Framers sought, and the Court has striven, to keep the term an open one, preferring that it take on concrete meaning through case-by-case determination. Thus, the main definition of dignity is the meaning given it by the Court in its jurisprudence. The Court has been rather freewheeling in this regard, consistent with its desire to set up proactively a new legal order.

Human Personhood and the Polity

The dignitarian jurisprudence of the Constitutional Court is replete with references to the nature of humankind and society.[6] The Court has frequently characterized man as a "spiritual–moral being," reflecting the Christian-natural law influence. The *Life Imprisonment Case* is again a good statement of this:

The constitutional principles of the Basic Law embrace the respect and protection of human dignity. The free human person and his dignity are the highest values of the constitutional order. The state in all of its forms is obliged to respect and defend it. This is based on the conception of man as a spiritual–moral being endowed with the freedom to determine and develop himself.[7]

Christian natural law is still influential in Germany. However, in recent times the Constitutional Court has moved away from such overt reference to Christian natural law. This may reflect the increasing secularization of German society. According to a 1998 poll, only 10 percent of Germans regularly attend church, down from 25 percent of the West German population in 1967.[8] In 1950, approximately 90 percent of East and West Germans claimed to be religious adherents. By 1989, when the Berlin Wall fell, only 36 percent of East Germans claimed that status.[9] This contrasts with 38 percent of the church-going American population in 1996 and 43 percent in 1995, according to two surveys.[10] In 1776, interestingly, only 17 percent of Americans regularly attended church.[11] In 1967, 68 percent of the West German population believed in God; today, 56 percent do. By contrast, 96 percent of Americans believe in God today.[12]

These statistics reveal, interestingly, that as Germans are becoming more secular, Americans are becoming more religious, especially as compared to their origins. This makes for a great irony from the standpoint of constitutional law, that German law resonates more with ideas of morality than the more neutral American law. Of course, religion is not the sole source of morals; Kantian morality and other ethical sources also influence German law.

A strongly Kantian view likewise invests the concept of personhood with rationality and self-determination, but also with duties and moral bounds. These strands of thought converge to form an integrated, whole person. As envisioned in German constitutional law, human beings are spiritual–moral beings who are to act freely, but their actions are to be bound by a sense of moral duty. Actions, in other words, are to be guided by a sense of social need, personal responsibility, and human solidarity.[13] Thus, as conceived in German constitutional law, the person is not to be just an autonomous individual acting egoistically, but also one constrained by reciprocal obligations to others and society. German constitutional law sets forth this vision as an ideal that people can, morally and spiritually, strive to realize.[14]

There is a strong linkage of the concept of personhood to the social community. The seminal case on artistic freedom, *Mephisto*, captured this thought well: "The human person [is] an autonomous being developing freely within the social community."[15] The human is not to be "an isolated and self-regarding individual," as he or she so often seems to be in the American social scheme.[16] Rather, the human is to be "related to and bound by the community."[17] The *Investment Aid Case* first advanced the concept of the human as a community-bound person: "The image of man in the Basic Law is not that of an isolated, sovereign individual; rather, the Basic Law has decided in favor of a relationship between individual and community in the sense of a person's dependence on and commitment to the community, without infringing upon a person's individual value."[18]

Once again, these statements bear the clear imprint of Kantian moral philosophy. Thus, we can see that the community envisioned by the Basic Law is one where individuality and human dignity are to be guaranteed and nourished, but with a sense of social solidarity and responsibility. Rather than a collection of atomistic individuals, people are connected to one another. Individual self-determination is offset by concepts of "participation, communication and civility."[19] In short, at the root of the German social vision is the Kantian proposition that humans are to be treated always as ends in themselves, and never as means, and that this is to be done within a moral social construct that both empowers and guides people. The *Life Imprisonment Case*, again, gives good voice to these thoughts:

This freedom within the meaning of the Basic Law is not that of an isolated and self-regarding individual but rather [that] of a person related to and bound by the community. In the light of this community-boundlessness it cannot be "in principle unlimited." The individual must allow those limits on his freedom of action that the legislature deems necessary in the interest of the community's social life; yet the autonomy of the individual has to be protected. This means that [the state] must regard every individual within society with equal worth. It is contrary to human dignity to make persons the mere tools [*blosses Objekt*] of the state. The principle that "each person must shape his own life" applies unreservedly to all areas of law; "the intrinsic dignity of each person depends on his status as an independent personality."[20]

We can thus see that the German idea of personhood relies strongly on a vibrant idea of community. Faced with the challenges of a changing pluralistic and multicultural society and forces of globalization, the German communal vision is harder than ever to realize today.

It is worth observing that the communal orientation reflects, in part, the Aristotelian idea of man as a social being, not an independent contractor. The Aristotelian ideal is yet central to European thought and tradition, reflected in modern time as the social dimension to life. Recall, for example, that the 1789 French Declaration of the Rights of Man and Citizen articulated rights within the context of duties, and listed social rights as well as individual rights. The French Revolution reverberated throughout Europe, including in the territory of Germany, where Kant, among others, was deeply moved by the French experience.

AMERICA

By comparison, American constitutional law has never really sought to define human dignity, nor human personhood or personality. Certainly there have been sketches of these concepts in American law, particularly in procedural due process, substantive due process, and capital punishment cases.[21] Moreover, in recent times the Warren Court, and particularly Justices Brennan and Marshall, sought to give life to these concepts.[22] Justice Brennan, in fact, sought to build a jurisprudence centered on human dignity. More recently, human dignity turns up with some regularity in the Supreme Court's discussions, particularly over autonomy rights and their role in preserving the integrity of individuality, and might even be considered a background theme of American law.[23]

In fact, the idea of dignity can be considered as implicit to the American constitutional scheme. Viewed from the eighteenth century, it was certainly an assertion of dignity to proclaim independence and found a social order dedicated to the proposition that individuals could best thrive within a scheme of limited government. Since then, the Court has emphasized, from time to time, that one purpose for limiting government was so that people could develop their faculties free from official interference. Justice Brandeis, in his famous concurrence in *Whitney v. California*, captured this thought especially well: "Those who won our independence believed that the final end of the State was to make men free to develop their faculties; and that in its government the deliberative forces should prevail over the arbitrary."[24] The self-realization component to dignity is well represented in American law, especially in substantive due process and free speech law.

Justice Brandeis, again in *Whitney*, is perhaps the best source for the vision of human nature or personhood that underlies the American constitutional scheme and is to utilize such freedom. In articulating his theory of free speech in *Whitney*, Justice Brandeis posits that the revolutionary generation "were not cowards ... [who] fear[ed] political change." They were instead "courageous, self-reliant men, with confidence in the power of free and fearless reasoning applied through the processes of popular government."[25] From this we can logically infer a vision of man, in free speech law and beyond, that is one of courage, self-reliance, and fortitude. This is the image of a lone ranger: hardy, self-sufficient, independent. Visions of community or human solidarity are not the regular vocabulary of the Court. It is to this ideal of human self-sufficiency that the range of American freedom is directed.

The ideal of self-sufficiency and hardiness resonates broadly in American law, especially free speech law, where it developed in the twentieth century. We might trace it even earlier to the freedoms of contract and property that marked the laissez-faire of the nineteenth century. When Justice Harlan speaks, hopefully, that "such freedom will ultimately produce a more capable citizenry," he has Justice Brandeis' portrait in mind.[26] Likewise, Justice Brennan framed the concrete "breathing space" protections of *New York Times v. Sullivan* from this idealized conception of human nature when he treated public officials, like judges, as "men of fortitude, able to thrive in a hardy climate."[27] The hardy soul of free speech law is an apt metaphor for the idea of American freedom. Exercise of American freedoms can be somewhat of a free-for-all, calling for hardy souls and those thick in skin. Americans believe that through freedom, the exercise of individual choice will manifest the "self-determining moral powers of a free person."[28]

Yet these ideas of American law are, at best, implications from the structure of liberty. Unlike German law, American law does not exhibit the same systematic attempt to come to basic definitional certitude over ideas of dignity, personhood, or personality. Instead, we must trace these ideas through the shadows left by the Supreme Court's pronouncements. It is an exercise more of implication and derivation than plain reading.

There are several explanations for this. First, dignity is textually mandated, in article 1, and personality, in article 2, of the Basic Law, whereas it is not mentioned at all in the American Constitution. Instead, the idea of dignity and personality must be implied from the promise of liberty in the due process clause or other textual authority. Such freehanded judicial creativity has been problematic in America, triggering a debate about the legitimacy of judicial review. Thus, the absence of a textual tie is especially disabling to American law. Second, and conversely, with the textual tie to dignity and personality it is more natural for the Constitutional Court to build a system of dignitarian jurisprudence. In this way, German law reflects the civil law orientation toward abstraction, systemazation, and classification. By comparison, American law reflects the common law orientation toward pragmatism and concreteness. Americans reason more from the bottom up, through the facts of the case, than the top down, from a philosophic mount. American pragmatism makes it hard to systematize and elaborate. Third, the idea of dignity implies commitment to its realization in the social order. But this calls for a proactive governmental role, as in Germany, but alien to America, which views government with skepticism, if not as threatening.

Whatever the reasons, the German social vision contrasts starkly with the American one. In the United States there is no consensus on core values, like Kantian morality, around which to organize the social order. While Americans can fundamentally agree on principles like individual freedom and democracy, these principles operate without stabilizing concepts of morality or community. Originally, of course, ideas like morality or community were or were to be invested with the animating force of civic republicanism, by which communities would select the right and proper values to be guided by. But this vision has long disappeared in any meaningful sense from regular American discourse. Moreover, the early consensus on religion and morality, which marked the founding generation has broken down. By now, Americans are so diverse in view and outlook as to be a verbal cacophony.

Instead, twenty-first-century Americans see themselves as autonomous people who themselves determine the norms and values that infuse the social order. In the United States, "rich cultural diversities" exist, all of which vie for influence and adherents.[29] "Many types of life, character, opinion and belief . . . develop."[30] These norms and values are almost always in flux, in competition and conflict with each other. In this climate, it is difficult for any one norm or value to predominate over another. No American principle demonstrates this more than the concept of free speech.[31] Through free speech, people argue out and determine who they are as a people, what norms will guide them, and what society they are or will become. Thus, individual freedom in America is somewhat unconnected to any one particular community, whereas in Germany it unfolds within a more shared sense of community, at least historically. Today Germany is becoming increasingly more diverse, religiously, culturally, and ethnically. Thus, the shared sense of community previously present is fraying. Germany is becoming more like the pluralistic society of the United States.

COMPARISON

The difference in makeup of community makes sense when one considers that Germany and the United States have different population mixes. Having started as a country of less than 4 million fairly homogenous people in 1791, America is now a country of over 260 million people that includes wide ethnic, religious, and cultural diversity.[32] While the dominant American racial group is European (80%), it comes from throughout Europe and beyond; 12 percent of Americans are African and 7 percent are of other races. America is a multicultural society. Seventy-five percent of Americans live in urban or suburban areas. In fact, America is rapidly becoming more suburban than urban. The reunited Germany has a population of about 84 million, which is 87 percent urban. Ethnically, German society is about 92 percent German. Turks comprise the largest ethnic minority group, consisting of just over 2 percent of the population. Thus, about 20 percent of Americans are minorities in relation to the majority population, as compared to about 8 percent of Germans. Moreover, the German influx of a minority population has been a recent, post–World War II phenomenon, quickening after the collapse of the Iron Curtain in the early 1990s. America, by contrast, has been a land of constant influx from throughout the world since the eighteenth century.

Both Germany and America are overwhelmingly Christian in religious orientation, although the complexion of belief differs. Germany, the birthplace of Protestantism, is primarily Lutherans and Catholics. Estimates of Germany's present Jewish population vary between 50,000 and 100,000, a very small percentage of the population. There are 2.5 million people of Islamic heritage in Germany, representing about 3 percent of the population. American Christians span all denominations, not just the mainstream groups of Catholicism and Lutheranism. Moreover, about 1.5 percent of Americans are Jewish, numbering 4.3 million people, almost as large as the Jewish population of Israel. Less than 2 percent of Americans are Islamic.[33]

Of course, since the United States was founded as a beacon of religious liberty, it makes sense that the American population would reflect tremendous religious diversity. Those unhappy or unwilling to conform to the strictures of the Old World emigrated to the New World, seeking a fresh start and a way to pursue their conscience unhindered.

These statistics reveal that the average German has much more in common, ethnically, religiously, and culturally, than the average American. This is not to say that German society is wholly homogenous. Increased immigration over the previous decade is quickly diversifying Germany's cultural makeup. The cultural divide between the peoples of the former East and West German states, in particular, remains pervasive. Nevertheless, Germans share a more common heritage than Americans. For example, unlike Germany, the United States has never had an aristocracy, monarchy, dominant state church, or unified educational system. It is not so surprising then that the culture reflected by German society reveals a more shared sense of values. This difference has dramatic consequences for the two social orders, as we will see. Of course, Americans, like the Swiss, share common political and democratic ideals. In this way, America is a land united more by ideas than ethnic affinity. In comparison, Germans have had just fifty years of the political and cultural affinity produced by the Basic

Law. Only since 1989 has the Basic Law been the integrative force of the two Germanies. Germany is more a land of blood and soil than ideas.

THE CONCRETE MEANING OF HUMAN DIGNITY

Germany

Since human dignity is a capacious concept, it is difficult to determine precisely what it means, in law, outside the context of a factual setting. It is one of those terms best understood through application and not definition. As the driving principle of the German legal order, however, and as a root of Kantian thought, it possesses a certain fixed content within Germany. At a minimum, for example, it means that the social order must reflect recognition of the equality of humankind. This concept is anchored in article 3 of the Basic Law, which provides,

(1) All persons shall be equal before the law.

(2) Men and women shall have equal rights. The state shall promote the actual implementation of equal rights for women and men and take steps to eliminate disadvantages that now exist.

(3) No person shall be favored or disfavored because of sex, parentage, race, language, homeland and origin, faith, or religious or political opinions. No persons shall be disfavored because of disability.

Equality means that persons are entitled to equal worth.[34] Certainly there can be no slavery or serfdom or gender, racial, or ethnic discrimination.[35] German equality has a stronger substantive bite than American. This seems warranted by the stronger textual language. American equality, rooted in the Fourteenth Amendment, simply states, "No state shall . . . deny to any person within its jurisdiction the equal protection of the laws." Only around 1954, with the landmark case of *Brown v. Board of Education*, did the Supreme Court seek to make equality a premier organizing principle of American society.[36] In recent times, the Court has been quite tentative in applying the concept of equality. This is quite remarkable in view of what seems the persistent structural inequality of American society, especially in matters of race, where wide gaps between majority whites and others over education, income, crime, and other matters of class yet exist.[37]

Second, dignity means respect of physical identity and integrity, which is textually specified in article 2(2) of the German Basic Law, which provides, "Every person shall have the right to life and physical integrity." This prohibits torture and corporal punishment and forbids imposing punishment without fault or levying disproportionate penalties.[38] There is no comparable American language. In the United States, these ideas are addressed, to an extent, under due process and the Eighth Amendment, which prohibits "excessive bail . . . excessive fines . . . [and] cruel and unusual punishments."

Third, dignity means respect for intellectual and spiritual identity and integrity.[39] This is manifested most dramatically in the protection of personality rights, specified in article 2 of the Basic Law and elaborated on in Chapters 3, 4, and 5 of this book. In American law, this idea also is developed in personality law and free speech law, covered in the next several chapters of this book.

Fourth, dignity means limitation of official power.[40] This is particularly evident in the commitment to the *Rechtstaat* and especially its guarantee of proportionality, which circumscribes governmental means to legitimate ends, and of procedural protections, which allow persons affected by official action to be heard and to be able to influence proceedings that concern them. Article 19(4) of the Basic Law is the textual tie for this, providing, "Should any person's rights be violated by public authority, he may have recourse to the courts." In America, this idea is handled, extensively, under procedural due process protections, harking back to the Magna Carta and the "law of the land."

Fifth, dignity means guarantee of individual and social existence. Tangibly, this is manifested in the article 2(2) right to life and in Germany's social welfare state, textually anchored in article 20(1) of the Basic Law.[41] American constitutional law does not speak to this social dimension. Instead, social issues are addressed through legislation and basic operation of the democratic process.

The main development of German dignitarian jurisprudence has occurred in conjunction with the more concrete freedoms of article 2 of the Basic Law. There are three specific freedoms in article 2 of the Basic Law. The first of these is the right to free development of personality, phrased in article 2(1) as, "Every person shall have the right to free development of his personality insofar as he does not violate the rights of others or offend against the constitutional order or the moral law." This idea is fundamentally a Kantian one, and Kant's influence resonates deeply in German law, both public and private. It is the clause most like the American concept of privacy rights, grounded in the due process clause. German personality rights include, among other things, protection of informational privacy, a right to have one's paternity established, and a right to have official records reflect a sex change.[42] These personality rights, both German and American, will be elaborated on in Chapers 4 and 5.

The second of the important article 2 freedoms is "the right to life and to physical integrity." The right to life clause is the source for the Constitutional Court's conclusion in the *Abortion Cases* that the state has a duty to protect life after conception, which resulted in strict limitation of abortion.[43] No right to life language exists in the American Constitution, which had a decisive effect on the Court's outcome in *Roe v. Wade*.[44] In *Roe*, the Supreme Court went to great lengths to emphasize that the constitutional idea of person applies only after one is born. The Court was thus not willing to imply a right to life for a fetus. The contrasting German and American treatment of abortion will be examined in Chapter 6. Apart from abortion, the Constitutional Court has not invoked the clause to place wide-ranging duties to protect life on the state. While recognizing a duty to protect life, the Constitutional Court has deferred to government's implementation of it. Normal politics is thus the main scene for determining the nature of governmental duties in this regard, as in America.

The "physical integrity" clause is mainly used as a source to guide criminal procedures, somewhat like American criminal due process jurisprudence.[45] It has also been used to limit invasions of the body that would cause pain, harm, disfigurement, or injury. For example, in the *Spinal Tap Case*, the Court invalidated a court-ordered sampling of a defendant's spinal column to test his involvement in a crime on the ground that this violated a person's physical integrity.[46] The Court has also invalidated use of polygraph tests to determine a defendant's veracity.[47] Attaching a person to a machine to force the truth out, the Court reasoned, is "an inadmissible invasion of a person's innermost self and a violation of human dignity." Man should not be "an object of experimentation," a manifestation of the Kantian injunction to treat people as only ends.[48] Efforts to apply the physical integrity clause outside the criminal context have not been successful. As this topic of physical inviolability is mainly a criminal one, it will not be addressed in this book.

The last of the article 2 freedoms provides that "Freedom of the person shall be inviolable." Mainly, this freedom protects free physical movement. It is somewhat akin to the English concept of habeas corpus, protecting against arbitrary restraints on physical liberty, and operates in conjunction with the other article 2(2) freedoms.[49] It too will not be extensively considered here.

Not surprisingly, human dignity, alone or in conjunction with the more particular freedoms of article 2, is a rich source of constitutional litigation, and is widely debated on and off the Court.[50] It directly poses the critical question of the role of a constitutional court in a democracy. Some believe that human dignity, like basic rights, should be determined through the operation of judicial review. Judicial intervention will check the excesses of majoritarian politics, as originally foreseen by the American Framers. Others believe that such a proactive judicial role intrudes too deeply into the democratic process, leading to a government of judges and not people. Instead, the democracy as a whole, through parliamentary democracy or legislative determination, expressing the supreme will of the people, should determine the meaning of dignity. In these ways, human dignity in Germany is most like the American concept of modern substantive due process, particularly rights of privacy. Both concepts are open ended and controversial, posing difficult questions for the role of the court within a democracy and the nature of the constitutional order. The remaining part of this book explores this topic as it relates to the development of human personality in Germany and America.

America

In comparison to the relatively specific framing of human dignity and its cognates in the Basic Law, it is striking how devoid of detail the American Constitution is on these matters. While the Constitution makes no mention of dignity, ideas of dignity might nevertheless be implied through articulation of basic freedoms. There are, however, only a few anchors in the text for this enterprise.

One source, the privileges and immunities clause, has effectively been rendered a dead letter, until quite recently, for purposes of enumerating basic rights since the Supreme Court's determination in 1873, in *The Slaughter-House Cases*, that the Fourteenth Amendment privileges and immunities clause only protects a narrow category of national rights, such as rights to assemble, petition, and use navigable waters.[51] That leaves only two textual pieces of support for this endeavor: the due process clause and the Ninth Amendment. The Ninth Amendment was not invoked by the Court until 1965 in the famous *Griswold v. Connecticut* case, and then only to lend support to the Court's enumeration of a right of privacy beyond the constitutional text.[52] Not surprisingly, therefore, the Court has mainly relied on the due process clause, which provides that no "state [shall] . . . deprive any person of life, liberty, or property, without due process of law," to found basic rights that empower development of personality.[53] Through due process, the Court has interpreted a range of privacy and autonomy rights that protect personal decision making in areas relating to marriage, procreation, contraception, family relationships, child rearing, and education.[54] These issues will be examined in Chapter 5. The movement of both Courts thus seems very much in the same general direction, notwithstanding different textual, historical, philosophical, and cultural settings.

NOTES

1. DONALD P. KOMMERS, THE CONSTITUTIONAL JURISPRUDENCE OF THE FEDERAL REPUBLIC OF GERMANY 305 (1989).

2. *Id.* at 305.

3. For brief description of this history, *see id.* at 308.

4. For elaboration of these theories, and their influence on human dignity, *see* 2 BODO PIEROTH & BERNHARD SCHLINK, GRUNDRECHTE STAATSRECHT 90–91 (10th ed. 1994).

5. 45 BVerfGE 187, 228 (1977), *translated in* DAVID P. CURRIE, THE CONSTITUTION OF THE FEDERAL REPUBLIC OF GERMANY 314 (1994).

6. Kommers, *supra* note 1, at 312.

7. 45 BVerfGE at 227, *translated in* Kommers, *supra* note 1, at 316.

8. Jack D. Shand, *The Decline of Traditional Christian Beliefs in Germany*, 59 SOCIOLOGY OF RELIGION 179 (1998).

9. Mary L. Gautier, *Church Attendance and Religious Belief in Postcommunist Societies*, 36 JOURNAL FOR THE SCIENTIFIC STUDY OF RELIGION 289 (1997).

10. David Briggs, *Study Says Estimates on Churchgoing are Inflated*, CLEVELAND PLAIN DEALER, May 20, 1998, at 1A; Shand, *supra* note 8.

11. Rodney Stark, *German and German American Religiousness: Approximating a Crucial Experiment*, 36 JOURNAL FOR THE SCIENTIFIC STUDY OF RELIGION 182 (1997).

12. Shand, *supra* note 8.

13. Kommers, *supra* note 1, at 313.

14. Winfried Brugger, Der moderne Verfassungsstaat. Rechtsvergleichunge Bemerkungen aus Sicht der amerikanischen und der deutschen Verfassung (1999) (unpublished manuscript, on file with author).

15. 30 BVerfGE 173, 193 (1971), *translated in* Kommers, *supra* note 1, at 428.

16. *Life Imprisonment Case*, 45 BVerfGE at 227, *translated in* Kommers, *supra* note 1, at 316.

17. *Id.*

18. 4 BVerfGE 7, 15–16 (1954), *translated in* Kommers, *supra* note 1, at 313.

19. Kommers, *supra* note 1, at 313.

20. 45 BVerfGE at 227–28, *translated in id.* at 316.

21. *See, e.g.*, Goldberg v. Kelly, 397 U.S. 254, 264–65 (1970) (Brennan, J., opinion) ("From its founding the Nation's basic commitment has been to foster the dignity and well-being of all persons within its borders"). *See also* Planned Parenthood of Southeastern Pennsylvania v. Casey, 505 U.S. 833, 851 (1992) ("These matters [decisions relating to marriage, procreation, etc.], involving the most intimate and personal choices a person may make in a lifetime, choices central to personal dignity and autonomy,

are central to the liberty protected by the Fourteenth Amendment"). *See also* Furman v. Georgia, 408 U.S. 238 (1972).

22. McClesky v. Kemp, 481 U.S. 279, 336 (1987) (Brennan, J., dissenting) ("Considering the race of a defendant or victim in deciding if the death penalty should be imposed is completely at odds with [the] concern that an individual be evaluated as a unique human being"); Miranda v. Arizona, 384 U.S. 436 (1966); Rosenblatt v. Baer, 383 U.S. 75, 92 (1966) (Stewart, J., concurring) ("The right of a man to the protection of his own reputation from unjustified invasion and wrongful hurt reflects no more than our basic concept of the essential dignity and worth of every human being—a concept at the root of any decent system of ordered liberty").

23. *See Casey*, 505 U.S. at 851; National Treasury Employees Union v. von Raab, 489 U.S. 656, 681 (1989) (Scalia, J., dissenting) ("In my view the Customs Service rules are a kind of immolation of privacy and human dignity in symbolic opposition to drug use").

24. 274 U.S. 357, 375 (1927).

25. *Id.* at 377.

26. Cohen v. California, 403 U.S. 15, 24 (1971).

27. 376 U.S. 254, 273 (1964).

28. David Richards, TOLERATION AND THE CONSTITUTION 243–44 (1986).

29. West Virginia State Board of Education v. Barnette, 319 U.S. 624, 642 (1943).

30. Cantwell v. Connecticut, 310 U.S. 296, 310 (1940).

31. Edward J. Eberle, *Hate Speech, Offensive Speech, and Public Discourse in America*, 29 WAKE FOREST L. REV. 1135 (1994) (through public discourse, we determine who we are as a people).

32. MARY ANN GLENDON, RIGHTS TALK: THE IMPOVERISHMENT OF POLITICAL DISCOURSE 36 (1991).

33. Statistics concerning the population of the United States are based on THE WORLD ALMANAC AND BOOK OF FACTS 832 (1998); THE STATESMAN'S YEARBOOK 1391 (134th ed. 1997–98). Statistics concerning the population of Germany are based on THE WORLD ALMANAC AND BOOK OF FACTS 790 (2001); *id.* at 767 (1998); STATESMAN'S YEARBOOK, *supra* note 33, at 548; THE TIME ALMANAC 222 (2000).

34. *Life Imprisonment*, 45 BVerfGE at 228.

35. Pieroth & Schlink, *supra* note 4, at 93.

36. 347 U.S. 483 (1954).

37. David E. Sanger, *Big Racial Disparity Persists Among Users of the Internet*, N.Y. TIMES, Jul. 9, 1999, at A12; Sheryl Gay Stolberg, *Racial Divide Found in Maternal Mortality*, N.Y. TIMES, Jun. 18, 1999, at A18; Erica Goode, *For Good Health, It Helps to Be Rich and Important*, N.Y. TIMES, Jun. 1, 1999, at D1 (28.4% of blacks live below poverty line as compared to 11.2% of whites; an average white male lives 5 years longer than a black male, an average white woman 3.7 years longer than a black woman); *Nation Still Divided Racially, Economically Study Finds*, PROVIDENCE SUNDAY JOURNAL, Mar. 1, 1998, at A3 (median family income of black and Hispanic Americans is only 55% of white Americans, and minorities are three times more likely to live below poverty line).

38. *Life Imprisonment*, 45 BVerfGE at 228; Pieroth & Schlink, *supra* note 4, at 93.

39. Pieroth & Schlink, *supra* note 4, at 93.

40. *Id.* at 94.

41. *Id.*

42. *Census Act Case*, 65 BVerfGE 1 (1983); *Right to Heritage II*, 90 BVerfGE 263 (1994); *Right to Heritage I*, 79 BVerfGE 256 (1988); *Transsexual Case*, 49 BVerfGE 286 (1978).

43. *Abortion II*, 88 BVerfGE 203 (1993); *Abortion I*, 39 BVerfGE 1 (1975).

44. 410 U.S. 113 (1973).

45. Kommers, *supra* note 1, at 343.

46. 16 BVerfGE 194 (1963). *See also Pneumoencephalography Case*, 17 BVerfGE 108 (1963) (Court invalidated court-ordered puncture of a person's vertebral canal for purposes of testing personality for crime).

47. *Polygraph Case*, 35 Neue Juristische Wochenschrift (NJW) 375 (1982) (decision of August 18, 1981). *See also* 17 BVerfGE 347 (1963).

48. Kommers, *supra* note 1, at 344.

49. See Pieroth & Schlink, *supra* note 4, at 110–11.

50. *See, e.g.*, Peter Badura, *Generalprävention und Würde des Menschen*, 19 Juristenzeitung 337 (1964) (examination of roots of dignity concept); Christoph Degenhart, *Das allgemeine Persönlichkeitsrecht*, 5 Juristische Schulung 361 (1992) (examination of general right of personality); Hasso Hofmann, *Die versprochene Menschenwürde*, 118 Archiv des Öffentlichen Rechts 353 (1993) (exploration of capacious concept of human dignity).

51. *See* 83 U.S. (16 Wall.) 36 (1873). In dramatic fashion, the Court recently interpreted the Privileges and Immunities Clause to contain a stronger core of substantive freedom that invalidates a state residency requirement on levels of welfare assistance. Saenz v. Roe, 526 U.S. 489 (1999). It remains to be seen whether *Saenz* augurs a reconception in the promise of liberty at the root of the clause. Cases before *Saenz* cautiously interpreted a certain range of freedom in the Article IV privileges and immunities clause, being careful not to ground the decision in the Fourteenth Amendment privileges and immunities clause, still viewed largely ineffective since *Slaughter-House*, but for the future that *Saenz* bodes. *See, e.g.*, United Building & Construction Trades Council v. Camden, 465 U.S. 208 (1984) (protecting national citizenship against set-aside work program imposed by municipality to protect residents); New Hampshire v. Piper, 470 U.S. 274 (1985) (rule limiting bar admission to state residents violates privileges and immunities); Hicklin v. Orbeck, 437 U.S. 518 (1978) (residential hiring preference violates privileges and immunities).

52. 381 U.S. 479 (1965) (relying on Ninth Amendment, and other amendments, for penumbras emanating from such specific guarantees). *See also id.* at 493 (Goldberg, J., concurring) ("the Ninth Amendment . . . lends strong support to the view that the liberty protected by the Fifth and Fourteenth Amendments . . . is not restricted to rights specifically mentioned in the first eight amendments").

53. *See, e.g., Roe*, 410 U.S. at 113 ("This right of privacy, whether it be founded in the Fourteenth Amendments concept of personal liberty, as we

feel it is, or in the Ninth, is broad enough to encompass a woman's decision whether or not to terminate her pregnancy"). Other cognates of privacy could be found in the Third Amendment's prohibition against "quartering troops in any house" and the Fourth Amendment's "right of the people to be secure in their persons, houses, papers and effects, against unreasonable searches and seizures."

54. Griswold v. Connecticut, 381 U.S. 479 (1965); Skinner v. Oklahoma, 316 U.S. 535 (1942); Carey v. Population Services International, 431 U.S. 678 (1977); Eisenstadt v. Baird, 405 U.S. 438 (1972); *Griswold*, 381 U.S. 479; Moore v. East Cleveland, 431 U.S. 494 (1977) (city cannot limit occupancy of dwelling to members of same nuclear family); Pierce v. Society of Sisters, 268 U.S. 510 (1925) (state cannot mandate public school attendance when parents desire to send children to private school); Meyer v. Nebraska, 262 U.S. 390 (1923) (state cannot mandate teaching of only English in schools).

3

Personality and Freedom of Action: The Outer World

INTRODUCTION TO PERSONALITY

Viewed from the perspective of an individual, human dignity means the ability to develop and realize one's talents, ambitions, and desires in life. Finding one's place in life is how most people would define their dignity. This includes a sense of self-respect and self-worth, ideas also central to one's conception of dignity. But the idea of dignity does not have to be just a focus on self. It can also include concern and respect for others and society. Thus, a fuller concept of dignity might couple the idea of self-realization with a sense of social obligation and solidarity with others. The way or ways in which law envisions the human person depends very much on the vision of human nature that animates it. In turn, these legal constructs reflect in true ways the underlying legal culture.

Central to the concept of human personhood is human personality, which is our focus in the next three chapters. We need to focus, specifically, on how law and legal culture conceptualize human personhood. Is man an actor intent only on self-development or egotistic pursuit of desire? Or is man also concerned with well-being and the plight of others? What conditions are present for achievement of human talent and capacity? Does the social order empower or constrain human freedom and human welfare? How well do conceptions of human personality equip us to deal with the challenges of our age?

These are the questions we need to probe and evaluate as we search for and uncover the idea of human personhood in the legal orders of Germany and the United States. Western man at the beginning of the twenty-first century is a constitutional being situated in a constitutional culture, vested with a range of personal rights that he or she may exercise to realize his or her ambition. How he or she exercises rights can make a difference, both in daily life and the broader world he or she inhabits. This is the portrait of modern man as we enter the twenty-first century.

This portrait did not, of course, emerge from whole cloth, but instead evolved from earlier visions of human nature. In the eighteenth century, man was hypothesized to exist, originally, in a state of nature. In this idealized state, thinkers conceived different visions of human nature, which served as the basis for elaboration of a social contract. Hobbes, for example, thought man to be a beast, in a perpetual state of war, who entered into society out of fear and self-interest, desiring preservation. Rousseau, by contrast, viewed man in benevolent terms, as being innately good. Civilization corrupted man, more than being a reflection of man's dark nature. Different premises followed from these assumptions. For Hobbes, man was possessive and self-interested; for Rousseau, man's rights and claims were to be mediated by concern for the common good. In the nineteenth century, thinkers envisioned man mainly in economic terms—*homo economicus*[1]—as a free trader by Adam Smith, an alienated soul by Marx, or a master of his fate, through laissez-faire, by Herbert Spencer. Modern man, situated at the beginning of this century, follows from these antecedents. He or she is a constitutional person—conceived in constitutional terms—with individual rights at his or her disposal to shape his or her world and society overall.

As we trace this idea of human personhood in the constitutional laws of Germany and the United States, we find its most vivid manifestation in the personality laws of the two countries, which will be our focus. In Germany, this is the subject of article 2 of the Basic Law and its right, according to official translation, to the "free development of personality." In American law, this topic is defined as autonomy law, including rights of privacy that emanate therefrom. These American rights are not set forth in any explicit manner in a way comparable to the textual enumeration in article 2 in the German law. Instead, they are implications from the promise of liberty of the due process clause, which provides, in the Fifth and Fourteenth Amendments to the Constitution, that "No person shall be . . . deprived of life, liberty, or property, without due process of law."

The difference in language is revealing. The German phrasing in article 2 is *Entfaltung*, which connotes more an "unfolding," like a bud from a rose, than "development," which is translated as *Entwicklung*.[2] Thus, German law is really a focus on the "free unfolding of personality" more than just the self-realization connoted by "development." The language of American law resonates with freedom. Americans speak of autonomy rights, rights to do things; for example, the right to choose over personal matters like abortion, family life, or reproductive choices. The American language of personality rights does not resonate with the idea of "unfolding" and the commensurate sense of well-being it implies.

We will trace this idea of personality through three main components integral to personality law. The first two components involve a contrast between inner and outer freedom. Outer freedom entails freedom of action, the ability to act in the world as one desires. Acting as one desires is a central ingredient of personal identity. As conceived in German law, freedom of action empowers one to do fundamentally what one desires insofar as it does not interfere with others or the constraints of the social order. This is the topic of this chapter.

As freedom of action is outward in focus, inner freedom connotes a personal, interior sphere that is inward in orientation. The personal sphere delimits an essential sphere of privacy within which one can fundamentally determine who one is and how one should relate to the world, if at all. One may choose to engage actively in the world, and thus avail oneself of freedoms of action. Or one may choose to withdraw from the world, retreating into oneself and concentrating on inner development. The focus of this inner freedom is a person's thoughts, beliefs, emotions, and yearnings, and the right to decide what to do with them. A person might, for example, choose to expose them to the world or some of its members. Or a person might instead opt to maintain them secret from the outside world, as part of an inner core of inviolate personality. Everyone needs this inner sanctuary of being in which to contemplate life and its dimensions. We will examine how the two laws have sought to create an inner, intimate sphere so that a core of personality might be developed and protected. The parameters of inner freedom is the topic of Chapter 4.

A final component to personality as envisioned in constitutional law are issues relating to identity, self-determination, and autonomy, the subject of Chapter 5. This area has been a central focus of both German and American law over the last thirty years. It provides the greatest overlap between the two laws, including coverage of such common issues as abortion, homosexuality, sexual freedom, marriage, and parenthood. The countries' treatment of such common topics will yield an especially rich perspective on the similarites and differences in legal culture.

The survey of personality conducted in these chapters will, in turn, yield an insightful portrait of our twenty-first-century constitutional man, illuminating who we are and, perhaps, who we might become. When added to the final trait examined in the book—freedom of expression—we will have an especially rich portrait of modern man. We will then be in a good position to assess more carefully the countries' contrasting views of human dignity and personality, and the comparative strengths of their constitutional visions.

FREEDOM OF ACTION: THE OUTER WORLD

Germany

The German law on the "free unfolding of personality" (*freie Entfaltung der Persönlichkeit*) is comprehensive and multifaceted. Grounded in human dignity and, specifically, Kant's theory of moral autonomy, the right is ordinarily read in conjunction with the more ultimate article 1 guarantee, the only right so tangibly linked to another in German law. Personality rights come into play, potentially, whenever an action is not protected by a more specific right. Theoretically, all claims or interests have the potential to be so protected. In this way, article 1 human dignity and article 2(1) rights interact to form comprehensive protection of human personality and personhood. The Constitutional Court captured the sense of these rights well in the *Eppler Case*: "They complement as 'undefined' freedom the special [defined] freedoms, like freedom of conscience or expression, equally constitutive elements of personality. Their function is, in the sense of the ultimate constitutional value, human dignity, to preserve the narrow personal life sphere and to maintain its conditions, that are not encompassed by traditional concrete guarantees."[3]

This "catch-all" function of personality rights is important. In view of "modern developments and the associated threats they pose to the protection of human personality," for example, personality rights serve as a last preserve of freedom, open to expansion.[4] How these rights have been expanded, and the human traits they capture, is the subject of our present examination as we sketch a portrait of human personality.

Textually, comprehensive rights are not clearly derivable from enumeration of a "right to the free development of personality," although the German text offers more tangible support for the effort than the American one. Notwithstanding the language, the fundamental thrust of the German Constitutional Court has been to enlarge the rights sought to be captured by the language, as compared to confining itself to strict application of the language of the text.[5] This proactive approach follows from the tools of German legal science (*Rechtswissenschaft*) and its emphasis on courts and scholars working collaboratively to provide a gloss on bare legal text so that there might be an open development of the law to meet social needs. The technique also brings into focus how, under German methods of constitutional interpretation, the primacy of the text controls in relation to present conditions. These developments also follow directly from the inspiration of German civil courts, which had interpreted personality law in just this manner. German personality law is thus a creature of the Constitutional Court, as rights of privacy are of the Supreme Court.

Elfes *and the General Right of Personality*

German personality law, in a constitutional sense, began with the groundbreaking decision of *Elfes* in 1957.[6] An earlier Constitutional Court case, the *Investment Aid Case*, had first begun the process of attempting to fix the definition of freedom of action.[7] As significant, the Federal Supreme Court (BGH), the supreme interpreter of the German Civil Code, had developed a right of personality within the context of the BGB as it relates to the Basic Law. For example, in one famous case the BGH derived a right of personality from articles 1 and 2 of the Basic Law in protecting the contents of a letter sent as commentary to a magazine.[8] Publication of the letter reflected the author's personality, the court reasoned. If printed out of context, the letter could shed unfavorable light on the author. Decisions such as these found a favorable audience in the legal literature. Thus, *Elfes* represented the Constitutional Court's approval of these developments of the BGH, thereby constitutionalizing the doctrine of a general right to personality.

Interestingly, this period of the 1950s represented one of significant judicial creativity by the Constitutional Court. The seminal case on freedom of expression, *Lüth*, was decided one year after *Elfes*.[9] This creativity also echoed in the United States. The 1950s marked the emergence of the Warren Court revolution, including momentous decisions like *Brown v. Board of Education;*[10] *Yates v. United States*, which for the first time invalidated the convictions of several members of the Communist Party, a courageous decision amidst the hysteria of the Red Scare;[11] and *Roth v. United States*, which for the first time proffered a definition of obscenity in the hope of finding an end point to free speech law.[12] As we look back at the twentieth century, the 1950s emerges as the fountainhead of the human rights movement. Human rights germinated both nationally, as our discussion of American and German law shows, and internationally, as the peoples of the world formed conventions, such as the 1948 U.N. Universal Declaration of Human Rights and the 1950 European Convention for the Protection of Human Rights and Fundamental Freedoms, which nations' adopted and implemented.

The setting in *Elfes* seemed an odd one in which to announce a general personality right. Elfes was active in right-wing politics, before and after World War II, enjoying some success, including election as a parliamentary representative as a member of the Christian Democratic Union.[13] In his political activities, he was a severe critic of West German defense policy and its policy toward reunification with Eastern Germany, having participated in conferences and demonstrations at home and abroad.[14] Seeking to continue spreading his message abroad, he sought extension of his visa to attend a foreign political conference, but was denied on the ground that his criticism constituted a threat to national security. During this infant stage of the Federal Republic, it was understandably sensitive to the dangers of the right wing and Nazis, present and former. The reassimilation of those who had been Nazis during the Hitler era into the free democratic order of the Republic, in particular, was a persistent and troubling problem.

Elfes first argued that his activities were protected by article 11, which guarantees Germans freedom of movement. However, the Court ruled that this provision applied only to inter-German travel, not foreign travel.[15] Thus, if Elfes was to succeed, another argument was necessary. Here to do service was the article 2 guarantee of personality. Even if foreign travel was not covered by article 11, it might yet be part of one's personal freedom of action, protected under article 2(1), so the Court determined. This illustrates the catch-all function of article 2 personality rights: They capture claims not protected by the more specific guarantees in the catalogue of basic rights. As the Court stated, "Insofar as specific life areas are not guaranteed through the specific protection of a basic right, an individual can call on article 2(1) for protection against incursions into his liberty by officials."[16]

By freedom of action, the Court meant the right to engage in activities necessary to the development and assertion of one's person: "seen from a legal perspective, [article 2(1)] is an independent basic right, that guarantees general human freedom of action."[17] Whether traveling abroad constituted freedom of action depended on resolving a theoretical dispute left open in the *Investment Aid Case* as to the reach of this freedom.[18] In the *Investment Aid Case* the Court had laid out two definitions of freedom of action, not choosing one over the other. Freedom of action could mean only a "minimal amount of this freedom of action without which an individual would not be able to develop herself as a spiritual–moral person," or freedom of action could be interpreted "in a broad, comprehensive sense."[19]

In *Elfes*, the Court decided that a broad interpretation better suited the text and purpose of the Basic Law. First, it seemed inconceivable how a definition limited to the "core area of personality" could ever result in violations of "the rights of others . . . the constitutional order . . . or morality," the textual limitations of personality set out in article 2(1). It seemed hard to envision how these textual restrictions could then have meaning. A broader interpretation thus seemed more sensible. Second, article 2 reflects radiation of human dignity, the ultimate constitutional value, as do all constitutional principles. Thus, a broad interpretation seemed more compatible with a view of persons as morally autonomous beings operating responsibly within the community. Third, an expansive interpretation also seemed more consistent with the Framers' intentions, who had originally used the language "everyone can do or not do what he or she likes," changing this for "linguistic" reasons, not legal considerations.[20]

A broad interpretation of freedom of action has important consequences for the German constitutional order. As intended by the Court, every form of activity related to personality, in principle, is covered by the concept. Restraints on personal freedom will come only from those imposed as a condition of the "constitutional order" or other textual limitations.[21] As stated in a later case, "Article 2 guarantees everyone a general freedom of action insofar as one does not violate the rights of others, the moral order, or the constitutional order."[22] This conception of freedom again resonates with the influence of Kant. For Kant, freedom should be enjoyed to the full subject only to the restraints imposed by others' pursuit of the same. Ideally, each person would discover his or her talents, but also his or her limits. The conception endows people with significant personal freedom, transforming the Basic Law into a very rights-protective charter. One might argue it is consistent with the concept of human dignity that infuses the Basic Law, calling on the state, as it does, "to respect and protect it."

In practice, however, the Constitutional Court has limited the reach of this freedom despite the expansive potential of the concept; it has applied freedom of action mainly to economic and recreational areas.[23] Yet the role of article 2 as the last preserve of individual freedom is an important principle. It serves as a residual vessel of freedom in a way that the Ninth Amendment of the U.S. Constitution as yet does not. Despite the Ninth Amendment's seeming authorization of rights beyond those textually enumerated, the Supreme Court has mainly eschewed the principle.[24] Thus, future developments, perhaps, await expansion of German freedom of action in a way that seems unlikely under the Ninth Amendment. In fact, it is interesting as a matter of comparative law that Germans have been quite expansive over the idea of freedom, whereas Americans have been rather stingy. In the 1986 case of *Bowers v. Hardwick*, the Supreme Court even theorized the end of substantive due process, the law that gives rise to personal freedom.[25]

Applying these principles, the Constitutional Court determined that foreign travel was within freedom of action.[26] This determination did not, of course, end the inquiry. Freedom of action is guaranteed only to the extent it is within the constitutional order and does not violate third-party rights or morality.[27] *Elfes* thus provided the Court with the occasion to interpret these textual limitations. At issue in *Elfes* was the constitutional order limitation, since security measures are taken to protect society. This is the most important limitation.

Rights of others entails the rights and claims of third parties.[28] Such claims might justifiably limit individual rights in Germany or in America. In German law, this restriction has been employed to ban arson and trespass, for example.[29] In the context of religious rights, the dignitarian rights of others were used to limit an atheist's attempt to coerce individuals to his view through use of cigarettes as bribery.[30] However, third-party rights are ordinarily evidenced in the legal and constitutional order, and thus unlikely to act as an independent restraint.[31]

Morality is no more self-defining in German law than American, although German law relies on more explicitly Christian law notions than American and also, with its rooting in German moral idealism, has a more pronounced moral grounding. Interesting for comparative purposes, morality has been used in both Germany and the United States to ban sodomy and homosexual activities.[32] However, notably, the major German case of 1957 has been held in disrepute for some time, whereas the more recent 1986 decision of *Bowers v. Hardwick* remains the law, having only recently been questioned, and then *sub silentio*, in the 1996 case of *Romer v.*

Evans.[33] Ironically, the Georgia sodomy law at issue in *Bowers* has recently been declared unconstitutional by the Georgia Supreme Court, under the Georgia Constitution.[34] Thus, ultimately, underlying legal systems in both Germany and America repudiated this stricture of law. Still, morality is mainly reflected in legal concepts, like "good morals" (*gute Sitten*) or "good faith" (*Treu und Glauben*), that make up the legal order.[35] As such, and especially with its roots in Kantian thought, morality becomes an important background principle for the legal system as a whole. As a practical matter, however, morality itself will not ordinarily restrain freedom of action.[36] This brings us back to the "constitutional order," of which much depended on its construction.

According to the Constitutional Court, the constitutional order means the general legal order as it conforms to the Constitution.[37] One interpretation of this would be that any law consistent with the Constitution, at least procedurally, could limit the basic right. In fact, this interpretation was the one in vogue under the 1919 Weimar Constitution. While textually plausible, this would effectively render the right meaningless.[38] Since the Federal Republic was founded as a social and democratic state committed to human dignity, this interpretation seemed inappropriate.

Rather, since the "Basic Law erected a value-oriented order . . . the independence, self-determination, responsibility and dignity of individuals must be guaranteed in a political community."[39] Thus, for laws to be consistent with the Constitution, they must conform to the value order of the Basic Law. At the top of this value order is, of course, human dignity, the ultimate constitutional value. In this context, dignity means, at a minimum, that the "intellectual, political and economic freedom of people may not be limited so that the essence of personhood is impaired."[40] From this it follows "that each citizen is afforded a sphere of private development . . . an ultimate inviolable realm of personal freedom, insulated against encroachment by public authorities."[41] No law impinging on the "inviolable realm" could be consistent with the Basic Law.

Laws must also conform substantively to "unwritten fundamental constitutional principles [of the free and democratic order], as well as the fundamental decisions of the Basic Law, especially the principles of the rule of law (*Rechtsstaat*) and the social welfare principle" (*Sozialstaatsprinzip*).[42] Through this interpretive technique, the Constitutional Court introduced significant background and even immanent, if not extratextual, authority. This appears to be a deliberate choice by the Framers and interpreters of the Basic Law. During the Nazi time, gross injustice was committed within a state committed to an extreme version of positivism. To avoid such injustice, the Framers sought to distance the legal order from such absolute sovereignty, providing, in article 20(3) that "the executive and the judiciary shall be bound by law and justice." Anchoring the legal order in natural law seemed appropriate in view of the mischief created by rule of men. Of course, like natural law, article 20(3) "justice" can operate as a freestanding conception. The decision of *Soraya* represents perhaps the furthest extension of this principle, suggesting as it does that fundamental concepts of justice as interpreted by the Constitutional Court might, in some circumstances, trump statutory enactments of Parliament.[43] Again, this underscores the Court's proactive interpretive stance, and also the rich context within which the Basic Law is to be interpreted.

The *Rechtsstaat* principle is especially significant in this regard. By *Rechtstaat*, Germans mean a state based on reason and the rule of law, as we have previously examined, but it now merits mention again. The idea has its roots in the law of Frederick the Great, limiting the discretion of the administration along standards of reason. Under this principle, laws must give fair warning and fair procedure, not be retroactive, and have a legal basis.[44] The concept of *Rechtsstaat* also embodies the Proportionality Principle, meaning, in essence, that laws must pursue proper ends through means that are suitable and "proportional" to the ends sought.[45] Proportionality is a stringent test, requiring that governmental actions be calculated to further a legitimate purpose and impose no more than a reasonable burden on basic rights. The essence of a basic right must yet be preserved, as textually mandated in article 19(2). Thus, at bottom, proportionality is a requirement of reasonableness. The Proportionality Principle is akin to means–end testing in American rights analysis, such as that used in heightened scrutiny methodologies. For example, under conventional American doctrine, violations of individual rights trigger strict scrutiny, an inquiry requiring government to justify its regulation as "necessary to serve a compelling state interest and . . . narrowly drawn to achieve that end."[46] Both methodologies guard against arbitrary government. Thus, the true impact of the Proportionality Principle is seen in case law, as in the United States, where it often settles the case, as will be amply seen.

It is thus apparent that the value-oriented nature of the Basic Law significantly influences the nature of the legal order. Laws must conform to this value order to be part of the constitutional order. Constitutional order is thereby rendered into a two-sided limitation. While the constitutional order can limit personality rights, this can occur only when laws themselves conform to the German value order. In essence, the Constitutional Court implied a limitation from the structure of the Basic Law on the express textual limitation of article 2(1), itself a notable but plausible act of judicial activism.[47] Significantly, this had the effect of transforming plain constitutional language into an open-ended, general clause. Much will always depend on judicial interpretation of article 2(1).

This technique of the Constitutional Court is quite like the techniques of the civil courts in interpreting the civil codes. For example, German civil courts, operating pursuant to article 242 (good faith) or 826 (good morals) of the BGB, frequently readjust contracts to enforce concepts of fairness to preserve the bargain. An example of this is standard-form contracts, which courts invalidate as contrary to good faith if they contain one-sided, unbargained-for terms. Thus, at bottom, the techniques of the Constitutional Court reflect the civil law orientation of the German legal order, as the jurisprudence of the Supreme Court reflects the common law orientation of the American legal system.

In *Elfes*, the Court found that Elfes's interests in foreign travel was part of his freedom of action, but that it was outweighed by the state security interests at issue.[48] Certainly, state security is a justifiable part of the constitutional order, which might be used in limitation of basic rights. However, the particular state interests at issue in *Elfes* did not seem particularly well drawn or persuasive. Elfes was an elected official in Germany. His views were well-known, at home and abroad. Thus, it seems unreasonable to find that another foreign trip would place the state in jeopardy. Perhaps the government desired to protect its image abroad. Perhaps it yet feared for the fragility of the new German experiment in democracy. *Elfes* seems to reflect the skittishness of Cold War times. In this way, *Elfes* is not unlike American cases of this genre; for example, cases that upheld registration and disclosure requirements of Communist activities or ones that prohibited the teaching of Marxist–Leninist doctrine.[49]

As a seminal case, it is notable that the Constitutional Court in *Elfes* did not attempt to set out any comprehensive definition of freedom of action. In fact, there is no case where the Constitutional Court has defined the full range of personality rights.[50] Instead, the Court has preferred to work out the specifics of what freedom of action means in concrete cases in view of current or developing social conditions.[51] Thus, the exact reach of the zone in which individuals may shape their lives awaits case-by-case developments, as in American autonomy law.[52]

However, *Elfes* did establish the methodology applied by the Constitutional Court to judge the reasonableness of governmental action seeking to limit personal interests. As applied in *Elfes*, this methodology is an ad hoc balancing test designed to test the weight of the personal interest against the strength of the official interest. The Constitutional Court did not engage in any comprehensive review of the lower court decision, preferring to look lightly at the court's results. The Constitutional Court looked only to see whether the lower court decision had a basis in law.[53] The Court seemed to be concerned that it not intrude too deeply into the domain of the ordinary courts. It would take later events before the Court would exercise a more intensive review of lower court cases to further fundamental rights. This development occurred mainly in connection with freedoms of expression, as in American law, which is itself notable from a comparative perspective, as explained in Chapter 7.

The reluctance of the Constitutional Court to preempt the work of the ordinary court has its roots in civil law. Germany, like other European countries rooted in the civilian system, has a specialized court system, with different tribunals for different areas, such as civil law, administrative, and tax courts. These specialized courts are, of course, expert in their areas. Thus, the Constitutional Court is generally hesitant to intrude into an area in which another court is expert. Moreover, the civil law, founded on Roman law roots, is the traditional field of German legal thought. Because of the traditional respect and prestige of the civil law, the Constitutional Court might be especially cautious to intervene in favor of the then relatively new constitutional law. The Constitutional Court is a specialized court as well, hearing only constitutional claims. This specialized constitutional court system is based on an Austrian model of the 1920s, and posits a different form of judicial review than the general jurisdiction of the American variety. The Constitutional Court also reflects the constitutional experience during the Weimar Republic.

In this capacity, the Constitutional Court is the supreme interpreter of the Basic Law. Other German courts refer constitutional questions to the Constitutional Court. The Constitutional Court then determines the constitutional issue, after which it remands the case back to the ordinary court for final disposition. Because the Basic Law effects the relations of private law through the doctrine of Third Party Effect, the Court's interpretation, in turn, effects the ordinary court's disposition of the case. While setting the tone, the Constitutional Court works closely with the ordinary courts to carry out the new legal order.

The relationship between constitutional and private law is a deeply interesting question, with strong roots in both history and modern theory. Interestingly, the approach in both countries has been to increasingly constitutionalize areas that historically form part of the private law. In Germany, this makes particular sense, since the adoption of the Basic Law signaled a new legal order for the country. Pursuant to the Basic Law, all law, public and private, must conform to the value order of the new charter. In America too, the trend of the Supreme Court has been to constitutionalize private law areas, most notably defamation law, through the landmark case of *New York Times v. Sullivan.*[54] Note, for example, Justice White's cry: "Using [the First] . . . Amendment as the chosen instrument, the Court, in a few printed pages, has federalized major aspects of libel law by declaring unconstitutional in important respects the prevailing defamation law in all or most of the 50 States. . . . These are radical changes in the law and severe invasions of the prerogatives of the States."[55] The constitutionalization of both laws may reflect, in part, the emergence of human rights after World War II. Still, the relationship between public and private law is more pervasive in Germany than America. For Germans, both are part of one integrated legal system.

Elfes is significant in another regard. The techniques employed by the Constitutional Court illustrate how it has been able to assume its role as guardian of the constitution and, correspondingly, censor of governmental action. The German Constitutional Court thus parallels the role of the Supreme Court, especially over matters of American constitutional substantive due process. In the modern era of human rights, the Supreme Court has judged the reasonableness of official action against the opaque language of "due process of law." Both the German and American Courts have set up legal regimes to anchor such operative terms in more solid ground. In Germany, we have seen how personality rights have become part of a general "freedom of action" limited only by third-party rights, morality, or the constitutional order. In the United States, the due process inquiry involves a quest for those "basic values implicit in the concept of ordered liberty," which itself involves a reasoned judgment "of respect for the liberty of the individual . . . [against] the demands of organized society."[56] In both countries, these decisions are ultimately acts of judicial judgment. We will be in a better position to gauge the quality, range, and validity of those judgments upon further examination of German law in relation to American law.

As in the United States, most measures challenged for violating personal freedoms pass constitutional muster.[57] In *Elfes*, for example, national security interests were held to justify limitations on foreign travel. Likewise, general freedom of action has been limited by price regulations and the freedom of action of a horse rider has been limited to assigned bridal paths out of deference to the rights of hikers and bikers to pursue their activities, in tranquility, secure from horse traffic.[58] Pursuing some semblance of peace and quiet amidst the bustle of the modern world seemed, to the Constitutional Court, a worthy objective.

However, the Constitutional Court has also invalidated measures for violating the Proportionality Principle. Thus, government cannot prevent persons from trying to arrange drivers for interested riders.[59] Likewise, parents do not have unlimited power to bind their minor children by contract.[60] One of the best examples of the Constitutional Court's technique in censoring state actions is the *Falconry Licensing Case*, where the Constitutional Court found government regulation unreasonable in requiring those engaging in the sport of falconry to demonstrate competence in the use of firearms.[61] As compared to *Elfes*, *Falconry Licensing* demonstrates a considerable tightening of the scrutiny devoted to incursion of freedom.

Falconry Licensing Case

At issue in the *Falconry Licensing Case* was a federal hunting law that required prowess in knowledge and operation of weapons, including guns, as a requirement to obtaining a hunting license. The plaintiff engaged in the ancient sport of falconry, which involves use of a falcon to hunt and retrieve prey. Since guns are not used in falconry, the plaintiff objected to being tested for weapon proficiency.[62]

Evaluating this claim, the Constitutional Court determined that the requirement of weapon proficiency "violates in an unconstitutional manner article 2 freedom of action, because denial of the ability to hunt without weapon proficiency contradicts the concept of the rule of law [*Rechtsstaat*]; therefore, the regulation is inconsistent with the constitutional order."[63] Why this is so requires closer examination of the *Rechtsstaat* principle: "The concept of *Rechtsstaat* demands, when viewed in conjunction with the presumptive zone of freedom article two bestows, that citizens are protected against unnecessary curtailment of their freedoms by official actions. For legal measures to be indispensable, they must use means to establish a legal end that are suitable and that do not excessively burden an individual."[64]

Applying this test of proportionality, the Constitutional Court determined that "weapon proficiency is incongruous with the legislative goal . . . [of] protection of wildlife and prevention of abuse of hunting birds."[65] These goals could be accomplished "through more precisely drawn measures." The problem was that "the requirement of weapon proficiency has nothing to do with the maintenance [and preservation] of hunting. . . . It is a violation of proportionality when weapon proficiency is demanded . . . that has no relation to the planned activity." Indeed, discharge of weapons "could frighten the falcons . . . and they might not return to the falconer."[66] Fortifying these conclusions was the Constitutional Court's observation that few open areas remain in modern life where falconry can be engaged in. Care must therefore be taken to preserve them.[67] Like the case of *Rider in the Woods, Falconry Licensing* is an example of the Constitutional Court carving out a sphere of protected liberty amidst the bustle of the modern world.

As we turn to American law, it is worthwhile to observe, by way of summary, that German law accords citizens a broad range of freedom of action. Through careful evaluation of action that would constrain such freedom, the Constitutional Court shows again how it has set itself up as a comprehensive censor of the reasonableness of government action.

America

In the United States, by comparison, there is no comprehensive constitutional concept of a general freedom of action entitling persons to do what they like within the constraints of the social order. The closest textual authority for such general freedom would be the Ninth Amendment to the Constitution, which the Supreme Court has refused to so broadly construe. Thus, freedom of action is more likely to be handled under general private law concepts, like tort, contract, or property, or pursuant to the criminal law. As a whole, therefore, ordinary American law maps out the zone for general freedom of action.[68] U.S. citizens can thus do what they like insofar as they do not violate the obligations of the general legal system. And as any American knows, the range of this freedom is quite broad indeed. Certainly, however, there is a significant difference, in both Germany and the United States, between constitutionalizing an area, with its accompanying higher status, and treatment pursuant to the ordinary law. This is especially the case with the United States, where the Constitution has attained near sacred status as a covenant among the generations.

At the constitutional level, in addition, the American approach under modern substantive due process has been much more selective, focusing on identifying those personal freedoms thought to be "fundamental," "implicit in the concept of ordered liberty," or "deeply rooted in the Nation's history and tradition," to name a few of the formulas.[69] Under these constructs, the Court has deemed "fundamental" activities relating to control over one's life, such as marriage, procreation, contraception, or child rearing;[70] or control over one's body, such as abortion or the ability to withhold medical treatment.[71] As in the German freedom of action cases, the American cases are, in a certain way, outer directed, focusing on issues of personal autonomy and self-determination in relationship to the world. On the other hand, this aspect of American law differs from German freedom of action in that American "fundamental" rights also partake of an element of personal identity. Marriage, procreation, and contraception, for example, are more personal topics, and more revealing of identity, than foreign travel, riding in the woods, or engaging in falconry.[72] In this way, American law has a certain resonance with the personal sphere of German law, discussed in Chapter 4.

A second focus of American substantive due process law has been the delineation of a certain zone of privacy, particularly in shielding disclosure of personal matters. This explains the privacy accorded the bedroom and the home in certain contexts.[73] However, as with American autonomy law, rather than any general or comprehensive right, this law has evolved narrowly as well, in response to discrete intrusions into individual privacy, usually amidst criminal prosecutions. At bottom, then, American law is episodic, a judicial response to "substantial arbitrary impositions," whereas German law is more systematic.[74] Undoubtedly, this reflects the American common law methodology, even in constitutional law, itself a continuing influence of English law. German systematization, by contrast, reflects the influence of Roman law, especially as transformed in high German legal science (*Rechtswissenschaft*).[75] Under German legal science, techniques of careful legal study and investigation were brought to bear on Roman law, attempting to uncover the essence of a system of law, and German customary law, in order to discover the basis of law itself. A high achievement of German legal science was the drafting of the German Civil Code of 1896. In short, the differing approaches of the law evidence a cultural distinction between common and civil law.

NOTES

1. Mary Ann Glendon, Rights Talk: The Impoverishment of Political Discourse 69 (1991).

2. *Id.* at 62.

3. 54 BVerfGE 148, 153 (1980).

4. *Right to Heritage I*, 79 BVerfGE 256, 268 (1988).

5. Christoph Degenhart, *Das allgemeine Persönlichkeitsrecht*, 5 Juristische Schulung (JUS) 361, 362 (1992).

6. 6 BVerfGE 32 (1957).

7. 4 BVerfGE 7 (1954).

8. *Schacht Case*, 13 BGHZ 334, NJW 1404 (1954).

9. 7 BVerfGE 198 (1954).

10. 347 U.S. 483 (1954).

11. 354 U.S. 298 (1957).

12. 354 U.S. 476 (1957).

13. He had been a member of the central committee of the party before 1933, police commissioner of Krefeld in 1927, and mayor of Mönchen-Gladbach, among other political activities; 6 BVerfGE at 32–33.

14. *Id.* at 33.

15. *Id.*

16. *Id.* at 37.

17. *Id.* at 36.

18. 4 BVerfGE at 7.

19. 6 BVerfGE at 36. The first definition is the so-called Core Theory (*Kernbereich Theorie*), by which is meant protection of only a core of personality that involves the essence of woman as a spiritual–moral person.

20. *Id.* at 36–37.

21. "Restraints on the free development of personality come from the constitutional order." *Id.* at 37.

22. *Falconry Licensing Case*, 55 BVerfGE 159, 165 (1980).

23. Donald P. Kommers, THE CONSTITUTIONAL JURISPRUDENCE OF THE FEDERAL REPUBLIC OF GERMANY 323 (1989). The *Falconry Licensing Case*, 55 BVerfGE at 159, is an example of how the Court has interpreted freedom of action to apply in recreational areas.

24. The Ninth Amendment provides, "The enumeration in the Constitution, of certain rights, shall not be construed to deny or disparage other retained by the people." Griswold v. Connecticut, 381 U.S. 479 (1965), is one of the few cases that interprets the Ninth Amendment, employing it as part of its decisional rationale.

25. 478 U.S. 186 (1986).

26. 6 BVerfGE at 41–42.

27. This is the text of article 2, and as interpreted by the Court. *Id.* at 36–37.

28. Bodo Pieroth & Bernhard Schlink, 2 GRUNDRECHTE STAATSRECHT 102 (10th ed. 1994).

29. David P. Currie, THE CONSTITUTION OF THE FEDERAL REPUBLIC OF GERMANY 317 (1994).

30. *Tobacco Atheist Case*, 12 BVerfGE 1 (1960).

31. Pieroth & Schlink, *supra* note 29, at 102.

32. *Compare Homosexuality*, 6 BVerfGE 389, 433–36 (1957) (relying on Christian law notions and other moral code limitations to find homosexual activity beyond article 2 protection, although noting that sexual activities are among the most intimate of human acts); *with* Bowers v. Hardwick, 478 U.S. 186 (1986) (homosexual activity not part of any protected right of privacy).

33. Pieroth & Schlink, *supra* note 28, at 103 (noting change in view of homosexuality toward acceptance since 1969). In fact, the criminal law

provision then enforced in the German case has long since been repealed. Romer v. Evans, 517 U.S. 620 (1996). Ironically, the majority never made mention of *Bowers*, preferring to gloss over the roadblock. *Id.* at 636 (Scalia, J. dissenting) ("In holding that homosexuality cannot be singled out for disfavorable treatment, the Court contradicts a decision, unchallenged here, pronounced only 10 years ago, *see* Bowers v. Hardwick, and places the prestige of this institution behind the proposition that opposition to homosexuality is as reprehensible as racial or religious bias").

34. Powell v. State, 510 S.E.2d 18 (1998), 1998 WL 804568 (Ga. November 23, 1998); *discussed in* U.S. Law Week, December 8, 1998, at 1327, and Kevin Sack, *Georgia's High Court Voids Sodomy Law*, N.Y. Times, November 24, 1998, at A16.

35. BGB art. 138(1), 242, 826. These are some of the famous general clauses of the BGB, which contain open language designed to bring the Code into conformity with contemporary needs as determined by courts and scholars.

36. Pieroth & Schlink, *supra* note 28, at 102.

37. 6 BVerfGE at 37–38.

38. *Id.* at 40–41.

39. *Id.* at 40.

40. *Id.* at 41.

41. *Id.*

42. *Id.*

43. 34 BVerfGE 269 (1973).

44. Currie, *supra* note 29, at 318–19.

45. *Id.* at 122.

46. Arkansas Writers' Project, Inc. v. Ragland, 481 U.S. 221, 231 (1987).

47. 6 BVerfGE at 37–41.

48. *Id.* at 42–43.

49. Communist Party v. Subversive Activities Control Board, 367 U.S. 1 (1961); Dennis v. United States, 341 U.S. 494 (1951).

50. *Census Act Case*, 65 BVerfGE 1, 41 (1984).

51. *Id.*; Pieroth & Schlink, *supra* note 28, at 98–99.

52. Justice Harlan phrased this dynamic of liberty, which resonates in both German and American law, especially well:

The full scope of the liberty guaranteed by the Due Process Clause cannot be found in or limited by the precise terms of the specific guarantees elsewhere provided in the Constitution. This "liberty" is not a series of isolated points pricked out in terms of the taking of property; the freedom of speech, press, and religion; the right to keep and bear arms; the freedom from unreasonable searches and seizures; and so on. It is a rational continuum which, broadly speaking, includes a freedom from all substantial arbitrary impositions and purposeless restraints, . . . and which also recognizes, what a reasonable and sensitive judgment must, that certain interests require particularly careful scrutiny of the state needs asserted to justify their abridgment.

Poe v. Ullman, 367 U.S. 497, 543 (1961) (Harlan, J., dissenting).

53. 6 BVerfGE at 43–44.

54. 376 U.S. 254 (1964).

55. Gertz v. Robert Welch, Inc., 418 U.S. 323, 370 (1973) (White, J., dissenting).

56. Griswold v. Connecticut, 381 U.S. 479, 500 (1965) (Harlan J., concurring) citing Palko v. Connecticut, 302 U.S. 319, 325 (1937); *Poe*, 367 U.S. 542.

57. Currie, *supra* note 29, at 319.

58. 8 BVerfGE 274, 327–29 (1958); *Rider in Woods*, 80 BVerfGE 137 (1989).

59. 17 BVerfGE 306, 313–18 (1964), noted in Currie, *supra* note 29, at 319.

60. 72 BVerfGE 155, 170–73 (1986).

61. 55 BVerfGE at 159.

62. He was simply not interested in shooting a gun. *Id.* at 163.

63. *Id.* at 165.

64. *Id.*

65. *Id.* at 165–66.

66. *Id.* at 166.

67. *Id.* at 168.

68. By ordinary law, I mean the general law; that is, all law—civil, criminal, or administrative—other than constitutional law. Thus, the ordinary law is the background against which constitutional law is applied.

69. *Palko*, 302 U.S. at 325; Moore v. East Cleveland, 431 U.S. 494, 503 (1977); *Griswold*, 381 U.S. at 506.

70. Loving v. Virginia, 388 U.S. 1 (1967); Skinner v. Oklahoma, 316 U.S. 535 (1942); Eisenstadt v. Baird, 405 U.S. 438 (1972); Meyer v. Nebraska, 262 U.S. 390 (1923).

71. Roe v. Wade, 410 U.S. 113 (1973); Cruzan v. Director, Missouri Department of Health, 457 U.S. 261 (1990) (competent people have constitutionally protected liberty interest in refusing unwanted medical treatment, although such liberty interest may fall short of "fundamental" right and does not apply, in whole, to incompetent people, who must rely on substituted judgment of family members).

72. *Elfes*, 6 BVerfGE at 32; *Rider in the Woods*, 80 BVerfGE at 137; *Falconry Licensing*, 55 BVerfGE at 159.

73. *Griswold*, 381 U.S. at 479 (right to use contraceptives); Stanley v. Georgia, 394 U.S. 557 (1969) (right to possess obscene material in privacy of home).

74. *Poe*, 367 U.S. at 542, 543.

75. Friedrich von Savigny, one of the seminal German legal theoreticians of the Code, described the aims of German legal science: "We want a national community whose scientific endeavors focus upon one and the same object . . . 'an organically progressive legal science which may be common to the whole nation.'" Savigny's legal historicism became "the fulcrum for the emergence of a national community of scholars." Reinhard Zimmerman, An Introduction to German Legal Culture, *in* INTRODUCTION TO GERMAN LAW, 1, 4–5 (Werner F. Ebke & Matthew W. Finkin, eds., 1996).

4

Inner Freedom:
The Personal Sphere

The flip side of freedom of action is a focus on the interior person. This is man's inner life, where thoughts, feelings, and emotions reside. We can think of this as his or her soul or innermost being, his or her inner sanctuary. Over this area he or she has ultimate dominion. We might envision this as a "private sphere or ultimate domain of inviolability in which a person is free to shape his life as he or she sees fit."[1] This is the way interiority is conceived by the German Constitutional Court. Or we might think of it as "the most comprehensive of rights and the right most valued by civilized men," namely, "the right to be let alone," as the Supreme Court has conceptualized the idea.[2] Thus, one's personal domain includes the right to retreat from the world, as one likes, and concentrate on inner development and inner awareness. Or one might decide to engage actively in the world, as covered by the idea of freedom of action developed in Chapter 3. There is not, of course, a clear conceptual line between the inner and outer worlds. Rather, both are components of an integrated, whole person. This chapter accents the interior component of human personhood as traceable in the constitutional laws of Germany and America, complementing Chapter 3's emphasis of man's exterior component.

It is interesting, as a matter of comparative law, that the call for a general right of personality, including this interior dimension, occurred rather contemporaneously in Germany and the United States, during the influential last decade of the nineteenth century, and through the same vehicle of tort law. The call met with great success in Germany, developing first comprehensively in tort and then into a full-blown constitutional right, but with only limited success in America, sounding in tort and only modestly so in constitutional law.

In America, the idea began with Samuel Warren and Louis Brandeis, law partners and friends, who, in their seminal article, *The Right to Privacy*, called for the establishment of a general right of personality based on the notion of "an inviolate personality," including a "more general right to be let alone," and "to the immunity of the person—the right to one's personality."[3] Warren and Brandeis were writing in response to the new technologies of their day, which included the phonograph and the camera, and their potential to capture, instantaneously, human emotion. Yet such technology could also be intrusive, especially to the rich, famous, or notorious. The *New York Times* of around 1902 notes, for example, how President Teddy Roosevelt felt like striking out at photographers who he felt hounded him, and that J. Pierpont Morgan, founder of the financial house of Morgan, felt captive to photographers angling for a shot.[4] In response to such new developments, Warren and Brandeis advocated a general right of personality that would include "legal recognition . . . [of] thoughts, emotions and sensations," and also "some retreat from the world," in recognition "that solitude and privacy have become more essential to the individual" given the "intensity and complexity of life attendant upon advancing civilization."[5] Warren and Brandeis sought to shield man's inner life—his personality—from an ever-prying public in the same way that property had been used 200 years before to mark off a personal domain of inviolability.

Warren and Brandeis's call for a new right of personality never really caught on in American law. There were some early attempts by courts to pick up the seeds laid by the two Bostonians. Other prominent scholars, such as Roscoe Pound of the Harvard Law School, furthered the call from time to time.[6] And Brandeis himself, now from his lofty perch on the Supreme Court, continued to sound the call, his own best ambassador, as evidenced by his advocacy, in *Olmstead v. United States*, of "the right to be let alone."[7] In spite of these efforts, a right of personality never developed in America in any comprehensive sense.

Rather, what came of Warren and Brandeis's original cry was a tort claim to privacy, recognized today in most states, that includes protections of unreasonable intrusion and public disclosure of private facts. The core of these rights resonates in German tort law too. So, we might speak of a certain congruence between the tort laws of the two countries. With the flowering of free speech freedoms in America, dating at least from the seminal 1964 case of *New York Times v. Sullivan,* however, most of these privacy claims have been eclipsed by the rights of free speech.[8] At the constitutional level, no right to personality exists. Instead, Warren and Brandeis's advocacy influenced development of a constitutional concept of "right of privacy," as articulated by the Supreme Court in the famous 1965 case of *Griswold v. Connecticut,* where the Court empowered a married couple to decide, themselves, on whether to use contraceptives in their private, sexual practices.[9] We shall need to look at *Griswold* and its influence more carefully later as we trace the range of autonomy central to personality in Chapter 5. What is significant for us at this stage is to recognize that while Warren and Brandeis's original advocacy of a "right to be let alone" was actually an umbrella concept for a more far-reaching right to development of personality, it has come to be understood in the generations that followed as a "right to privacy," not a right to inviolability of personality.

Let us now continue exploring how personality, and especially its interior component, came to be, and how it then developed in the two laws. In Germany, during the late 1800s, scholars and commentators too were echoing the call of Warren and Brandeis for establishment of a general right of personality. Like those Bostonians, Germans were responding to the sometimes intrusive and outrageous prying of cameramen and newspapermen, especially the sensationalistic press, and the developing age of rapid communication. For example, Germans were outraged over photographs circulated in the popular press of images of the dead Otto von Bismarck in 1899, which photographers obtained by bursting into the room where Bismarck died.[10]

The German origins of the right have a deeper lineage too. The right of personality is based originally on Kant and his work on moral personality. For Kant, development of a person's capacity and talent is central to realization of moral autonomy. Hence, one could think of development of personality as a moral "right," with accompanying obligation. Endowed with talent and capacity, in other words, a person shall develop and use them. Each person should so make their way in the world. Kant's reasoning had a deep influence on German thought and legal philosophy. In 1791–1792, Wilhelm von Humboldt, Germany's preeminent university reformer, worked out some of the political implications of Kant's thoughts in a short book on government in which he set forth the idea that the highest purpose of the state "was to promote conditions favoring the free and harmonious unfolding of individuality."[11] Von Humboldt's book had a profound influence in Germany and beyond, including on John Stuart Mills, who credited von Humboldt for the idea of development of individuality in his famous essay *On Liberty*.[12] Mills would later find dedicated apostles in Oliver Wendall Holmes and Louis Brandeis, architects of American concepts of freedom and individuality.[13]

Kant also influenced Friedrich Karl von Savigny and other formulators of German private law. Von Savigny, Germany's preeminent jurist of the nineteenth century, for example, stated that "the goal of all law . . . is directed to the secure and independent development of the personality."[14] The drafters of the 1896 German Civil Code suggested, in fact, that the law recognize a "general right of personality."[15] However, the drafters ultimately did not adopt such a right, although the Swiss Code of 1907 did. Instead, the German civil courts developed a comprehensive general right of personality, including a highly pronounced interior component, in conjunction with their interpretations of the German Code. To a significant extent, German law picked up the suggestions by Warren and Brandeis, although German law appears to have developed by its own impetus, without apparent influence by Warren and Brandeis. German tort law echoes the essence of the American tort claim to privacy, but then goes beyond it.

The impetus for the full flowering of German personality law, however, was the adoption of the Basic Law in 1949 and its anchoring of the social order to the concept of human dignity and corresponding unfolding of personality. As we now trace the idea of personality comparatively through the lens of the German and American Constitutional Courts, it is notable that German law has accented the interior component of human personality, a focus American law has not as yet developed in a comprehensive way.

The theme of preserving human personhood is a timeless one, the subject of philosophical and ethical speculation through the ages. It is also an idea put to the acid test of hard experience. Every age presents its challenges to human personality and human freedom. Technology, especially, presents unique and often unanticipated challenges. The development of the printing press, combustion engine, and airplane are just some of the technological developments that revolutionized their ages. Innovation can be a cause for the betterment of mankind or its captor. All depends on how it is handled and used. We can see this clearly in the history of the late 1800s already described. The invention of the camera and its ability to unerringly capture human conduct and emotion was a great challenge for the legal systems of that era.

Our age presents its own challenges, which seem of an unprecedented nature. We live in the computer age. The computer is our camera. It has the potential to gather, store, transmit, and use information of unlimited scope and variety. Much of this information is personal: information about us. Today there is evidence that government in the United States may possess hundreds of files per citizen; by comparison, a 1983 study estimated that the U.S. government had "an average of fifteen files on every citizen."[16] Those computers contain information about a person's finances, spending patterns, tax data, family history and status, medical history, and life experience. Each time we make a credit card purchase, enter the hospital, or subscribe to some service, we enter some database. Recently, a computer was sold that contained confidential pharmacology files of patients. The files disclosed sensitive information about people's present and past medical histories, such as treatment for AIDS, depression, or sexually transmitted diseases.[17] The invention of the Internet, especially, introduces a vast new marketplace of ideas, services, and offerings with great potential for tapping personal information. A recent survey by the American Federal Trade Commission revealed that few consumer Web sites told consumers if they would maintain confidential personal information disclosed, and how they would use such information.[18] Web sites often survey consumers, inquiring about spending patterns, tastes, plans, income levels, family members, and other sensitive information, including children. Computers easily capture the tracings of our habits, if not our belief or attitudes. They can be a portal to our inner personalities.

Of course, computers are not the only technological development that captures the dimensions of personality. Security cameras ubiquitously record all movement and, sometimes, sound in buildings, rooms, or at desks. They provide us with our last, haunting look at Princess Diana as she exits the Ritz hotel in Paris. Helicopters are a regular tool of law enforcement to observe behavior not accessible otherwise behind enclosed fences. Intrepid entrepreneurs even clandestinely photographed, from a helicopter, the otherwise private, off-limits wedding of Madonna to Sean Penn. DNA testing is now regularly used to establish guilt or innocence or trace the presence or past of diseases. DNA testing established President Clinton's involvement with Monica Lewinsky. Themes of past science fiction are becoming our everyday realities.

Much about us is discoverable. The patterns of our life are traceable. We are in many ways an open book, although we may not know that to be the case. Control over this information is power, such power that has the potential to shape political and social events and the events of our lives. For example, "use of computerized criminal history records affects both the chances for employment of ex-convicts and the balance of power between attorney and prosecution."[19] Release by American Republican politicians of the Starr report on the Internet in the fall of 1998 instantaneously framed the debate on President Clinton's impeachment. Thus, as we focus now on German and American law, we need to see how the two laws respond to these challenges.

GERMANY

I start with German law because it is more highly developed on these points than American law and thus provides a benchmark with which to measure protection of personality. Starting from the same time frame of the 1890s, the two laws have taken different paths in the ensuing 100 years, notwithstanding a similar social and technological milieu.

Establishment of Interiority in German Law

Microcensus

Focus on the interior component of human personality in German constitutional law began comprehensively with the important *Microcensus Case*, which concerned the constitutionality of a federal questionnaire or "microcensus" designed to elicit a portrait of the German population.[20] The questionnaire sought information over personal habits, including vacation practices, occupation, standard of living, and whether mothers worked or remained home to rear children, among other topics.[21] In this context, the Court carved out a private, personal sphere for citizens to inhabit, free from unwarranted incursion.

The fact that the statistical survey sought personal information necessitated inquiry into the domain of personal rights protected within article 2 of the Basic Law. Here the Constitutional Court raised the barricade of human dignity, that "the state could take no measure, or enact any law, which would violate . . . or otherwise infringe upon the essence of personal freedom as encompassed within the limits of article 2."[22] The significance of this became immediately clear: "The Basic Law thereby guarantees individual citizens an inviolable area of personal freedom in which one can freely form one's life, the effect of which is to remove all official power [from this realm]."[23] This is the personal sphere in which one is free to determine and structure one's life. As the Court stated later, "The right to free development of personality and human dignity guarantees everyone an autonomous area of private life formation, in which one can develop and protect one's individuality."[24]

This intimate sphere is a critical part of the human vision that lies at the root of the Basic Law, bestowing self-worth, social value, and respect. As the Constitutional Court observed, "In the light of this image of man, the human achieves social value and respect in society."[25] The Constitutional Court's statement also shows how concepts of human dignity, humanity, and community are interlinked in German law. Through this interaction, dignity takes on a more concrete meaning: "It would be inconsistent with human dignity for the state to force people to register and catalogue their whole personalities, even if done anonymously through a statistical survey, and thereby treating man as an object, which is accessible in every manner."[26] Insistence on respect for human dignity is thus instrumental to preservation of human autonomy.

With this background, the Constitutional Court went on to elaborate the Inner Sphere. "Such a [pervasive] penetration in the personal area through a comprehensive inspection of the personal relationships of a citizen is also denied the state because individuals must have an Inner Space [*Innenraum*] in which to develop freely and self-responsibly their personalities, an Inner Space in which they themselves possess and in which they can retreat, banning all entrance to the outer world, in which one can enjoy tranquility and a right to solitude."[27]

The presence of an ascertainable Inner Space in German personality law is a notable achievement and a dramatic contrast with American law. It is wholly a creation of the Constitutional Court in pursuit of its perception of the vision underlying the Basic Law. Textually, it is certainly not self-evident that "the dignity of man" or "the right to the free development of his personality" would yield this emphasis. Rather, it reflects the Constitutional Court's desire to preserve and protect the integrity of human personality by applying the concept of human dignity to meet changing social conditions, such as the development and use of computer technology in *Microcensus*. In this way, human autonomy and capacity are safeguarded and nourished against the challenges posed by modern social, economic, and technological change. Like the invention of the camera in 1890, the Constitutional Court appears intent on keeping its constitution "in tune with the times."[28] In a general way, this contrasts with the Supreme Court, which has normally sought to anchor fundamental rights in timeless or constant principles, such as natural law or its subset, inalienable rights, or from verifiable sources, like tradition or history, partly as a way of deflecting the argument that the Court is overstepping its bounds.

Considering that law is a reflection of culture, it is interesting to decipher the cultural traits evidenced by this German accent on the interior life. For one thing, this focus is quite compatible with German history and culture, which has placed extraordinary emphasis on the world of the mind and of the artist. Emphasis of culture has predominated over public life through most of German history. This contrasts with American law and American life, which has emphasized public life, a natural outgrowth of the central role played in the United States by democracy, often over cultural life. The high valuation of free speech reflects, in part, the instrumental role Americans perceive that speech plays in promoting democracy. American substantive due process law reflects this as well. The thrust of American cases has either been autonomy to be exercised in the world over life-affecting decisions (abortion, child rearing, family relationships), or privacy from a prying world (contraception, procreation, marriage). But under American privacy, unlike German personality, the Supreme Court has not sought comprehensively to define or nourish an interior sphere so much as to shield the outside world from invasion of that private zone. In this way, American law resonates more with Brandeis's idea of a "right to be let alone" than any right to develop one's talent or character.[29] By contrast, the German focus on interiority reflects, again, a Kantian emphasis on the autonomy of the individual and the unfolding of human capacity.

As a matter of doctrinal law, the Constitutional Court's carving out of a private, intimate sphere has produced distinct strands of personality law. Perhaps most notable is the general control over personal information that has resulted in a right to informational self-determination, discussed next in connection with the *Census Act Case*.[30] Related to informational self-determination is the right to control portrayal of one's person, including certain rights to control presentation of one's own image and spoken word, and rights, in some circumstances, not to have false interviews or statements attributed to one's person as yields a false portrait. The idea of freedom has this inner dimension, which bestows control in the person over matters that reflect personality. These ideas, in fact, germinated first in German tort law, paralleling the course originally set out by Warren and Brandeis. But we are getting ahead of ourselves, as these are all matters meriting separate development later. What is significant for our purposes is that the German strand of interior personality has led to a distinct evolution of personality law compatible with the original thinking of Warren and Brandeis but quite different from American law, and that seems, at least at first glance, equipped to deal with the challenges of the computer and information age.

In reference to *Microcensus*, the question for the Constitutional Court was whether this "microcensus" so deeply impinged upon this sphere of intimacy as to violate article 2 personality rights. Certainly "not every statistical survey of personal data violates personal dignity . . . or disturbs self-determination over the innermost [private] areas of life."[31] Characteristic of the German regime of rights, everything is a question of balance and proportion. No one's right is extended to the detriment of other rights, as, for example, in the American preferencing of free speech. Thus, personality rights—even over intimate areas—are mediated in relationship to other values of the social order. A person's obligations as "community-connected and community-bound" citizens entail a certain cooperation with officials in matters that call for state planning, like a census.[32]

This inquiry necessitates a closer evaluation of the case. Survey questions principally threaten self-determination rights when they impinge upon the "personal intimate area of life, which by nature is confidential." For "the modern industrial state, this is a barricade to prevent administrative–technical depersonalization."[33] However, statistical surveys inquiring only over human behavior will not generally violate the intimate realm. This is especially so when anonymity is used, as in the *Microcensus* survey, since this obscures any personal connection, thereby hindering, if not preventing, any catalog of human personality.[34] The chances that personal information could be exploited are thereby reduced.

In *Microcensus*, the key issue turned on inquiry into vacation and recreational habits. While such inquiries implicate the private sphere, they do not "force disclosure of information arising from one's intimate sphere, nor allow the state access to relationships that are ordinarily beyond outside scrutiny or of a confidential nature."[35] This type of information could be obtained from general sources, "although with greater difficulty."[36] Thus, the inquiry did not constitute a constitutional violation. Likewise, resort to the *Rechtsstaat* principle did not yield relief, since the legal norms at issue were sufficiently definite and the measures taken satisfied the Proportionality Principle, being suitable means to accomplish legitimate ends.[37] *Microcensus* thereby illustrates the same methodology used by the Court in the outer-directed freedom-of-action cases: evaluation of the intensity of the rights violation, and then testing of the case against *Rechtsstaat* principles, especially that of proportionality.

Informational Self-Determination

The most notable concretization of the aim to preserve an intimate realm to life is the concept of informational self-determination. Information self-determination means, fundamentally, a right to control access to and dissemination of personal data, including protection against revelation of one's private affairs. As the Constitutional Court announced, "The general personality rights anchored in articles one and two guarantee . . . control over . . . personal details of one's life."[38] The right is rooted in a desire to preserve the integrity of human personality against unwarranted intrusion, such as prying eyes or, especially, the onslaught of the technological age and its accompanying multifarious challenges. Thus, the Constitutional Court has sought to carve out an area of inviolable human interiority as a secure haven. "The Constitutional Court has recognized a last inviolable area of private life formation from which all public power is disseized."[39] In a sense, this represents adjustment of the Kantian ideal of moral autonomy to the conditions of the modern age.

Census Act Case

No case better represents this aspect of the Constitutional Court's jurisprudence than the famous *Census Act Case.*[40] Building on *Microcensus, Census Act* strives to preserve the inviolability of human personality amidst revolutionary changes in the computer age during the period of the 1980s. The case is prescient enough to anticipate many of the challenges posed by the continuing revolution in computers, including the Internet.

The controversy concerned the Federal Census Act of 1983, which required the collection of comprehensive data concerning the Federal Republic's demographic and social structure. The act set the parameters for the country's population count and also required rudimentary personal information, such as name, address, gender, marital status, nature of household occupants, religious affiliation, job occupation, and work setting.[41] The act also required citizens to fill out detailed questions concerning their sources of income, educational background, mode of transportation to and from work, and use of dwelling, including method of heating and utilities.[42] The act further allowed information obtained to be transmitted to local government, which could then use the information for purposes of planning, environmental protection, and redistricting. Local government could even compare information to housing registers and, if necessary, correct them.[43]

Although passed without controversy by the Bundestag, the law triggered a storm of protest. Hundreds of citizen-initiative groups called for a boycott of the census. Günter Grass, the Nobel Prize–winning author, called the law a "monster." Even a high census official admitted that the questionnaire "was written in an exceedingly authoritative and frightfully unclear language."[44] Over 100 persons filed suit against the act, complaining that the act's intrusiveness threatened their privacy rights.[45] The Constitutional Court agreed, at least temporarily, and suspended the census until its constitutionality could be determined. The case was one of the few times when individuals directly pursued claims to the Constitutional Court without having to exhaust legal remedies because of an immediate threat to a fundamental right.

At the heart of *Microcensus* and *Census Act* (the *Census Cases*) is the concern that intrusive and comprehensive surveys of the population will yield personality profiles that, with the aid of modern computing techniques, will facilitate the state's ability to access such information at will and use it as seen fit. For example, the Constitutional Court in *Census Act* observed that modern computing techniques can gather and store practically limitless information about people, which is accessible "in seconds." This "information . . . can produce a . . . personality profile, which the person affected cannot control . . . and induces psychological pressure on behavior."[46] From the Kantian perspective, this carries the danger of converting human beings into mere objects of statistical survey, depersonalizing the human element. From the standpoint of human autonomy, the Constitutional Court feared that gathering, storing, and using personal information would threaten human liberty. The more that is known about a person, the easier it is to control the person.[47] Control might include channeling or manipulation of human behavior or outright coercion as government seeks desired norms of behavior. Control like this has the potential to shape political, social, or economic events or the events of daily life. There is great potential for molding human character. These concerns are especially heightened with the advance of modern computing technology and its capacity to access human habit and capabilities.[48] The amount of personal information stored in and accessible by computers is staggering, including information about credit history, taxes, social security, and travel plans.[49]

The background of German personality law provides the theoretical base for these concerns. Since the "focus of the constitutional order . . . is the value and dignity of the person, who operates in free self-determination as a member of a free society," these values must be sustained "in view of modern developments and their accompanying threats to human personality."[50] Human dignity must be preserved amidst changing economic and social conditions if human personhood is to remain inviolate in modern society. In this way, the Constitutional Court acknowledges that changing social conditions require ingenuity in the application of core concepts.

Just this motivation led the Constitutional Court to announce a general right of informational self-determination, by which it meant

the authority of the individual to decide fundamentally for herself, when and within what limits personal data may be disclosed. [T]his decisional authority requires a special measure of protection under present and future conditions of automatic data processing. [For example,] the technological capability of storing [highly] personalized information concerning specific people is practically unlimited and retrievable in seconds . . . without concern for distance. [T]his information, when connected to other data sources . . . can produce a complete or partial personality profile, which the affected individual cannot control or confirm its truth. The possibilities of acquiring information and exerting influence have increased to a degree never previously known.[51]

The rise in technological capability poses severe threats to human personality and human autonomy. "An individual's right to plan and make decisions freely may be severely curtailed, if she does not know or cannot predict adequately what personal data is known or may be disclosed."[52] It is unhealthy for society "where citizens do not know who knows what about them, and when they know it."[53] Not knowing others' knowledge of your affairs may lead citizens to curtail their activities or "refrain from exercising rights . . . like associational rights," or expression, religious, or occupational freedoms. People may not undertake desired activities when they know that such activities may be observed, recorded, and entered into a computer database, accessible instantaneously, at any time, without the person's knowledge. For example, people undergoing treatment for sensitive medical conditions, such as mental illness or AIDS, may forego or adjust treatment if they do not believe such treatment is confidential. The pain of unknown eyes prying into personal affairs may chill human conduct.

Certainly official possession of detailed personal information carries a serious threat of abuse, including coercion and manipulation of people and their autonomy.[54] This carries the specter of Big Brother, as predicted presciently by George Orwell in his book *1984*, ironically the date of the *Census Act* decision. As recognized by Orwell, such control "would damage an individual's personal development, and also the common good, because self-determination is an elementary condition of a free democratic society based on citizens' ability to act and to participate."[55] Accordingly, data use that has the potential to influence people must be strictly controlled. Against these dangers, "An individual must be protected against unlimited collection, storage, use and transmission of personal data . . . as a consequence of the free development of personality under modern conditions of data processing."[56] In essence, informational self-determination follows from human autonomy; in the modern information age, control of information is power. Thus, control over personal information is the power to control a measure of one's fate, which is indispensable to the free unfolding of personality.

The right to informational self-determination, like all basic rights, is not absolute in the carefully calibrated value order of the Basic Law.[57] Since persons "develop within the social community . . . personal information is also a reflection of social reality."[58] Thus, there is a social dimension to personal data as well, posing a tension between personal and social components to information. Government and other actors in society, such as banks or companies, need information about people to plan and serve the public weal. Democracy itself depends on the free flow of information.[59] "The Basic Law . . . has resolved the tension between individuality and society by constituting individuals as community-bound and community-related."[60] Therefore, "individuals must . . . accept limitations on their right to informational self-determination for reasons of overriding public interest [*überwiegenden Allgemeininterresse*].[61]

The Constitutional Court has stated this principle in a different case as follows: "Limitation of freedom can occur when justified by overriding public interest, because individuals enter into communication with others in the social community, and their conduct effects others and can disturb the personal sphere of others or the interests of the community."[62]

Just what an "overriding public interest" is can only be determined by resorting to standard German norms. First, the law must have a (constitutional) legal basis, which makes clear the conditions and reach of the limitations on freedom and thereby satisfies the *Rechtsstaat* command that norms be clearly stated.[63] Second, the law must satisfy the Proportionality Principle, which, as we know, mandates that freedom be limited only to the degree necessary to satisfy public interests. Because "of the dangers of automatic data processing . . . the legislature must, more than ever, adopt organizational and procedural safeguards to diminish violations of individual personal rights."[64] Only then can one test the strength of the public interest.

Testing the act against these principles entailed a detailed and comprehensive analysis, filling seventy-one pages of the official report. While the Constitutional Court concluded that it was legitimate to perform a census for social and economic planning, collection and storage of data for other purposes would be constitutionally suspect.[65] The Constitutional Court "carefully scrutinized the nature of the information collected, the methods of its storage and transmission, and its particular uses" in order to assure that the stated uses properly fell within police powers and did not pose undue threat to human liberty.[66] Protection of information thus depended on a distinction "between personality-related information that is gathered and processed in an individually nonanonymous manner and data that is census-related."[67] Protective measures must be in place to assure that personality profiles of individuals cannot be obtained. Cloaking information in anonymity is the key safeguard. Persons are not to be treated as "mere information-objects"; individuals are not to be depersonalized as information sources without losing their essence as "spiritual–moral" persons.[68] The Constitutional Court ultimately sustained most of the act, although it invalidated several provisions, including one that allowed local officials to "compare census data with local housing registries" on the ground that combining these statistics might allow officials to identify particular persons, thereby violating the core of personality.[69]

In the wake of *Census Act*, it is worth observing what a remarkable act of judicial activism the case represents.[70] First, the Constitutional Court suspended the act until its constitutionality could be determined, ultimately requiring the German Bundestag to amend certain provisions before the census could be carried out. This delayed the census for four years at notable cost.[71] Second, the Constitutional Court established concretely a right of informational self-determination from the textual authority of articles 1 and 2. That language, of course, does not self-evidently bestow citizens' control over personal data. Rather, the Constitutional Court extended the principle animating the provisions to carve out this radiation of autonomy. In this way, the Constitutional Court acted in a manner quite like the Supreme Court, in *Griswold v. Connecticut*, in inferring a right of privacy from the Bill of Rights.[72] At the root of the Constitutional Court's decision was the vision that human dignity and autonomy must be preserved against the onslaught of the modern computer age. Thus, measures need be taken to assure that the collection, storage, and use of personal data is justifiable pursuant to the *Rechtsstaat*, and that this power not be abused.

Interestingly, in 1993 when Germany reevaluated the Basic Law following German reunification, the Constitutional Commissioners decided not to codify explicitly informational privacy, seemingly preferring court-created law.[73] In this way, the Constitutional Commissioners paralleled the course of the drafters of the Civil Code, who decided against codification of a general right of privacy. Thus, like informational self-determination, a general right of privacy has been a court-created doctrine, as in the United States. Indeed, this brings into clear relief the role of German courts as active participants in the creation of the law.

AMERICA

The closest American constitutional case, in a substantive way, to the German concept of informational self-determination is *Whalen v. Roe*, which involved a patient-identification requirement in a statute providing for a centralized computer file of all persons who obtained drugs, both legal and illegal, pursuant to a doctor's prescription.[74] Although the Supreme Court recognized, like the Constitutional Court, that there was a "threat to privacy implicit in the accumulation of vast amounts of personal information in computerized data banks or other massive government files,"[75] the Supreme Court nevertheless held that "neither the immediate nor the threatened impact of the patient-identification requirements . . . is sufficient to constitute an invasion of any right or liberty protected by the Fourteenth Amendment."[76] The American Court hesitated to declare any substantive right, preferring to wait and see whether case law would present an actual intrusion into privacy rights. In this manner, American law, reflecting common law orientation, represents a tentativeness not characteristic of German law.[77]

It is interesting to speculate why American law has not taken a turn similar to the Germans, even though, of course, the growth of data and data processing parallels, if not eclipses, that in Germany. Thus, the threats to human autonomy posed by the information age are at least equal, if not greater, than in Germany. Textually, the American Constitution seems about as illuminative of such a right as the German. The First Amendment, for example, plausibly bestows certain rights to knowledge of how information, especially personal information, is to be gathered or used.[78] The Fourth Amendment confers certain rights of privacy against discovery of personal information, especially that over which one has a "reasonable expectation" of privacy.[79] The due process clause protects against arbitrary intrusion into matters of personal security and liberty.[80] Human dignity too has been a theme of the American Bill of Rights, including especially its cognates of self-determination and autonomy.[81] Together, these rights would seem to convey a certain zone of privacy, which, it might be argued, covers informational privacy. In this way, a right to informational privacy and self-determination plausibly could exist to safeguard human liberty and self-government in the information age.

Yet American law has not developed along these lines.[82] Perhaps this is because the Supreme Court feels less compelled to address changing social and economic conditions. Perhaps this is because the Supreme Court feels more restrained in declaring rights to be fundamental in the absence of clear textual or historical support. Perhaps this is because *Whalen*, like all substantive due process cases, is anchored in privacy, not autonomy as *Census Act*, and privacy confers less power or control than autonomy. Or perhaps it is because the American Constitution is less endowed with an underlying philosophic base, such as the influence of Kantian morality on the Basic Law, yielding correspondingly less substance.

The Supreme Court might also believe that Congress or legislatures have sufficiently protected these rights, leaving little for the Court to do.[83] In fact, the threat to privacy posed by the information age has been a constant topic of American legislative politics over the past few years. Yet no comprehensive statutory regime has been forthcoming. Certain legislative enactments target specific areas, such as the 1994 Driver's Privacy Protection Act that prohibits most disclosures of personal information about an individual in connection with a motor vehicle record, or the Privacy Act of 1974, which prohibits disclosure, without consent, of official records maintained on people. But these measure are episodic, not encompassing. They form more a quilt of specific, narrow legislative responses to identified privacy problems than a comprehensive framework.

In lieu of legislation or constitutionalizing, self-policing by industry has been the preferred solution. This has had decidedly mixed results. For example, there is mounting concern that banks and other financial institutions misuse the reams of personal information collected on consumers and their spending patterns.[84] U.S. companies have had difficulty complying with an European Union privacy directive on transmitting data electronically.[85] Americans prefer self-policing; Europeans prefer rights of informational self-determination. However these approaches work out in practice, there is, of course, a significant difference between resolution of an issue pursuant to normal politics as compared to constitutional treatment and its accompanying higher status, especially in Germany and the United States, two countries with an elevated sense of "higher" law. Thus, as a matter of comparative law, it is worth observing that the German Constitutional Court is addressing this aspect of the computer age in a more rights-protective manner than the U.S. Supreme Court.

CONFIDENTIALITY

The concept of informational privacy—with its root base in control of personal information—extends beyond data processing and resonates generally in German law and, to an extent, in American law. Frequent application of the doctrine occurs in the context of confidentiality over personal matters. Good examples of this strand are confidentiality over medical files, general inquiries into mental and physical health, and divorce records.[86] In German law, these cases are grounded in the theory of German personality law already described. People are spiritual–moral beings who possess an inviolable core of privacy that is to be safeguarded as an inner sanctuary. Personal files are records of intimate details, scrutiny of which does not ordinarily extend beyond those whose lives are reflected. Entry is thus barred into this private sphere unless justified by overriding public need, and the measure is proportional to the end sought. In these cases the information sought—divorce records and patient files—was considered within a person's private sphere, as a record of intimate, personal details, but not an inviolable sphere beyond any inquiry.[87] Such incursions, therefore, required justification pursuant to the *Rechtsstaat* principle of proportionality, and both failed.[88] Along similar lines, the Constitutional Court has protected as confidential unauthorized recordings of private conversations.[89] Conversation, like private matters, reflects human personality; therefore, it is not accessible unless consented to or justified along proportionality grounds. Under German constitutional law, it is doubtful that Linda Tripp could surreptitiously record conversations with Monica Lewinsky, especially if intended for use against the president.

The German focus on this right of privacy has general resonance in American law. Confidentiality rights have historically been the subject of common law privilege (e.g., attorney–client priviledge) or statutory law (e.g., doctor–patient priviledge). However, the Supreme Court, in recent years, has announced certain confidentiality rules as a matter of federal evidence law in a variety of settings, most notably in attorney–client relations, spousal relations, and psychotherapist–patient relations.[90]

A difference between the laws is that American law is grounded in privacy, whereas German law is part of human personality. This has a number of consequences, the most important of which is that American privacy mainly protects only against official attempts at discovery. By comparison, German personality rights protect the individual per se so that he or she might flourish.[91] Thus, any unauthorized inquiry may by prohibited, whether from official or private sources. Another important difference is that the source for American claims is statutory (physician–patient) or by the common law (attorney–client), but not constitutional. This speaks to the status of the right, but not, of course, its character.

REPUTATIONAL INTEREST

A more innovative aspect of informational self-determination is the right it endows individuals to control the portrayal of facts and details of their lives, even if uncomfortable or embarrassing. In

German law, this idea has developed into a right that empowers people to shield hurtful truths from public scrutiny in order to safeguard reputation or other personality interests, such as well-being or self-identity.

As a matter of human nature, reputation is integral to personality because it forms part of the reflection of one's image, even self-image, and thus can constitute a window to one's soul. This is the internal dimension to reputation. Reputation is also important because it represents others' images of a person. The views others have, in turn, effect internal conceptions of self-worth. Reputation thus has both internal and external dimensions that are integral to personality. For these reasons, German law has recognized that individuals should be able to exercise some control over how they are viewed by others, externally in the world.

German law contrasts dramatically with American law over these points. In American law, reputational interests have historically been treated by the common law concept of defamation, consisting of libel and slander. But American defamation law has never contained a highly developed concept of personality to protect sensitive personal information from an intrusive world. Moreover, in the personal areas where First Amendment expression freedoms reach, those expression freedoms are likely to take precedence over a person's interest in shielding private information. This is another example, comparatively speaking, of how American law is committed to the idea of free expression more than any other value. Thus, we shall see again how German law accents the integrity of human personhood, reflecting its focus on the centrality of people to the social order.

Germany

Drunkard Case

A good example of personal control over truthful but harmful information is the *Drunkard Case*, where the Court prohibited the public announcement of persons legally determined to be incapacitated because of drunkenness, drug addiction, being a spendthrift, or other such disfavored status.[92] The purpose of such public announcements was protection of the general public, who otherwise might unwittingly transact business with such persons. However, control of the gathering and use of such personal information, including "the act and status of being placed under legal guardianship," is protected constitutionally because it is deeply revealing of personality.[93] To the Constitutional Court, release of information over one's status is analogous to use (or misuse) of computerized personal data.

A second aspect of the *Drunkard Case* distinguishes German law from American: "Public notice of being placed under guardianship on account of alcoholism or being a spendthrift is a severe violation of [informational self-determination]."[94] This "severely impacts the person in her entirety," "places a negative stamp" on reputation, "and complicates application of the Social State Principle [*Socialstaatsprinzip*] oriented support measures [*Hilfsmassnahmen*] designed to assist recovery from addiction and facilitate social reentry."[95] Indeed, such notification impacts on the person "at an especially critical phase in his beginning reentry into society."[96]

Reputation and its radiation to human personality is an important reflection of the state of the human condition in modern society. Over these matters, *Drunkard* echoes the essential teaching of German law: Human personality and its nurturing is a core concern of the constitutional order. Because of the centrality of personality, adjustments must be made to the legal order to further its facilitation, as in guardianship law in *Drunkard* and expression law in *Lebach* and related cases, as discussed later in this chapter. Moreover, the dignitarian radiation of the Basic Law necessitates a reaching out and nurturing of the weaker members of society, such as rehabilitated criminals or troubled souls. Human dignity, as it were, calls for application of the golden rule: considering how you would want to be treated if you were in that state, and the quality of society is to be judged by how it treats its weaker members. Individuals are not just independent contractors; they are "community bound" and "community connected." Thus, community as a whole has obligations to these persons, just as individuals are to be responsible as rights holders. Dignity, in other words, acts as a "higher law" by which individuals and society are judged and guided. Thus, it is appropriate to prefer the interests of rehabilitated persons as they readjust to their place in society.

America

A brief look at American law underscores deep cultural differences over these points. At the constitutional level, the cases most like *Drunkard* are *Wisconsin v. Constantineau* and *Paul v. Davis*, both treated under procedural due process.[97] It is noteworthy that public posting of a disfavored status (such as drunkenness in *Drunkard* or *Constantineau* or shoplifting in *Paul*) is treated in American law as only raising a procedural inquiry as to whether the person affected had adequate notice and participatory rights in determining whether the measure was justifiable. There was no inquiry into the effect of such posting on a person's well-being, phrased in American law as privacy rights, despite the obvious tarnishing of reputation that occurs, especially from a posting that turns out to be in error. This would seem to reflect the lack of focus in American law on the centrality of personality. There seems little solicitude for weaker social members who might seek to restore some semblance of ordinary life. In this respect, American outcasts encounter a pretty harsh world.

The difference in treatment between German and American law is also attributable to the difference between positive and negative approaches to the Constitution. Grounded in a positive dimension to liberty, the German constitutional order equips government to act proactively on behalf of human welfare. By comparison, acting mainly as a negative limitation on government, the American Constitution urges government to be neutral and more observer than actor. Rather, people are to fight their own battles, devising their own solutions to appropriate degrees of satisfaction.

PROTECTING REPUTATION FROM DEFAMATION OR INSULT

Germany

Mephisto

A person's right to his or her reputation encompasses protection of personal honor as an outgrowth of personality.[98] As such, these rights can, in certain cases, be extended to eclipse other basic rights, including, most notably, article 5 expression guarantees. Protection of honor and reputation in Germany is itself a highly valued manifestation of human dignity, with a long pedigree. The reputational component is grounded in the long-standing German focus on personality rights. The high estimation of honor is rooted in Germany's aristocratic past.[99] No case represents the German view better than the famous *Mephisto* case, a seminal case of artistic freedom, where the Constitutional Court split 3–3 in upholding an injunction against publication of Klaus Mann's novel of the same name on the ground that it defamed the memory of a famous deceased actor who had been quite active in the theater during the Nazi time.[100]

All basic rights, including artistic rights protecting Mann's novel, must be interpreted within the value order of the Basic Law, according to the Constitutional Court. Since the Basic Law is founded on the view "of the human person as an autonomous being developing freely within the social community," artistic freedom must also be measured against article 1 human dignity, the supreme value.[101] To the extent artistic or communication freedoms conflict with human dignity, they may have to yield, depending on the concrete balancing of the freedoms at issue. For example, in *Mephisto*, it might be argued that the tangible effect of Mann's novel was to tarnish the memory of the deceased actor. Disparagement of the dead could be thought to be inconsistent with human dignity.[102] "An artist's use of personal data about people in his environment can affect their social rights to respect and esteem."[103] To that extent, communication freedoms may have to yield to the superior value of dignity, as manifested in this interest in honor and reputation.

In this manner, the Constitutional Court implied limits on the seemingly boundless guarantee of artistic freedom, as it previously had implied limits to the apparent express limitation of personality rights in *Elfes*. In both cases, the Constitutional Court acted on behalf of its vision of human dignity; in *Mephisto* this limited expression rights, in *Elfes* it limited restriction of freedom of action. Human dignity thus becomes the glue between both rights-enhancing and rights-constricting interpretations. This is an illustration of the Constitutional Court's creative interpretation in service of the Court's vision of the new German constitutional order. Of course, the Supreme Court has also sometimes displayed a creative side.[104]

America

The Constitutional Court's reasoning points to a fundamental contrast with American law. Anchoring reputational rights in the capacious concepts of human dignity and accompanying personality allowed the Constitutional Court, in essence, to imply a constitutional right to be free from defamation. This could be justified from the "objective" theory of constitutionalism, requiring the state, as it does, to realize the norms of the value order. By contrast, American law is founded on the concept that "public" persons (public officials or those well known in the public eye) are to be treated as "men of fortitude, able to live in a hardy climate," consistent with Americans' image of themselves as tough, self-reliant, and courageous.[105] Accordingly, public men and women in the United States are expected to endure the insults and abuses common to public life. Based on such thinking, the Supreme Court has widely immunized speakers from defamation claims.[106] Under American principles, Gründgens, the actor, would qualify as a public figure, thereby subjecting him to these immunity rules.[107] In this way, one notices that American public persons are left alone to confront criticism or disparagement, lacking any claim to official protection, whereas Germans can call on communal support. In Germany, self-esteem is valued for the inner self-worth it can bolster, and also the tone of mutual respect it sets for the society. Constituting community on a core of values makes a big difference.

Movement of German Law in Direction of American

Protecting honor or reputation, especially when rooted as a tangible manifestation of human dignity and accompanying personality rights as in Germany, is likely to result in a preferencing of such reputational interests over other claims, even, most notably, expression rights. This is the balance *Mephisto* represents. This was also the balance present in American law before the time of *New York Times v. Sullivan* in 1964, which ushered in a new, preferred status of free speech that predominated over the reputational interests pricked by defamation. Yet *Mephisto* represents only part of the German picture. Both during the time of *Mephisto* and especially its aftermath, German law has evolved in the direction of American law.

German law has, for example, gone partway down the path of American law through the latitude it accords certain polemic communicated in matters of public significance pursuant to both the Counter-Attack Theory (*Gegenschlag*), which provides that a harsh public attack merits a reply in kind to counter its impact on the formation of public opinion, and by its assumption that public figures must endure sharp scrutiny and critique. This last point is especially pronounced in the development of case law since *Mephisto*.

The case marking the new approach most vividly is the *Stern–Strauss Interview Case*.[108] In this case, a prominent German writer, in an interview published in the leading magazine *Stern*, used the late Bavarian politician Franz Josef Strauss as an illustration of his view that not all German politicians were true democrats; some were "opportunistic democrats" (*Zwangsdemokraten*), those who, out of political necessity or opportunism, proclaimed democracy and democratic ideals even though they might prefer to act more dictatorially.[109] Responding to Strauss's successful suit for libel, the Constitutional Court redefined defamation. Purposeful denigration and insult do not themselves constitute libel, the Court reasoned, in a move in the direction of American law.[110] Rather, the line between protected speech, even if sharp and insulting, and unprotected libel lies at the point at which the statement primarily defames the person without any other substantive value. Like the Supreme Court, the Constitutional Court has construed this definition very narrowly out of concern that loose interpretation will detrimentally chill the exercise of expression rights. Thus, we can see that in a general way the Constitutional Court has recalibrated the equation between expression and reputational interests to preference expression rights. We can explore these aspects of personality more closely in Chapter 7 on expression.

What is significant for our purposes in exploring the aspect of personality radiated through reputation is that German law has significantly moved in the direction of American law over how to value reputation when juxtaposed against free speech. We still might say that German law places a higher premium on reputation than American, but this is certainly changing. As yet, German law has not fully adopted the more absolutist position of American law, which, for public persons, presumptively immunizes defamation claims.

RIGHT TO HONOR AND RIGHTFUL PORTRAYAL OF SELF

Germany

The German idea of personality encompasses a certain proactive element by which a person can defend himself or herself or ward off undesired intrusions. This idea is part of a more general right to control presentation of one's self in the world, as for example in a case like *Drunkard*. In one sense, of course, this is an outgrowth of the German theory of informational self-determination. However, the idea is additionally grounded in a more fundamental right of self-determination over one's position and social standing, a right "fundamentally to decide how to present oneself to third parties or the public, whether and to what extent outsiders can have access to one's personality."[111] In this way, both informational self-determination and this "image self-determination" are grounded in control over one's private, intimate core of personality. German law, again, reveals its concern for preservation of an inner dimension to human life.

In so interpreting article 2 personality rights, the Constitutional Court relied upon lines of doctrine developed by the Federal Supreme Court, the supreme interpreter of the German Civil Code. The BGH had developed a jurisprudence of personality rights in connection with interpretation of the BGB.[112] Over time, the BGH extended such rights to cover specific emanations of personality, including control over distribution of one's own writings (such as personal letters or diaries), secrecy in relation to medical records, or rights to one's spoken word, developments advocated by Warren and Brandeis and, later, confirmed by the Constitutional Court.[113]

In reliance on this work, the Constitutional Court recast the private law interests of reputation or privacy into the capacious language of human dignity and personality, thereby constitutionalizing the doctrine. This certainly made for a more secure anchoring of the concepts in the legal order, as the Court recognized.[114] Preservation and nourishing of human personality is a central aim of German law, notwithstanding the challenges of modern life. No cases demonstrated the power and reach of these new constitutional developments more than the famous *Soraya* and *Lebach* decisions.

Soraya: Right to Control Against Attribution of False Statements

In *Soraya*, the Court upheld an award of damages for publication of a fictitious interview in a tabloid newspaper with the former wife of the Shah of Iran. The fictitious interview fabricated intimate details of her private life. The award was predicated on this newly created constitutional right of personality, derived from the influence of objective constitutional principles on the private law.[115] Recast as constitutional values, privacy, personality, and dignity became obligations of the state to preserve and protect under objective constitutionalism. State organizations like the Constitutional Court thereby became obligated to create the proper conditions for their realization. These values now moved to the very center of the legal order:

The personality and dignity of an individual, to be freely enjoyed and developed within a societal and communal framework, stand at the very center of the value order reflected in the fundamental rights protected by the Constitution. Thus an individual's interest in his personality and dignity must be respected, and must be protected by all organs of the state [see articles 1 and 2 of the Constitution]. Such protection should be extended, above all, to a person's private sphere, *i.e.*, the sphere in which he desires to be left alone, to make . . . his own decisions, and to remain free from any outside interference. Within the area of private law such protection is provided . . . by the legal rules relating to the general right of personality.[116]

The constitutional right of personality entitles a person to be left fundamentally alone, free from unauthorized interference, whether from public or private actors, if so desired. A person should be able to control his or her personal affairs, including those that reflect especially personality, such as personal writings, words, or physical or psychological state. This control might reasonably include who, when, and under what conditions such personal information can be accessed or used. It is this kind of inner citadel that German personality rights are designed to protect.

Moreover, this right is enforceable as a private cause of action by which one private individual can enforce a right to privacy against another private individual, developments the Constitutional Court adopted from the ordinary courts. This development equips the inner citadel to defend against intrusion from the outside. In *Soraya*, these privacy interests operated to limit publication of the interview by the Axel Springer publishing house, publisher of the tabloid. "An imaginary interview adds nothing to the formation of real public opinion. As against press utterances of this sort, the protection of privacy takes unconditional priority."[117] Faced with a conflict among rights, the Constitutional Court favored personality in this setting.

As novel as these results were, even more pathbreaking were the methods used to obtain them. In constitutionalizing these innovations of the BGH, the Constitutional Court seemed to call into question parliamentary supremacy. Naturally, this would follow from the BGH's approach, since it created a damage remedy for intangible interests despite the wording of the Civil Code, which forbade such practice in the absence of an authorizing statute.[118] Responding to this, the Constitutional Court suggested that judges were not wholly bound by statutory law after all.[119] The Basic Law, in article 20(3), had altered the traditional civilian law limitation of the judge to statutory law, rejecting a "narrow positivism."[120] "Statutes [*Gesetze*] and laws [*Recht*] . . . are not necessarily always identical." "Law is not synonymous with the totality of written statutes."[121] Law (*Recht*) can, under some circumstances, include additional norms or concepts, derived from "the constitutional order as a whole" and "functioning as a corrective to the written law."[122] Thus, rather than being "bound by the strict letter of the law, the role of the judge is to realize in case law . . . the values immanent in the constitutional order, [even if] not written or clearly expressed in written law."[123] Judges should so fill in statutory gaps based on "practical reason" and "well-founded general community concepts of justice."[124]

However, in the case at hand there was no real statutory gap to fill, since the Bundestag had expressly rejected a law authorizing damages for intangible harms.[125] Now the Constitutional Court resorted to the tools of German legal science (*Rechtswissenschaft*) in authorizing this "creative law-making" (*schöpferischer Rechtsfindung*).[126] Social conditions must often take priority over statutory text.[127] Rather than being static, norms reflect the context of social relations in their societal–political milieu; their content varies under these circumstances.[128] The Constitutional Court observed that this is especially the case today, as contemporary society has witnessed dramatic social and legal change. In this context, a judge cannot simply consult written law and meet his or her obligation to declare the law. Instead, the judge "has a free hand" to interpret law in view of "substantive justice" and "changed social conditions."[129]

The Constitutional Court's interpretation comes pretty close to authorizing judges to determine themselves the applicability of statutory norms; those perceived to be outdated or not relevant can seemingly be replaced with a judge's own view of justice. Not surprisingly, this position engendered wide discussion in German legal circles.[130] On the other hand, the free hand of the judge might be more apparent than real, as German judges work within the techniques of interpretation authorized by the law. German law, in particular, has focused carefully on methodology and process. A major aim of German legal science has been to impart the process of interpretation so that even, for example, the German Civil Code could be interpreted out of itself to yield an independent system of law. The process of reasoned judgment might, therefore, not be unrestrained but instead cabined within the texture of law.

Still, if courts are to be bound by "justice" as well as enacted law, article 20(3) would seem, by this interpretation, to constitutionalize natural law as a source for rendering decisions.[131] If so, one might argue, judges should reject unjust law. Alternatively, one might say outmoded or misguided law should be corrected by judges striving for just results, as seemed the goal of the *Soraya* Court.[132] Certainly, *Soraya* injects a degree of free judicial creativity into constitutional law not seen so explicitly in the United States since, perhaps, *Calder v. Bull* and its famous debate between Justices Chase and Iredell.[133]

Nevertheless, natural law can be a perilous course as well as an enriching one, as American battles over the theory attest.[134] Recognizing this, the Constitutional Court has mainly sought to cabin the temptation to authorize judicial usurpation of parliamentary supremacy. In *Soraya*, for example, the Court was "careful to couch its reasoning" in authorizing judges to fill a gap left by the Civil Code "in terms of statutory interpretation, not of any right to defy the legislature."[135] The Court has applied this technique, in reliance on *Soraya*, to other cases as well.[136] But the Court has, in other cases, been clear in recognizing the obligation of judges to adhere to statutory law, thereby reining in judicial discretion.[137]

Contrasting this creative interpretivism with American law, it is worth observing that American law does not resonate with the language of "creative law-making," as in German law. Constitutional strategy in the United States is couched in the language of interpretivism, even if activist results are thereby reached.[138] Perhaps the German Court is simply more forthright about the judicial enterprise, although the American Court has its moments of candor too.[139] Maybe the Court is more comfortable with the techniques authorized by its legal system. Or perhaps the Constitutional Court, as a new court striving to create a new legal order, feels more justified in acting so proactively. Still, as a matter of comparative law, it is worth observing that German constitutionalism advocates a degree of judicial creativity more pronounced than the American variety. The German Court thus seems more a leader of democracy than an interpreter of its ways, traditions, or mores. In these respects, Germany poses a version of judicial review different from the American kind.

Lebach: *Right to Personal Honor and Control Over Presentation of One's Self in Society*

Later in the year, the Constitutional Court concluded in the *Lebach* decision that the privacy interests recognized in *Soraya* outweighed any public speech interest in publicizing an individual's role in a crime for which he or she had already paid the penalty.[140] Here a convicted robber was able to halt a planned television broadcast of a documentary film depicting, accurately, his and others' participation in a notorious armed robbery of an army munitions depot that resulted in the death of four soldiers.[141] The Constitutional Court grounded its decision in the felon's personality right in being let alone, free from publicity, so that he could concentrate on his reentry to society. The concern for rehabilitation took precedence even over highly ranked expression freedoms, as personality interests had trumped expression in *Soraya*.

In the 1970s the Constitutional Court tended to prefer values of human dignity and personality over communication, which it was able to accomplish through its comprehensive but ad hoc balancing process. The balancing process is a method by which the Court tries to achieve equilibrium among competing rights at issue. *Mephisto*, *Soraya*, and *Lebach* are emblematic of this approach. Today the Constitutional Court attaches far more significance to expression rights, even in relationship to concepts of honor or reputation. Free expression is itself now viewed more emphatically as an intrinsic element of human dignity. In this sense, expression and reputation are separate emanations of dignity. Still, dignity places limitations on expression that would be out of place in the United States, such as limiting hate speech or horror films. These matters will be explored more carefully in Chapter 7 and its discussion of expression.

At the heart of *Lebach* was the need to preserve the integrity of human personality against the sometimes intrusive influence of the outside world. "The rights to the free development of one's personality and human dignity secure for everyone an autonomous sphere in which to shape one's private life by developing and protecting one's individuality."[142] These values are threatened by public reporting of the crime, according to the Constitutional Court, "which publicizes his misdeeds and conveys a negative image of his person in the eyes of the public."[143] The film depicted the felons' homosexuality, and the Constitutional Court was concerned that this would resonate negatively in the public, complicating the felon's reentry into society.[144] The need to anchor personality is so strong, it seemed to the Court, that others could be prevented from examination of such truthful but personal events. Personality rights "include the right to remain alone, to be oneself within this [autonomous] sphere, and to exclude the intrusion of or inspection of others."[145] So the Constitutional Court explains how and why the inner sanctuary merits safeguarding.

From this, it is not much of a step to the general right of informational self-determination, developed as a concrete manifestation of this focus on interiority: "It also encompasses the right to one's own likeness and utterances, especially the right to decide what to do with pictures of oneself. In principle, everyone has the right to determine for himself whether and to what extent others may make a public account of either certain incidents from his life or his entire life story."[146] Of course, these privacy rights ran directly counter to the broadcasters' expression rights, guaranteed in article 5.[147] Expression rights are highly valued in Germany, as in America, and themselves reflections of human dignity. Thus, the Constitutional Court was faced with resolving the conflict between the two fundamental rights.

In such cases, the Constitutional Court strives to achieve concordance (*Konkordanz*) between the rights, attempting to interpret both in a manner such that the essence of each can be preserved and, hopefully, optimized. The idea of concordance as an interpretive technique follows from the objective ordering of values in the Basic Law, which is calibrated to steer society. It also follows from classical natural law, where natural rights, which people enter into society to secure, might reasonably be limited only by rights of others asserted in the circumstance. German thinkers, notably Kant and Hegel, contributed significantly to these ideas. To resolve such conflicts among rights, a careful assessment and application of the rights at issue is required. This would seem to work better in theory than practice. It is not always possible to achieve such harmony in the hard realities of the case. It was not possible in *Lebach*.

The Constitutional Court chose personality rights. Ordinarily, the public has a significant interest in learning of a crime. However, there is an important difference between a crime that is ongoing and one that is past.[148] If the crime is ongoing or yet being prosecuted, then the public has a real need to know of the danger it may be in, the need to solve it, and the need to bring people to justice. Such crimes are therefore an "overriding" public interest, as medical epidemics or public unrest, that may justify incursions of rights.[149] However, in *Lebach* the crime was past and the felon had paid his price. Thus, the only public interest was in publicizing an event that had already occurred.

From the felon's view, his or her "right to be let alone" increases to the extent the public has no interest in receiving current, vital information, according to the Constitutional Court.[150] This follows from the Proportionality Principle. "The invasion of the personal sphere is limited to the need to satisfy adequately the [public's] interest in receiving information, while the harm inflicted upon the accused must be proportional to the seriousness of the offense or to its importance otherwise for the public."[151] Consequently, it is not always permissible to "disclose the name, release a picture, or use some other means of identifying the perpetrator."[152] Moreover, crucial to the development of the felon's personality was his reintegration into society so that he might find himself again and thereby better reach his potential.[153] These factors combined to outweigh the broadcasting rights at issue.

Lebach thus illustrates how assertion of dignitarian rights can operate to limit other fundamental rights, even especially highly valued ones like expression freedoms. The limiting influence that rights may have on one another is mainly foreign to American law.[154] American law is no longer fully grounded in natural law, having given way in the last century more to positivism and its propensity to balance constitutional rights against social interests. The outcome in *Lebach* also demonstrates how this technique of concordance operates, weighing conflicting rights with sensitivity, nuance, and balance. How personality measures against expression depends more on the hard realities of the case than any categorical rule. *Lebach* further illustrates the communitarian bent of German law; the Constitutional Court's concern for reintegrating the felon into society took precedence over individual and social interests in expression.[155] Viewed in a different light, the felon's personal autonomy can only be effectively exercised in a social context, and this took precedence. On its face, *Lebach* too is a remarkable act of judicial activism: extending privacy rights from the textual enumeration of personality beyond textually secure expression rights.

America

It is hard to find a more dramatic contrast with American law than *Soraya* and *Lebach*, illustrating the strength that dignity and personality radiate in German law and society and, by comparison, their relative undervaluation in American law. Certainly one does not ordinarily find such solicitude for individual welfare in American law.[156] Assessing these cases against the backdrop of American law, it is quite remarkable how they empower individuals to control dissemination of truthful information about their personal affairs.[157] It is astounding, frankly, from the American perspective, to think that accurate reporting of an event, especially one with public significance, could be considered an invasion of personality. This goes well beyond any American action for libel or invasion of privacy. Under American law, expression interests would probably predominate in a case like *Lebach*. For example, the Supreme Court has held that a rape victim's name, publicly available, may be published in a newspaper, as can, more generally, the names of crime victims.[158] American newspapers regularly run stories covering the details of crimes, from perpetrators' suicide attempts to victims' sexual history. The American press, generally, manically pursued the salacious details of President Clinton's affair with Monica Lewinsky, a pursuit and publication horrifying to Europeans. As we take stock of German and American law, we can now see how the Constitutional Court has developed the line of privacy jurisprudence advocated by Warren and Brandeis, an argument that never fully developed in the United States.[159] In fact, the American position is the converse of the Germans: Speech values predominate over dignitarian values.

Böll: Right to Personal Honor and One's Own Words: Right Not to Be Misquoted

The reasoning of *Soraya* was later picked up in *Böll*, where the Court determined that false quotations are not protected by free expression guarantees because they too mischaracterize one's personality.[160] In *Böll*, a television commentator criticized the Nobel Prize–winning author Heinrich Böll for allegedly making statements that aided terrorism, then a problem in Germany.[161] In making his charge, the commentator misquoted Böll, and Böll asserted that the misquote invaded his sphere of personality. A state supreme court agreed, but the Federal Supreme Court dismissed the action.[162]

Uncovering new ground, the Constitutional Court determined that the dismissal of the suit violated Böll's personality rights on the grounds that an individual has a constitutional interest in not being misquoted:

[A misquote impairs a person's] constitutionally guaranteed general right to an intimate sphere. Among other things this right includes personal honor and the right to one's own words; it also protects the bearer of these rights against having statements attributed to him which he did not make and which impair his self-defined claim to social recognition.[163]

The Constitutional Court went on to say, "The use of a direct quotation as proof of critical evaluation is . . . a particularly sharp weapon in the battle of opinions and very effective in undermining the personality right of the person being criticized."[164] In essence, a speaker becomes a "witness against herself" in the contest for public opinions.[165] Such misappropriation of words demeans individuality. A person has a hard time restoring his or her stature. These wounds were particularly grievous because the personal attack was made on television, thus assuring broad dissemination.[166]

America

The contrast with American law over the use of false quotations is dramatic. In the recent Supreme Court case of *Masson v. New Yorker*, the Supreme Court determined that the use of deliberately falsified quotations in a published interview was protected speech because such conduct did not rise to the standard of proscribable actual malice falsity, established in the landmark case of *New York Times v. Sullivan*.[167] Lacking such malice, the speaker and social interests in "uninhibited, robust and wide-open" public discourse were more important.[168] The contrast between *Böll* and *Masson* thus further illuminates the differing value structures of the two countries. In Germany, at least during the 1970s and early 1980s, personal honor, rooted in article 1 human dignity and accompanying article 2 personality rights, outweighed expression rights in certain circumstances.[169] In the United States, by contrast, such personality interests never outweigh public discourse unless one can prove the speech fits the narrow category of actual malice falsity for public persons or other such enumerated exception to protected speech. In this way, human dignity, sometimes with its particular radiation of personal honor, seems the ultimate value of the German legal order, whereas free speech seems to play this role in the United States.

Another aspect of *Böll* illustrates a further contrast with American law. In comparison to established German doctrine, the violation of Böll's personality rights arose from a court's nonaction in foreclosing Böll's right to redress, as compared to the more conventional official action which invades the right. In German law this could be justified from the positive dimension of rights, which obligates the state to create the conditions in which rights can thrive—here, Böll's right to the integrity of his personality. Lacking this positive conception of rights, American law is unlikely to yield an outcome as in *Böll*. The Constitutional Court then found that there was no article 5 protection for false statements, such as the misquote. Thus, Böll's personality rights prevailed.[170]

SUMMARY

As we take stock of the development of German and American law over the idea of inner freedom, we can see that the two laws both converge and diverge from one another. The two laws converge over the treatment as confidential of certain personal matters, such as divorce and private conversations, and the protection of interests of honor and defamation because they are concrete radiations of personality and standing in society and, therefore, significant to a concept of individuality. Of course, German law values such reputational interests more highly than American law. And the American undervaluation of these interests, comparatively speaking, mainly reflects the country's preferencing of free speech, but also its lesser emphasis on this aspect of individual personality. Perhaps the long-standing commitment to democracy in the United States, and its tendency to level claims to personal status, also helps explain this, in contrast to Germany's feudal and aristocratic past.

The divergences are more pronounced than the similarities. The most notable divergence is the strong development in German law of an inner realm to freedom, as manifested especially in the idea of informational self-determination. This strand of interiority in German law is directed at shoring up the inviolability of human character amidst the challenges of the modern world. American law, by contrast, does not emphasize this interior component to freedom. Instead, except for the privacy interests protected by confidentiality, the American notion of freedom is mainly outer directed.

Deciphering the pattern of culture revealed by the two laws, we come back to their starting points. German law, as we recall, started from the premise of the inviolability of personality. Focusing, therefore, on the centrality of personality, German law strives to capture the multifarious radiations of human character. This helps explain why a person's writings, words, thoughts, and emotions are considered central to self-identity. American law, by contrast, does not focus on personality so much as privacy. The two focus points are revealing. The German focus on personality results in a desire to preserve and nourish the well-being of people. The American focus on privacy is grounded in the idea of a "right to be left alone." While aloneness is good for solitude, an important dimension to human life, it does not address the well-being of life in all its dimensions. Interior life that becomes known is sacrificed to the public. Thus, our examination of inner personality reveals two paths to freedom. German freedom is personal oriented, attempting to further the healthy unfolding of personality. American freedom is privacy oriented, mapping out ways people can be alone.

NOTES

1. Donald P. Kommers, THE CONSTITUTIONAL JURISPRUDENCE OF THE FEDERAL REPUBLIC OF GERMANY 328 (1989).

2. Olmstead v. United States, 277 U.S. 438, 478 (Brandeis, J., dissenting).

3. 4 HARV. L. REV. 193, 205–07 (1890).

4. Mary Ann Glendon, RIGHTS TALK: THE IMPOVERISHMENT OF POLITICAL DISCOURSE 49 n. 7 (1991).

5. Warren & Brandeis, *supra* note 3, at 195–96.

6. Roscoe Pound, *The Interests of Personality*, 28 HARV. L. REV. 343 (1915).

7. 277 U.S. at 478.

8. 376 U.S. 254 (1964).

9. 381 U.S. 479 (1965).

10. Glendon, *supra* note 4, at 50.

11. Glendon, *supra* note 4, at 71, *citing* Wilhelm von Humboldt, THE LIMITS OF STATE ACTION 16, 20–21 (J. C. Coulthard trans., Cambridge Univ. Press 1969).

12. The history is recounted in Glendon, *supra* note 4, at 71–72.

13. *Id.* at 72, 75.

14. 1 Friedrich Karl von Savigny, SYSTEM DES HEUTIGEN RÖMISCHEN RECHTS [SYSTEM OF MODERN ROMAN LAW] 103 (Scientia Verlag 1981) (1840–1851) (8 vols.) *cited in* William Ewald, *Comparative Jurisprudence (1): What Was It Like to Try a Rat?* 143 U. PA. L. REV. 1889, 2035 (1995).

15. Otto von Gierke, 1 DEUTSCHES PRIVATRECHT 702 (1895) *cited in* Harry D. Krause, *The Right to Privacy in Germany—Pointers for American Legislation?* DUKE L. J. 481, 485 (1965). Von Gierke is the direct source of the German idea.

16. Mary Jo Obee & William C. Plouffe, Jr., *Privacy in the Federal Bankruptcy Courts*, 14 NOTRE DAME J. L., ETHICS & PUB. POL'Y. 1011, 1015 (2000) (local, muncipal, state, and federal government entities "maintain hundreds, probably thousands, of computerized databases on individuals"); Paul Schwartz, *The Computer in German and American Constitutional Law: Towards an American Right of Informational Self-Determination*, 37 AM. J. COMP. L. 675, 677 n. 12 (1989).

17. John Markoff, *Used Computer Bares Old User's Secrets*, N.Y. TIMES, April 4, 1997 at A14.

18. Joel Brinkley, *FTC Surfs the Web and Gears Up to Demand Privacy Protection*, N.Y. TIMES, September 21, 1998 at C1. Some progress on privacy is being made in the United States. A recent Georgetown University survey reveals that about two-thirds of 364 Web sites surveyed posted some notice about their privacy and information-gathering practices. *Nearly Two-Thirds of Surveyed Web Sites Post Privacy Notices, Study Reports*, 67 U.S. LAW WEEK at 2728.

19. Schwartz, *supra* note 16, at 678 n. 16.

20. 27 BVerfGE 1 (1969).

21. *Id.* at 32.

22. *Id.* at 6.

23. *Id.*

24. *Right to Heritage I,* 79 BVerfGE 256, 268 (1988).

25. *Microcensus,* 27 BVerfGE at 6.

26. *Id.*

27. *Id.*

28. *Griswold,* 381 U.S. at 522 (Black, J., dissenting).

29. *Olmstead,* 277 U.S. at 478 (Brandeis, J., dissenting).

30. 65 BVerfGE 1 (1984).

31. 27 BVerfGE at 7.

32. *Id.*

33. *Id.*

34. *Id.* Moreover, as additional precautions, the statute prohibits publication of information gathered and binds census takers to confidentiality.

35. *Id.* at 8.

36. *Id.*

37. *Id.*

38. *Criminal Diary,* 80 BVerfGE 367, 373 (1980).

39. *Id.*

40. 65 BVerfGE at 1.

41. *Id.* at 4–7, 12–13.

42. *Id.* at 5.

43. *Id.* at 7–8.

44. Schwartz, *supra* note 16, at 688. The *Census Act* decision, and the 1983 Federal law that gave rise to it, did not occur in a legal vacuum. As early as 1970, state laws were enacted to provide for the transmission and processing of data and its protection. All states subsequently adopted legal regimes. Later laws were fashioned at both the federal and state levels that granted individuals certain rights to be informed of data banks and to comment and correct false information contained in them. Thus, the 1983 Federal Law arose amidst a legal culture already well accustomed to data protection. Protests, accordingly, reacted against what were well-focused and understood dangers associated with processing of information. *Id.* at 688–89.

45. Kommers, *supra* note 1, at 333.

46. 65 BVerfGE at 42.

47. Schwartz, *supra* note 16, at 676.

48. Since the 1969 decision of *Microcensus,* the Court observed, the advance of computer technology and capability has changed radically. Before, information was entered manually by keypunch and stored in separate areas, accessible mainly by expert personnel, making it more difficult to fashion together and obtain a personality "portrait." Today, information is entered and retrievable electronically by almost anyone, which facilitates instantaneous access to far-ranging information. 65 BVerfGE at 4, 17, 42.

49. Schwartz, *supra* note 17, at 677. In America, Professor Schwartz cites authority that "since the federal government's entry into the taxation of social welfare spheres, increasing quantities of information have been elicited from citizens and recorded." Many hospitals' resources are "devoted to the task of recording information about patients." *Id.* at 677 n. 14 (citations omitted).

50. 65 BVerfGE at 41.

51. *Id.* at 42.

52. *Id.* at 43.

53. *Id.*

54. *Id.*

55. *Id.*

56. *Id.*

57. *Id.*

58. *Id.* at 44.

59. Schwartz, *supra* note 16, at 701.

60. 65 BVerfGE at 44.

61. *Id.*

62. *Criminal Diary Case*, 80 BVerfGE 367, 373 (1980).

63. *Census Act*, 65 BVerfGE at 44.

64. *Id.*

65. *Id.* at 47.

66. Kommers, *supra* note 1, at 335. While it was necessary for state purposes to collect information, the Court stipulated that data may be collected only when "suitable as well as necessary." 65 BVerfGE at 46. While recognizing that certain data for statistical purposes, including that necessary for operation of the social welfare state, necessitated a stockpiling of data for future use, limits must still be set concerning such information. Clear goals for use of such information must be identified. *Id.* at 47–48. To better assure confidentiality, surveys could be returned through the mail at the cost of government. *Id.* at 60. Attributes identifying people were to be deleted as soon as possible and, until then, held confidentially on a need-to-see basis. *Id.*

67. 65 BVerfGE at 45.

68. *Id.* at 48. Other safeguards included confidentiality obligations and a prohibition of employing census takers in locales where they lived. *Id.* at 49–51, 60.

69. *Id.* at 64. Other deficiencies identified in the law were a lack of clarity in certain provisions, which therefore failed to place citizens on adequate notice of the law; failure to specify clearly projected uses of the information; and failure to obtain permission for transmission to authorities of certain information, such as religious affiliation. *Id.* at 64–66.

70. Since *Census Act*, government and courts have generally striven to meet the challenges of the case and conform the law to constitutional standards. The German judiciary has invalidated laws that do not adequately spell out projected uses of data or grant citizens satisfactory inspection rights. Schwartz, *supra* note 16, at 698–99. Federal and state laws now generally provide for extensive notification, inspection, and informational rights, responding to the Constitutional Court's "call for greater involvement of the citizen in his role as data subject." *Id.* at 699. *Census Act*, not surprisingly, also inspired an outpouring of scholarly commentary. Yet, Professor Schwartz notes, there have been setbacks too. Legal regulation of data use by police and antiterrorist agencies has been lax, probably on account of the majoritarian pressure to fight crime and terrorism. German

authorities responded harshly to protests of the next census, approved by the Constitutional Court after *Census Act. Id.* at 700–701.

71. Kommers, *supra* note 1, at 332. After *Census Act*, the government decided to abandon the census. Instead, the Bundestag drafted a new census bill, which the Constitutional Court approved. *See, e.g.*, BVerfGE, NJW 707 (1989); BVerfGE, NJW 2805 (1987).

72. 381 U.S. at 484 ("specific guarantees in the Bill of Rights have penumbras, formed by emanations from those guarantees that help give them life and substance. . . . Various guarantees create zones of privacy").

73. David P. Currie, THE CONSTITUTION OF THE FEDERAL REPUBLIC OF GERMANY 321 n. 324 (1994).

74. 429 U.S. 589, 591 (1977).

75. *Id.* at 605. For example, the "collection of taxes, the distribution of welfare and social security benefits, the supervision of public health, the direction of our Armed Forces, and the enforcement of the criminal laws all require the orderly preservation of great quantities of information, much of which is personal in character and potentially embarrassing or harmful if disclosed." *Id.*

76. *Id.* at 603–604. Applying German concepts, "the Court should have applied the right of informational self-determination by first asking if the State had decided what it planned to do with the data. Although New York had recorded 100,000 prescriptions each month during the twenty months that the law had been in effect, it had used this information in investigations of exactly two persons. . . . Protection of human autonomy . . . require[s] judicial inquiry into the influence on the individual of having his personal information used in a specific system or indefinitely stored for future application." Schwartz, *supra* note 16, at 684.

77. The position of Justice Brennan most approximates the German one. He observes that an individual has a privacy "interest in avoiding disclosure of personal matters," and that "broad dissemination by state officials of such information . . . would clearly implicate constitutionally protected privacy rights." 429 U.S. at 606 (Brennan, J., concurring). Moreover, the "central storage and easy accessibility of computerized data vastly increases the potential for abuse of that information, and I am not prepared to say that future developments will not demonstrate the necessity of some curb on such technology." *Id.* at 607. However, Justice Stewart, responding to Justice Brennan, seems to articulate the sense of the Court in dampening any recognition of "a general interest in freedom from disclosure of private information." *Id.* at 609 (Stewart, J., concurring).

78. *See, e.g.*, Roe v. Wade, 419 U.S. 113, 209 (1973) (Douglas, J., concurring) ("'liberty'" as used in the Fourteenth Amendment [includes] . . . autonomous control over the development and expression of one's intellect, interests, tastes, and personality"); Shapiro v. Thompson, 394 U.S. 618 (1969) (Marshall, J., dissenting) (because education affects ability of child to exercise First Amendment rights as receiver of information and ideas, there is intimate relationship between personal interest and exercise of rights justifying constitutional protection); *Griswold*, 381 U.S. at 482 ("The right of freedom of speech and press includes not only the right

to utter or to print, but the right to distribute, the right to receive, the right to read and freedom of inquiry, freedom of thought, and freedom to teach").

79. Katz v. United States, 389 U.S. 347, 361–62 (1967); Murphy v. Waterfront Commissioner, 378 U.S. 52, 55 (1964) ("respect for the inviolability of the human personality").

80. *See, e.g.*, Planned Parenthood v. Casey, 505 U.S. 833, 851 (1992) ("Our law affords constitutional protection to personal decisions relating to marriage, procreation, contraception, family relationships, child rearing, and education").

81. *See, e.g., Casey*, 505 U.S. at 851 ("These matters, involving the most intimate and personal choices a person may make in a lifetime, choices central to personal dignity and autonomy, are central to the liberty protected by the Fourteenth Amendment"); National Treasury Employees Union v. Von Raab, 489 U.S. 656, 681 (1989) (Scalia, J., dissenting) ("In my view the Customs Service rules are a kind of immolation of privacy and human dignity in symbolic opposition to drug use"); McClesky v. Kemp, 481 U.S. 279, 336 (1987) (Brennan, J., dissenting) ("Decisions influenced by race rest in part on a categorical assessment of the worth of human beings according to color, insensitive to whatever qualities the individuals in question may possess"); Goldberg v. Kelly, 397 U.S. 254 (1970) ("From its founding the Nation's basic commitment has been to foster the dignity and well-being of all persons within its borders"); Rosenblatt v. Baer, 383 U.S. 75, 92 (1966) (Stewart, J., concurring) (individual's right to the protection of his own good name "reflects [our] basic concept of the essential dignity and worth of every human being—a concept at the root of any decent system of ordered liberty").

82. Under American law, the privacy on which informational self-determination most logically could be based would be either as a matter of constitutional law under the due process clause or as a matter of tort law. Under due process, *Whalen v. Roe* is the main case. Under tort law, the concept would rest on privacy torts. Most states recognize an invasion of privacy action for public disclosure of private facts, through common law or by statute. State definitions of public-disclosure torts, covering matters like AIDS, abortion, or mental illness, parallel the Restatement (Second) of Torts section 652 D (1977). Jonathan B. Mintz, *The Remains of Privacy's Disclosure Tort: An Exploration of the Private Domain*, 55 MARYLAND L. REV. 425, 432–36 (1996) (describing scope of state protections). Some scholars have picked up the charge. *See, e.g.*, Edward J. Bloustein, *Privacy as an Aspect of Human Dignity: An Answer to Dean Prosser*, 39 N.Y.U. L. REV. 962, 1000–1001 (1964) (privacy represents freedom from public scrutiny and includes "prohibiting the disclosure of confidential information obtained by government agencies"); Charles Fried, *Privacy*, 77 YALE L. J. 475, 483 (1968) (arguing that "privacy . . . is control over knowledge about oneself"). *But see* Richard A. Posner, *The Right of Privacy*, 12 GA. L. REV. 393, 408 (1978) (we "have no right, by controlling the information that is known about us, to manipulate the opinions that other people hold of us"). Recently, an emerging tort of "breach of confidence" has been the focus of

scholarly attention. Mintz, *supra*, at 465. *See, e.g.*, Randall P. Bezanson, *The Right to Privacy Revisited: Privacy, News, and Social Change, 1890–1990*, 80 CAL. L. REV. 1133, 1135 (1992) (defining breach of confidence as "a concept of privacy based on the individual's control of information rather than on generalized social controls on information, and . . . an enforceable obligation of confidentiality for those possessing private information rather than . . . a duty visited on publishers").

83. This seems to be a basis on which *Whalen*, 429 U.S. at 594, was decided, as the Court noted precautions taken, like a locked wire fence, alarm system, and that computer tapes were kept in locked cabinets. However, precautions are only as good as the people who implement them. *See* Markoff, *supra* note 17 (noting how a sold computer contained confidential pharmacology files of patients, disclosing sensitive information, such as treatment for AIDS or depression).

84. *Working Group of Attorneys General Investigating Banks' Privacy Practices*, 68 U.S. LAW WEEK 2199 (1999).

85. *Daley Confident U.S. Privacy Efforts Will Be "Adequate" to Satisfy EU Directive*, 15 INTERNATIONAL TRADE REPORTER 1353 (1998). One difference between Americans and Europeans is over individuals' rights of access to personal information. Europeans favor such rights; Americans fear that the right will lead to excessive costs for U.S. business. *US Voluntary Approach to Data Privacy Is Inadequate According to EU Document*, 38 *id.* 1637 (1998). The difference points out a stark contrast in conceptions in the two areas.

86. *Medical Records*, 32 BVerfGE 373, 379 (1972); EuGRZ 415, 419 (1993) (BVerfGE); *Divorce Records*, 32 BVerfGE (1972); 27 BVerfGE 344 (1969).

87. *Medical Confidentiality*, 32 BVerfGE at 279–80; *Divorce Records I*, 27 BVerfGE at 351.

88. 32 BVerfGE at 279–80; 27 BVerfGE at 351.

89. *Tape Recording*, 34 BVerfGE 238, 245–51 (1973).

90. Upjohn Co. v. United States, 449 U.S. 383, 389 (1981); Trammel v. United States, 445 U.S. 40, 47, 51, 53 (1980); Jaffee v. Redmond, 116 S. Ct. 1923, 1928–29 (1996).

91. George P. Fletcher, *Human Dignity as a Constitutional Value*, U. W. ONTARIO L. REV. 171, 179 (1984).

92. 78 BVerfGE 77, 78 (1988).

93. *Id.* at 84.

94. *Id.* at 87.

95. *Id.*

96. *Id.* Those who desire that the notification be rendered can so choose, consistent with the idea of control over personal information.

97. Wisconsin v. Constantineau, 400 U.S. 433 (1971). In *Constantineau*, the Court invalidated a statute that allowed the posting of a notice in liquor stores forbidding sale of liquor to a person, without notice or hearing, because this impaired a person's good name without fair determination. Paul v. Davis, 424 U.S. 693 (1976). In *Paul*, the Court dismissed a suit brought over a police chief's posting of a person as an "active shoplifter," despite the contrary determination in *Constantineau*.

98. There is a long history, going back to the early twentieth century, of civil court protection through interpretation of the Civil Code, especially section 823, of interests of honor and reputation as part of personality rights. Thus, as noted previously, the Constitutional Court has "constitutionalized" most of these developments of the civil court. *See* Harry D. Krause, *The Right to Privacy in Germany—Pointers for American Legislation?* DUKE L. J. 481, 486–8, 499, 500 (1965).

99. Montesquieu thought that honor was the basis for monarchy, because "it is the nature of honor to aspire to preferments and distinguishing titles . . . and a Monarchial government supposeth . . . preeminences, ranks, and likewise a noble descent." MONTESQUIEU, THE SPIRIT OF THE LAWS 121–22 (D. W. Carrithers ed., 1977). Thus, honor seems particularly well-suited to an aristocratic society, like Germany for much of its history. In America, the development was different. For a time the civic republican emphasis on reputation and virtue animated a strong concept of honor. But eventually the revolutionary idea of equality among all peoples completely upturned any concept of nobility. Gordon S. Wood, THE RADICALISM OF THE AMERICAN REVOLUTION, 39, 207, 233, 285 (1991). Honor still persists in America as a legal concept, primarily through state defamation laws, but only to the extent not eclipsed by the landmark case of New York Times v. Sullivan, 376 U.S. at 254, which redefined the relationship between honor, furthered in state libel law, and the First Amendment. From the standpoint of today, honor might be thought of as "the personal reflection of the status which society ascribes to his social position." Robert C. Post, *The Social Foundations of Defamation Law: Defamation and the Constitution*, 74 CAL. L. REV. 691, 700 (1986). In America, reputation seems, therefore, more rooted in personality than honor.

100. 30 BVerfGE 173 (1971). The central character of the novel was an actor named Hendrik Höfgen, whom Klaus Mann, the son of the great German writer Thomas Mann, portrayed as having made his name by playing the devil in Goethe's *Faust* during the Nazi period. While other artists were prosecuted, Höfgen "betrayed his own political convictions and cast off all ethical and humanitarian restraints to further his career by making a pact with . . . [those in] power in Nazi Germany." *Id.* at 174. The story was based on a real-life actor, Gustaf Gründgens, whose career paralleled the fictitious Höfgen in important respects. The suit was brought by Gründgens's son to protect the honor and dignity of the dead, illustrating the extraordinary protection afforded honor in Germany.

101. 30 BVerfGE at 193, *translated in* Kommers, *supra* note 1, at 428.

102. 30 BVerfGE at 194. "It would be inconsistent with the constitutional guarantee of the inviolability of human dignity . . . if a person's general claim to respect . . . could be degraded or debased even after his death." *Id.* This point became important, because Gründgens died shortly after the commencement of the suit. His adopted son then continued the action, proceeding under BGB § 823(1), a general tort provision, that provides recovery for actions that "intentionally or negligently, and unlawfully, injures the life, body . . . liberty . . . or any other right of another person," seeking redress for harm to the memory of his father. This inter-

est was within the concept of dignity, according to the Court. The Court observed, however, that this protection diminishes as memory of the deceased recedes. *Id.* Again, this illustrates the Court's use of concordance, or balancing, as it attempts to bring some equilibrium to rights that otherwise conflict with one another. American law generally refuses recovery for reputational harm after death. Peter E. Quint, *Free Speech and Private Law in German Constitutional Theory*, 48 MD. L. REV. 247, 296 n. 162 (1989).

103. 30 BVerfGE at 195. The Court reasoned that a work of art could harm human dignity by misusing facts of a person's life. Whether this is so or not depends on the nature of the portrait drawn, particularly its truth or falsity. Reputational interests must then be balanced against artistic values to see which is weightier in the circumstance. This test involves a "weighing of all circumstances of the case." *Id.*

104. *See, e.g., Griswold*, 381 U.S. at 479 (deriving right of privacy from penumbras that emanate from specific rights).

105. New York Times Co. v. Sullivan, 376 U.S. at 273 (quoting Crain v. Hurney, 331 U.S. 367, 376 [1947], and discussing published criticism of government officials, such as elected city commissioners).

106. *Id.* at 283 is the leading case.

107. Gründgens would likely be "an individual . . . [who] achieve[d] such pervasive fame or notoriety that he becomes a public figure for all purposes and in all contexts," the essential test for public figures established in Gertz v. Robert Welch, Inc., 418 U.S. 323, 351 (1974).

108. 82 BVerfGE 272 (1990).

109. *Id.* at 273–74.

110. *Id.* at 283.

111. *Eppler*, 54 BVerfGE 148, 155 (1980).

112. First, the BGH found a general right of personality, derived from the influence of articles 1 and 2, that carried over into civil law so that everyone could enforce a certain privacy in their private legal relations. The path-breaking case was *Schacht-Letter*, 13 BGHZ 334, NJW 1404 (1954), where an attorney, on behalf of his client, Dr. Hjalmar Schacht, a former economics minister under Hitler, had written a letter to a newspaper demanding that it correct certain statements it had previously published concerning Schacht. The newspaper published this letter, along with other correspondence, without replying to it or correcting its earlier publication. The attorney successfully complained that the incomplete publication of the letter falsely depicted him to the public as making a personal stand when he actually was acting for his client. Breaking with precedent, the BGH found that a person's letters were protected, even in the absence of copyright, on account of this new found "general right of personality," rooted in section 823 I of the BGB. Krause, *supra* note 98, at 488. For an English translation of *Schacht-Letter, see* BASIL S. MARKESINIS, A COMPARATIVE INTRODUCTION TO THE GERMAN LAW OF TORTS 191–95 (1986); *id.* (3d ed. 1994). The revolutionary change marked by *Schacht-Letter* was attributable to the change in the German legal order marked by the value-ordered nature of the Basic Law, particularly articles 1 and 2. Prior to the Basic Law, the civil courts had been careful to limit claims for harms based on

intangible injury, such as presentation in a false light. *Soraya*, 34 BVerfGE 269, 270–71 (1973). With *Schacht-Letter*, the influence of the Basic Law as an objective statement of values on the civil law and, indeed, all law has become prominent. Under this theory of Third Party Effect (*Drittwirkung*), a certain content of the Basic Law affects all legal relationships, public or private. This contrasts with American law, where, ordinarily, the Constitution does not affect private law. The next step of this development was even more revolutionary. In the famous *Herrenreiter Case* of 1958, the BGH interpreted articles 1 and 2 to mean not only a legal command to respect human dignity and personality, but also to provide affirmative protection of personality against its incursion. *Herrenreiter* (Gentleman Rider), 26 BGHZ 349 (1958). In *Herrenreiter*, a picture was taken of an amateur horseman jumping in a competition, and the picture was used to advertise a product reputed to improve sexual potency. In assessing money damages, the BGH reasoned that the conduct must be appropriately sanctioned to reflect the seriousness of the harm to personality. *Id.* at 356. *Herrenreiter* thus gave rise to the doctrine of compensation for "moral" harms. For an English translation of *Herrenreiter, see* MARKESINIS at 195–201. These developments are also covered in *Soraya*, 34 BVerfGE at 270–73.

113. *See, e.g., Medical Records*, 32 BVerfGE at 373 (protection of medical records); *Divorce Records*, 27 BVerfGE at 344 (protection of confidential information of marriage relationships); *Böll*, 54 BVerfGE at 208 (right not to be misquoted). The BGH widely developed these rights of personality even though codification of them through amendment of the BGB was rejected. *See generally*, Krause, *supra* note 98, at 489, 495, 499–500.

114. 34 BVerfGE at 282.

115. *Soraya*, 34 BVerfGE at 281.

116. *Id.*

117. *Id.* at 283–84, *translated in* Currie, *supra* note 73, at 198. "The degree of care that must be expended to avoid dissemination of an imaginary interview is never too much to expect." *Soraya*, 34 BVerfGE at 286, *translated in* Currie, *supra* note 73, at 198 n. 95.

118. Currie, *supra* note 73, at 117–18. The critique is noted in *Soraya*, 34 BVerfGE at 276, 278.

119. 34 BVerfGE at 286.

120. *Id.*

121. *Id.* at 286–87.

122. *Id.* at 287. *See also* Currie, *supra* note 73, at 117.

123. 34 BVerfGE at 287.

124. *Id.*

125. The history is covered in Krause, *supra* note 98, at 488–96.

126. 34 BVerfGE at 287.

127. *Id.* Civil law is a good example of this. The BGB was adopted in 1900, but is made relevant to current times through the collaborative work of judges and scholars applying the methods of German legal science. In *Soraya*, the Court noted these techniques. "Interpretation of a statutory norm cannot always be tied to its original meaning." *Id.* at 288. This is especially the case as a codification grows older, such as the BGB; then judges'

"freedom to develop law creatively increases." *Id.* One must also consider what reasonable function language serves at the time of its application.

128. *Id.* at 288.

129. *Id.* at 289.

130. *See* Currie, *supra* note 73, at 118, 118 n. 90–91 (authorities collected). The seeds of the problem lie in article 20(3), which binds the executive and judiciary to "law [*Gesetz*] and justice [*Recht*]." *Gesetz* ordinarily means statutory law. *Recht* means justice or the totality of law. The Court interpreted *Recht* as written and unwritten law, and even immanent principles. 34 BVerfGE at 286–87. Such immanent principles might, for example, include the roots of Kantian idealism, a decisive influence on the Basic Law. The binding of the executive and court on *Recht* is a reaction to the horrors caused by extreme positivism during the Nazi period.

131. There is some basis for this, since Christian natural law was an important influence on the Basic Law. However, the debates over the framing of the Basic Law do not reflect this. Currie, *supra* note 73, at 119.

132. *Id.*

133. 3 U.S. (3 Dall.) 386 (1798). *Compare* Justice Chase's natural law foundation, "There are certain vital principles in our free republican governments," *id.* at 388, *with* Justice Iredell: "It has been the policy of all the American states, [and] of the people of the United States, [to] define with precision the objects of the legislative power, and to restrain its exercise within marked and settled boundaries. . . . The ideas of natural justice are regulated by no fixed standard." *Id.* at 399.

134. *Compare* Lochner v. New York, 198 U.S. 45 (1905) (invalidating statute regulating work hours based on view of business as liberty of individual) *with Griswold*, 381 U.S. at 486 (finding "right of privacy older than the Bill of Rights").

135. Currie, *supra* note 73, at 120. *Soraya*, 34 BVerfGE at 290 (judges could "thereby fill the gap in codified sanctions that was evident respecting this violation of personality law").

136. *See, e.g.*, 82 BVerfGE 6, 11–15 (1990) (applying principles of *Soraya* to validate, by analogy, live-in partner's right to assume deceased partner's lease, even though law spoke only of spouses).

137. *See, e.g.*, 49 BVerfGE 304, 320 (1978) ("It is not the business of a judge who is bound by the statute and laws to cut back claims for liability that the statutes afford"). Currie, *supra* note 73, at 120–21. Whether natural law or its cognates is a justifiable measure of constitutionality is heavily debated in the scholarly literature. Letter from Dr. Bodo Pieroth, Professor of Law, University of Münster, Germany, to Edward J. Eberle (May 21, 1997).

138. Like the German Basic Law, the American Constitution contains many vague words that lend themselves to open interpretation. Note, for example, "necessary and proper," U.S. CONST. ART. I, § 7, cl. 18; "due process," *id.* amend. V and XIV; "equal protection," *id.* amend. XIV.

139. *Casey*, 505 U.S. at 849 ("The inescapable fact is that adjudication of substantive due process claims may call upon the Court in interpreting the Constitution to exercise that same capacity which by tradition courts always have exercised: reasoned judgment").

140. 35 BVerfGE 202 (1973).

141. *Id.* at 204–05.

142. *Id.* at 220, *translated in* Kommers, *supra* note 1, at 414–15.

143. 35 BVerfGE at 226, *translated in* Kommers, *supra* note 1, at 416.

144. Because of the effect of mass media and the illusion of reality that a documentary film conveys, the Court worried that the film would reinforce public hostility to homosexuality, especially its connection to a horrific crime. 35 BVerfGE at 228–31, 233–35.

145. *Id.* at 220.

146. *Id.* at 220, *translated in* Kommers, *supra* note 1, at 415.

147. Freedom of reporting is expressly guaranteed in article 5(1), which provides, "Freedom of the press and freedom of reporting by means of broadcasts and films shall be guaranteed. There shall be no censorship."

148. 35 BVerfGE at 220–21, 223–31, 233–34.

149. *Medical Confidentiality*, 32 BVerfGE 373, 380 (1972).

150. 35 BVerfGE at 233–34. "Once [a] criminal is convicted . . . [the] public ordinarily has no interest in repeated invasion of a criminal's [private] sphere." *Id.*

151. *Id.* at 232, *translated in* Kommers, *supra* note 1, at 416.

152. *Id.*

153. *Id.* at 235–36, *translated in* Kommers, *supra* note 1, at 417 ("The criminal's vital interest in being integrated into society and the interest of the community in restoring him to his social position must generally have precedence over the public's interest in a further discussion of the crime"). This concern follows from the Social State Principle. 35 BVerfGE at 236.

154. A notable exception under American law is trial publicity, a protected free speech activity, which may nevertheless impugn due process. *See, e.g.*, Sheppard v. Maxwell, 384 U.S. 333 (1966).

155. 35 BVerfGE at 235–36 ("Not only must the reformed felon be prepared to return to free, human society, but also society must be ready to accept him. Constitutionally this follows, self-evidently, from a society in which human dignity stands in the center of its value order and is obligated by the principles of the Social State. As a rights bearer of human dignity, the felon too must have a chance to reintegrate into society").

156. *See, e.g.*, DeShaney v. Winnebago County Dept. Social Services, 489 U.S. 189 (state not required to protect life, liberty, or property against invasion by private citizens); *but see* Goldberg v. Kelly, 397 U.S. 254, 261 (1970) ("Suffice it to say that to cut off a welfare recipient in the face of . . . brutal need without a prior hearing of some sort is unconscionable, unless overwhelming considerations justify it").

157. Judge Posner captures the sense of American law well: "We have no right, by controlling the information that is known to us, to manipulate the opinions that other people hold of us." Posner, *supra* note 82, at 408.

158. Florida Star v. B.J.F., 491 U.S. 524, 527 (1989) (refusing to enjoin disclosure of rape victim's name available in sheriff department's pressroom report); Cox Broadcasting Corp. v. Cohn, 420 U.S. 469, 472–73 (1975) (may publish rape victim's name taken from open criminal records).

159. Perhaps American law never developed as German law due to conceptual confusion as to what privacy is. As Professor Keeton observes, "To date the law of privacy comprises four distinct kinds of invasion of four

different interests of the plaintiff [appropriation of, for example, one's name or likeness, unreasonable intrusion, public disclosure of private facts, and false light in the public eye], which are tied together by the common name, but otherwise have almost nothing in common except that each represents an interference with the right of the plaintiff 'to be left alone.'" PROSSER AND KEETON ON TORTS 851 (W. Page Keeton, Dan B. Dobbs, Robert E. Keeton, & David G. Owen, eds., 5th ed. 1984) [hereinafter PROSSER AND KEETON ON TORTS). Conceptuality, such privacy is grounded in a mix of concepts: property (appropriation), confidentiality (unreasonable intrusion and public disclosure of private facts), and harm to feelings (false light). In comparison to German law, American privacy lacks an architectonic concept, such as human dignity or personality, which may have facilitated its natural growth. Today, moreover, First Amendment considerations have eclipsed the tort rights of public disclosure and false light. The tort of appropriation is grounded in the market economy, protecting against unauthorized use for money or profit. Thus, it exists as property, not a personality emanation. That leaves only unreasonable intrusion as a sound protection of the person. Today, little remains of Warren and Brandeis's original aim. Harry Kalven, *Privacy in Tort Law—Were Warren and Brandeis Wrong?* 31 LAW & CONTEMP. PROBS. 326 (1966); MINTZ, *supra* note 82, at 425; Diane L. Zimmerman, *Requiem for a Heavyweight: A Farewell to Warren and Brandeis' Privacy Tort*, 68 CORNELL L. REV. 291 (1983).

160. 54 BVerfGE at 208.

161. The commentator stated, "Heinrich Böll characterized the liberal state [*Rechtsstaat*]—against which the [terrorists'] violence was directed—as a 'pile of dung,' and said that he saw only 'the remnants of decaying power, which are defended with ratlike rage.' He accused the state of pursuing the terrorists 'in a pitiless hunt.'" *Id.* at 209, *translated in* Quint, *supra* note 102, at 332 n. 265. Since the turbulent decades of the 1960s and 1970s, there have been several notable terrorist attacks as well, such as the assassination of Alfred Herrhausen, head of Germany's largest bank, Deutsche Bank, in 1989, and of Detlev Rohwedder, leader of the Treuhandanstalt, the agency set up to privatize assets of former East Germany, following reunification in 1990. Timothy Aeppel, *Murder Heightens Eastern German Crisis*, WALL ST. J. (April 3, 1991 at A17).

162. 54 BVerfGE at 211–13.

163. *Id.* at 217, *translated in* Kommers, *supra* note 1, at 419.

164. 54 BVerfGE at 217, 421.

165. *Id.* at 218.

166. *Id.* at 216.

167. Masson v. New Yorker, 501 U.S. 496 (1991).

168. 376 U.S. at 270.

169. Edward J. Eberle, *Public Discourse in Contemporary Germany*, 47 CASE W. RES. L. REV. 797, 807, 841–43 (1997).

170. 54 BVerfGE at 217–218; Quint, *supra* note 102, at 333–34. On remand, the BGH upheld the decision in Böll's favor. NJW 635 (1982). The case of *Eppler*, 54 BVerfGE at 148, an important case for the theory and reach of the personal sphere, provides an interesting contrast with *Böll*.

Decided on the same day, Eppler, a well-known politician, "sought an injunction prohibiting opponents from repeating their charge that Eppler . . . desire[d] to 'test the endurance of the economy'" through his social policies. Quint, *supra* note 102, at 334 n. 273. The statement implied that Eppler was willing to take undue risks with the economy. Accordingly, Eppler viewed the statements as an attack on his constitutional right of personality. As in *Böll*, a lower court dismissed the suit. Unlike *Böll*, however, the Constitutional Court found that the remarks did not violate his "private, secret or intimate sphere," 54 BVerfGE at 154, and, therefore, were not an infringement of Eppler's constitutional right of personality. *Id.*

5

Identity, Self-Determination, and Autonomy

A final strand of personality law relates to attributes of identity and personal self-definition. By this idea of identity I mean who one is and how one defines oneself in the world through exercise of personal choice over issues material to human existence, as reflected within a constitutional context. This strand too is grounded in the innermost reach of personhood, where it takes conception, as with those other strands emanating from the personal sphere discussed in Chapter 4. For example, decisions over procreation, contraception, or abortion are existential matters, speaking centrally to how one conceives oneself as a person and reflecting inner convictions, feelings, and emotions. Yet decisions like these also help define who one is in relationship to the world, both for oneself—as a matter of self-determination—and as one is perceived by others—as a matter of how one forms personal identity. These decisions thus entail elements of self-realization and autonomy.

The idea of autonomy is particularly pronounced in American law, as personal choice over issues like abortion or contraception forms a central exercise of personal freedom. This notion of autonomy is also highly stressed in German law for reasons that overlap, in part, with American law. In German law the range of autonomy has been concretized over matters that resonate in American law as well, such as abortion, sexual choice, and sexuality, and also over matters that do not strike as common a chord, such as the right to discover one's biological heritage or live by one's chosen name. In fact, this strand of German law has the greatest commonality with American law of all the strands discussed in this book. It is thus a particularly good subject to study for comparative purposes. Both laws will be discussed in tandem, illuminating points of convergence and divergence, as we search for deeper insight into the nature of personality as conceived in modern constitutional law.

The search for meaning in human existence has been a central quest of the twentieth century. In the twentieth century, more than others, man and woman have confronted themselves starkly, on their own terms, without edifice or pretence, shorn of a religious, moral, or social ideal that might offer some support or comfort, as was more prevalent in earlier ages. The effect of two decisive world wars shattered illusions about the rationality, goodness, and progress of humankind, legacies more of the nineteenth century—ideas that people, left to their own devices, would realize a higher, ever better, quality of human existence. It also shattered, for a time, faith in government, especially for Germans, as the world observed how the German nation, and the Russian nation, could be put in service of a government's ideology with disastrous consequences. The first half of the twentieth century harkened back to old themes of human nature, of good and evil, pleasure and terror, themes particularly resonant in earlier times, like perhaps the Middle Ages or, as we might imagine, the Stone Age. With the wars in Yugoslavia, these themes arose again, uneasily, at the close of the twentieth century.

In the face of the despair and disillusionment present so often in the first part of the twentieth century, we as people have sought to rebuild a stable society and culture so that people could better recognize and contain the demons in man's soul and found a culture where humanity might be preserved and, hopefully, where human potential and capacity might again thrive and blossom. These aims of the nineteenth century, sounded by von Humboldt, Warren, and Brandeis, among others, have not been easy to achieve. With the upheaval of two world wars, only the time after World War II presented sufficient social stability to pursue this vision.

Our time is one of significant change as well, making it more difficult to realize this vision. Economically, our world has changed from one of mass industrialization to a consumer society and service economy and now to an information world situated in an interdependent, global economy. Socially, we have experienced the decline of rural and agrarian society through mass migration to the cities, transforming society into a great metropolis. Today less than 25 percent of Americans live in rural areas, compared with over 50 percent in 1910.[1] Increasingly, America is becoming a suburban society as people seek sanctuary from urban ills. Contemporary Germany is 87 percent urban. Urbanization presents its allures, but also its blights, including aloneness and, sometimes, alienation of the human soul. Interestingly, despite the heavy urbanization of German society, Germans still try to hold on to the nature that yearns in their soul, ringing their cities with parks and greens, wandering paths, and bike lanes. Our world is one of unprecedented mobility as well, especially in the United States, where people move their residences and change jobs with frequency.

The constitutional laws of both the United States and Germany reflect man's search for meaning, identity, and autonomy amidst the bustle of the modern world. The period from the end of World War II to our time has witnessed an unprecedented development in constitutional jurisprudence of protection of the human person, and his or her personality and privacy, as both cultures have seen fit to vest man and, with the search for equality, woman with significant autonomy over life-affecting decisions that help define a person's existence. These decisions entail a search for meaning in life. Decisions over matters like procreation, preventing conception of life, aborting developing life, or ending life itself are ones fraught with consequences, for the decision maker, those affected thereby, and society as a whole. This chapter examines a person's search for meaning in life, his or her existentialism, as the person defines his or her existence through exercise of choice. We trace the pattern of those choices, and the process by which a person decides, over such life-affecting decisions, as evidenced in the two constitutional laws.

THE THEORY OF GERMAN AND AMERICAN AUTONOMY LAW

German and American law proceed from different root assumptions. Examining the essence or core of law can sometimes yield a direct path to understanding and uncovering its motivations or animating force. That is the intention here. Understanding the philosophy of law helps explain how the two countries, in some notable cases, reach different conclusions on similar topics.

Germany

German autonomy law, like the other strands of personality law we have examined, is animated by dignity, the core principle of the German legal order, not privacy. Following the horrors of World

War II, rooting the social order in human dignity seemed the best course to secure human freedom and human capacity, as we have seen. Dignity, in conjunction with its cognate of the article 2 free unfolding of personality, contains an idea of autonomy too. As the Constitutional Court has stated, "The right to free development of personality and human dignity guarantees every individual an autonomous area of private life formation in which one can develop and protect one's individuality."[2] German autonomy law is concerned with an individual's development and formation of identity. As the Court elaborated, "Article 1 of the Basic Law protects the dignity of a person, as a person understands himself in his individuality, and becomes aware of himself. Included here is that a person can himself decide his affairs, on his own, and mold his own fate self-responsibly."[3] The German notion of autonomy bestows, self-evidently, a fair measure of freedom, as a person is to take care of himself or herself and assume responsibility for his or her own fate. Yet this idea of autonomy is not so much a freedom from something—as American law shields people from government and majoritarian forces—as a freedom for—here, freedom for empowerment of human capacity in all its richness. Personal claims of liberty are thus to be exercised within the context of a holistic conception of personhood that includes attributes of self-determination, equal worth, and respect, but also bounds and responsibility.

In this way, autonomy rights, like the other emanations of German personality law, reflect the same driving force of human dignity. "Their function is, in the sense of the ultimate constitutional value, human dignity, to preserve the narrow personal life sphere and to maintain its conditions, that are not encompassed by traditional concrete guarantees."[4] German personality law is remarkably consistent. Human dignity and its realization are the common denominators of personality law, animating freedom of action, inner freedom, and autonomy rights. With such a clear and common construct, German law can unfold in a seamless, integrated way, like a tapestry.

America

The same cannot be said for American autonomy law, which proceeds from different root assumptions than German law. American law exists on multiple justifications, including twin main assumptions of privacy, as developed originally in *Griswold v. Connecticut,*[5] and liberty, as privacy became redefined in *Planned Parenthood of Southeastern Pennsylvania v. Casey.*[6] There is also a third justification, history and tradition, which can yield, ironically, both autonomy-enhancing and constricting outcomes.

Privacy means, specifically, freedom from government, an idea with particular resonance in America with its commitment to limited government. Free from government, a person can pursue his or her vision of who he or she is, secure, with the establishment of a "right," that government will not interfere. This is the empowering notion of personal autonomy at the root of American law. This idea took root especially in the twentieth century, as a search for meaning following the horrors of World War II. With the securing of freedom in Europe, a new search for freedom at home seemed warranted. The transformation of American government from limited scope to the New Deal and then the Great Society was a motivation too. As the reach of government extended, creation of more private space seemed more urgent, a new form of check to counter the growth of new power.

American autonomy law represents one of the radical transformations of twentieth-century law, along with other transformations, such as the growth of the administrative state and the rise of the modern presidency. It marks a coming of age of American constitutional existentialism, of control over one's fate. The story begins with *Skinner v. Oklahoma*, where the Supreme Court, in an opinion by Justice Douglas, protected a person's right to procreate as "one of the basic civil rights of man" against a state law requiring sterilization of "habitual criminals."[7] Procreation, like marriage, is "fundamental to the very existence and survival of the race."[8] So defined, it is hard to imagine a more "natural" right than procreation. Natural law in the twentieth century might reasonably be viewed as that which is intrinsic to human existence. Being so grounded in attributes of fundamental human existence, *Skinner* might plausibly serve as a doctrinal base for similar such existential questions central to life, like decisions over contraception, abortion, marriage, or the ending of life itself through suicide.[9] Viewed in this light, *Skinner,* decided in 1942 amidst knowledge of the Holocaust, addresses acutely a central dilemma of humanity in the twentieth century: defining the terms of human existence. Yet bereft of strong textual support, and lacking clear analytical justification, *Skinner's* assertion of "basic civil rights," without more, was not altogether convincing, ringing hollow to many. Lacking strong doctrinal support, why should the Court declare "basic civil rights," many asked, instead of society, acting through the democratic process?

These were the difficult questions taken up by the Warren Court, in *Griswold v. Connecticut*, one of the landmark decisions of the twentieth century, where the Court worked out the theory of American autonomy law, referred to, doctrinally, as substantive due process law.[10] There were two main theories to choose from.[11] Justice Douglas wrote the opinion for the Court, as he elaborated the sketch he set out in *Skinner*. There was still natural law, as Douglas concluded by stating, "We deal with a right of privacy older than the Bill of Rights."[12] But he buttressed his conclusion with a textual defense, "by the letter or penumbra of the Bill of Rights," of a "zone of privacy created by several fundamental constitutional guarantees" that created a private sphere—"rights of privacy and repose"—beyond government control.[13] Through such reasoning, *Griswold* became the heir to Warren and Brandeis's right of privacy, transforming their thought into constitutional doctrine. Grounded in the Constitution as a right, a person now had constitutional protection over life-affecting decisions, such as those over procreation, contraception, marriage, or raising children. In this way, Warren and Brandeis's focus on thoughts, emotions, and feelings was transformed into decisional authority over everyday issues.

Justice Harlan, in a concurring opinion, offered an alternative doctrinal justification for this private, personal freedom. According to Harlan, this freedom is rooted in "basic values 'implicit in the concept of ordered liberty'" contained within the due process clause, which "stands . . . on its own bottom."[14] Due process liberty is not easy to define or cabin because it speaks to the innately human cry for freedom.[15] As such, there can be no end point to human freedom, as there can be no limit to the human spirit.

So, with the opinions of Douglas and Harlan, we have two paths to American autonomy law. For Douglas, a person may define attributes of personality found by the Supreme Court to be "fundamental," as part of one's privacy. Privacy here means freedom from government, a private sphere of freedom empowering one to choose. For Harlan, such personal choice is not privacy but liberty: "Respect for the liberty of the individual."[16] As part of one's personal liberty, a person can define fundamental life-affecting decisions.

So things stood, doctrinally, until the Supreme Court protected a woman's right to have an abortion in *Roe v. Wade,* which triggered the cultural war over who, the Court or the people acting through the community, should define basic values for the society.[17] Fought mainly over abortion, school prayer, and bussing, issues that originated in the 1960s and 1970s and yet perculate today, the cultural wars forced the Supreme Court to reconsider the whole enterprise in *Planned Parenthood of Southeastern Pennsylvania v. Casey,* where the Court rethought abortion law.[18] In *Casey,* the Supreme Court ruled for Harlan, finding "a promise of the Constitution that there is a realm of personal liberty which the government may not enter."[19] Defined as personal liberty free from governmental interference, a person can make his or her "most basic decisions about family and parenthood" and other existential matters.[20] Following

Harlan's lead, the Supreme Court reconceived the idea of freedom. Instead of freedom from government—the idea of a right of privacy—freedom was transformed into a positive right, a right to choose, constitutionally, over "personal decisions relating to marriage, procreation, contraception, family relationships, child rearing and education" and the like.[21] As such, this right became one

> to be free from unwarranted governmental intrusion into matters . . . fundamentally affecting a person. . . . These matters, involving the most intimate and personal choices a person may make in a lifetime, choices central to personal dignity and autonomy, are central to the liberty protected by the Fourteenth Amendment [due process]. At the heart of liberty is the right to define one's own concept of existence, of meaning, of the universe, and of the mystery of human life. Beliefs about these matters could not define the attributes of personhood were they formed under compulsion of the State.[22]

We can now see clearly that American autonomy law rests on twin foundations of a negative liberty, a right to privacy from unwarranted government interference, and, so shielded, a positive personal liberty to choose affirmatively one's vision over intimate life decisions. The tenor of an individual and the tone of society turns, in part, on emphasis of such a choice as one of privacy or of liberty. There is no code or predetermined formula guiding choice over such matters. It is a personal decision. For the Supreme Court too, the boundaries of choice are unclear. It is, in fact, the reasoned judgment of the Court, illuminated again by Justice Harlan, that directs the way:

> Due process has not been reduced to any formula; its content cannot be determined by reference to any code. The best that can be said is that through the course of this Court's decisions it has represented the balance which our Nation, built upon postulates of respect for the liberty of the individual, has struck between that liberty and the demands of organized society. If the supplying of content to this Constitutional concept has of necessity been a rational process, it certainly has not been one where judges have felt free to roam where unguided speculation might take them. The balance of which I speak is the balance struck by this country, having regard to what history teaches are the traditions from which it broke. That tradition is a living thing. A decision of this Court which radically departs from it could not long survive, while a decision which builds on what has survived is likely to be sound. No formula could serve as a substitute, in this area, for judgment and restraint.[23]

There is also a third dimension to American autonomy law, that of history and tradition. History and tradition are part of the calculus of factors to be consulted by the Supreme Court in reaching these fundamental decisions, as noted by Justice Harlan in his description of the Supreme Court's process of judgment. Resort to history and tradition thus can buttress the legitimacy of the Supreme Court's pronouncements on substantive due process. For example, in *Moore v. City of East Cleveland,* the Supreme Court looked to history to found support for the family in choosing who, among family members, to live with in a dwelling, finding "the institution of the family is deeply rooted in this Nation's history and tradition."[24]

More often, however, use of history and tradition is the weapon of choice for those fighting the counterattack on the Supreme Court's substantive due process enterprise. In *Bowers v. Hardwick*, history and tradition was used to supplant "judge-made constitutional law having little or no cognizable roots in the language or design of the Constitution."[25] In the recent *Washington v. Glucksberg* case, the Supreme Court "examin[ed] our Nation's history, legal traditions and practices" to find no constitutional justification for a person's right to choose to end life through suicide.[26] For proponents of this idea of judicial restraint, the goal is to prevent "the Judiciary [from] necessarily tak[ing] to itself further authority to govern the country without express constitutional authority."[27] Thus, to the extent the debate is over history or tradition, much will depend on how a judge views these sources—as living or dead, fluid or fixed.

We can now see that American law is, in a sense, at war with itself. Advocates of self-sovereignty, proponents of *Griswold* or *Roe,* are opposed by those rooted to history and tradition, proponents of *Bowers* or *Glucksberg.* In the United States, constitutional politics is high theory and high theater. The debate over *Roe*—over substantive due process—is the second in the United States questioning the role of the Supreme Court, after *Lochner v. New York.*[28] The debate is over whether the Court, as interpreter of the Constitution, is empowered even to declare society's fundamental values insofar as its decision can plausibly be tied to the Constitution or, alternatively, whether such constitutes the Court acting as "superlegislature," supplanting the decisions of the democratic process.[29] This debate is most likely one never to be resolved. Instead, each generation picks up the cause, trying to make sense of its time.

Let us now turn from theory to practice, as we trace the practical results reached by the two Courts' search for dignity and personal freedom in the last half of the twentieth century. There are many themes to autonomy law in the two countries. In German law these themes include the right to know one's parenthood and heritage;[30] the right to determine one's sexual identity, including having official records changed to reflect one's chosen gender;[31] and certain rights to choose one's name.[32] Some of these themes have resonance in American law. For example, rights to know one's heritage and sexual autonomy have been major themes of American law.[33] However, as we have examined, the American cases proceed from an assumption of privacy, not dignity or personality, and reach conclusions different than the German. Abortion has been a prominent issue in the laws of both countries over the past thirty years. On account of its significance, we will examine abortion separately in Chapter 6. Other American themes do not echo as clearly in German law. For example, decisions relating to procreation and contraception resonate prominently in American law, but less markedly in German law. From the German standpoint, however, this may reflect the Constitutional Court's lack of opportunity to enumerate these rights. The Basic Law and case law seem to offer sufficient textual and precedential authority to support this endeavor. These points are best brought out through a comparative look at the two laws.

SEX, SEXUALITY, AND SEXUAL INTIMACY

Sexuality is "a sensitive, key relationship of human existence, central to family life, community welfare, and the development of human personality," and is, appropriately, a major topic in German and American law.[34] German law views sexuality as integral to personal self-definition and identity, like other highly valued personality rights. "The Basic Law has placed the intimate and sexual domain of human activity under the constitutional protection of article 2(1) in conjunction with article 1(1). These provisions of the Basic Law guarantee to an individual the right to determine oneself one's view of sexuality."[35] In America, sexuality is conceived primarily as part of privacy, not personality.[36] Privacy, in this sense, is a freedom from unwarranted governmental interference. "If the right of privacy means anything, it is the right of the *individual*, married or single, to be free from unwarranted governmental intrusion into matters so fundamentally affecting a person as the decision whether to bear or beget a child."[37] Thus, acts like procreation, contraception, and abortion are conceptualized as part of privacy rights over which one can exercise autonomy. As reconceived in *Planned Parenthood of Southeastern Pennsylvania v. Casey*, such autonomy becomes the "liberty relating to intimate relationships."[38]

In a sense, German and American law are of the same chord in defining sexuality as private. In both laws, private means beyond governmental interference. Yet there is also a difference between the two laws. In American law, privacy is all there is. Privacy is linked to the liberty of freedom from government. So conceived, liberty is a matter of personal choice, empowering individuality. We can thus see how liberty might become sexual freedom. By contrast, German law connects privacy to personality. Rooted to personality, sexuality forms another path to explore the mystery and wonder of human existence. This path leads more to self-discovery than freedom. I mean freedom, in this sense, as freedom for freedom's sake. As we can see, different consequences might flow from the different conceptions animating the two laws. Let us now explore this more carefully.

America

Sexuality is a major topic in the United States. It is also an especially appropriate topic to begin discussion of autonomy law, since American cases on this topic—*Skinner* on procreation, *Griswold* on contraception, *Roe v. Wade* on abortion—initiated, in significant part, the search for personal identity marked by this branch of law. Two opinions by Justice Douglas on behalf of the Court, *Skinner* in 1942 and *Griswold* in 1965, formed the origins of this aspect of American personality law. These cases and their progeny also traced, in law, the sexual revolution occurring in society in the 1960s and beyond, worldwide, but with special fervor in the United States. Sexual politics tracked the upheaval of domestic politics, especially concerning the Vietnam War then raging. The 1960s also formed the fulcrum by which women would emerge as equal citizens in society. Decisions over procreation, contraception, and abortion came to be seen, for the gender revolution, as significant as those establishing the right to vote, enter a profession, or live where one chose, matters crucial to the civil rights revolution. Autonomy law thus reconceived gender relationships in society. Women came to be seen as equal to men in their right to decide vital matters of their destiny.

Skinner: *Procreation*

Skinner, Justice Douglas observed, "touches a sensitive and important area of human rights. Oklahoma deprives certain individuals of a right which is basic to the perpetuation of a race—the right to have offspring."[39] It is hard to imagine a matter more crucial to human existence. In 1942, the time of the decision, this was no exercise in idle speculation. *Skinner*, addressing statutory legacies of the eugenics movement, was decided at the time that Nazi Germany was implementing its Final Solution, the Holocaust, which also became a holocaust of the German soul. Starkly phrased, the choice was over who should control the decision concerning reproduction, an individual or the state. Could the state mold citizenry along desired genetic patterns, or was this a matter of free will to be exercised according to individual choice? The Supreme Court seemed well aware of what was at stake.[40]

The Supreme Court ruled for the individual, finding this decision to "involve one of the basic civil rights of man."[41] As Justice Jackson observed, "There are limits to the extent to which a legislatively represented majority may conduct biological experiments at the expense of the dignity and personality and natural powers of a minority—even those who have been guilty of what the majority define as crimes."[42] The Supreme Court's announcement that "marriage and procreation are fundamental to the very existence and survival of the race," and therefore protected as rights under the Constitution constitutes a dramatic and prescient affirmation of human liberty and human dignity.[43] The true significance of *Skinner* can be seen when contrasted with decisions then being made in Germany, during the Nazi time. In fact, Germany was not alone among European countries in pursuing racial policies. Sweden conducted a campaign of forced sterilization, targeting people, mostly women, considered to be racially or socially inferior for forty years, from 1936 to 1976.[44] A total of 63,000 people were sterilized, many against their will.

In this context, *Skinner* sets a base line for human liberty, transcending national borders. Choice over procreation is a life-affecting decision entailing part of one's existence, one's basic dignity. This is the choice of a person to be recognized as a human being in the eyes of the law, on one's own terms, over matters central to life's meaning and mystery, free from state coercion. This is also the choice of a person to be recognized for equal worth. This is especially the case with *Skinner*, as the case involved a differentiation in the law of similar crimes for members of different economic classes. The law targeted petty criminals, not all criminals.[45] Part of dignity is recognizing that even the lowly in status have equal claims to self-worth and choice. As a reflection of American law, *Skinner* further illustrates the natural skepticism Americans have about government and its power to coerce human personality. In this way, we can see why Americans cherish the negative liberty marked out by a zone of privacy shielding one from state interference.

Griswold: *Contraceptive Choice*

The idea of privacy as a human right, initiated constitutionally in *Skinner,* percolated in the American mind and reached fruition in the early 1960s, foreshadowing the sexual revolution that would later follow under its banner. Searching itself for its proper role within the constitutional scheme, especially as reconceived in the post–New Deal era, the Supreme Court decided, on substantive terms, that the basis of a "right of privacy which presses for recognition" is legitimate, having previously dismissed the issue several times on jurisdictional grounds.[46]

Griswold presented the Supreme Court with one of those momentous occasions in constitutional law. To decide for the right of married persons to choose over their use of contraceptives was to risk the Court's prestige and legitimacy, as it was not self-evident that such a right was manifest in the text of the Constitution. To some, this was the Court acting "as a super-legislature to determine the wisdom, need, and propriety of laws that touch . . . social conditions."[47] According to Justice Black, for example, *Griswold* involved "the same natural law due process philosophy found in *Lochner v. New York*" and later repudiated.[48] For Justice Black, it is preferable to be ruled by the people, as compared to the Court acting as "Platonic Guardians."[49]

However, to decide against the right would seem to denigrate the integrity of human personhood, disrespecting individual choice over "an intimate relation of husband and. wife," and placing it in the hands of legislatures, then comprised almost entirely of white males.[50] Why should the state, authorized by the legislature, decide how a person should conduct his or her sex life? The Supreme Court choose for people. "Would we allow the police to search the sacred precincts of marital bedrooms for telltale signs of the use of contraceptives? The very idea is repulsive to the notions of privacy surrounding the marriage relationship."[51]

In so doing, the Supreme Court empowered people with choice—with the means, in a constitutional structure, of deciding basic terms of existence—of life (procreation) or its prevention (contraception). In this way, *Skinner* and *Griswold,* mirror opposites in result of choice, form complimentary emanations of the self-sovereignty at the root of American law. Later cases liberated the right of privacy from the marriage relationship, transforming it into an inalienable aspect of individual liberty.[52] The range of this personal liberty has, over time, become quite extensive, mapping out the perimeters of individual freedom. As the Supreme Court commented,

This right of personal privacy includes "the interest in independence in making certain kinds of important decisions." While the outer limits of this aspect of privacy have not been marked by the Court, it is clear that among the decisions that an individual may make without unjustified government interference are personal decisions "relating to marriage; procreation; contraception; family relationships; and child rearing and education." The decision whether or not to beget or bear a child is at the heart of this cluster of constitutionally protected choices.[53]

Personal choice over matters intimate to human existence is a prominent feature of American law. These choices mark out personality attributes, central to individuality. The full reach of this individual liberty remains undefined, awaiting enumeration in both American and German law.[54] Interestingly, both laws have not capped human freedom, choosing, instead, to let the human spirit find its own measure.

Germany

German law seems in accord with American law on matters relating to sexual intimacy, at least as a matter of theory. Forced sterilization violates the article 2(2) guarantee of bodily integrity, the core of the *Skinner* holding.[55] In the *Homosexuality* case, the Constitutional Court flatly stated, "This right [of personality] comprises also the free sexual activity of persons," including consensual homosexual conduct.[56] In 1957, however, the Constitutional Court was willing to read morality as a constraint on such free sexual activity.[57] Later cases removed the constraint. In the *Sex Education Case*, which as its name implies dealt with sex education in the schools, not sex among adults, the Constitutional Court observed, "The Basic Law has placed the intimate and sexual domain of human activity under the constitutional protection of article 2(1) in conjunction with article 1(1). These provisions of the Basic Law guarantee to an individual the right to determine oneself one's view of sexuality."[58] In a still later case, the Constitutional Court confirmed this valuation of the sexual domain as intrinsic to privacy. "The Basic Law has placed the sexual domain, as part of a person's private sphere, under the protection of article 2, in conjunction with article 1. Restrictions in this area are, without more, incompatible with the Basic Law."[59]

The tenor of these cases seems broad enough to encompass concrete sexual activities, including those of procreation and contraceptive choice. *Homosexuality* provides the theory; later cases bring the theory to fruition. Certainly the text of the Basic Law, with its emphasis on human dignity and the free unfolding of personality, seems sufficient to support the concept of sexual autonomy. Interestingly, the German cases focus on personality, whereas the American ones highlight specific acts. Despite this difference in emphasis, German and American law seem in general accord on protecting sexual intimacy as a matter of individuality, although the precise enumeration of sexual freedoms differs in the two laws. The next topic brings this point out in bolder relief.

SEXUAL SELF-DETERMINATION AND SELF-IDENTITY

The themes of sexuality are broad in German and American law. Control of one's own sexuality—of sexual acts and self-identified gender—is another measure of human personality captured in the two laws. German law has taken a proactive stance, empowering human capacity. American law, apart from procreation and contraception, has been more tentative, uncertain over whether to extend the promise of liberty at the root of *Griswold*. American constitutional law seems unwilling to view sexuality as integral to human personality.

Germany

Transsexual Case

Perhaps no German case voices the theme of sexual autonomy better than the *Transsexual Case*, which, living up to its name, concerned a born male who desired to live as a female.[60] The plaintiff acted on his urge and underwent a sex-change operation, which transformed him to a her as far as biologically possible. However, German records still listed her as him. The listing became the question of the case: The woman sought official recognition of her acquired sex.

The question of sexual identity "belongs to the most intimate areas of personality, where all official power is removed," the Constitutional Court observed, consistent with its view of sex as a matter of privacy.[61] Only the most compelling public interest would justify intrusion therein. "Human dignity . . . and free development of personality require . . . that one be allowed to determine what sex one belongs to, according to one's psychological and physical constitution."[62] Physical traits, legal regulation of gender, or sexuality itself are not decisive.[63] Rather, decisive is "the striving toward unity of psyche and body."[64] These concerns for human welfare outweigh any moral or legal limitation of such self-realization.[65] So the Constitutional Court reconceived sex, liberating it from its earlier, more restrained view in *Homosexuality*. For these reasons, a person is entitled to have his or her chosen sex registered in official records. A person has a right to live according to the sex he or she chooses. Sexual identity thus becomes a matter of personal choice, radiating another aspect of inherent human dignity.

Transsexual Equal Protection

Based on the *Transsexual Case*, the Constitutional Court later invalidated, in *Transsexual Equal Protection*, an age requirement of twenty-five years before sex changes could officially be registered.[66] This violated equal protection, since adults under twenty-five were treated differently without justification as compared to older adults. The decisive event was the operation, according to the Constitutional Court, not the age.[67]

These two decisions thus highlight the inclusion of sexuality, including sexual choice and preference, as an important part of human personality. Choosing one's sex, one's gender, or one's sexual activity seems, in the German view, an important part of individual existence. This has involved an evolution in thought. Modern cases prefer personal choice over these matters as part of human dignity, in comparison to the constraints of conventional mores predominating in earlier cases. German cases thus capture the coming of age, in matters of sexual self-determination, of modern times, beginning with the sexual revolution of the 1960s.

America

These cases on transsexuality contrast dramatically with American law. No idea of transsexuality appears in American law. The closest American case at the constitutional level to the German cases is *Bowers v. Hardwick*, which, of course, dealt with consensual homosexual activity in the privacy of the home.[68] When Michael Hardwick looked up from the privacy of his bedroom, he was shocked to find a policeman at the door. "What are you doing in my bedroom?" he asked.[69] The policeman answered by arresting Hardwick based on a law against sodomy. The law was over 170 years old, modeled on old English law, and influenced by religious beliefs.[70] It had not been applied consistently in the last 100 years. It was not even applied consistently in *Bowers*, selectively targeting homosexual but not heterosexual acts of sodomy, as Justice Stevens observed.[71] The authorities were not even interested in pressing the case. But Michael Hardwick was, as a test case for gay rights. And an ambitious Georgia State attorney general, Michael Bowers, was, hoping to further his name among proponents of family values.

The Supreme Court's decision was, therefore, going to be significant in the ongoing culture wars. The Court did not disappoint. Relying on tradition, the Supreme Court upheld the sodomy law, asserting that "proscriptions against . . . [sodomy] have ancient roots";[72] therefore, homosexual acts could receive no constitutional protection as privacy rights. Chief Justice Burger put the moral point starkly: "Condemnation of . . . [homosexual conduct] is firmly rooted in Judeo–Christian moral and ethical standards."[73] Attorney General Bowers could not have made the point better. So the Supreme Court eliminated any claim to privacy or protection from governmental intrusion in a person's bedroom.[74] Otherwise, Chief Justice Burger claimed, it would "cast aside millennia of moral teaching."[75]

Yet the Supreme Court appeared to miss the critical constitutional question. This "was not what Michael Hardwick was doing in his bedroom, but rather what the state of Georgia was doing there," wrote Mr. Hardwick's attorney.[76] In fact, *Bowers* stands uneasily at odds with the protection of a person's bedroom that lies at the core of *Griswold*. The difference might only be explained as one between heterosexual and homosexual activity. Upon reflection, so also thought Justice Lewis Powell, who changed his mind after having cast the decisive vote for the state in *Bowers*: "I think I probably made a mistake" commented Powell. "I thought the dissent had the better of the arguments."[77] Justice Powell's odyssey illustrates the startling, and sobering, "human dimension at the heart of the judicial enterprise."[78] Judges are, after all, human too, wrestling uneasily with difficult decisions. Unfortunately for Hardwick and proponents of privacy, *Bowers* seemed to signal the death knell of personal privacy rights. In fact, *Bowers* became notable, in the time before *Planned Parenthood of Southeastern Pennsylvania v. Casey*, as the second death of substantive due process following the demise of *Lochner v. New York*.[79] For gay rights activists, *Bowers* was the *Plessy v. Ferguson* (which had established the doctrine of "separate but equal" in matters of race) of sexual equality.[80]

Comparing the two laws, it would seem, at first glance, that the 1986 case of *Bowers* is in accord with the 1957 *Homosexuality* case, where the Constitutonal Court similarly read morality as convention, rooted in traditional religious beliefs, to constrain homosexual activity. However, in comparison to *Bowers, Homosexuality* has been held in disrepute for some time, whereas *Bowers* has only recently been questioned.[81] This would seem to underscore a difference in culture.

The difference seems attributable, in part, to the role played by morality and tradition in the two laws, which now reveals itself to be a defining trait in the two legal orders. American morality seems to be grounded more in convention and mores of the past and their perceived wisdom for guiding the present. As we see in *Bowers*, such tying to the past constrains personality. The dead hand of history can operate to stultify the living. German morality, by contrast, reflects deep roots in Kantian idealism: dignity, self-determination, equal worth, and respect, the standard root force we have been examining. This operates to emancipate human capacity and self-determination. One might say America is backward looking in its tethering of liberty to tradition and convention, whereas Germany seems forward looking, embracing modern social attitudes insofar as they fit concepts of moral autonomy. For American law, the past rules; for German law, the idea—moral autonomy—rules. In this way, American law is cautious and, at times, constraining. German law, by contrast, is dynamic, equipping modern man and woman to meet the needs of their time. Human nature, in German law, is timeless. Only the issues that people require to satisfy their quality of life change. American law, by contrast, is more concerned about trying to measure human nature by an ideal of the past.

A further difference is over sexual activity generally. In *Bowers*, the Supreme Court went out of its way to reject any basis, in American privacy law, for protection of consensual sexual activity.[82] German cases, by contrast, stand for this very proposition as a consequence of commitment to human autonomy. Thus, whereas American law protects only specific points of privacy as enumerated quite carefully according to common law methodology, German law empowers human capacity. Sexual autonomy thus reveals itself to take on different meanings in the two laws. Summarily stated, American law is rooted in privacy; German law in dignity.

RIGHT TO KNOW ONE'S HERITAGE

The right of a person to know his or her heritage, including biological parents, has been a major theme of personality law, especially German law. Two major cases of the German Constitutional Court have addressed this topic: the *Right to Heritage II Case*, which built on the earlier *Right to Heritage I Case*.[83] The idea animating these cases is that knowledge of one's heritage is integral to healthy personality development and self-identity. Knowledge of one's origins facilitates a harmonious unfolding of personality. In the United States, the Supreme Court, in *Michael H. v. Gerald D.*, has reached conclusions contrary to the German Constitutional Court, rejecting a personal search for biological origin.[84] Let us examine the differing approaches of the Courts on this important topic.

Germany

At issue in both German cases were provisions of the family law, book four of the German Civil Code.[85] The concern in *Right to Heritage I* was that these provisions did not allow a child who had newly acquired majority status to pursue judicially a declaration of his or her legitimacy or illegitimacy so that he or she could determine his or her heritage except when parents were divorced or separated for three years.[86] Because these circumstances might not be present, young people's ability to ascertain their identity might be foreclosed; this constricted their personality rights too severely.

The problem in *Right to Heritage II* involved a two-year statute of limitation period in which a young adult could seek a judicial declaration of (il)legitimacy.[87] If judicial process was not sought within this period—because the young person was not aware of his or her background or because his or her legal guardian pursued no process—then the young person might lose any opportunity to learn of his or her origin. This would seem to curtail his or her freedom over this important matter of human identity.

Right to Heritage I

In this context, the Court announced a substantive right to learn one's heritage, viewing the right as indispensable to healthy personality development. "It is a violation of general personality rights . . . to limit a majority age child's ability to determine her heritage to the statutorily enumerated circumstance."[88] Relying on the sphere of interiority established as part of inner freedom in *Microcensus*, the Court observed, "The right to free development of personality and human dignity guarantees every individual an autonomous area of private life formation in which one can develop and protect one's individuality. Knowledge and development of individuality are closely bound with certain constitutive facts. Among these is included one's heritage."[89] Knowledge of heritage is decisive because it reveals genetic origin and is central to individual identity. It is a "key factor for individual self-discovery and self-understanding. . . . As an individual character trait, ethnicity and knowledge of heritage offer individuals . . . important connections to understanding and development of one's own individuality. Therefore, personality rights include knowledge of one's heritage."[90] Yet because there still might be cases where it would be impossible to determine biological origin, "article 2 in conjunction with article one, confers no [absolute] right to obtain knowledge of one's heritage, rather they protect against the withholding of attainable information."[91] The substantive right thereby becomes an informational right; a right to obtain all relevant accessible information.

Measured against these requirements, the family law provisions were untenable. The law had been constructed to facilitate family peace, a concern grounded in the article 6 guarantee of marriage and family, which claims the state's "special protection."[92] A harmonious family is important, and in cases in which a marriage would be destroyed or seriously harmed, children's process rights might justifiably be limited.[93] However, the Bundesrat had drawn the measure too centered on the concerns for family peace, so that these interests overshadowed those of the children.[94] It is easy to envision cases where determination of paternity would not disrupt family peace, particularly when the child has reached majority status. For example, the child, together with his or her mother or stepfather, might want to find out. Or the child may already have established relations with his or her biological father, and now wants to have this legally determined. For these reasons, it was up to the legislature to craft a solution that would have a less restrictive (*durch mildere, aber gleich wirksame Mittel*) impact on young adults' personality rights.[95]

Right to Heritage II

In the second case, the Constitutional Court invalidated the two-year statute of limitation period in which newly aged adults could seek judicial declaration of their biological origin, because the law might operate to foreclose any possibility of young people discovering their heritage. Discovery of one's heritage could only occur, in most cases, if a child's legal guardian (usually the mother), or the child, pursued legal process within the relevant time frame. However, legal guardians might not act or might not inform their children that they are illegitimate out of concern for family tranquility. There was a clear conflict of interest between the child's best interests and the family's.[96] If children did not know of their status, they would not know to pursue legal process. In this way, all opportunity to learn of one's heritage could be extinguished.[97] "The impossibility of clarifying one's own heritage can be a considerable burden and can undercut one's [inner] security."[98] In view of this, the law must be changed, consistent with personality rights, so that a child might learn his or her identity. These conclusions are important, reflecting the concern in German law for the nurturing of young adult life. German law extends special solicitude to its young members.

A further significance of *Right to Heritage II* lies in the methodology the Constitutional Court used to reach it conclusions. The case evidences a noticeable tightening of the scrutiny employed by the Constitutional Court to test incursion of personality rights. A law curtailing personality rights is "permissible only when it serves to protect a weighty end, is necessary, and when the end is so significant that it justifies intrusion on personality rights."[99] Such heightened scrutiny represents a distinct tightening of the relationship between means and ends, and strikes general resonance with American heightened scrutiny regimes. In German law, this tightened methodology is traceable to developments in rights analysis generally, particularly free expression rights. It represents a more rights-protective approach as compared to earlier more deferential methodologies such as that employed in *Elfes,* or the *Deutschland–Magazin* variable standard of review of the 1970s, employed in cases like *Lebach* or *Böll.*[100]

Applying the methodology demonstrates the bite of tightened proportionality. The statute of limitations provisions "serve legal security . . . [which] is an important goal. . . . Certainly it is a considerable burden when those interested must consider who legally is the father of a child. . . . It also serves the public interest" to clarify this.[101] However, "it seems questionable whether it is necessary to tie a young adult's possibility of clarifying his origin to this concern for legal security."[102] Less restrictive alternatives could be employed. For example, the Bundestag could arrange for a young adult "to clarify his heritage . . . without effect on his relatives."[103] Perhaps the young person could find this out in secret or in camera, thereby saving his or her relatives from disruption. Or a child's knowledge of his or her status could become the tolling event for the statute.[104] A closer fit between means and the end must be structured.

As presently structured, however, the law "considerably limits the right to know one's own heritage."[105] Consistent with the Proportionality Principle, therefore, "the interest in legal security does not weigh so hard so that it can justify this severe incursion of personality rights."[106] Thus, at bottom, there is no justification for so curtailing personality interests.

It is interesting to observe that announcement of this heightened methodology parallels the development of American law. Whereas in American law we can trace heightened scrutiny in rights analysis to the early free speech cases and, formally, to the 1942 *Skinner* case, if not the famous *Carolene Products* footnote of 1938, strict scrutiny has, since the 1950s, become a standard part of the American legal landscape.[107] In Germany, the path has been more circuitous. As in the United States, the origins of heightened scrutiny lie in free expression law. The seminal 1958 *Lüth* case, for example, evidences the Constitutional Court's independent analysis.[108] However, after *Lüth*, expression cases went through several metamorphoses—from a low-level deferential approach of the 1970s, to a variable standard of review in *Deutschland–Magazin* in the 1980s, to, finally, the intensive approach of today.[109]

Tracing this development in personality, the Constitutional Court has preferred it as a seminal value of the legal order since *Microcensus* in 1969, and especially in the 1970s, starting with *Mephisto* and then *Soraya*, where the Constitutional Court preferenced personality rights even over expression. Still more intensive scrutiny of personality rights is evident in the 1983 *Census Act Case* and the 1988 *Right to Heritage I* case.[110] Yet with *Right to Heritage II* we have a formal statement of "strict" scrutiny, as we did in the United States in the 1942 *Skinner* case.[111] Thus, both Courts have devised similar rationales and methodologies for rights analysis.

These concerns led the Constitutional Court, in *Right to Heritage II*, to confront more generally its role with respect to the legislature. The Constitutional Court must strive to respect the law maker. Where possible, laws should be interpreted in a "constitutionally conforming" manner.[112] But there are limits to such deference; for example, when "the text and intent of the legislature are in contradiction."[113] "Respect for the democratically legitimate legislature forbids," in such circumstances, the Constitutional Court from rewriting the statute.[114] However, "norms inconsistent with the Basic Law are invalid."[115] The Constitutional Court thus has no choice: The law must be invalidated, and the Bundestag must remedy the defect; in this case, "by the next legislative session."[116]

The posture of the Constitutional Court mirrors the role of the Supreme Court in the American constitutional scheme. *Skinner, Griswold*, and *Roe v. Wade* attest to the battle over the proper role of the Court in a constitutional democracy. Both Courts, it is apparent, have staked out positions as last preserves of individual liberties, even when the decisions of the majoritarian process must be supplanted. However, it also seems clear that the Constitutional Court has assumed this role with more confidence than the Supreme Court. Unlike the Supreme Court, the Constitutional Court seems less constrained by concerns over "caution and restraint."[117] Perhaps this is because of its liberation from the past, empowering it proactively to realize a new constitutional order. Perhaps it is because of the texture of German law and its greater textual authorization.

America

The closest American Supreme Court case to the two *Right to Heritage* cases is *Michael H. v. Gerald D.*, which also dealt with the right to determine legitimacy.[118] The focus of the American case was the biological father's rights, Michael H., who initiated the lawsuit, and not the child, Victoria D., who sought to maintain a relationship with her biological father. Victoria D. was the child of an affair between an international model and her neighbor, Michael H. Michael H. was one of several men that the mother cohabited with, including her husband. Thus, to observers it was never quite clear who Victoria D.'s father was, although Michael H. often represented that he was.[119] For Justice Scalia, these facts "are, we must hope, extraordinary."[120]

Putting aside these questions of propriety and turning to the child, Victoria D. did not fare too well. In comparison to the solicitude given children by the German Court, Victoria D. got short shrift: The law gave her no chance to establish her origin, and the Supreme Court was wholly unconcerned with this state of affairs.[121] Rather than establishing children or natural parental rights, the Supreme Court valued more highly "the integrity of the marriage union," protecting it against claims that children or biological fathers might assert as to origin. Otherwise, the state might have to "recognize multiple fatherhood [which] has no support in the history or traditions of this country."[122] Viewed from the perspective of the Germans, *Michael H.*, in reaching an opposite outcome, seems to have sacrificed children's welfare for the sake of judicial restraint.[123] In this way, we observe again how history and tradition can operate to straitjacket personality, whereas the German personality is free to develop in view of modern conditions, seeking its own measure.

Youth, as conceptualized in *Michael H.*, is viewed as dependent on family. This contrasts with German law, where youth is treated as a personality in its own right, capable of making vital decisions. In this limited view, German law places more trust in the promise of youth than American. We will need to keep an eye on this issue as we continue our exploration of the dimensions of the two laws in the next several chapters.

IDENTITY: RIGHT TO ONE'S OWN NAME

Germany

In a fashion similar to the *Transsexual Cases*, the Constitutional Court has also determined that a person has a right to choose one's name as a reflection of personality. This conclusion arose in the *Name Change Case,* where a German national wished to keep his birth name rather than be registered under his Austrian wife's maiden name.[124] "A name protects against anonymity and dissolution of personality in mass, modern industrial society."[125] It is thus part of one's personality rights. However, while personality rights must be respected, such rights are not unlimited, but must be measured within community constraints. Thus, strangely, the Constitutional Court upheld the German customary requirement, reflected in the then relevant provision of the Civil Code, that married couples must maintain a common family name, which usually was the husband's.[126] Yet while that family name must be used for "official" purposes, a person was free to use the name of his or her choice in personal settings.[127] One could thus have two names, one for official and one for personal use, certainly an uneasy compromise between freedom and social order. Since the *Name Change Case,* the Civil Code has been changed.

America

No American case exists at the constitutional level over the right to use one's chosen name. Given the Supreme Court's reservation of use of substantive due process for important life-affecting decisions like procreation or contraception, it seems unlikely that the Court would risk its capital on the relatively less-significant matter of a personal name. This may explain why the Supreme Court has not pursued this avenue of personality rights. As a matter of ordinary law and ordinary useage, Americans freely choose the name they desire. Thus, both legal systems reach similar results, though only German law addresses this as a matter of constitutional law.

RIGHT TO DIE

A final issue of identity, self-determination, and autonomy relates to a person's choice to end life by euthanasia or suicide. From the standpoint of life's cycle, the decision to end life, round life's midnight, is the ultimate issue of autonomy, the final decision to make about life, bringing to a close the range of matters initiated at life's dawn relating to procreation and contraceptive choice. Interestingly, treatment of these matters in constitutional law parallels, chronologically, their unfolding in life's cycle. In American autonomy law, for example, *Skinner,* dealing with procreation, begins the jurisprudence; acting to end life has just recently turned up in the jurisprudence of the Supreme Court, in *Washington v. Glucksberg*, where the Court openly debated the proper course on suicide.[128] So law mirrors life's course.

America

In *Washington v. Glucksberg*, the Supreme Court, acting cautiously, declined the invitation to recognize any general right to assistance in committing suicide. This issue presented the Court once again with an opportunity to determine the direction of American autonomy law. The argument for a right to end life as another point on the continuum of personal liberty has a certain appeal.[129] Suicide, like other matters central to identity, such as procreation or abortion, is a "basic and intimate exercise of personal autonomy."[130] It is of vital significance to a person that he or she be able to control his or her last days. The character of personality is revealed in this final episode too. A person might choose to fight for each last breath or, instead, opt for a pain-free and humane end.

But the Supreme Court rejected these autonomy arguments and their premise of "broad, individualistic principles."[131] A person's decision to end life can be viewed, alternatively, in communitarian and not simply individual terms. That ultimate decision affects others, especially close friends and family members, as, indeed, it may affect the community as a whole. Suicide rights, as other autonomy rights, are as much a reflection of community and the values there cherished as of individual personality. As Justice Stevens observed, "The value to others of a person's life is far too precious to allow the individual to claim a constitutional entitlement to complete autonomy in making a decision to end that life."[132] Who calls the shots on determination of these values—an individual or a community—largely determines the complexion of constitutional law.

In deciding the point, the Supreme Court turned to history and tradition, where it "confronted . . . a consistent and almost universal tradition that has long rejected the asserted right . . . even for terminally ill, mentally competent adults."[133] This history, essentially, is present "in almost every State—indeed, in almost every western democracy."[134] "Our Nation's history, legal traditions, and practices thus provide the crucial 'guideposts for responsible decisionmaking.'"[135] *Glucksberg* thus evidences the Supreme Court's present desire to approach issues of substantive due process with caution and restraint, in a manner more like *Bowers* and less like *Casey*. "We 'have always been reluctant to expand the concept of substantive due process because guideposts for responsible decision making in this uncharted area are scarce and open-ended.' . . .

We must therefore 'exercise the utmost care whenever we are asked to break new ground in this field.'"[136] The Supreme Court is of split minds, again, as to this judicial enterprise.

As we enter the new millennium, it seems clear that the Supreme Court does not want to get too far in front of the democratic process over controversial issues that stir up society, even if they relate to intimate matters of personal autonomy. Rather, it prefers to await resolution of such issues pursuant to normal politics, reserving constitutional determination for other matters. "Americans [should] . . . engage in an earnest and profound debate about the morality, legality, and practicality of physician-assisted suicide."[137] And so, on issues of personal autonomy, at least in an "uncharted area," the Supreme Court prefers to follow the lead of society, allowing issues to gestate, as compared to showing the way.[138] On this issue, at least, democratic control seems preferable to Platonic guardianship. There are, as we have seen, merits and demerits to each position.

The process of the common law reinforces the caution of the Supreme Court. Unlike civilian legal systems, including techniques employed by the Constitutional Court, the Supreme Court is uncomfortable deducing conclusions from abstract concepts like personal autonomy.[139] The Supreme Court, at least at present, prefers to follow the more cautious, step-by-step working out of details, typical of the common law, "seeking to understand old principles afresh by new examples and new counterexamples."[140] Grounded in the ways of the common law, the Court is leery about abstraction, a tool more compatible with the civilian tradition. By contrast, for Germany, in particular, abstraction provides the added benefit of freeing the legal order from the past, empowering the Constitutional Court to set up a new legal order free from the ideological baggage of history. Thus, legal methodology makes a difference.

While the Supreme Court rejected any general right to committ suicide in *Glucksberg*, five members of the Court seem prepared to recognize, in the right circumstance, the ability of a dying person to die with dignity when faced with unnecessary and unavoidable pain or physical suffering.[141] In such a case, this majority appears to favor personal control over the time and manner of death so long as a person acts rationally and voluntarily. Put in this light, *Glucksberg* can be read to reject any general right to commit suicide, but not to foreclose the possibility of dying with dignity when faced unavoidably with pain and imminent death. Thus, there is dissention on the Supreme Court on this issue, as in society.

Interestingly, *Glucksberg* evidences a growing desire to enrich the dialog of the Court by looking across borders for treatment of similar issues. In its opinion, the Supreme Court explored the Dutch experience with euthanasia, which ultimately reinforced the Court's preference for judicial restraint.[142] Comparative law has not been a common pursuit of the Supreme Court, unlike other national courts, such as the Canadian or German Courts. Thus, the Supreme Court's peek outside its own legal system is a notable development, evident also in other recent cases.[143] Chief Justice Rehnquist and Justices Breyer, Ginsberg, Kennedy, and O'Connor, in particular, are wise to the benefits of comparative insight. Perhaps American participation in cross-fertilization across national boundaries, long a European custom, is a closer reality than had been assumed.

Germany

There are no German cases by the Constitutional Court on issues relating to a right to end life. As compared to the American Constitution, the German Basic Law contains more direct textual reference for this issue, including article 1 human dignity and article 2 personality and right to life provisions. How exactly these are to be harmonized is a matter of some speculation, which is heavily debated in the scholarly literature.[144]

There appears to be some support for a person's right to end life, and that this right is grounded, as a matter of free will, in human dignity.[145] Nevertheless, as with *Glucksberg*, difficult questions remain, not all of which have been worked out. For example, active euthanasia is viewed as an incursion on the right to life, especially on account of the Nazi experience.[146] However, assisted suicide (*Sterbehilfe*), sometimes considered as passive euthanasia, is to be distinguished from euthanasia. As a general matter, a person facing imminent death can, of their own volition, make the decision to end life, enlisting even active help from doctors and medical personnel.[147] Thus, medical treatment, or the foregoing of such, that would hasten death is possible if performed voluntarily, with patient consent. Also, assisted suicide in cases where the person is suffering greatly from a fatal illness may be possible under appropriate constitutional safeguards.[148] While we can observe some similarity between German and American law over a right to die, both laws are in the process of evolving. Thus, any comparisons are premature at this stage.

SUMMARY

The direction of American law over identity, self-determination, and autonomy has been different, in some notable ways, from German law. In American law the root construct for these rights has been privacy, not dignity or personality, as in German law. From the privacy construct, the Supreme Court has afforded constitutional protection to a range of personal decisions relating to marriage, procreation, contraception, abortion, and family relationships, among others. Yet these decisions, being grounded in privacy, facilitate individual freedom from undue state interference. Thus, their concern is freedom as an individual right, not the particular quality of the choice resulting from that freedom nor the well-being of the right holder. Unlike German law, there is no real focus on the quality of human life and personality. Instead, the American focus is, preeminently, on "the right to be let alone."[149] These privacy rights thus map out how we can be free to be alone from official interference. As alone individuals, Americans are then free to choose the values with which to constitute themselves and govern. And these "values [become] central to personal dignity and autonomy."[150]

However, the two legal orders differ fundamentally on the conception of dignity in this regard. For Americans dignity means the right to choose. Worth and stature follow from respect for choices. Germans certainly share this aspect of self-determination. Yet the difference lies in how self-determination unfolds. In America, personal autonomy is simply the right to choose. Personal autonomy is thus the value itself, an integral part of one's rights. In this way, American law is grounded in dignity.

In Germany, by contrast, personal autonomy is an aspect of human dignity. Dignity imposes obligations as well as endows freedom. Thus, personal autonomy is relevant to shaping one's character and personality, but that shaping is to occur not in isolation but within a social and moral community. True autonomy, in the German view, is to unfold in a manner consistent with moral obligations, which themselves are reflected in the Basic Law as individual and social duties. The state, official actors like the Constitutional Court, and society are all responsible partners working cooperatively with individuals to achieve this moral vision.

One might say the difference between the two cultures is between American "rights talk" and German Kantian philosopher-kings.[151] German law is, indeed, ruled by the Platonic guardians feared by Justice Black.[152] Put another way, the difference is over the conception of autonomy with (German) and without (American) the limiting construct of a workable definition of morality.

The sharpness of this distinction has been smoothed somewhat by a trend evident in certain recent cases to appreciate the communitarian dimension to personal choices.[153] Thus, there is some discernible movement in American law away from the view of rights holders as mere lone rangers and toward a conception of persons who may exercise rights in ways that connect to community. In this way, American law is moving in the direction of German law.

Deciphering the pattern of choices and personality attributes reflected in autonomy law, we achieve a better sense of how the two countries conceive modern personhood. In the United States it is noteworthy that the main theme of autonomy law is sexuality: procreation, contraceptive choice, abortion, and free sexual activity. There are other attributes of human personality reflected in American law as well, including issues relating to marriage, family, and bodily control, matters not covered extensively in this book.[154] But matters relating to sexuality—*Skinner, Griswold, Roe*, and *Bowers*—constitute the focal point of American law.

Choice over these matters, as we have seen, is mainly an aspect of individuality as a privacy right. As such, the emphasis is on self-sovereignty, with little attention to the quality of choices that might result and their effect on others or the rights holder himself or herself. In this sense, American law is somewhat one-dimensional; man as actor, not as molder of community.

By contrast, German law represents a more complete conception of human personhood. Deciphering the messages of German law, we observe that sexuality is also a frequent topic. Yet German cases on sexuality do not focus on the acts of sex, but instead on the impact of sexuality on formation of human personality. Thus, the emphasis is more on the quality of human life and its well-being. For example, the driving force in the *Transsexual Case* was not so much any right of privacy to engage in particular sex acts, as human welfare in "striving toward unity of psyche and body."[155] Sexuality is one of many parts of the human experience, not a discrete exercise of privacy, as in America. Kantian sovereignty reigns in Germany; self-sovereignty in America.

The other topics of German law also unfold within this fuller concept of human personhood, where man and woman are conceived as rational actors, but also as beings with obligations to others and society. Comparing treatment over a right to discover a person's biological heritage illustrates this. In the German cases, the central concern is discovery of origin for the value it will yield for self-discovery and psychological health.[156] Yet that desire must be mediated against competing claims to family peace and marriage union, as many have a stake in the outcome. The value of human discovery of place, as a matter of personal meaning and human dignity, receives priority.

By contrast, in *Michael H.* the inquiring child and biological father are viewed as lone right holders, posing threats to family tranquility and society.[157] Tradition is more important than the personal seach for well-being. We can now see how German personality is multidimensional; American is more one-dimensional. German law focuses on well-being; American on liberty.

The contrast between the two countries' treatment of a person's right to live by his or her chosen name also underscores some differences in culture. In Germany, the Constitutional Court's willingness to recognize such a right bespeaks its concern for the centrality of the human person, which influences the unfolding of the law. Choosing one's name is a matter of personal welfare; therefore, it is appropriately recognized in the law. By contrast, American substantive due process reserves its prestige for relatively weighty issues, usually of some existential dimension, like procreation, abortion, or suicide. We thus see how German law strives for completeness; American law is episodic, a response to a specific incursion of personal autonomy. This is a final difference between conceiving law as personality or privacy.

Emphasis of these differences should not obscure the clear convergence in attributes of personality covered in the two laws. Sexuality, heritage, and suicide are pronounced characteristics of human personhood that resonate prominently in both laws. The common occurrence of such similar traits suggests something transcendent about modern human personality, as situated in constitutionalism. We will be in a position to explore these points more carefully upon examination of the next set of traits explicated in the two laws.

NOTES

1. Lamar Graham, *Where Have All the Small Towns Gone?* PROVIDENCE SUNDAY JOURNAL (December 13, 1998), PARADE at 6.

2. *Right to Heritage I*, 79 BVerfGE 256, 268 (1988).

3. *Transexual Case*, 49 BVerfGE 286, 298 (1978).

4. *Eppler*, 54 BVerfGE 148, 153 (1980).

5. 381 U.S. 479 (1965).

6. 505 U.S. 833 (1992).

7. 316 U.S. 535, 536, 541 (1942).

8. *Id.* at 541.

9. *Griswold*, 381 U.S. at 479; Roe v. Wade, 410 U.S. 113 (1973); Zablocki v. Redhail, 434 U.S. 374 (1978); Washington v. Glucksberg, 521 U.S. 702 (1997).

10. 381 U.S. at 479.

11. Justice Goldberg, in his concurrence, also proferred a theory of unenumerated rights based on "the concept of liberty . . . supported by numerous decisions of this Court, . . . and by the language and history of the Ninth Amendment." *Griswold*, 381 U.S. at 486–87 (Goldberg, J., concurring). Such rights are to be found, in Goldberg's view, through looking to "'traditions and [collective] conscience of our people' to determine whether a principle is 'so rooted [there] . . . as to be ranked as fundamental.'" *Id.* at 493, *citing* Snyder v. Massachusetts, 291 U.S. 97, 105 (1934).

12. 381 U.S. at 486.

13. *Id.* at 499 (Harlan, J., concurring), 485 (Douglas, J., concurring).

14. *Id.* at 500.

15. The full scope of the liberty guaranteed by the Due Process Clause cannot be found in or limited by the precise terms of the specific guarantees elsewhere provided in the Constitution. This "liberty" is not a series of isolated points pricked out in terms of the taking of property; the freedom of speech, press, and religion; the right to keep and bear arms; the freedom from unreasonable searches and seizures; and so on. It is a rational continuum which, broadly speaking, includes a freedom from all substantial arbitrary impositions and purposeless restraints, . . . and which also recognizes, what a reasonable and sensitive judgment must, that certain interests require particularly careful scrutiny of the state needs asserted to justify their abridgment. Poe v . Ullman, 367 U.S. 497, 543 (1961) (Harlan, J., dissenting from dismissal on jurisdictional grounds).

16. Poe v. Ullman, 367 U.S. at 542 (Harlan, J., dissenting).

17. 410 U.S. 113 (1973).

18. 505 U.S. 833 (1992).

19. *Id.* at 847.

20. *Id.* at 849 (citations omitted).

21. *Id.* at 851 (citations omitted).

22. *Id.*

23. Poe v. Ullman, 367 U.S. at 542 (Harlan, J., dissenting.).

24. 431 U.S. 494, 503 (1977) (plurality).

25. 478 U.S. 186, 194 (1986).

26. 521 U.S. 702, 710 (1997).

27. *Bowers*, 478 U.S. at 195.

28. 198 U.S. 45 (1905) (invalidating state statute limiting work week of bakers to sixty hours on ground this limited parties ability to engage in freedom of contract).

29. *Griswold*, 381 U.S. at 482.

30. *Right to Heritage II*, 90 BVerfGE 263 (1994); *Right to Heritage I*, 79 BVerfGE 256 (1988).

31. *Transsexual Case*, 49 BVerfGE 286 (1978).

32. *Name Change Case*, 78 BVerfGE 38 (1988).

33. Michael M. v. Gerald D., 491 U.S. 505 (1989); *compare* Bowers v. Hardwick, 478 U.S. 186 (1986) *with* Eisenstadt v. Baird, 405 U.S. 438 (1972).

34. Paris Adult Theatre I v. Slaton, 413 U. S. 49, 63 (1973).

35. *Sex Education*, 47 BVerfGE 46, 73 (1977); *Homosexuality*, 6 BVerfGE 389, 432 (1957) ("This right [of personality] comprises also the free sexual activity of persons").

36. Carey v. Population Services, 431 U.S. 678, 685, 688–89 (1977) (describing reach of protection of sexuality under right of privacy). *But see* Bowers v. Hardwick, 478 U.S. at 191 (no right to engage in homosexual conduct).

37. Eisenstadt v. Baird, 405 U.S. at 453 (emphasis in original).

38. 505 U.S. 833, 857 (1992).

39. 316 U.S. 535, 536 (1942).

40. "The power to sterilize, if exercised, may have subtle, farreaching and devastating effects. In evil or reckless hands it can cause races or

types which are inimical to the dominant group to wither and disappear." *Id.* at 541.

41. *Id.*

42. *Id.* at 546 (Jackson, J., concurring).

43. *Id.*

44. *Sweden Plans to Pay Sterilization Victims*, N.Y. TIMES, Jan. 27, 1999, at A6.

45. As the Court observed, "Sterilization of those who have thrice committed grand larceny [blue collar criminals], with immunity for those who are embezzlers [white collar criminals], is a clear, pointed, unmistakeable discrimination." 316 U.S. at 541. In the face of such inequality, the Court decided *Skinner* on equal protection grounds.

46. 381 U.S. at 485; *see, e.g.*, Poe v. Ullman, 367 U.S. 497 (1961); Tileston v. Ullman, 318 U.S. 44 (1943).

47. *Griswold*, 381 U.S. 479, 482 (1965).

48. *Id.* at 515 (Black, J., dissenting).

49. *Id.* at 526.

50. *Id.* at 482.

51. *Id.* at 485–86.

52. It is true that in *Griswold* the right of privacy in question inhered in the marital relationship. Yet the marital couple is not an independent entity with a mind and heart of its own, but an association of two individuals each with a separate intellectual and emotional makeup. If the right of privacy means anything, it is the right of the *individual*, married or single, to be free from unwarranted governmental intrusion into matters so fundamentally affecting a person as the decision whether to bear or beget a child.

Eisenstadt v. Baird, 405 U.S. 438, 453 (1972); Carey v. Population Services, 431 U.S. 678, 687 (1977).

53. Carey v. Population Services, 431 U.S. at 684–85.

54. *Compare id. with Eppler*, 54 BVerfGE 148, 153 (1980).

55. Bodo Pieroth & Bernhard Schlink, GRUNDRECHTE STAATSRECHT II 105 (10th ed. 1994).

56. 6 BVerfGE 389, 432 (1957).

57. *Id.* at 432–33.

58. 47 BVerfGE 46, 73 (1977).

59. *Transsexual Equal Protection*, 60 BVerfGE 123, 134 (1982).

60. 49 BVerfGE 286 (1978). The plaintiff had married, but the marriage ended in divorce after eleven years. A child came from the marriage, although the plaintiff later learned the child was not his. The plaintiff started to feel increasingly like a woman. These feelings were accelerated when one of his testicles was removed due to an accident; later the other testicle was amputated too. *Id.* at 290.

61. *Id.* at 298.

62. *Id.*

63. The Court canvassed the latest scientific research on sex and identity before settling on the human spirit as the decisive factor.

64. 49 BVerfGE at 299. Viewed in this way, the sex-change operation would be the "realization of this goal." *Id.*

65. Even a future marriage to a male would not violate the morality limitation of article 2(1). *Id.* at 300.

66. 60 BVerfGE 122 (1982).

67. *Id.* at 133. Under the article 3 equal protection guarantee, the Constitutional Court has striven to achieve more substantive equality than the Supreme Court under the Fourteenth Amendment. David P. Currie, The Constitution of the Federal Republic of Germany 322–28 (1994).

68. 478 U.S. 186 (1986).

69. *Striking Down the Sodomy Laws*, N.Y. Times, Nov. 25, 1998, at A24.

70. *Id.*

71. 478 U.S. at 218–19 (Stevens, J., dissenting).

72. *Id.* at 192.

73. *Id.* at 196 (Burger, C. J., concurring).

74. *Striking Down the Sodomy Laws, supra* note 69, at A24.

75. 478 U.S. at 197 (Burger, C. J., concurring).

76. *Striking Down the Sodomy Laws, supra* note 69, at A24.

77. Linda Greenhouse, *When Second Thoughts In Case Come Too Late*, N.Y. Times, Nov. 5, 1990.

78. *Id.*

79. *Compare* Planned Parenthood v. Casey, 505 U.S. 848 (1992) ("Neither the Bill of Rights nor the specific practices of States at the time of the adoption of the Fourteenth Amendment marks the outer limits of the substantive sphere of liberty which the Fourteenth Amendment protects") *with* Bowers v. Hardwick, 478 U.S. at 194 ("The Court is most vulnerable and comes nearest to illegitimacy when it deals with judge-made constitutional law having little or no cognizable roots in the language or design of the Constitution"); Lochner v. New York, 198 U.S. 45 (1905).

80. 163 U.S. 537 (1896).

81. Professors Pieroth and Schlink observe that *Homosexuality's* proscription has been invalid since 1969. Pieroth & Schlink, *supra* note 55, at 103. In fact, the criminal law limitation enforced in *Homosexuality* has since been repealed, as noted previously. *Transsexuality's* reconsideration of the morality limitation concerning sexual attitudes is further proof of this. 49 BVerfGE at 299–300 (1978). On *Bowers, see* Romer v. Evans, 517 U.S. 620 (1996). More recently, the Georgia Supreme Court declared the Georgia statute at issue in *Bowers* unconstitutional as a matter of law under the Georgia Constitution. Powell v. Georgia, 510 S.E. 2d 18, 1998 West Law 804568 (November 23, 1998), *discussed in* US L. Wk., Dec. 8, 1998, at 1327. Ironically, the concept of liberty is broader in some states than nationally.

82. *Bowers*, 478 U.S. at 191.

83. 90 BVerfGE 263 (1994); 79 BVerfGE 256 (1988).

84. 491 U.S. 110 (1989) (plurality opinion).

85. BGB §§ 1593–1596, 1598.

86. 79 BVerfGE at 257. Under German law, such (il)legitimacy can only be determined pursuant to judicial proceedings as in American law. *See* BGB § 1593. *Cf.* R.I. Gen. Laws § 33–1–8 (1995).

87. 90 BVerfGE at 265; BGB § 1598.

88. 79 BVerfGE at 268. Note that the question of determining heritage implicates other constitutional guarantees too. Equal protection provides that "No person shall be favored or disfavored because of . . . parentage, race . . . homeland and origin. . . ." GG article 3(3). Article 6 provides for certain marital, family, and parental rights, including parental control of child rearing, GG Article 6(2), and also that "children born outside of marriage shall be provided by legislation with the same opportunities for physical and mental development and for their position in society as are enjoyed by those born within marriage." GG article 6(5). The Basic Law thus provides explicitly what the Supreme Court has implied from the Constitution. *See, e.g.,* Moore v. City of East Cleveland, 431 U.S. 494 (1971) (plurality) (fundamental freedoms inhere in marriage and family relationships); Pierce v. Society of Sisters, 268 U.S. 510 (1925) (liberty of parents to direct upbringing of children).

89. 79 BVerfGE at 268.

90. *Id.* at 269. The Court noted that biological origin is not the only determinant of personality. More "significant are multiple [life] events and experiences." The Court also saw significance in knowledge of heritage for individual self-discovery beyond what is documented empirically, as a matter of science. *Id.*

91. *Id.*

92. *Id.* at 270. Note again how the Basic Law protects specifically marriage and family, GG art. 6, rights that American law has implied from the promise of liberty in the due process clause. *See, e.g., Moore,* 431 U.S. at 494 (family); Loving v. Virginia, 388 U.S. 1 (1967) (marriage).

93. 79 BVerfGE at 270.

94. *Id.*

95. *Id.* at 271–74.

96. 90 BVerfGE 263, 273 (1994).

97. *Id.* at 272–73.

98. *Id.* at 271.

99. *Id.*

100. Under *Deutschland–Magazin,* 42 BVerfGE 143 (1976), the Court applied a variable intermediate standard of review. The degree of protection varied with the severity of the rights incursion. This led to some inconsistency in application. *See* Edward J. Eberle, *Public Discourse in Contemporary Germany,* Case W. Res. L. Rev. 797, 843–52 (1997).

101. 90 BVerfGE at 271.

102. *Id.* at 272.

103. *Id.*

104. *Id.* at 276.

105. *Id.* at 272.

106. *Id.* at 273.

107. *See, e.g.,* Lovell v. Griffin, 303 U.S. 444 (1938) (invalidating ordinance limiting leafletting); Near v. Minnesota, 283 U.S. 697 (1931) (invalidating as prior restraint statute regulating speech as public nuisance). Skinner v. Oklahoma, 316 U.S. 535, 541 (1942) ("We [emphasize] . . . our view that strict scrutiny of the classification in which a State makes in a

sterilization law is essential"). *See also* Korematsu v. United States, 323 U.S. 214 (1944). United States v. Carolene Products Co., 304 U.S. 144, 152 n. 4 (1938). *See, e.g.*, Griswold v. Connecticut, 381 U.S. 479 (1965) (right of privacy); Cohen v. California, 403 U.S. 15 (1971) (free expression); Brown v. Board of Education, 347 U.S. 483 (1954) (equal protection).

108. 7 BVerfGE 198 (1957). *Lüth* is examined comprehensively in Eberle, *supra* note 100, at 808–27.

109. Eberle, *supra* note 100, at 807–08.

110. 65 BVerfGE 1, 44–51, 64–66 (1983); 79 BVerfGE 256, 270–73 (1988).

111. 90 BVerfGE at 271.

112. *Id.* at 275. This is an example of striving to conform legislation to the higher law of the Basic Law. This involves a process of actualization (*aktualisiert*) of the values of the Basic Law. *See* Winfried Brugger, *Legal Interpretation, Schools of Jurisprudence, and Anthropology: Some Remarks from a German Point of View*, 42 Am. J. Comp. L. 395, 398 (1994).

113. 90 BVerfGE at 275. Means–end testing pursuant to the Proportionality Principle will usually uncover this.

114. *Id.*

115. *Id.* at 276.

116. *Id.* at 276–77.

117. Moore v. East Cleveland, 431 U.S. 494, 502 (1977).

118. 491 U.S. 110 (1989) (plurality opinion).

119. *Id.* at 113–14.

120. *Id.* at 113.

121. *Id.* at 130–31. Michael H. was trying to rebut the presumption of legitimacy that attaches to a child of an unmarried couple. Michael H. was the biological father, Victoria D. the product of an adulterous affair. Michael H. wished to establish his paternity of Victoria D. Victoria D. wished to maintain a relationship with her natural father.

122. *Id.* at 131.

123. *Id.* at 121–23 (Court explaining need for judicial restraint in interpreting reach of substantive due process).

124. 78 BVerfGE 38 (1988). Under German customary law, as codified in section 1355 of the BGB, a married couple must maintain a common family name. The name chosen for the family can be either that of the husband's or the wife's. This German customary requirement is not consistent with international practice. *Id.* at 40. In this case, the Austrian wife registered her family name in Austria so that she could preserve it under Austrian law. German authorities interpreted this to mean that the couple had chosen the wife's name as the common family name. The suit was over the couple's right to maintain their own names, at least officially.

125. The right to bear and control one's name has deep roots in German law. BGB §§ 12, 823, 1004.

126. 78 BVerfGE at 38–39, 49 (interpreting BGB § 1355).

127. The Court determined that a common family name was a highly valued legal interest, constituting an important public law relationship, and also guaranteeing the "unity of the family," which has constitutional

dimension under article 6. Families are a unit, and not a collection of individual members, revealing, again, the communitarian bent of German law. *Id.* at 49. Thus, the German customary norm satisfied the Proportionality Principle. *Id.* at 49–50. Still, since use and choice of name lies within the protection of personality rights, one is free to use the name of one's choice in personal or business relations. *Id.* at 50–52.

128. 521 U.S. 702, 117 S. Ct. 2258 (1997).

129. The argument was successful in the U.S. Court of Appeals for the 9th Circuit. Compassion in Dying v. Washington, 79 F.3d 790 (1996).

130. *Glucksberg*, 521 U.S. at 724, *citing Casey*.

131. *Glucksberg*, 521 U.S. at 724.

132. *Id.* at 741 (Stevens, J., concurring).

133. *Id.* at 723.

134. *Id.* at 710.

135. *Id.* at 721 (citations omitted).

136. *Id.* at 720.

137. *Id.* at 735. "The States are currently engaging in serious, thoughtful examinations of physician-assisted suicide and other similar issues." *Id.* at 719.

138. *Id.* at 720.

139. *Id.* at 722.

140. *Id.* at 770 (Souter, J., concurring).

141. Justices Breyer, Ginsburg, O'Connor, Souter, and Stevens, in their concurrences.

142. 521 U.S. at 734. While the evidence from The Netherlands was equivocal, as noted by Justice Souter, *id.* at 787, the Court read the evidence to reveal abuses in the practice of euthanasia, particularly for the vulnerable, like the disabled and elderly. *Id.* at 734.

143. *See, e.g.*, Printz v. United States, 521 U.S. 898, 976–77 (1997) (Breyer, J., dissenting) (analyzing extensive inventory of comparable federal systems, including those of Switzerland, Germany, and the European Union, in seeking illumination of the proper relationship between the American federal and state governments); *Casey*, 505 U.S. 833, 945 n. 1 (1992) (Rehnquist, C. J., dissenting) (evaluating Canadian and German cases on abortion). *But see Printz*, 521 U.S. at 921 n. 11 (opinion by Scalia, J.) ("We think such comparative analysis inappropriate to the task of interpreting a constitution, though it was of course quite relevant to the task of writing one").

144. Horst Dreier, 1 GRUNDGESETZ KOMMENTAR 125 (Horst Dreier, ed. 1996).

145. *Id.*

146. Pieroth & Schlink, *supra* note 55, at 105.

147. Dreier, *supra* note 144, at 125.

148. *Id.*

149. Olmstead v. United States, 277 U.S. 438, 478 (1928) (Brandeis, J., dissenting).

150. *Casey*, 505 U.S. 833, 851 (1992).

151. MARY ANN GLENDON, RIGHTS TALK: THE IMPOVERISHMENT OF POLITICAL DISCOURSE (1991).

152. Griswold v. Connecticut, 381 U.S. 479, 526 (1965) (Black, J., dissenting).

153. Examples of this include *Casey*, 505 U.S. at 852 (observing that the act of abortion is one "fraught with consequences for others"), and *Glucksberg*, 521 U.S. 702, 738, 741 (1997) (Stevens, J. , concurring).

154. Zablocki v. Redhail, 434 U.S. 374 (1978); Moore v. East Cleveland, 431 U.S. 494 (1977) (plurality); Cruzan v. Missouri, 457 U.S. 261 (1990).

155. 49 BVerfGE 286, 299 (1978).

156. *Right to Heritage I*, 79 BVerfGE 256 (1988); *Right to Heritage II*, 90 BVerfGE 263 (1994).

157. 491 U.S. 110 (1989) (plurality).

6

Abortion

No discussion of dignity, privacy, and personality in German and American law would be complete without an evaluation of abortion law. This is particularly the case because abortion has been the subject of heated debate in both countries for over thirty years, starting with the original abortion decisions, issued within two years of each other:[1] The Supreme Court decided *Roe v. Wade* in 1973;[2] the Constitutional Court decided *Abortion I* in 1975.[3] In the 1990s, moreover, both Courts fundamentally rethought both decisions; the Supreme Court in 1992, in *Planned Parenthood of Southeastern Pennsylvania v. Casey*,[4] and the Constitutional Court, in 1993, in *Abortion II*.[5] Thus, abortion is certainly a unique opportunity to compare and contrast the constitutional visions of two leading constitutional courts in two important Western democracies.

The work of the Courts is not easy. Abortion is perhaps the searing issue of our age, stoking fires on both sides of the fight over whose choice should control. For over thirty years in America, abortion has occupied center stage in politics, driving presidential elections, the controversies over nominations to the Supreme Court, and even American foreign policy, including the politics of who assumes ambassadorships. Abortion now transcends mere normal politics, becoming a defining issue of our day, as slavery was in the mid-nineteenth century and civil rights was in the decades of the 1950s and 1960s. "We're in a war," says Don Treshman, national director of Rescue America, an antiabortion group. "The only thing is that until recently the casualties have only been on one side. There are 30 million dead babies and only five people on the other side, so it's really nothing to get all excited about."[6]

And a war it has been. In the past few years, at least seven people have died at the hands of antiabortionists. The dead have included three doctors performing abortions along with one of their bodyguards, and two employees at a Boston abortion clinic. Recently, a Buffalo doctor, marked by antiabortion groups, was shot in the back while relaxing with his family in their kitchen upon returning from their synagogue. For those warring on the pro-life side, these casualties are "justifiable homicide." "God says that 'if man sheds blood, then by man shall his blood be shed,'" wrote Paul Hill, a former minister and convicted killer of an abortion doctor, in jail, responding to questions from schoolchildren.[7] Work at abortion clinics is dangerous; death threats have risen markedly, and clinics have regularly been picketed and bombed.[8]

Abortion racks the nation's psyche as slavery did in the mid-nineteenth century. "I accuse the land of my nativity of insulting the majesty of Heaven with the greatest mockery that was ever exhibited to man" said abolitionist William Lloyd Garrison.[9] In 1857, Frederick Douglass stated, "The struggle may be a moral one; or it may be a physical one; or it may be both moral and physical, but it must be a struggle."[10] As with slavery, abortion is seen in primarily moral terms, as preserving the sanctity of life or the quality of choice, depending on one's view. America's holy war on abortion involves participants on all sides. The high ground of the pro-life movement is asserted most eloquently by Pope John Paul II who, in his 1995 encyclical on the issue, called abortion "crimes that no human law can claim to legitimize."[11] For Catholics and others of faith, abortion is a wrenching conflict of conscience, placing people between the doctrine of their church and the law of their land.[12]

Less eloquently, but more graphically, the *National Pro-Life Newsletter* offered a new year's message of an America of "abortion clinics as a world of death camps, contract killers and mass murder."[13] "Blood will run in the streets like nobody has ever seen," warned Daniel Ware, an antiabortion leader, if Paul Hill, the killer of an abortion doctor quoted earlier, was executed, as sentenced.[14] Operation Rescue, an antiabortion group, posts war criminal posters of abortion doctors.[15] An antiabortion Web site, the Nuremberg Files, maintains files on doctors who perform abortions. "The site includes a color key indicating whether the doctor is 'working' or 'wounded'. A line crossed through the name indicates a 'fatality.'"[16] German feminists capture the emotions on the other side. The decision of the German Constitutional Court invalidating a liberal abortion law was decried as "violence against women."[17] It is hard to find the middle ground in abortion.

In time, the raw emotions of abortion may abate, as happened in past issues in America. It took the Civil War to settle the issue of slavery, but not of equal rights for citizens. Determined Southern resistance to civil rights for all people, including black Americans, continued for over 100 years after the Civil War. Only in the last thirty years has such resistance ceased in any major way. Yet the battle for equal rights still continues. Eventually the law too will accommodate the passions of abortion in America.

Abortion in Germany is also an emotional issue. As pro-choice women decry what they perceive as restrictive abortion laws, those in the pro-life movement display their moments of candor as well. The Catholic archbishop of Cologne held a mass for unborn life in protest of the liberalized abortion law adopted by the Bundestag.[18] Yet Germans do not kill, bomb, or intimidate their countrymen on the other side of the debate.

Bombings and killings do occur in Germany, although rare, but over the place of foreigners in German society, not over abortion. This is the evil work of neo-Nazis and other right extremists, raising anew the ugly spectre of the 1930s. Germany has had difficulty adjusting to a multiracial society and to the reunification of East and West. Over 7 percent of the German population is immigrant.[19] Unfortunately, the problem of right-wing violence, especially in response to the presence of foreigners in the country, has been a Europeanwide problem, in Belgium, Britain, and France, among others.

In Germany, abortion is a divisive issue as a matter of religion, politics, and region, a festering wound of reunification. Abortion has deepened the division between Catholics and Protestants.[20] Catholics, in particular, are torn between church doctrine and German law, which condemns but permits abortion. German Catholics are a main opponent of abortion. Politically, Catholics tend to belong to the conservative Christian Democratic Union (CDU) or its Bavarian sister party, the Christian Social Union (CSU). The "Christian" in the parties' names attests to the continuing religious influence in the formation of policy and morals in Germany and, for that matter, Europe. The United States severed this influence, formally, with the radical experiment in separation of church and state, originated with the country's founding. The recent reunification fortifies this split. Most of Eastern Germany's 17 million residents are Protestant, while the 62 million West Germans are split between Catholics and Protestants.[21]

Nationally, abortion divided East and West Germans, forming another thorn in the difficult transition to forming one nation. East German law allowed abortions on demand in the first trimester and without charge to all women who wanted them.[22] West German law was stricter; abortion was allowed only if physicians certified that continued pregnancy would be detrimental to the mother or child. What to do about abortion became one of the most divisive issues between East and West Germany as the two states moved to reunification.[23] The debate over how to meld the two laws was so sensitive that the 1990 unification treaty allowed each German state to keep its law in place until an all-German parliament could resolve the issue.[24]

The solutions brought no lasting peace. After rancorous debate, the all-German Parliament adopted a liberal abortion law, allowing abortion in the first trimester if the woman declared she was in distress and underwent counseling.[25] This brought German law into step with the views of the population and also the laws of its neighbors.[26] The law was a compromise between the restrictive West German and more permissive East German statutes. Within a year, however, the Constitutional Court, composed entirely of West Germans, struck down the law, in *Abortion II*. The Constitutional Court favored the more restrictive approach to abortion that had been in place in West Germany.

The Constitutional Court's decision incensed feminists in both the East and the West, but particularly exacerbated open wounds in the East. Already anxious over the dismantling of the East German social state, which provided extensive day care, liberal maternity leave, child leave, and one day off a month for "housework," East German women, in particular, felt threatened by the encroaching West German social and legal culture, which washed away the last remnants of East German life and, with it, their sense of security.[27] Abortion in Germany is not only a divisive issue of religion and politics, as in America, but it also cuts to the heart of national identity, dividing the country by region.[28]

In both the United States and Germany, abortion forms one of the central issues over which women have raised their voices, asserting their identities as free and equal citizens. Abortion politics, more than any other issue, has given rise to the women's movement. Abortion, together with other issues of reproductive choice, procreational freedom, and equality in the workplace, have been the fronts in the battle fought over women's equality in society, constituting the anvils on which modern woman's identity has been forged. How to accommodate the proper decisional sovereignty of women with the competing rights of developing life, in particular, is the central matter of the abortion cases. This chapter addresses these questions as we continue to trace the nature of human personality and its assertion in constitutional culture.

Our focus shall be on the conflict between a woman's right of self-determination and a fetus's right to life as specific manifestations of dignity and personality and as specific balances drawn between liberty and community in the two legal orders. The two legal orders evaluate the issue differently. German law condemns abortion; American law legalizes it. Yet despite such different pronouncements, there is some resemblance in practical terms in the outcome that a pregnant woman can achieve. In the most recent major cases on the topic, *Casey* and *Abortion II*, the two Courts allowed a woman's choice to have an abortion, provided that she evaluated the consequences of the act from the perspective of the fetus, others affected (such as the father, family, or attending medical personnel), and the community, interests made manifest in counseling, waiting periods, and related regulations. Thus, both in Germany and America, society is justified in circumscribing abortion to address these concerns, reflecting balance between individual liberty and community. We will examine the nature of the balance struck in each society.

THE DIFFERENT PREMISES OF
GERMAN AND AMERICAN ABORTION LAW

German and American constitutional law proceed from different premises, illuminating two paths to accommodation of self-determination and respect for life. We shall first concentrate on explicating the difference in constitutional vision before moving on to examining the similarities and differences of the two abortion laws.

Germany

In Germany, the explicit textual enumeration of human dignity once again provides the starting point. "Developing life also partakes of the protection of human dignity," the Constitutional Court asserted in *Abortion I,* since "where human life exists, human dignity attaches."[29] Human dignity does not depend "on birth or a developed personality," issues that have been hotly contested in the United States.[30] "Everyone shall have the right to life," echoes the text of article 2(2), and this guarantee extends to "developing life in the mother's womb," according to the Constitutional Court.[31]

"Everyone" thus includes the yet unborn person; a fetus has a right to life. "Life in the sense of individual existence . . . begins according to undisputed biological and physiological knowledge . . . 14 days after conception."[32] Once begun, life is "a continuous event, which knows no sharp phases and does not contain distinct boundaries between the different stages of development."[33] The German approach to life is holistic. By this reasoning, the Constitutional Court established that an unborn person is entitled to human dignity and the article 2 guarantee of a right to life, as an independent legal value.

In the next step of the development, the Constitutional Court transformed these provisions, through objective constitutionalism, into positive commands of the German constitutional order; the state became positively charged with the duty to protect life (*Schutzpflicht*). "This duty of protection has its basis in article 1(1)," which, after all, calls on the state "to respect and protect" human dignity as "the duty of all state authority."[34] "The object and scope of this duty is more specifically determined by article 2(2)," the right to life guarantee.[35] As we have seen previously, articles 1 and 2 function in tandem to protect the centrality of the human experience. Thus, we can now observe that German protection of fetal life derives from the radiation of human dignity, as reflected in the right to life clause, which the Constitutional Court then transformed into a positive command of the state to protect. These developments follow especially from the Nazi experience, particularly the Holocaust and the Federal Republic's reaction against it, in founding the social order on human dignity. Owing to this unique crystallization of values, Germany, as a matter of comparative law, can view with plausible skepticism the experiences of other lands over abortion, including its European neighbors and the United States, countries, for the most part, with more liberal abortion schemes then and now.[36] The German experience with abortion is thus distinctive, as is any matter involving life itself, like capital punishment.

The duty of protection of life is all encompassing. "The duty to protect the unborn is owed each individual, not just to human life in general," pronounced the Constitutional Court, echoing the dignitarian concern of treating each person as a unique and worthy being.[37] This duty is imposed on all levels of state authority, especially the legislature, which makes the laws.[38] Accordingly, "the legal order must guarantee the appropriate legal foundation for the development of the unborn in relation to its own right to life."[39] How to do this is a matter of legislative discretion. However, under German constitutional democracy the legislature operates pursuant to Constitutional Court direction, a more overtly steering function than is common in America. At a minimum, the Constitutional

Court directs, the Bundestag must declare abortion to be illegal and must require that women carry the unborn to term.[40] These pronouncements reveal how German abortion law might be characterized as restrictive. As so conceived, the duty to protect obligates government to act to intervene against forces or people who would terminate life, and to create the proper social and economic conditions for life to thrive. To fortify this mission government must, in addition, raise public consciousness through education, informational campaigns, or other means, such as public broadcasting, that the unborn have a right to life.[41] The German approach is designed to protect the interests of the unborn. The approach certainly constitutes a remarkable assertion of proactive government power.

Yet Germany is also a country committed to protection of privacy and personality rights. Thus, right to life guarantees cannot be applied in isolation, as if there were no other values or concerns that mattered; there can be no absolute right to fetal life.[42] Countering the exercise of fetal right to life guarantees are a pregnant woman's rights of human dignity too, as radiated in her personality rights that protect her decisional autonomy; her right to life, which protects her health and well-being against undue risk in the pregnancy; and her right to physical integrity, guaranteed also in article 2(2), which safeguards her bodily integrity against unconsented touching, violation, or forced bodily service. Thus, under the German Basic Law, abortion triggers an epic conflict among these seminal values, a conflict that certainly is not easy to resolve.

In German law, a conflict among constitutional rights triggers application of the fundamental principle of concordance (*Konkordanz*), a balancing technique that attempts to maximize the realization of all the values at issue through careful interpretation. We have seen application of this principle before, in, for example, the conflict between personality and expression rights, particularly in cases like *Soraya* and *Lebach*. Resolution of the conflict in those cases was difficult, at best. In the *Abortion* cases, the conflict is even more severe. Attempting to achieve balance between fetal rights to life and women's ability to choose seems theoretically impossible. One cannot honor a woman's choice and yet sustain a fetus's life in all cases. Such was the essential conclusion of the Constitutional Court.

The Constitutional Court resolved the dilemma by concluding that while abortion must be treated as wrong, as a violation of the values of the legal order, it might nevertheless be available in limited circumstances.[43] In both *Abortion* cases the Constitutional Court recognized that fetal life must be preferred over women's self-determination as a matter of constitutional priorities.[44] However, in both *Abortion* cases the Constitutional Court recognized that respect for the woman's dignity as radiated in the matrix of article 2 guarantees necessitated that the duty to protect life not be preferred in all circumstances. In certain circumscribed circumstances, such as danger to the mother's life or health, rape, or other concerns appropriate to achieving quality of life, women's dignitarian interests might prevail in the careful balance to be performed.[45] Performance of the balance thus might result in women's access to abortion, upon justification, in Germany, notwithstanding the legal order's commitment to the value of life. The German approach is considerate and nuanced. Quite apart from specific results reached, the Constitutional Court's pronouncements validating human life constitute statements of constitutional priorities, communicating the values of the social order. We shall soon explore the parameters of the balance.

America

Abortion in the United States proceeds from different premises as a matter of constitutional law. A woman's right to choose is grounded in the privacy rights, rooted in Fourteenth Amendment liberty, established by the Supreme Court in *Griswold v. Connecticut*. "This right to privacy, whether it be founded in the Fourteenth Amendment's concept of personal liberty as we feel it is, or . . . [in] the Ninth Amendment's reservation of rights to the people, is broad enough to encompass a woman's decision whether or not to terminate her pregnancy."[46] As a constitutional right, the right to choose is entitled to significant constitutional protection. Under the rights methodology prevailing at the time of *Roe*, measures limiting abortion rights were subject to judicial "strict scrutiny," the standard test applicable to rights.[47] Under this tough standard of review, the Supreme Court invalidated numerous state laws, including ones calling for abortions to be performed in hospitals, written informed consent provisions, twenty-four-hour waiting periods, and regulations calling for physicians to inform women of the risks attendant in the abortion procedure.[48]

Yet abortion is not just a matter of exercise of individual liberty, as with other American fundamental rights. The act of abortion affects others, touching their claims and rights, which may conflict with those of the mother. It also affects the tone of society. For example, it was important for Germany to assert the value of life, notwithstanding the particulars of the balance struck. The *Casey* Court also seemed to recognize the uniqueness of abortion:

It is an act fraught with consequences for others: for the woman who must live with the implications of her decision; for the persons who perform and assist in the procedure; for the spouse, family, and society which must confront the knowledge these procedures exist, procedures some deem nothing short of an act of violence against innocent human life; and, depending on one's beliefs, for the life or potential life that is aborted.[49]

Yet unlike in Germany, there is no American fetal right to life after conception, nor is there any state duty to protect life, although the state may act to protect life after the point of viability.[50] As a matter of constitutional text and interpretation, the American position has merit, as the text makes no mention of the unborn or of any right to life. Moreover, as the Supreme Court concluded based on exhaustive research, the whole concept of person in the American Constitution is a postnatal one.[51] Still, it sounds harsh, as a matter of rhetoric, to treat developing human life as an interest, not a human being. Rather than a state duty to protect life, there is a "potentiality of human life" that the state is justified in protecting.[52] Under *Roe* this "grows in substantiality as the woman approaches term and, at a point during pregnancy . . . becomes compelling."[53] Thus, in *Roe*, the Supreme Court balanced the compelling points of abortion rights against developing fetal rights.

Roe has widely been decried for elevating the ability of women to choose above the competing claims of the fetus or society. Yet even in *Roe* the Supreme Court recognized that "the pregnant woman cannot be isolated in her privacy. She carries an embryo and, later, a fetus."[54] The Supreme Court fixed the balance between autonomy and life pursuant to the trimester scheme: "The abortion decision and its effectuation must be left to the medical judgment of the pregnant woman's attending physician" in the first trimester; in the second trimester "the State [could] . . . regulate the abortion procedure in ways that are reasonably related to maternal health"; and, finally, the state could "regulate, and even proscribe abortion except where it is necessary, in appropriate medical judgment, for the preservation of the life or health of the mother" in the third trimester.[55] The trimester scheme in *Roe* has been perhaps the most derided aspect of the case. Critics viewed it as more the work of the legislature than the court. Proponents of *Roe*, in response, saw it as a tool necessary to protect the right. As with politics, so with law: It seems difficult to find a middle position in abortion.

When the *Casey* Court reconsidered *Roe* thirty years later, it dispensed with the trimester scheme, replacing it with an undue burden standard.[56] The difference in legal standard signals a difference; the Supreme Court in *Casey* is more solicitous of fetal interests than the *Roe* Court.[57] Courts, like legislatures, are prone to place their stamp on the handiwork of their predecessors. Nevertheless, the Supreme Court drew the line circumscribing a woman's autonomy at the same point of fetal viability as the *Roe* Court. Ironically, upon careful consideration, both Courts ended up in essentially the same spot. The difference in time frame reflected medical developments that had, in the ensuing twenty years, pushed fetal viability back four weeks.[58]

As we now take stock of both countries' treatment of abortion, we can observe that in the United States there is only one constitutional right at issue, a woman's autonomy right to choose over this existential issue, as compared to the constellation of rights at stake in Germany, balancing women's autonomy with the fetal right to live. Conceiving the conflict as one between women's rights and fetal interests—as in the United States—pronounces constitutional priorities quite different from that of viewing the conflict as one between women's and fetal rights as in Germany. Balancing interests against rights will generally result in favoring rights. Balancing among rights, by contrast, is likely to yield careful, albeit difficult, accommodations. As a matter of law, therefore, the American position favors abortion rights. By contrast, German law favors fetal rights, although it leaves room for a woman's choice in certain justifiable circumstances. At bottom, the German approach requires a careful, nuanced consideration of the relevant rights and interests at issue.

The difference is also one of rhetoric. Condemning abortion, as in Germany, imparts a message of wrongness. By contrast, legalizing abortion, as in the United States, conveys permissibility. The tenor and tone of language make a difference, especially insofar as language has an educative function.A closer look at the decisions of the two Courts illustrates how they balanced dignity, personality, and privacy in abortion law. The specific portrait of human personhood, both as a rights chooser and in its formative stage, comes into better focus as we look at the tangible results of the two laws.

THE ABORTION DECISIONS

Germany

Abortion I

The 1975 *Abortion I* decision of the Constitutional Court, a long and complicated case filling ninety-five pages of the official reporter, invalidated a federal statute that would have decriminalized abortion in the first trimester, provided the woman received counseling and medical advice and the procedure was performed by a licensed physician.[59] After the first trimester, abortion would have been permitted if the pregnancy threatened the life of the woman or serious damage to her health, and within twenty-two weeks if the child would be born with severe birth defects.[60] In these respects, the German Parliament had intended to bring German law more into step with that of its neighbors in Europe. The federal statute was a product of the center–left coalition between the Social Democrats and Free Democrats.[61] During this period, center–left coalitions were more the rule than the exception in Europe.

Acting pursuant to the procedure for abstract judicial review, the conservative Christian Democrats in the Bundestag, and several Länder, challenged the statute.[62] Deciding the issue anew after the legislative consensus, the Constitutional Court held that decriminalization of abortion during the first trimester violated the state duty to protect the life of the fetus (*Schutzpflicht*), as guaranteed by human dignity and the right to life.[63] These conclusions were controversial because the Constitutional Court had not previously announced such a broad duty to protect life in connection with the right to life clause. Discovering the right now, in this setting, left the Constitutional Court open to a charge of judicial activism. And, in fact, as a matter of legislative politics the abortion issue created what seemed unseemly incentives, illustrating the perils of constitutional democracy. In politics, the Christian Democrats and its sister party in Bavaria had lost the battle on abortion to the Social Democrats and Free Democrats. Now, however, through the second opportunity presented by abstract judicial review, the Christian Democrats were able to accomplish judicially what they were unable to accomplish politically. As in the United States, commitment to independent constitutional review necessitates occasional supplanting of the majoritarian process. In such a system, we can only hope the Court acts wisely, in either America or Germany.

As rethought by the Constitutional Court, the state must apply criminal sanctions to protect fetal life in order to realize the value structure of the Basic Law, at least in the absence of suitable alternative protective measures.[64] Abortion implicates the value of life itself, a premier value of the legal order. Therefore, the state must protect it through criminal measures. Abortion is an "act of killing," which the legal order must condemn in strong terms as a way of educating the nation on the value of life.[65] Nevertheless, certain exceptional circumstances demanded too much from pregnant women, who, after all, had certain dignitarian and personality rights too. In reaching this balance, therefore, the Constitutional Court approved certain of the "indications," or safe harbors, for legal abortion provided for in the statute as a way of providing some balance among the rights. Safe harbors included threats to women's health or life and severe birth defects. The Constitutional Court also declared an indication for pregnancy resulting from sex crimes, such as incest or rape, and, more broadly, for a "general situation of need" indication when "continuation of the pregnancy would impose extreme hardship on the woman comparable in intensity to the other indications."[66] Otherwise, abortion must be made a crime. "The constitutionally commanded legal disapproval of abortion must clearly be reflected in the legal order."[67] These pronouncements reflect, again, the rhetorical function of German law, steeped in European culture, where a purpose of law is to impart morals and right standards for conduct.

The Bundestag passed a new law that implemented these teachings. In practice, most women could obtain an abortion if they desired under one of the indications, especially the general situation of need. Implementation of the law also varied by region. So, women in more restrictive regions, such as Bavaria, traveled to more permissive areas of Germany to obtain an abortion, or abroad, especially to the Netherlands. This state of affairs led supporters of *Abortion I* to argue that new, stricter legislation was required. Supporters of abortion rights, by contrast, argued that the resulting legislation was too restrictive of abortion rights.[68] One might plausibly conclude that *Abortion I* did not settle the abortion controversy in West Germany, as *Roe* did not in the United States.

Abortion II

The Constitutional Court was presented with a wholly different problem in 1993, when it was asked again to review the constitutionality of abortion as provided in the Pregnancy and Family Assistance Act (1992 Abortion Reform Act).[69] With the unification of the two Germanies came the necessity of reconciling the more restrictive West German law with the more liberal East German one. The law of East Germany granted women the right to have an abortion during the first trimester. The Unification Treaty made special provision for abortion, permitting East German law to remain in effect in the East until new, unified German legislation could be worked out. Many expected that the East German law would provide the basis for compromise.

In fact, the 1992 Abortion Reform Act was the product of compromise between the Social Democrats and Christian Democrats of the West and the parties of the East. The new law eliminated the requirement of third-party determination of indications during the first trimester of pregnancy.[70] Abortion, instead, would be "not unlawful" (*nichts rechtswidrig*) if the woman choose to terminate her pregnancy after mandatory counseling designed to induce her to "make her own decision of conscience with awareness of responsibility," and after a three-day waiting period, designed to reinforce the importance of choice.[71] These provisions reveal, again, a purpose of German law to impart civic and personal responsibility. After the first trimester, indications excusing the unlawfulness of abortion could only be met upon professional determination that a serious birth defect or threat to the woman's own life or death was present. Abortion due to birth defects also required counseling, and was not permissible after twenty-two weeks.[72] In essence, the 1992 Abortion Reform Act had converted the criminal provisions of the 1975 Act into mandatory counseling ones, substituting persuasion for the sanction of the criminal law. Moreover, the 1992 Abortion Reform Act spoke to abortion in the context of broad-ranging social protection of women and children, including provisions providing for day care, vocational training and placement for primary-care parents, housing and rent control, and increased welfare benefits for pregnant women and single parents, measures designed to encourage women to bring their pregnancies to term.[73] In these ways, the law attempted to encourage and bolster a pro-life position, but not order it.

In a 6–2 decision filling 164 pages of the official reporter, the Constitutional Court reaffirmed the essential core of its 1975 *Abortion I*. The ruling galvanized the country. An East German state secretary for social affairs, Regine Hildebrandt, denounced the ruling as a "return to the Middle Age."[74] "This is a catastrophe," said Hildebrandt. "This is just impossible at the end of the 20th century." On the other side of the debate, Catholic bishops praised the decision, issuing a statement that "the real winner is humanity."[75]

The Constitutional Court felt compelled to defend the value structure of the Basic Law, notwithstanding the handiwork of democracy. "Dignity attaches to the physical existence of every human being . . . before as well as after birth. . . . Unborn life is a constitutional value that the state is obligated to protect that attaches to each human life, not life generally" pronounced the Constitutional Court.[76] In keeping with this holding, the Court found that the provisions of the 1992 Abortion Reform Act that made all abortions legal during the first trimester were unconstitutional. Returning to the conception of *Abortion I*, the Constitutional Court further held that the statute must make clear that "as a matter of general principle abortion is, in fact, illegal and that the pregnant woman has a legal duty, again as a matter of principle, to carry the child to term. The fundamental prohibition of abortion and the fundamental duty to carry the child to term are two inseparably bound elements of the constitutionally commanded duty of protection."[77] The duty to protect life stands at the very core of the social order.

The major change in *Abortion II* was that the state, in fulfilling its duty to protect life (*Schutzpflicht*), did not have to criminalize all illegal abortions. Therefore, an abortion, while formally "illegal," might nevertheless be available, although only upon justification, such as pursuant to medical, eugenic, or criminal indications. Moreover, an abortion, under what had been the social indication, could be obtained without punishment if the state or others, such as the church, created a comprehensive counseling system with the goal of convincing the pregnant woman to carry the child to term.[78] To be effective, counseling must be backed up with social support measures designed to encourage women to have children. The criminal-based system of *Abortion I* had proved ineffectual, creating antagonism among women; the state felt a counseling system would be more effective, appealing to women's sense of responsibility and trust.[79] Thus, the counseling system actually represented an adjustment of the law to meet changed social conditions. In the ensuing twenty years since *Abortion I*, women had been more assertive and self-deterministic; the law recognized this changed reality.[80] Thus, we can see how abortion became a central issue for feminism and the idea of gender equality.

From an American perspective, the counseling system set up in Germany is content-based advocacy, questionable from a First Amendment view because of its one-sided message designed to educate women about their maternal responsibilities.[81] "The counseling . . . must necessarily be directed to the protection of unborn life. . . . The counseling should encourage, not frighten; enhance understanding, not instruct; reinforce responsibility, not patronize."[82] Counseling is a built in safeguard to protect the unborn's right to life. It would be unusual for American law to so openly proselytize. In Germany, this seems more justifiable, given the Basic Law's commitment to human life.

Yet these counseling provisions had the significant effect of recognizing, for the first time in Germany, that a woman could have an abortion during the first trimester of her pregnancy without fear of criminal punishment:

The state may validly conclude that in view of the reality of abortion in modern society, the more effective solution to the problem of unwanted pregnancy is to stay the hand of the would-be prosecutors, to make an ally and friend of the women in distress, to foreswear threats of punishment, and to induce her to cooperate voluntarily without fear of retribution or loss of personal integrity.[83]

So the concern for preserving life was transformed from an iron fist to a velvet glove.

The Constitutional Court then scrutinized the counseling provisions to assure that they were sufficiently attentive to the fetus's right to life. Several of the provisions were struck as being insufficiently so attentive. For example, they did not adequately proclaim the right of the fetus to live and protect it; they did not describe adequately the social welfare and public support measures that would encourage a woman to bring the fetus to term and thus were a necessary support of the counseling system; they did not guarantee with enough clarity the right of the woman to return to her job after the pregnancy; they did not sufficiently encourage the woman to state her reasons, resolve her conflict, and preserve anonymity; and they did not sufficiently provide for support, or protect against outside pressures, of family or friends supporting or militating against pregnancy.[84] Moreover, the counselor, not the woman, had to certify when the counseling was complete.[85] For these reasons, the Constitutional Court ordered the Bundestag to rework the counseling provisions.

America

From its start, *Roe* was a controversial decision.[86] The ensuing nineteen years did nothing to lessen the controversy.[87] *Casey*, like *Abortion II*, provided the occasion for the Supreme Court to rethink fundamentally its original decision on abortion, which the Court did in a long and complicated opinion of ninety-four pages, echoing the length, if not the complexity, of the German cases. The Supreme Court sought to end the long-simmering controversy:

Where, in the performance of its judicial duties, the Court decides a case in such a way as to resolve the sort of intensely divisive controversy reflected in *Roe* and those rare, comparable cases, its decision has a dimension that the resolution of the normal case does not carry. It is the dimension present whenever the Court's interpretation of the Constitution calls the contending sides of a national controversy to end their national division by accepting a common mandate rooted in the Constitution.[88]

The Supreme Court felt obligated to act, on reason and principle, consistent with the role it saw for itself as a constitutional guardian, acting in its "capacity to exercise the judicial power and to function as the Supreme Court of a Nation dedicated to rule of law."[89]

To the surprise of many, the *Casey* Court confirmed the essential holding of *Roe*:

(1) a recognition of a woman's right to choose to have an abortion before fetal viability and to obtain it without undue interference from the State . . .

(2) confirmation of the State's power to restrict abortions after viability, if the law contains exceptions for pregnancies endangering a woman's life or health . . . ; and (3) the principle that the State has legitimate interests from the outset of the pregnancy in protecting the health of the woman and the life of the fetus that may become a child.[90]

Yet the Supreme Court also redefined the balance between women's autonomy rights and fetal rights as exercised by the state. The Supreme Court replaced *Roe's* trimester framework with an "undue burden" test, by which the Court would evaluate the interference with women's autonomy to determine if it placed "a substantial obstacle in the path of the woman seeking an abortion of a nonviable fetus."[91]

The Supreme Court devised the "undue burden" test for *Casey*, which bears some resemblance to the "unreasonable burden" (*unzumutbare Belastungen*) standard of the Constitutional Court, just as the Constitutional Court had applied an enhanced state duty of protection of life in the *Abortion* cases.[92] Perhaps abortion is, indeed, a unique act. Or perhaps it is an issue over which it is simply too difficult to treat as other cases and apply standard rights methodologies. As with the *Abortion* cases, elaboration of the right or rights would depend on its application in concrete circumstances. In *Casey*, this called for application of the undue burden standard.

Applying the undue burden test to the Pennsylvania law at issue, the Supreme Court invalidated a spousal notification requirement but validated the other four provisions: informed consent, twenty-four-hour waiting period, reporting, and parental consent requirements.[93] Of these provisions, informed consent and the twenty-four-hour waiting period are noteworthy, since they were invalidated under the *Roe* approach and thus provide the most graphic contrast between the two cases and, also, the greatest similarity with *Abortion II*.[94]

The informed consent provision required the physician performing the abortion to inform the woman of the nature of the procedure, the attendant health risks, the gestational age of the fetus, and the availability of state information concerning social welfare programs, such as "information about child support from the father, and a list of agencies which provide adoption and other services as alternatives to abortion."[95] The provision bears some resemblance to the mandatory counseling provision validated in *Abortion II*.[96] Like that provision, the informed consent requirement is not value neutral but "designed to influence the woman's informed choice between abortion or childbirth."[97] Under American free speech principles the requirement could quite plausibly be considered content based as well, and, therefore, subject to heavy justification under strict scrutiny analysis. Likewise, if the choice over abortion was considered to be a fundamental right, the counseling provision would also ordinarily be subject to strict scrutiny proof. This, in fact, had been the Supreme Court's conclusion under the *Roe* regime.[98] In these ways, *Casey* signals a different course.

A similar analysis applies to the twenty-four-hour waiting period. The provision also bears some resemblance to the three-day waiting period validated in *Abortion II*, although, obviously, the provisions differ by two days.[99] Both waiting periods are designed to force the woman to reflect carefully on the consequences of her choice. Combined with the laws' mandatory counseling provisions, the requirements are designed to influence the woman to carry the fetus to term, if at all possible. As with the informed consent provision, waiting periods also were previously infirm under the *Roe* approach.[100]

CONVERGENCE AND DIVERGENCE IN ABORTION LAW

In assessing abortion law in both countries, what seems most noteworthy is the growing convergence of the two laws in practical terms, notwithstanding their different constitutional premises. Comparing *Abortion II* with *Casey*, both countries provide for qualified access to abortion during the first trimester, if desired, provided that the pregnant woman undergoes mandatory counseling designed to convince her to have the child and that she consider this possibility for a specified short period of one or several days prior to undergoing the abortion procedure.

This element of convergence seems especially noteworthy given that the two Courts confronted very different precedents in the 1990s. *Abortion I* was a very autonomy-rights restrictive, pro-life protective decision; *Roe* was the opposite. The contrast between *Abortion I* and *Roe* was itself quite fascinating: Both Courts acted quite countermajoritarian in achieving opposite outcomes; they regulated with precision the extent of abortion "rights" and "duties" in a manner that plausibly left them open to attack for overstepping separation of powers by acting "legislatively."[101] Starting from these divergent precedents, the Constitutional Court in *Abortion II* ameliorated some of the harshness of *Abortion I*, from the woman's perspective, by decriminalizing abortion and thereby allowing women, for the first time, to have abortions during the first trimester provided they followed the statutory requirements. In this way, the Constitutional Court moved in the direction of *Roe*.[102] In *Casey*, the Supreme Court restructured the equation set in *Roe* to address more fully state and community interests in protection of fetal life along the lines of the *Abortion* cases. It might be said that *Casey* thereby recognized the magnitude of a fetal claim to life and the community's interest therein for the first time, as the Constitutional Court had done in 1975 in *Abortion I*. Such a communal strain is unusual for American law. In these ways, the two Courts moved closer to one another in their treatment of abortion.[103]

Notwithstanding the resemblance in outcome that can be achieved, the two laws differ substantially as a matter of legal substance and tone. In Germany, a constellation of rights apply, and these rights are coupled with duties. On behalf of the fetus, human dignity and the right to life combine to impose on the state an obligation to protect life. The state speaks for the unborn child. Fetal rights exist in counterpoise to a woman's autonomy rights, as derived from her guarantee of human dignity, rights to personality, and bodily integrity. Especially when viewed with the positive state duty to protect and nurture life, these rights illustrate the twin positive and negative dimension of German rights. We can thus see that German rights are holistic, operating together in a carefully synchronized system. Any given right is never quite absolute and detached from others in the constellation. The catalogue of rights, each representing different aspects of human personality, functions as a whole: Integrated rights complement a concept of an integrated human personality. In the United States, the equation seems simpler: A constitutional right of privacy, conferring limited decisional autonomy, is balanced against the potentiality of life, represented as an interest of the state, not as a right.

The most notable difference in the enumerated values of the two Constitutions is the right to life. In Germany this is explicitly enumerated in article 2(2). The Constitutional Court interpreted this protection, in conjunction with human dignity, to encompass fetal life.[104] By contrast, the American Constitution is silent over a right to life generally, including that for a fetus. Moreover, through textual exegesis, the Supreme Court in *Roe* determined that rights apply postnatally, not for developing life.[105]

The pro-life focus in Germany is a product, preeminently, of Catholic natural law and the country's reaction to Hitler's politics of annihilation. In the wake of the Nazi experience, Germans reached deep into their tradition, notably Christian and Kantian morality.[106] Ironically, abortion was outlawed in Hitler's Germany, becoming, in 1943, a capital offense.[107] These influences help explain why the Constitutional Court felt compelled to label abortion as "wrong" in the eyes of society, even if it might be allowed in certain limited circumstances. Consistent with its conscious pro-life stance, the Basic Law also outlaws capital punishment, as did the 1848 Frankfurt Constitution, another important influence.[108] Moreover, article 1 of the Basic Law obligates the state "to respect and protect" human dignity. Thus, the essence of the value order is a commitment to the value of life. Kantian idealism, with its emphasis on the value of each life, fortifies this concept. In this light, then, is radiated the pro-family and pro-child social welfare provisions coupled around abortion regulation in the 1992 Abortion Reform Act, reflecting the social state directive and, of course, the pragmatic desire to influence the choice over abortion. Germany thus reveals itself to be consistently pro-life and deliberately child friendly. Human welfare and its flourishing seem central.

Another distinguishing trait of the two countries is the objective constitutionalism of German law. Under article 1, the German state is obligated to respect and protect human dignity. In combination with the article 2(2) provision for the right to life, the Constitutional Court, for the first time in *Abortion I*, implied a positive obligation of the state to protect life, which became the concrete anchoring of a fetus's right to life. As a matter of interpretation, the implication of this positive state duty is plausible, but not self-evident. Human dignity, right to life, and objective constitutionalism provide some foundation for the duty. Yet even within German law, the assignment stands out as an act of judicial activism.

A comparative evaluation of other right to life cases puts this into bold relief. Apart from abortion, the Constitutional Court has not invoked the clause to impose duties on government to protect life. In several cases, the Constitutional Court has recognized that a duty to protect life exists, but in these cases the Constitutional Court has refused to impose duties on government to act. The closest case factually to the *Abortion* cases is the *Schleyer Kidnaping Case*. In the case, the Constitutional Court recognized a duty to protect where a victim was kidnaped, but refused to impose duties on government to rescue the victim or prevent kidnaping out of concern that government be able to implement its own policy.[109] Likewise, the Constitutional Court refused to impose duties on government to act in a range of situations where the threat to life was more remote. These case include threats posed by the storage and transportation of chemical weapons or nuclear reactors, or risks posed by aircraft noise and highway noise.[110] In these cases, the Constitutional Court seemed quite cautious about extending any claim to governmental obligation as a matter of constitutional law to ensure safety or life, a caution echoed in the American regime. Accordingly, the Constitutional Court deferred substantially to legislative determinations, in bold contrast to its intensive scrutiny of the parliamentary determinations at issue in the *Abortion* cases.[111]

The Constitutional Court's differing treatment of the duty to protect life suggests that it differentiated factually among these cases. Kidnapping and abortion, for example, are distinct events. The more intensive scrutiny employed in the *Abortion* cases might be justified by the need to protect the overriding value of fetal life.[112] For one thing, the Constitutional Court would appear to be the only institution willing to act on behalf of unborn life. Alternatively, preferred treatment of fetal life may suggest that cases involving abortion are treated differently than other cases. In view of the *Casey* Court's use of a newly minted undue burden standard to judge abortion, there is evidence of preferred treatment of fetal life in the United States as well. Both countries ultimately treat abortion as sui generis. Perhaps this reflects the high value placed on fetal life by both Courts.

In view of the American concern for limited government and rejection of affirmative state obligations, it is hard to envision how the Supreme Court would impose any positive duty to act on government.[113] The difference in conception of state power thus reveals itself to be another distinguishing trait in the two legal orders.

It is worth pointing out, however, that the positive German state obligations help facilitate the communitarian bent of German law, as illustrated in the *Abortion* cases. Rights are not just a matter of individual exercise in the German scheme, but are to unfold in a manner consistent with the value order of the Basic Law. Rights are thus coupled with responsibilities. By contrast, the American Constitution is silent about these matters.[114] Rights, seemingly, can be exercised outside the context of a value order or even a sense of responsibility, except as that which a person might recognize. The two legal orders thus differ on the role rights play in constituting community.

Viewed from a different perspective, the two countries differ over conceptions of individuality as well. The German cases circumscribe women's decisional authority out of respect for fetal life. German basic rights possess a clear social dimension; women must consider the effect of their choice on others. By contrast, the American cases are premised fundamentally on women's self-determination, which is more apparent in *Roe* than *Casey*. German abortion rights exist within a richer constellation of rights and, accordingly, must be considered against the competing claims of these other rights. American abortion rights exist in isolation, not mediated by other rights claims. Accordingly, American abortion rights can be exercised more absolutely, according to the wishes of the rights chooser. Through this review of abortion, we can now see that the two countries have achieved a different balance among personality, liberty, and order within society.

NOTES

1. Even the Courts recognized this. *Abortion II*, 88 BVerfGE 203, 214 (1993); *Casey*, 505 U.S. 833, 844 (1992).

2. 410 U.S. 113 (1973).

3. 39 BVerfGE 1 (1975).

4. 505 U.S. 833 (1992).

5. 88 BVerfGE at 203.

6. Catherine S. Manegold, *Anti-Abortion Killings: The Movement; Anti-Abortion Groups Continue Radical Talk*, N.Y. TIMES, Jan. 1, 1995, at A26.

7. Timothy Egan, *The Roots of Terror; Is Abortion Violence a Plot? Conspiracy Is Not Confirmed*, N.Y. TIMES, June 18, 1995, at A1.

8. *Id.*

9. Katherine Hessler, *Early Efforts to Suppress Protest: Unwanted Abolitionist Speech*, 7 B. U. PUB. INT. L. J. 185, 200 (1998), *quoting from* William Lloyd Garrison's The Liberator, first published Jan. 1, 1831.

10. *Id.* at 216, *quoting* Frederick Douglass, Remarks in a speech about freedom (1857).

11. Allan Cowell, *Obeying Pope, German Bishops End Role in Abortion System*, N.Y. TIMES, Jan. 28, 1998, at A3.

12. *Id.*

13. Manegold, *supra* note 6, at A26.

14. *Id.*

15. Egan, *supra* note 7, at A1.

16. Jim Yardley & David Rohde, *Abortion Doctor in Buffalo Slain; Sniper Attack Fits Violent Pattern*, N.Y. TIMES, Oct. 25, 1998, at A1.

17. Stephen Kinzer, *German Court Restricts Abortion, Angering Feminists and the East*, N.Y. TIMES, May 29, 1993, at A1.

18. Ferdinand Protzman, *Germany Widens Abortion Rights After Fierce Debate in Parliament*, N.Y. TIMES, June 26, 1992, at A6.

19. Craig R. Whitney, *German Aide Faults Policy on Foreigners*, N.Y. TIMES, May 29, 1994, at sect. 1, p. 9 (reporting 7% of German population as immigrant, but not formal citizens).

20. Cowell, *supra* note 11, at A3.

21. Ferdinand Protzman, *Broader Abortion Law Leaves Germans Somber*, N.Y. TIMES, June 27, 1992, at A3.

22. Stephen Kinzer, *supra* note 17, at A1.

23. Marlise Simons, *A Divisive Issue of German Unity; How to Reconcile Abortion Laws*, N.Y. TIMES, July 19, 1990, at A1.

24. Protzman, *supra* note 21, at A1.

25. *Id.*

26. At the time the Bundestag acted, 75 percent of all Germans, male and female, supported the right of a woman to choose an abortion during the first trimester. *Id.*

27. Simons, *supra* note 23, at A1.

28. Recent data indicate that the cleavage between East and West over abortion yet persists, although it is lessening; Eastern women yet take a more pro-choice attitude, as compared to Western women. This seems at-

tributable to Eastern women's greater participation in the labor market and higher levels of education. The attitudes of Eastern men, however, approximate more closely those of their Western counterparts. This may be attributable to their preoccupation with job prospects and, also, the discernibly greater influence of religion in the East as a result of reunification. Lee Ann Banaszak, *East–West Differences in German Abortion Opinion*, 62 PUB. OPINION Q. 545 (1998). Thus, the melding of East and West, following reunification, is slowly changing German society.

29. 39 BVerfGE 1, 41 (1975).

30. *Abortion II*, 88 BVerfGE 203, 251 (1993).

31. *Abortion I*, 39 BVerfGE at 41, 46.

32. *Id.* at 37; *Abortion II*, 88 BVerfGE at 251 ("The Basic Law obligates the state to protect human life. The unborn belong to human life. They also receive the protection of the state").

33. 88 BVerfGE at 37; *Abortion II*, 88 BVerfGE at 244 ("From a biological perspective, life is a continuum, that begins with the joining of egg and semen and ends with the death of the person").

34. *Abortion II*, 88 BVerfGE at 203.

35. *Id.*

36. In *Abortion I*, the Court observed that Germany would not be unduly influenced by the abortion experiences of other countries on account of the uniqueness of the German value order and the country's history with Naziism. 39 BVerfGE at 60. In particular, the Court looked to the experiences of England and East Germany, countries with much more liberal abortion regimes then. *Id.*

37. *Abortion II*, 88 BVerfGE at 203, 252.

38. *Id.* at 252.

39. *Id.* at 203.

40. *Id.* at 203, 253. "The fundamental prohibition of abortion and the fundamental duty to carry a child to term are two indispensable, inseparable elements of the constitutional commanded protection." *Id.* at 253.

41. *Id.* at 261. "The state also had to reinforce the general public's consciousness of the claim of the unborn to protection—this duty obliged the schools, public information and counseling offices, and both public and private broadcasting." Gerald L. Neuman, *Casey in the Mirror: Abortion, Abuse and the Right to Protection in the United States and Germany*, 43 AM. J. COMP. L. 273, 281 (1995).

42. 88 BVerfGE at 253–54 ("Protection of life is not absolutely commanded in the sense that it will take precedence without exception over other legal values; the language of article 2(2) demonstrates this. The obligation to protect does not mean that any measure can be taken in its service. Instead, the idea is that the range of protection is to be determined in view of the importance and need for protection of the underlying legal value—here the unborn human life—in comparison to the legal values in conflict").

43. "Condemnation of abortion must be clearly expressed in the legal order." *Abortion I*, 39 BVerfGE 1, 44 (1975).

44. *Abortion I*, 39 BVerfGE at 42–43; *Abortion II*, 88 BVerfGE at 252–55.

45. *Abortion I*, 39 BVerfGE at 49–50; *Abortion II*, 88 BVerfGE at 255–58.

46. Roe v. Wade, 410 U.S. 113, 153 (1973).

47. "Where certain 'fundamental rights' are involved, the Court has held that regulation limiting these rights may be justified only by a 'compelling state interest,' . . . and that legislative enactments must be narrowly drawn to express only the legitimate state interests at stake." *Id.* at 155. Strict scrutiny is, of course, still the prevailing methodology for rights analysis, although there have been notable departures from it, such as in *Casey*.

48. Akron v. Akron Center for Reproductive Health, Inc., 462 U.S. 416 (1983).

49. 505 U.S. 833, 852 (1992). Even in *Roe*, the Court recognized that abortion was different than other situations involving rights. *Roe*, 410 U.S. at 159 (noting "situation . . . is inherently different").

50. The *Roe* Court considered carefully and rejected the notion of a fetal right to life. 410 U.S. at 156–58. "The unborn have never been recognized in the law as persons in the whole sense." *Id.* at 162.

51. *Id.* at 157–58.

52. *Id.* at 164.

53. *Id.* at 162–63.

54. *Id.* at 159.

55. *Id.* at 164–65.

56. "A finding of an undue burden is a shorthand for the conclusion that a state regulation has the purpose or effect of placing a substantial obstacle in the path of a woman seeking an abortion" of a nonviable fetus. *Casey*, 505 U.S. at 877.

57. "The woman's liberty is not so unlimited, however, that from the outset the State cannot show its concern for the life of the unborn, and at a later point in fetal development the State's interest in life has sufficient force so that the right of the woman to terminate the pregnancy can be restricted." *Id.* at 869.

58. "We conclude the line should be drawn at viability, so that before that time the women has a right to choose to terminate her pregnancy." *Casey*, 505 U.S. 833, 870 (1992).

59. Neuman, *supra* note 41, at 274, *citing* Fünftes Gesetz zur Reform des Strafrechts, 1974 BGB 1, I sec. 1297. As a matter of comparative law, it is interesting to note that the German justices, particularly Justice Ernst Benda, were quite familiar with Roe v. Wade and American constitutionalism. Justice Benda had been a student at the University of Wisconsin in the 1950s. Donald P. Kommers, *The Constitutional Law of Abortion in Germany: Should Americans Pay Attention?* 10 J. CONTEMP. HEALTH L. & POL'Y, 1, 6 (1994).

60. Neuman, *supra* note 59, at 274–75.

61. *Id.* at 274.

62. Abstract judicial review is a procedure under which the Constitutional Court may decide questions concerning the interpretation or compatability of federal or state law with the Basic Law in the "abstract," or outside the context of a real legal dispute, at the request of the federal or state government or of one-third of the members of the Bundestag. GG

arti. 93(1). In this case, the Länder of Bavaria, Baden-Württemberg, Rheinland-Pflaz, Saarland, and Schleswig-Holstein filed suit. 39 BVerfGE 1, 18 (1975). Abstract judicial review is thus most like the notion of an advisory opinion in American law, which, since the founding of the Republic, the Supreme Court has refused to issue, preferring instead to rule only in the context of a real dispute between parties. From the German standpoint, abstract judicial review facilitates the integration of the Basic Law into society through the Court's interpretation of the Basic Law. It helps the Court steer society pursuant to the strictures of the Basic Law. The Court's concern is to assign an objective meaning to the constitutional rule at issue, in keeping with the objective nature of German constitutionalism, as compared to settling the legal dispute between the parties. For elaboration of these points in the context of *Abortion I, see* Kommers, *supra* note 59, at 5–6.

63. 39 BVerfGE at 42–43.

64. *Id.* at 45–47. The Constitutional Court noted that how to protect unborn life was fundamentally a decision for the legislature. *Id.* at 44.

65. *Id.* at 46.

66. *Id.* at 49–50.

67. *Id.* at 53.

68. Neuman, *supra* note 41, at 276. In the context of further abortion litigation, the "Court has held that payment for abortion by public medical insurance carriers does not violate any right of fellow beneficiaries, and that the requirement of wage continuation for employees undergoing abortions does not violate the property rights of employers." *Id.* at 276–77 (citations omitted). This contrasts with the American experience. *See* Harris v. McRae, 448 U.S. 297 (1980) (upholding Hyde amendment, which prohibited use of federal Medicaid funds for abortion except where life of mother in danger); Maher v. Roe, 432 U.S. 464 (1977) (state regulation may deny funding for nontherapeutic abortions). Coverage of abortion under public insurance illustrates how abortion politics involves issues of class. Rich woman can always obtain an abortion. Poor women, dependent on insurance, are at the mercy of the prevailing political climate.

69. The formal name of the act was a mouthful: Act for the Protection of Prenatal Developing Life, for the Promotion of a More Child-Friendly Society, for Assistance in Pregnancy Conflicts and for the Regulation of the Termination of Pregnancy. 1992 BGB I 1398, 1402 (amending §§ 218–19 of the German Criminal Code or *Strafgesetzbuch* [StGB]). These amended sections constitute the 1992 Abortion Reform Act.

70. 1992 Abortion Reform Act, 218 (a)(2) StGB.

71. *Id.* § 219(1); 88 BVerfGE 203, 299 (1993).

72. *Id.* § 218a (2, 3) StGB. The provisions are discussed in Kommers, *supra* note 59, at 13–14; Neuman, *supra* note 41, at 277–78.

73. 1992 Abortion Reform Act, art. 1–16.

74. Kinzer, *supra* note 17, at A1.

75. *Id.*

76. 88 BVerfGE at 252.

77. *Id.* at 253.

78. *Id.* at 257–58.

79. Neuman, *supra* note 41, at 282. This had been the position of Justice Rupp von Brünneck in her dissent in *Abortion I*, 39 BVerfGE 1, 76, 85–86 (1975).

80. Kommers, *supra* note 59, at 19 (noting how social context had changed radically since 1975; 1990 opinion polls indicated most Germans supported easing restrictions on abortion).

81. The Court noted that counseling can only have a chance if the end result remains open. The counseling must be designed to help the woman to resolve her dilemma whether to have the child or not. 88 BVerfGE at 282.

82. *Id.* at 282–83.

83. Kommers, *supra* note 59, at 20, *citing id.* at 282.

84. 88 BVerfGE at 301–09. For detailed discussion of these provisions, *see* Neuman, *supra* note 41, at 282–84. The state's obligation to protect unborn life also required it to take measures that prevented situations which would place undue burdens on pregnant women. Thus, the state should protect against educational and job discrimination, and compensate through social security law long periods of uncompensated child rearing and family subsidies as a means of preventing abortion, among other measures. In short, the state needed to create a "child-friendly" society. 88 BVerfGE at 258–61. *See also* Neuman, *supra* note 41, at 280–81.

85. 88 BVerfGE at 286.

86. *See, e.g.*, John Hart Ely, *The Wages of Crying Wolf: A Comment on Roe v. Wade*, 82 YALE L. J. 920 (1973). Like the German *Abortion* cases, *Roe* too was long, filling sixty-five pages in U.S. Reports.

87. *Casey*, 505 U.S. 833, 844 (1992) ("Liberty finds no refuge in a jurisprudence of doubt. Yet 19 years after our holding that the Constitution protects a woman's right to terminate her pregnancy in its early stages, Roe v. Wade . . . that definition of liberty is still questioned").

88. *Id.* at 866–67.

89. *Id.* at 865. The Supreme Court elaborated,

The Court must take care to speak and act in ways that allow people to accept its decisions on the terms the Court claims for them, as grounded truly in principle, not as compromises with social and political pressures having, as such, no bearing on the principled choices that the Court is obliged to make. Thus, the Court's legitimacy depends on making legally principled decisions under circumstances in which their principled character is sufficiently plausible to be accepted by the Nation. *Id.*

90. *Id.* at 846.

91. *Id.* at 877.

92. The Court, in *Abortion II*, 88 BVerfGE 203, 257 (1993), described the test as follows: "Unreasonableness can, to be sure, not arise out of circumstances that remain within the realm of normal pregnancy. Rather, burdens must exist that demand a measure of sacrifice of one's own life values, that are not to be expected from women." *Casey*, 505 U.S. at 857 ("Finally, one could classify *Roe* as *sui generis*").

93. *Id.* at 879–900. The spousal notification requirement was invalidated on the basis of equality between the sexes and the belief its implementation would lead to domestic violence and abuse. *Id.* at 891–98.

94. *Compare* Akron v. Akron Center for Reproductive Health, Inc., 464 U.S. 416 (1983) (invalidating informed consent, twenty-four-hour waiting periods, and other provisions as imposing excessive burdens on access to abortion).

95. *Casey*, 505 U.S. at 881.

96. 88 BVerfGE at 257–59, 282–84.

97. *Casey*, 505 U.S. at 881, *citing Akron*, 462 U.S. at 444. Under the provision, the physician "must inform the woman of the availability of printed materials, published by the State describing the fetus and providing information about medical assistance for childbirth, information about child support from the father, and a list of agencies which provide adoption and other services as alternatives to abortion." *Casey*, 505 U.S. at 881.

98. So Justice Blackmun noted, 505 U.S. at 929–30 (Blackmun, J., concurring and dissenting in part); *accord* Thornburgh v. American College of Obstetricians and Gynecologists, 476 U.S. 747, 760 (1986); *Akron*, 462 U.S. at 442–49.

99. *Abortion II*, 88 BVerfGE at 227, 299–300, *construing* § 218(a) StGB.

100. *Akron*, 462 U.S. at 450.

101. Webster v. Reproductive Health Services, 452 U.S. 450 (1989) (plurality) ("rigid *Roe* framework is hardly consistent with the notion of a Constitution cast in general terms"); Doe v. Bolton, 410 U.S. 179, 222 (1973) (White, J., dissenting) (deploring "exercise of raw judicial power"). The German dissenters echoed these thoughts. *Abortion I*, 39 BVerfGE 1, 70 (1975) (Rupp von Brünneck, J., and Simon, J., dissenting) ("The Court must not . . . assume [legislative functions] . . . and thereby endanger constitutional review").

102. *Roe*, 410 U.S. 113, 164 (1973).

103. American constitutional law is pretty well known in Germany, both among scholars and judges. Justice Benda, in particular, was quite cognizant of *Roe* in structuring *Abortion I.* Justice Dr. Dieter Grimm is well-versed in American law, especially free speech law. See Dieter Grimm, *Die Meinungsfreiheit in der Rechtsprechung des Bundesverfassungsrericht*, 48 NEUE JURISTISHE WOCHENSCHRIFT 1697 (1995). Likewise, Justice Dr. Paul Kirchhof is knowledgeable of American law. PAUL KIRCHHOF & DONALD P. KOMMERS, GERMANY AND ITS BASIC LAW: PAST, PRESENT AND FUTURE—A GERMAN–AMERICAN SYMPOSIUM (1993). It is not uncommon for the Constitutional Court to cite American cases. *See, e.g., Lüth*, 7 BVerfGE 198 (1958), *citing* Palko v. Connecticut, 302 U.S. 319, 327 (1937). By contrast, the Supreme Court almost never consults the work of another country's jurisprudence, although recent cases may signal otherwise. *See, e.g.*, Printz v. United States, 521 U.S. 898, 976–77 (1997) (Breyer, J., dissenting) (extensive inventory of comparable federal systems, including those of Switzerland, Germany, and the European Union, in seeking illumination of the proper relationship between the American federal and state governments); Washington v. Glucksberg, 521 U.S. 702, 734 (1997) (extensive review of other

countries' treatment of assisted suicide, and especially the Dutch experience, in rejecting constitutional right to die). *But see* Justice Scalia for the Court: "We think such comparative analysis inappropriate to the task of interpreting a constitution, though it was of course quite relevant to the task of writing one." *Printz*, 521 U.S. at 921 n. 11.

104. *Abortion I*, 39 BVerfGE at 36–37.

105. *Roe*, 410 U.S. at 157–58.

106. *Abortion I*, 39 BVerfGE at 36 ("The express inclusion in the Basis Law of a self-evident right to life—different as compared to the Weimar Constitution—is explainable primarily as a reaction against the 'annihilation of life valued unworthy,' of a 'final solution' and 'liquidation' that was pursued as official policy by the Nazi regime").

107. Rita J. Simon, ABORTION: STATUTES, POLICIES, AND PUBLIC ATTITUDES THE WORLD OVER 5 (1998). Hitler believed that use of contraception violated womenhood and motherhood. *Id.*

108. GG art. 102.

109. *Schleyer Kidnaping Case*, 46 BVerfGE 160 (1977) (deference to state and to legislature on how to prevent and solve kidnaping cases; no judicially imposed duty).

110. *Chemical Weapons Case*, 77 BVerfGE 170 (1987) (rejecting any constitutional claim that storage and transportation of chemical weapons violated Basic Law); *Mülheim-Kärlich Nuclear Reactor*, 53 BVerfGE 30, 57–60 (1979); 56 BVerfGE (1981) (aircraft noise); 79 BVerfGE 174 (1988) (highway noise).

111. Neuman, *supra* note 41, at 300.

112. *Abortion II*, 88 BverfGE 203, 262–63 (1993).

113. DeShaney v. Winnebago County Dept. of Social Services, 489 U.S. 189 (1989). If *DeShaney* were decided according to German law, it is probable that the Constitutional Court would value quite highly the young boy's right to life, especially with the state on notice of his abuse, and therefore impose affirmative obligations on government and scrutinize with care asserted state interests in juxtaposition to the right to life, as it had done in the *Abortion* cases.

114. In this light, the Court's discussion in *Casey* of the consequences of the abortion act, injecting a communitarian dimension, stands in contrast to much of American law.

7

Freedom of Expression

A final trait of human personality captured in human rights is freedom of expression. Through exercise of freedom of expression, men and women speak their minds, communicating their beliefs, opinions, ideas, or ideologies. People may utter truths or falsities, conjectures or facts, praise or profanity. What people say and how they say it reveals much about the truth of who they are and, ultimately, the tenor of society. For example, advocating resistance to a war is one thing; displaying the message "Fuck the Draft" another.[1] Expression is deeply revealing of personality.

Like a snapshot, speech portrays in an instant who we are. Our thoughts and speech also contain the threads by which we imagine and re-create ourselves as we might like to be. As we articulate our hopes and aspirations, we hold out the possibility of transforming our lives. The communications we make influence others, including their perception of us, forming part of the image others have of us. Like a looking glass, speech displays our selves, part of our inner psyche. The information we impart enables others to better fashion their lives. These are some of the ways in which speech constitutes and reveals human personality.

Speech or expression, umbrella terms for the process of thought and communication at the core of human personhood, are, in many ways, the most fundamental of liberties. In the realm of the mind and soul, a person formulates thought, the driving force of life and its manifestation in concrete behavior. Thought and its communication is the first step in realizing human capacity. It is the indispensable wellspring for human dignity, its conception, and its elaboration; for formation of personality and freedom of action, described in Chapter 3; for the personal sphere of human personhood, covered in Chapter 4; and for the concept of human autonomy, identity, and self-determination, as elaborated on in Chapters 5 and 6. In this sense, all "words are . . . triggers of action."[2]

Today we take for granted the indispensability of speech as a condition of a free person and of a free and just society. But the securing of freedom of the mind, historically, has been a long struggle, having only recently, in the twentieth century, been achieved. In the course of history, battle for control of the mind and its moral content and beliefs was an original front for assertion of individuality and human dignity. Past rulers sought control over the mind as part of their realm, requiring loyalty and obedience in spirit as well as behavior. Rulers sought to safeguard their domains from dangerous or seditious opinions, in their view, which might threaten their authority. The invention of the printing press facilitated the spreading of words, and this increased significantly the threat of dissemination of divergent opinions. In England in 1476, the crown exercised control of the printing press as its prerogative.[3] Soon the crown set up a system of censorship. Manuscripts first had to be submitted to officials for approval before they could be published. "This system of 'prior restraint' remained in effect until 1694."[4] In 1635, Massachusetts Bay authorities banished Roger Williams from the colony for "new and dangerous opinions."[5] Williams's "opinions" included the radical assertion that the land of the New World belonged to Native Americans and not to the crown, which had granted title to the white English settlers of Massachusetts Bay. The quest for freedom of expression was a hard-fought struggle, over time, to secure the integrity of a person's thought process, beliefs, and conscience. This was an early struggle for individuality, for control of oneself free from the coercion of the ruler.

In the United States today, free speech is one of the first freedoms, owing symbolically to its pride of place as one of the set of fundamental liberties enumerated in the First Amendment.[6] Although the First Amendment's position was an historical accident, free speech indeed resonates as the first freedom in American society in the hearts and minds of Americans and in the jurisprudence of the Supreme Court, which has privileged extraordinarily the status of expression.[7] There is, perhaps, no other right Americans so dearly associate with, considering it their birthright to speak freely their minds, with vigor, exuberance, and utter abandon. Free speech captures the spirit of being American.

The flowering of speech as a fundamental individual right is mainly a twentieth-century phenomenon, like most of the other rights elaborated on in this study. In the United States, speech first caught the attention of the Supreme Court in the great controversies over American involvement in the Great War raging in Europe at the start of the twentieth century. Over issues like the drafting of American soldiers for the war effort and the American invasion of Russia following cessation of hostilities in World War I—matters testing the loyalties of citizens, as those earlier episodes with the English crown—the Supreme Court began formulating modern free speech theory.[8] Incorporated into the idea of due process in 1925, the first of the civil rights so to be transformed, free speech became the premier fundamental freedom applicable to the country as a whole, reinforcing its status as the first freedom.[9] Since then, the Supreme Court has constructed speech as a presumptively protected zone of freedom, free from ordinary restraints, such as those applicable to conduct, in which citizens are able, quintessentially, to think, feel, and say what they like without fear of punishment. In this sense, it is the archetypal American liberty, representing the idea of freedom.

Free expression in contemporary Germany also is marked by an open, vibrant, sometimes caustic exchange of the central issues of the day. As in the United States, freedom of expression guarantees are central to the constitutional order and structure of German society. Unlike speech freedoms in the United States, German communication rights are carefully circumscribed by distinct textual, legal, cultural, and civility limits. Nevertheless, within those limits, contemporary German expression is a spirited and sophisticated body of law that presents both lessons and pitfalls to an observer of a system of free expression. In the last decade especially, German expression has followed the course of American, conceiving speech as a presumptively protected realm of freedom where people are free to speak their minds without fear of the censor. The Constitutional Court has been instrumental in charting this course.

This chapter explores the concept of free expression in Germany and America with a view especially toward comparing German law to its American counterpart. With its early origination and full flowering, it makes particular sense to use American law as the standard. We will especially examine how citizens discuss issues common to themselves as a people and a society. By this idea of public discourse, I mean public discussion of issues, personalities, or general concerns of interest to members of society. Through this critical exchange of ideas, a democracy determines its purposes and a culture is constructed.[10] Through exploration of the quality and range of communication in each country, we can derive important insight as to the role free expression plays, or should play, in comparable Western constitutional democracies. We shall also decipher the cultural messages imparted through speech, seeking insight into the sense of society. The quality of free expression captures human personality, radiating the expressive dimension to human dignity. We shall see how the two countries constitute personality over this expressive component.

We will first examine the conception and structure of expression in both countries, concentrating especially on the idea of public discourse. Then we will examine specific issues of speech that resonate in both societies, setting out a good basis to observe similarities and differences in the two laws, and also in the conceptions of human personhood and community. These issues include defamation, offensive speech and hate speech, and treatment or mistreatment of national symbols, such as the flag or anthem.

PUBLIC DISCOURSE: THE STRUCTURE OF EXPRESSION

America

American speech is an exercise in free individuality. Citizens, quite simply, are free: free to speak their minds; to assert ideas, opinions, or critiques; and to form associations, as they wish. Freedom to speak one's mind is basic to being American. Thus, it is not surprising that American free speech involves a "profound national commitment to the principle that debate on public issues should be uninhibited, robust and wide-open, and that it may well include vehement, caustic, and sometimes unpleasantly sharp attacks on government and public officials."[11] And while public discourse relates to matters concerning the public, political and otherwise, the range of American speech generally is broad and wide open, also embracing topics private and personal. Absent exigent circumstance, such as a threat of violence or tangible harm to children, people themselves are entrusted with the power to determine the nature and quality of communication without government intervention or communal restraint.

In 1940, Jesse Cantwell, a Jehovah's Witness, walked down the street in New Haven, Connecticut, then a heavily Catholic area, and played a phonograph that attacked religion generally and Catholicism particularly.[12] The message was highly offensive to Cantwell's Catholic audience, some of whom "felt like hitting" or "throw[ing] Cantwell off the street."[13] Cantwell was charged with breaching the peace, but the Supreme Court protected the speech, finding it to be Cantwell's prerogative as an individual to express himself as he saw fit.

In 1991, Margaret Gilleo, unhappy with American participation in the Gulf War, placed a sign on her front lawn displaying the words "Say No to War in the Persian Gulf, Call Congress Now."[14] The city sought to enforce its ordinance that prohibited homeowners from displaying signs on their property out of concern it would become "visual clutter."[15] The Supreme Court ruled for Gilleo: "Displaying a sign from one's own residence often carries a message quite distinct from placing the same sign someplace else, or conveying the same text or picture by other means. Precisely because of their location, such signs provide information about the identity of the 'speaker.'"[16]

With the First Amendment as a shield against official intervention, people are able to speak freely, to comment, to criticize, or to "invite dispute . . . induce . . . unrest, create dissatisfaction . . . or even stir people to anger" as they wish on matters of concern.[17] This is the free spirited nature of American law, and it is particularly appropriate for the country. In the United States, "rich cultural diversities" exist, and these groups vie for influence and adherents, attempting to corner the marketplace of ideas.[18] "The constitutional right of free expression is powerful medicine in a society as diverse and populous as ours."[19] "Many types of life, character, opinion and belief . . . develop unmolested and unobstructed" beneath the shield of the First Amendment.[20] These lives and opinions, in turn, influence others, forming collective clusters of believers. Any such community of belief or allegiance forms on its own as the product of voluntary associations, not of official or majoritarian compulsion.[21]

Government may not properly intervene in this competition for influence; its role is not to inhibit or prejudice a person's ability to persuade others.[22] Instead, the reach of the idea is determined by its ability to attract support. The only effective counter is the force of a stronger idea. In the competition for influence, government remains on the sidelines, a neutral observer, which the Supreme Court actively polices through its commitment to the core First Amendment principle that government must be neutral with respect to the content of expression. In these ways, people are entrusted with the responsibility of making judgments about the use or abuse of speech, its effect and reach, and its limitation, if any, short of an exigency. Free speech is democracy in action.

Americans believe or accept this image of themselves as independent, autonomous, self-determining people. Recall again, from Chapter 2, the ideal of self-reliance posited by Justice Brandeis in his great *Whitney v. California* concurrence: The founders "were not cowards . . . [who] fear[ed] political change." They were, instead, "courageous, self-reliant men, with confidence in the power of free and fearless reasoning applied through the processes of popular government."[23] This is the image, in American law, of the hardy, self-sufficient soul. Sometimes the person acts as a lone ranger, like Jesse Cantwell or Margaret Gilleo. Sometimes a person acts as a rebel. Unhappy with the policies of the administration of President Reagan in 1984, Gregory Johnson protested outside the Republican convention then taking place. He doused kerosene on an American flag and set it on fire, leading to his prosecution under a Texas flag-desecration statute. The Supreme Court, in a close decision, overturned the conviction, finding it to be protected speech.[24]

Our pattern of speech is constructed on this ideal of hardiness and self-sufficiency. Again we return to Justice Brandeis:

> Those who won our independence believed that the final end of the State was to make men free to develop their faculties; and that in its government the deliberative forces should prevail over the arbitrary. They valued liberty both as an end and as a means. . . . They believed that freedom to think as you will and speak as you think are means indispenable to the discovery and spread of political truth; that without free speech and assembly discussion would be futile; that with them, discussion affords ordinarily adequate protection against the dissemination of noxious doctrine; that the greatest menace to freedom is an inert people; that public discussion is a political duty; and that this should be a fundamental principle of the American government. . . . It is the function of speech to free men from the bondage of irrational fears.[25]

So constituting free speech as a safe haven underscores Americans' commitment to freedom. It also reveals Americans' distrust of government. Americans prefer citizen control over official direction.

Animated by principles of limited government and peoples' self-determination, the Supreme Court has sketched out a broad realm for free discourse. Constitutional immunity encompasses speech about public matters, like "religious faith," "political belief," or other subjects in which "sharp differences arise."[26] These differences may appear "the rankest error to [one's] neighbor."[27] For example, we saw how Jesse Cantwell offended his Catholic audience. In attempts to win converts, people like Cantwell may "resort to exaggeration, . . . vilification of men," and even "false statements."[28] Despite "the probability of excesses and abuses," the justification for this protected realm of public discourse is that, in "our diversified country, these liberties are . . . essential to enlightened opinion and right conduct on the part of the citizens of democracy."[29]

By "putting the decision as to what views shall be voiced largely into the hands of each of us," we "hope that use of such freedom will ultimately produce a more capable citizenry."[30] The hope is that free thought and communication will facilitate development of human capacity so that people will become concerned and active citizens and open-minded and tolerant individuals. Free speech encourages vital, independent, brash people. "No other approach would comport with the premise of individual dignity and choice upon which our political system rests."[31]

From the perspective of an individual, speech presents the opportunity to reevaluate and reconstitute one's life. Thought and expression always contain the "possibility of transcending what is taken for granted" or who we are at any given moment, or how society or community presently stand, as we search for a better understanding of ourselves, our world, and our future.[32] In *Ladue*, Margaret Gilleo was able to transcend the moment, seeing beyond the country's commitment to war and questioning its utility or justness. Free speech is inextricably linked to personal decision making and self-realization of capacity, attributes of human dignity that we have been examining.

Another goal of open discussion is achievement of a more "perfect polity."[33] This goal may be realized through a more democratic, informed, and fairer society. That would seem to be the intent of Paul Cohen, wearing his jacket attacking the draft, or Gregory Johnson, burning the flag, however crudely expressed. From a societal perspective, open discourse provides the communicative process necessary for formation of public opinion and the common will. As ideas impact on one another, they modify or limit one another. Out of this process a common consensus or collective "self-determination" is achieved.[34] This is especially vital to America, where speech is the introduction to the "melting pot" by which diverse and pluralistic citizenry begin to assimilate into one nation. In this sense, expression is rooted in democratic self-government, again indispensable to the American experiment in popular sovereignty. Speech provides the medium through which democracy determines its purposes. As trends, celebrities, and new developments and phenomena are discussed, the culture is formed as well. For example, we now communicate through e-mail and e-commerce, new phenomena that have seeped into the culture. Speech is integral to formation of politics and culture.

In public discourse, these ideals sometimes seem more valuable as aspirations than actually attainable goals. Indeed, one might reasonably question whether all people are sufficiently mature or enlightened to shrug off debased ideas and perceive the germ of truth or the better angelic qualities of human nature amidst the swirl of public debate. For example, how many of us could shrug off the acts of a group of teenagers who, one summer night in 1990, spent the predawn hours taping broken chair legs together to form a cross. Once completed, they placed their crudely made cross inside the fenced yard of a black family that lived near the house where one of the teenagers was staying and set the cross aflame.[35] Despite the horrific nature of the conduct, the Supreme Court, applying the First Amendment, invalidated the city ordinance that prohibited bias-motivated conduct under which the boys were prosecuted, on the grounds that the ordinance was content based and thus improperly constituted the city taking sides in the open debate.

Even though the reality may differ from the ideal, the ideal is nonetheless important. The ideal transcends reality, living on in the hearts and minds of Americans. The ideas and ideals we believe in are an important aspect of individual and national identity. America is deeply committed to the principle that government must be neutral with respect to the content of expression, notwithstanding the horrible truths of hatred, offense, or outrage that may be communicated. Among the widely divergent cultures and traditions of American society, this robust trade in ideas provides an indispensable means by which all citizens speak to or about one another, however civilly, rudely, or passionately, before deciding what to do, what values to adopt, and what ends are worth pursuing. Public discourse thus forms an important connection among all American citizens. Structurally, the First Amendment provides the protected forum for this critical dialogue.[36]

In the United States, expression is presumptively protected and cannot ordinarily be regulated, unless it fits into one of the narrowly enumerated exceptions to free discourse, such as public defamation, advocacy of violence, fighting words, or obscenity. Over the past fifty years, the Supreme Court has both narrowed, with precision, the topics that can constitute exceptions from free discourse (for example, obscenity, incitements to violence, child pornography), and, concurrently, rejected arguments for the creation of new categories beyond the protection of the First Amendment.[37] The result of this analytical dynamic is that the rules of American speech are well drawn, and these rules facilitate the ability of Americans to express freely their thoughts on almost any topic in substantially the manner they choose. The clearly demarcated playing field provides wide scope for free discussion. Rather than silencing speech on the basis of its content, majoritarian preferences must be expressed through regulation of conduct, education, or counterspeech remedies unless exigent circumstances manifesting clear, present, and serious dangers to individuals or society make such remedies wholly unworkable. In this way, the Supreme Court has carved out expression as a presumptively protected realm of activity, immune from government regulation unless justified by such exigent circumstances.

So Americans engage in their birthright, freely speaking their minds, like Jesse Cantwell, Margaret Gilleo, or those teenagers in St. Paul. Free speech appeals to the rebel, dreamer, or outcast among or within us. For many citizens, it is the best chance to speak out and be heard, to protest, dissent, or challenge convention or authority. A function of speech is to promote a vision of who we would like to be or can become.

Germany

As in America, freedom of expression occupies a central place in the constitutional order of Germany. Unlike America, expression does not hold the premier position. Human dignity is the premier value in Germany, as we have been exploring. In this way, the two constitutional edifices of free speech are constructed on different foundations.

German expression law similarly values expression along both individual and social dimensions, although their contours differ. As developed by the Constitutional Court in *Lüth*, the foundational German case on expression guarantees, the Supreme Court values communication both as an end in itself and as a means to accomplish other worthy ends:

As the most immediate manifestation of the human personality in society, the basic right to free expression of opinion is one of the noblest of all human rights. . . . To a free democratic constitutional order it is absolutely basic [*schlechthin konstituierend*], for it alone makes possible the continuing intellectual controversy, the contest of opinions that forms the lifeblood of such an order. In a certain sense it is the basis of all freedom whatsoever, "the matrix, the indispensable condition of nearly every other form of freedom.[38]

Lüth, we recall from our discussion in Chapter 1, involved a Hamburg press official, Erich Lüth, who called for the boycott of a new film by an infamous film director, Veit Harlan, who had worked under the general direction of Nazi propaganda minister Josef Goebbels, producing Nazi propaganda and anti-Semitic films, some of which were later determined to be crimes against humanity.[39] Lüth was active in a group seeking to repair relations between Christians and Jews. Incensed by Harlan's reemergence on the

German film scene, Lüth's call for a boycott was motivated by his desire to demonstrate to the world that the new German cinema was free from the darkness of the Nazi period. He believed Harlan's Nazi past would bring moral condemnation to Germany, inside and outside.[40] The case thus seemed a worthy factual setting to fashion new thought and speech freedoms for the new German constitutional order.

Viewed as an intrinsic value, communication is an important human characteristic. Free expression is an immediate and tangible manifestation of human character that is necessary for spiritual and moral growth. Expression reflects the basic human desire that one's opinion count for something, that one be able to influence the world.[41] The linkage of communication to human personality has deep roots in modern German law. We have already examined in previous chapters how article 1 human dignity and article 2 rights to free development of personality coalesce to form a certain sphere of inviolable human autonomy. Now we can see that human communication is another radiation of this core; expression is constitutive of human being, like the desires for freedom, identity, and autonomy.

The German valuation of communication for its own intrinsic worth has close parallels to American law. In American law, various nonconsequential justifications for speech have been put forth, including the views that speech is an integral part of personal development; is necessary to the achievement of control over our destinies;[42] is a constituent element of our moral autonomy that entitles us to dignity and respect;[43] or provides a basis for self-determination or self-realization in defining who we are.[44] These are all ways of expressing a concept of human dignity.

This personal dimension of communication entails the individual rights to speak, think, and inform oneself freely. For example, a number of protestors against the German army and militarism displayed placards or signs stating, "Soldiers are Murderers," in a deliberate insult, triggering a firestorm of criticism in the country about honor, duty, and the licentious of speech. Nevertheless, the Constitutional Court protected the critique: "The right to freedom of opinion guarantees everyone the right to assert freely their opinion: Everyone has the right to say what she thinks, even when she does not provide or cannot provide any verifiable reasons for her view."[45] Historically, this individual strand has been rooted in the human need for intellectual and spiritual communication and dialogue. Recent cases of the Constitutional Court markedly emphasize the importance of speaker autonomy as an integral component to the unfolding of human personality (*Persönlichkeitsentfaltung*), a distinct rooting of free speech in human personality rights.[46] The enhanced commitment to an individual's right to speak one's mind is a notable characteristic of German law in the 1990s, illustrating how German law is following the pattern set by American law.

Nevertheless, while enjoying enhanced prominence in recent years, the individual strand of German communication law has historically been subordinate to its more highly valued social component. The main German consequential rationale, strikingly, mirrors the American one: the promotion of democracy. In German law, free communication is absolutely constitutive (*schlechthin konstituierend*) to a free democratic order, as we observe again from *Lüth*.[47] Communication facilitates the ongoing public dialogue necessary for the success of democratic society. The articulation of an opinion (*Meinungsäusserung*) has an immediate "intellectual effect on the world . . . that helps build public opinion and attempts to convince adherents."[48] American law has similarly viewed democratic self-government as a central justification for speech.[49] In this way, both societies see communication as a preferred freedom: indeed, "the matrix, the indispensable condition of nearly every other form of freedom."[50] The difference in the two societies, again, is that free speech is the preferred legal value in America, whereas it is an important, but not the preeminent, value in Germany; human dignity is the most favored German value.

In view of the German focus on communication as central to the functioning of democracy, it is not surprising that public speech lies at the core of article 5 protection. In the German world of speech, communication is at the zenith to the extent it contributes to the battle of opinions (*Meinungskampf*) over matters of public concern, especially what the Constitutional Court views as fundamentally essential questions (*wesentliche berührende Frage*).[51] As in the United States, speech is thus valued most highly to the extent it aids democratic self-government, facilitating discussion and formation of the public will.[52]

In part, this reflects the value-ordering function basic rights perform in Germany, including communication rights. There is a distinct hierarchy of speech in German law, valued according to its utility in promoting desirable ends. At the top of this hierarchy is public or political speech because it is essential to the operation of democracy. German courts view communication through the prism of its contribution to "public" dialogue. A central determination in German law, accordingly, is whether communication contributes to the formation of public opinion. To the extent speech possesses "public" importance, it is presumptively protected through operation of the Presumption Principle (*Vermutungsprinzip*), a key tool by which the Constitutional Court structures public discourse. Specially prized is communication with important political or social content. A consequence of this preferencing of public speech is that it can impact detrimentally on private rights. For example, in *Lüth* the high value of the public communication concerning Harlan's reemergence in German culture eclipsed the specific private right issues of Harlan's reputation and business interests.

Or the speech may trigger harsh exchange. In the *Schmid–Spiegel* case of 1961, a high-ranking state judge (Schmid) lambasted the German press, asserting that it favored employers in labor strikes.[53] The famous German weekly newsmagazine, *Der Spiegel*, responded, characterizing the judge as having communist sympathies, even though it had information to the contrary. Judge Schmid struck back, writing in a daily newspaper and accusing the magazine of lying about him and comparing its political reporting to pornography. *Der Spiegel* was able to secure a libel judgment against Schmid, which became the basis of the lawsuit.[54]

Following *Lüth*, the Constitutional Court concluded that the lower courts had inadequately valued communication protections as compared to its interpretation of the private law rules regulating defamation. In view of the intrinsic and social value of communication, such freedoms are entitled to heightened protection in the general balancing of interests test employed by the Constitutional Court to gauge freedom of expression:

Only a free public discussion over all matters of general significance guarantees the free building of public opinion that is necessary to a free democratic state. This dialogue necessarily occurs pluralistically involving contrasting views arising from contrasting motives, freely disseminated. Above all, it consists of speech versus counterspeech. Every citizen is guaranteed the right through Article 5 to take part in this public discussion.[55]

As with the reputation of the German film industry in *Lüth*, the personal politics and trustworthiness of an important judge is a matter of deep public significance entitled to presumptive protection under the application of the Presumption Principle.

In structuring public discourse, the Constitutional Court added an important doctrinal tool, the concept of counterattack (*Gegenschlag*), that complements the Presumption Principle. As developed in the case, the harsh nature of the *Spiegel* article justified Schmid's harsh public reply to counter its impact on the formation of public opinion.[56] That a sharp attack merits a reply in kind has become a central feature of German law. *Schmid–Spiegel* also announced the now central doctrine that false statements of fact, in comparison to value judgments (*Werturteil*), are a verifiable limit on public discourse.[57] False facts can mislead or distort and thus hinder the quality of public discourse. This truth–falsity dichotomy has general resonance in American law.[58]

To an American observer, the Constitutional Court's structuring of public discourse as an open, robust, even caustic dialogue is reminiscent of American doctrine.[59] In both American and German law, the remedy for sharp or harsh speech is not suppression but more speech; speech is to be countered by speech in the American "marketplace of ideas" or the German "intellectual struggle of opinions" (*geistigen Meinungskampf*).[60] Unmistakably, the German Constitutional Court is pursuing its own "marketplace of ideas" metaphor. "Only in an equal competition of viewpoints can public opinion be realized, and can individual members of society form their personal views."[61] Choice of this metaphor seems designed mainly to facilitate the structure of public discourse, especially for achievement of a political will, as compared to seeking any more central value, like truth or advancement of knowledge more common to the American scheme. Both countries are committed to entrusting the nature of this aspect of public discourse to the people. The "marketplace of ideas" is the forum for ascertainment of truth or satisfaction, not government, community, or custom.

While such public or political communication is perhaps most prized in Germany, art, academic, research, or scientific communication also enjoy high status. In this way, German and American law have developed similarly, at least at first glance, since U.S. law also considers these categories of speech to be the most highly valued. In both countries, speech is valuable to the formation of political will necessary to democratic self-government and the discussion of general social matters necessary to the building of culture.

Conversely, speech that concerns private or self-interests, such as commercial or economic goals, is considered to be of lower value. Such communication will often yield to higher-valued constitutional principles, such as human dignity or personality rights, the topics we have been examining. An example of this is publication of the false interview of Princess Soraya, which constituted a violation of her inner personality.[62] The public–private distinction is a central determination in German communication law.

Pure commercial speech in the American sense of advertisement is not principally protected. However, expression of commercial topics is protected to the extent it involves opinion or is covered under press rights, which include publication of certain informational advertisements.[63]

Many of the content-based restrictions on communication are designed to safeguard German democracy from extremism, thereby helping safeguard it. Article 5(3) requires teachers to be loyal to the Basic Law. The ban on speech advocating Nazism and militarism, which was instituted in the denazification period following World War II, remains beyond constitutional attack.[64] In Germany, it is against the law to wear a swastika, give the Nazi salute, sell Hitler's books, or disseminate Nazi materials over the Internet.[65] Likewise, limitations on group defamation, incitement of hate, and hate speech are designed to safeguard the social order and promote social harmony.[66] And, of course, article 5 communication freedoms are themselves expressly subject to the triad restrictions of the general laws and laws protecting youth and personal honor. Other content-based exceptions include expression that threatens the democratic social order and violence, especially its accessibility to youth.[67] Most of these exceptions are attributable to the German preoccupation with preventing the reoccurrence of totalitarianism and the rise of extremist groups, and also to preserve social harmony. Justifying their need, of course, is the fundamental German concept of a "militant democracy" (*streitbare Demokratie*), which underlies the Basic Law. As we have previously examined, this term refers to government's obligation actively to protect society against threats to its stability or well-being, such as the recent crackdown on right-wing violence.

Moreover, these developments reflect the German reaction to the totalitarian control of information by the Nazi regime, which formed a main motivation for the drafters of the Basic Law; they sought to guarantee broad expression and informational rights as a means to prevent any reoccurrence of totalitarianism. By contrast, in the United States the struggle over the law of seditious libel—both at the beginning of the country over the transition from the administrations of Presidents Adams and Jefferson and at the beginning of the twentieth century over the cause of World War I—formed an important background to the development of American law.[68]

The German exceptions from free discourse stand in dramatic contrast to American law, which protects seditious libel, hate speech, and group defamation and places expression beyond the limitations of the general law. This observation again points out an influence of the value-ordered nature of the German Constitution as compared to the value-neutral American one. Of course, there is certainly more justification for such content-based exceptions in Germany than the United States. The world outside Germany rests a little easier knowing that Nazi hate cannot be disseminated there, notwithstanding the limitation of expression it represents.

But Nazi hate can be distributed in America. In 1977 American neo-Nazis, in uniforms reminiscent of Hitler's minions, obtained permission to march in Skokie, Illinois, a Chicago suburb with a large Jewish population, including 5,000 survivors of the German concentration camps.[69] Today, in America, Nazi materials are readily available over the Internet, even to German customers, much to the consternation of German authorities.[70] In fact, the leading purveyor of anti-Semitic and Nazi literature in Germany over the past twenty years has been an American, Gary Lauck, operating from America's heartland within the sanctuary of free speech.[71] Unlike Germany, the United States never experienced as severe a threat to its stability as Nazism and its ensuing horrors. Thus, the United States seems better positioned to handle the racial hatred of American neo-Nazis or teenagers who burn crosses in the dead of night on the property of despised neighbors. Despite industrial and technological revolution, there is still some sanctuary in being "kindly separated by nature and a wide ocean."[72] Certainly Gary Lauck made use of that sanctuary, losing it only after venturing beyond the country's borders, where he was arrested in Denmark and put on trial in Germany for purveying hate. The countries' contrasting treatment of Gary Lauck is one graphic difference between the two laws.

Some of the difference between American and German law is attributable to the different textual provision of expression guarantees. Choice of language reveals drafters' intentions and the legal culture sought to be constructed. American law notably tends to absolutism, consistent with its phrasing of expression guarantees. As Justice Black famously said, "The phrase 'Congress shall make no law' is composed of plain words, easily understood. . . . [The] language [is] absolute."[73] The German Basic Law, by contrast, contains a number of distinct provisions that protect expression freedoms, and these are subject to more overt constraints. The main provision is article 5, which contains seven separate freedoms.[74] The most important of these are the freedom of opinion clause, freedom to inform oneself, and the rights to pursue freely art, science, teaching, and research. In addition, article 5 provides for freedom of the press and reporting through broadcasts and film, and prohibits censorship. Article 5 is thus notable for its specificity and provision of modern communicative methods, in comparison to the older and more generally phrased First Amendment.[75] Freedoms of opinion, information, press, and reporting are textually subject to the limitations "of general laws . . . provisions for the protection of young persons, and in the right to respect for personal honor," while artistic, research and scientific freedoms are textually unbounded.[76] The textual limitation of the main communication freedoms would seem to mean that expression should not be an absolute value. Instead, the text qualifies the reach of expression through the triad of limitations.[77]

Article 8 protects the right of assembly, while article 9 secures rights of political association. Article 17 provides for the right of petition and article 21 guarantees rights of political parties, which are to participate in the formation of the public will. The German enumeration of all these freedoms encourages separate analytical treatment of each right.[78] By comparison, the American Constitution groups all expressive freedoms, including those of press, assembly, and petition, in the First Amendment. The Supreme Court has tended to develop all First Amendment freedoms within the same basic construct of a fundamental right to expression and thought.[79]

Despite the differing political, philosophical, and historical traditions from which freedom of expression arose in both countries, today it occupies a central place in each society. Interestingly for comparative purposes, the free speech law of both countries arose substantially at around the same time, the period immediately following World War II, consistent with the worldwide flowering of human rights.[80]

With this background, we are now in a good position to examine more carefully the quality of expression. Let us turn to an examination of specific topics that arise in both American and German law so that we can get a better sense of the similarities and differences in the two laws and their impact on human freedom and personality. There are many topics to choose from. For our purposes, in surveying a portrait of human personhood we will concentrate on a sampling of topics that especially reveal the nature of both laws: defamation, offensive speech and hate speech, and denigration of national symbols, such as a flag or anthem.

DEFAMATION

America

The empowering capacity of American law is facilitated especially by the rules that apply to defamation law, the body of expression where one person's speech tarnishes another's honor or reputation. For example, during a highly charged murder trial in which a policeman was convicted of killing a youth, a publication of the John Birch Society, an arch-conservative political group, ran an article accusing Elmer Gertz, the lawyer for the victim's family, of orchestrating a frame-up of the policeman, and stated that Gertz had a criminal record and long-standing communist affiliations.[81] None of this was true, and Gertz secured a libel judgment against the organization. But *Gertz* shows us how defamation can harm a person's good name. When juxtaposed against defamatory but important commentary, difficult conflicts arise between a person's right to engage in speech and the personal interest in maintaining one's good name and reputation. How this conflict is resolved sheds important insight into the assumptions and preferences of a legal culture. We have been tracing, so far, how the laws of each country empower people to develop their capacities, and these capacities have mainly been surveyed along a group of interests that can be called personality. In the United States, however, the law has developed so that free speech generally prevails over these personality interests. In Germany, by contrast, such personality interests exert far greater limitation on speech. Of course, as a reflection of thought and emotion, expression is a radiation of personality. So the real conflict is between these different radiations of personality.

The free rein of individuality at work in American law is partly a consequence of the Supreme Court's structuring of the rules that govern public defamation law. Central to the American idea is the belief that a main purpose of expression is the ability to criticize the government and its officials, a form of speech sanctioned, through history, as seditious libel.[82] The ability to criticize one's government is a central test of a country's commitment to communication freedoms, as demonstrated by recent experiences in China, the old Soviet Union, or Myanamur (the old Burma). It is also a main way by which people communicate with one another, forming the common will necessary to the governing of the country. To serve these values of democratic self-government and individual enlightenment, the Supreme Court has created a zone of immunity for speech involving public officials, public figures, or other matters of public interest.

New York Times Co. v. Sullivan is the central case that establishes these outcomes.[83] Under the *New York Times* and its progeny, people can speak ill of public officials and public figures, immunized from the sanction of tort law, insofar as they do not speak with "actual malice—that is, with knowledge that [the statement] was false or with reckless disregard of whether it was false or not."[84] Simply stated, this means that a public official must prove that a statement tarnishing his or her reputation was made with actual malice for it to be sanctionable. If the public official cannot prove that, the statement is protected. The *New York Times* is a paradigm of the American technique of categorization; by establishing clearly defined categories of proscribable speech, the zone between protected and unprotected speech is well marked, providing decision makers with clear guidelines to render dispositions on speech and thereby avoid the dangers of misapplication of doctrine and the resulting chilling of the exercise of expression freedoms that might occur.

The dynamic of categorization is a main structural technique of American expression law. Other safe havens for individual expression are clearly marked out too. Under the *Brandenburg v. Ohio* test for incitement, for example, advocacy of any idea is protected "except where such advocacy is directed to inciting or producing imminent lawless action and is likely to incite or produce such action."[85] Under this rule of *Brandenburg*, most forms of political dialogue are protected, including discussion of political theories, forms of governmental structure, and even insurgent or insurrectionist speech.

Within the safe harbors of actual malice, incitement, or other haven, people may openly comment and criticize government and its officials and public figures, resorting even to exaggeration, vilification, false statements, and insurrectionism, as long as they not do it deliberately or recklessly with respect to the truth.[86] As a consequence, individual speech rights predominate widely over the personality interests of reputation and honor. For example, in *Associated Press v. Walker* the Supreme Court reversed jury awards of $800,000 for a news report stating that Walker, a retired army general, had led a charge against federal officials enforcing a court decree ordering integration of the University of Mississippi.[87]

For these targets of defamation, public persons, like General Walker, personal interests in reputation must, for the most part, be sacrificed for the free exchange of ideas. As with Justice Brandeis's vision of "courageous, self-reliant men," such targets are viewed as "men of fortitude, able to thrive in a hardy climate."[88] In the United States, speech is for the free in spirit, thick in skin, and hardy in soul.

We can see that American defamation law groups protections according to one's status as a public or private person. A person in the public eye yields certain privacy, a price to be paid for fame. Those who enter public debate and comment become themselves objects of discussion. The public right to know and speak is preferred, on account of its central speech value, over personal privacy interests. Public persons can also defend themselves better through their more common access to the press. As conceived in German law, a public person can better fight an attack on personal reputation with a counterattack.[89] The *New York Times* rules do not apply to those not in the public eye. These private persons have a far easier time protecting their reputations and privacy.[90] In this way, a person's status matters; protection varies along the public–private fault line.

Hustler Magazine v. Falwell and Strauss Political Satire

The free individuality of American law can best be seen through the exercise of comparing, as has been the technique of this book. Here the specific contrast is between *Hustler Magazine v. Falwell* and the German case of *Strauss Political Satire*, decided around the same time.[91] In the Supreme Court case, the Court protected the expression of *Hustler* magazine, an adult-oriented, graphic sex offering. The magazine parodied a Campari liquor advertisement describing people's first time enjoying the liqueur. The magazine depicted Reverend Jerry Falwell, prominent leader of the Moral Majority, a right-wing political group, as having his first sexual encounter with his mother in an outhouse in an inebriated state. The caricature could not plausibly be viewed as a statement of fact, nor could it reasonably be construed as intentionally false sufficient to make out "actual malice," the standard for unconstitutionality appropriate to a figure of Falwell's prominence.[92] The only other grounds left to sanction the speech were hurt feelings and asserted emotional harms. According to the Supreme Court, these are pains to be borne in service to the American ideal of unfettered discourse.[93]

The *Strauss Political Satire* case contrasts dramatically with American law. In this case, caricatures of Franz Josef Strauss, a prominent national politician from Bavaria, were published that depicted him as a sexually active pig, copulating with other pigs dressed in judicial robes meant to portray "justice." The Constitutional Court found that this ribald satire exceeded the bounds of propriety.[94] The crude depiction can only be viewed as a sharp, scurrilous attack on Strauss, the Court reasoned. Sexual acts are intimate components of human dignity, as we have previously examined in Chapter 5. Depicting humans as animals, especially performing sexual acts, is a severe intrusion on human personality. By such reasoning, the Constitutional Court found a violation of Strauss's dignity as a person.[95] The case thus illustrates how human dignity and personality rights can limit individual speaker rights. In these respects, German and American law contrast dramatically over the limiting influence that personality rights have on expression.

There is more that can be said about *Falwell.* By rejecting "outrageousness" as a category of proscribable expression by which to sanction the parody, the Supreme Court explicitly rejected any official role in arbitrating acceptable norms of community, a theme presaged in earlier cases.[96] In part the Supreme Court's conclusion was based on the inherent subjectiveness of terms like "outrageousness" or "offensiveness."[97] Such terms present dangers to the First

Amendment because they allow juries or communities to sanction speech based on personal dislike of particular expression.[98] This can "cleanse public debate to the point where it is . . . palatable to the most squeamish among us."[99] But such a cleansing would be detrimental to the free exchange of ideas and the ideals to which Americans aspire. Accordingly, the Supreme Court has removed such value judgments from jury or community determination.[100] Instead, courts protect the communicative structure of speech by focusing jury deliberations on legal concepts such as the *New York Times* actual malice standard, and narrowly circumscribe community control of expression.

The deeper lesson of *Falwell*, therefore, is that concepts like "outrageousness" or "offensiveness" are inappropriate standards by which to measure the constitutionality of speech because they can be determined only by reference to "commonly accepted norms of a particular community."[101] But many culturally diverse communities exist in the United States. There is no one overarching, commonly accepted norm or set of norms constituting community. Rather, norms differ among people and among communities. "One man's vulgarity is another's lyric";[102] "One man's amusement teaches another's doctrine."[103] In America, norms or cultural standards always seem open to debate. The First Amendment safeguards this possibility of recognizing new truths and making more satisfactory choices.

Böll and Masson v. New Yorker Magazine, Inc.

A further contrast in defamation law can be derived from assessing how the two countries treat false quotations. We have previously examined this from the perspective of personality interests in Chapter 4. Now we examine this from its flip side of expression.

In the German case, *Böll*, the Constitutional Court determined that false quotations are not protected by free expression guarantees because they mischaracterize one's personality.[104]

[A misquote] impairs [a person's] . . . constitutionally guaranteed general right to an intimate sphere. Among other things this right includes personal honor and the right to one's own words; it also protects the bearer of these rights against having statements attributed to him which he did not make and which impair his self-defined claim to social recognition.[105]

Such misappropriation of words demeans individuality. In the American case of *Masson v. New Yorker*, the Supreme Court determined that the use of deliberately falsified quotations in a published interview was protected speech because such conduct did not rise to the standard of proscribable actual malice falsity.[106] Lacking such malice, the speaker and social interests in "uninhibited, robust and wide-open" public discourse were more important.[107] The contrast between *Böll* and *Masson* thus further illuminates the differing value structures of the two countries: In Germany, personality interests curtail speech more heavily; in America, the positions are reversed.

Germany

Notwithstanding these differences, German law is, increasingly, more similar to American law than different. Like American law, German defamation law is intimately bound up with the central issues of the day. In German law, we have already seen how *Lüth* introduced these ideas of speech. Under *Lüth* speech is essential, "immediately constitutive" (*schlechtin konstituierend*), for the new German order and facilitation of human capacity. But the path of German expression did not unfold as predictably as the step-by-step progression of American law.

That path, of course, begins with *Lüth*, which, as we have seen, can fairly be characterized as a speech protective regime. By the time of the 1970s, however, the speech protective design of *Lüth* had seemed to run its course, at least when speech interests came into conflict with those of personality. Under the approach initiated in the famous *Mephisto* case, the Constitutional Court tended to defer to the ordinary courts' balancing of expression rights against countervailing rights of personality.[108] With the resurgence of personality rights during this era, these rights tended to predominate over communication rights. The approach went so far in *Mephisto* that even the memory of a deceased actor, tarnished by Klaus Mann's depiction, eclipsed the artistic rights of the writer. In America it would be rather stunning if the honor of the dead affected artistic merit. Emblematic also of this approach were cases like *Soraya*, where the inner core of personality predominated over the speech interests of a fabricated interview, and *Lebach*, where, likewise, personality won out over the showing of a documentary film.[109] We have previously examined, in Chapter 4, how the nature of these personality interests outweighed expression rights, and how the positions would be reversed in the United States. Later, in the 1980s, the Constitutional Court moved away from the extreme deference of *Mephisto* and sought to strike a middle position between such deference and the heightened approach of *Lüth*.[110] The case that marked this third phase was *Deutschland–Magazin*, where the Constitutional Court announced a variable standard of review: The degree of the Court's scrutiny depended on the severity of the incursion of the constitutional right.[111]

With this background, we can see that German communication law stood at a threshold as it approached the 1990s. The value of communication would seem to depend on the sense of the German Constitutional Court. The Constitutional Court could employ the variable standard to enhance communication freedoms.[112] Conversely, it could attach more importance to other constitutional rights, like article 2 personality rights, which would then have the effect of trumping communication rights, as in *Böll*. Thus, German law in the 1990s faced a choice: whether to prefer communication or personality rights.

The way chosen by the Constitutional Court, decisive for the development of modern German law, was to preference communication rights. The Constitutional Court embarked upon this task in a remarkable series of decisions that initiated the 1990s. Two of these important cases were libel judgments involving the prominent and controversial German politician, Franz Josef Strauss.[113] Two other cases involved denigration of national symbols, one involving the national flag and the other the national anthem.[114] One of the two *Strauss* cases we will examine now, both for its conception of expression freedoms and for the idea of defamation posited; the two national symbol cases we will examine later in this chapter.

Stern–Strauss Interview

The case marking the shift most dramatically was *Stern–Strauss Interview*, which involved an interview with a prominent writer, Ralph Giordano, published in the leading magazine, *Stern*, to mark the death of Rudolph Hess, the former Nazi leader.[115] In the course of the interview Giordano used Strauss as an illustration of his view that not all German politicians were true democrats; some were "opportunistic democrats" (*Zwangsdemokraten*), those who out of political necessity or opportunism proclaimed democracy and adopted democratic ideals, even though they might prefer to act more dictatorially.[116] "For me Franz Josef Strauss is the personification of this type. . . . This type—which I want to depersonalize, because it in no way concerns only Franz Josef Strauss—is very active in the Federal Republic."[117] As powerful men and personalities, these people appeal to the "not yet resolved German desire for a strong man, the so-called German version [*Verschnitt*] of a national socialism Leadercult [*Führerkult*]."[118] Giordano, who was a Jewish survivor of a concentration camp and had a long history of opposition to the reestablishment of Nazism in Germany, viewed such "opportunistic democrats" as a danger to German democracy.[119] The lower courts accepted Strauss's argument that he had been libeled, enjoining further use of his name to personify the term "opportunistic democrat."[120]

In exercising constitutional review, the Constitutional Court signaled its return to the view that communication was special, as expressed in *Lüth*.[121] While it is true that freedom of opinions rights are limited by the general law, the Constitutional Court noted that the general law, in turn, is subject to the fundamental values of the Basic Law according to the Reciprocal Effect Theory.[122] The lower courts failed to adequately take this constitutive value of the Basic Law into account. To assure compliance with the Basic Law, the Constitutional Court therefore found it necessary to heighten its scrutiny. Intensive, full-scope judicial scrutiny will occur upon the lower courts' misinterpretation of the meaning and range of fundamental rights, the Court asserted.[123] When communication freedoms are at issue, intensive review will apply when those freedoms are incorrectly understood or evaluated. This may arise when courts wrongly interpret a communication; assign a meaning to a communication that it does not objectively have; or when a court interprets a communication in a way that leads to a finding that it may be regulated, without adequate substantiation of the reasons underlying its choice, including the reasons why other plausible, legal interpretations were dismissed. Communication rights are also denied when courts misclassify opinions as unprotected factual assertions, libel, or defamation.[124]

As phrased, this test of full-range review (*in vollem Umfang überprüfbar sein*) posits a limited but intensive role for the Constitutional Court.[125] The role is limited in that the Constitutional Court regularly defers to the ordinary courts' fixing of procedure, establishment and evaluation of the facts, and interpretation of the ordinary law, as is customary in the German constitutional order. However, the role is intensive in that the Court noticeably sharpens its review of the lower courts' interpretation of constitutional norms, as already described. This is an important change compared to earlier, more deferential versions of judicial review, such as that in *Mephisto* or even *Deutschland–Magazin*.[126]

Notwithstanding its tightening of review, the Constitutional Court yet insists that the balancing of interests take place in the ordinary courts. The Constitutional Court's stance appears to be out of deference to the traditional distinction in Germany between public and private law, and the distinction since 1949 of the Constitutional Court and the ordinary courts. The main role of the

Constitutional Court in the constitutional order thus remains unchanged: to exercise close supervision of the ordinary courts' balancing of constitutional norms to assure that those values are adequately taken into account. Under this regime, it is common for the Constitutional Court to remand decisions to the ordinary courts for a reapplication of the balancing test in view of the factors prescribed by the Court. This is what happened in the *Stern–Strauss Interview*. Thus, as before, the ordinary courts will often have the last word, subject to the Constitutional Court's directives on interpretation and application of constitutional principles.[127]

To an American observer, the standard of review announced in *Stern–Strauss Interview* is more reminiscent of American "hard-look" administrative law review than American strict scrutiny constitutional law review. As in American hard-look review, the German Constitutional Court looks to see whether the lower courts have correctly fixed the procedure, assessed the facts, interpreted the general law and the Basic Law accurately, and thoroughly explained its conclusions.[128] If these factors are correctly applied, the Court will normally uphold the lower court decision, even if it would have reached a different conclusion. True to its continental roots, the German Court will not ordinarily substitute its judgment for that of the lower courts. This attempt to respect the authority of ordinary courts and yet uphold constitutional norms probably explains the Constitutional Court's choice of this form of intensive review as compared to the stricter scrutiny of American courts.[129] The German Court is somewhat more constrained by its desire not to intrude too deeply into the province of the ordinary courts, a hesitation not always shared by the U.S. Supreme Court. Still, by forcing ordinary courts to make their reasoning transparent, the Constitutional Court better performs its assigned role as guardian of the constitution.

Acknowledging the lower court's recognition of the prevalent view that communication rights are qualified by personality rights, the Constitutional Court in *Stern–Strauss Interview* found it necessary to recalibrate speech freedoms within the German constitutional order. Communication freedoms are essential to the free development of personality, with which they are closely linked, the Constitutional Court reasoned.[130] So defined, communication is an important part of human dignity. The Court thereby reasserted the importance of the individual component of expression. By this reasoning, the Constitutional Court set out to recapture the earlier prominence of communication as developed in cases like *Lüth* or *Schmid–Spiegel*. Reemphasis of this individual component still compliments the democratic component of expression as regulated by the conventional Presumption Principle favoring political speech.[131] Indeed, the Constitutional Court went on to sketch the contours of public discourse in a way previously envisioned by the U.S. Supreme Court in cases like *New York Times v. Sullivan* or *Cantwell v. Connecticut*.[132] "Especially in public dialogue [*öffentliche Auseinandersetzung*], including political campaigns, criticism must be accepted, even exaggerated [*überspitzt*] and polemical [*polemisch*] forms, because otherwise there is a danger of chilling [*Lähmung*] or limiting [*Verengung*] the process by which opinion is formed."[133] Public persons naturally must expect criticism.[134]

Assessing the facts anew against this revised doctrinal framework, the Constitutional Court found fault with the interpretation of the lower court. The comments about Strauss could be viewed as denigrating. Labeling anyone a Nazi in postwar Germany is a very low blow.[135] Measured against the German version of hard-look review, however, this was not the only interpretation of the statement. It is much more likely that the statement was directed to the German people as a warning that their longing for a strongman was dangerous to German democracy. Strauss was merely an object of this longing. This seemed especially likely to the Constitutional Court because Giordano had previously, in a book, counted Strauss as an "opportunistic democrat" and an object of the German longing for a strongman, but specifically rejected any comparison of Strauss with Hitler.[136] Moreover, the author had sought to depersonalize the reference to Strauss. Thus, viewing the statement "objectively," it simply did not have the defamatory meaning ascribed to it by the lower court.[137] Rather than defamation, the statement was an important contribution to the free formation of opinion, protected under the Presumption Principle because of its value to German democracy.[138]

This reassessment of the communication forced the Constitutional Court to redefine libel for purposes of article 5 freedoms. Purposeful denigration and insult (*überzogene und selbst eine ausfällige Kritik*) do not themselves constitute libel, the Constitutional Court reasoned, in a move in the direction of American law.[139] Rather, the line between protected speech (even if sharp or insulting) and unprotected libel lies at the point where the statement primarily defames the person without any other substantive value. Obviously, such a distinction is not an easy one to make, and one might question the ability of the Constitutional Court or any court in working out such an obtuse standard.[140] The Constitutional Court ought to delineate clearer boundaries between protected expression and unprotected libel or defamation. A useful legal transplantation in this context would be the technique of categorization employed by the Supreme Court in cases like *New York Times v. Sullivan*. In the absence of sharpening legal definitions, the standard must, most likely, await clarification through case application, not unlike the American common law method.

Applying this test, the Constitutional Court interpreted the statement as primarily concerning the role of opportunistic politicians in German public life, not a defamatory personal attack on Strauss. "In the foreground was the objective statement and [Strauss] came into play only as an illustration of the type."[141] "The statement was primarily a warning that it is necessary to protect and safeguard the German democratic order from threats."[142] Since the appellate court had inaccurately interpreted the statements, the Constitutional Court remanded the case with instructions to reperform the balancing of interests with greater attention to expression values.[143] By such reasoning, the outcome in *Strauss Political Satire*, just three years earlier, might turn out differently. Certainly freedoms of expression are being placed ahead of those of personal honor.

GROUP DEFAMATION

A group of people may be tarnished by speech as well as an individual. Ordinarily, this would occur when speech attacks a characteristic or trait people have in common, such as ethnicity, nationality, gender, or other status. It might also occur when people are targeted for the associations they form or status they assume. This was the case when protestors attacked German soldiers as murderers in the cases of that name, as we shall examine. The idea of group defamation presents a significant contrast between the two laws.

America

There is no idea of group defamation in American law. Why this is so goes to the rubrics of American speech. First, American fundamental rights are conceived as individual, personal rights, not group rights. On this reasoning, a right to be free from group defamation has long been rejected.[144] Second, even conceived as individual rights, America may be the only land which tolerates hate speech and other extremist speech to such an extent. Cases like *R.A.V. v. St. Paul* or *Collins v. Smith* are explainable only as commitments to the American ideal of unfettered public discourse.[145] These ideals are worth adhering to, in the American view, despite the painfully high price to be borne in service to them. Third, American concepts of human dignity and personality rights are underdeveloped in relation to Germany. Thus, in America, expression has a relatively free rein, less encumbered by such civility norms. Freedom to speak one's mind, however crudely or rudely, is quintessential to being American.

Germany

In modern Germany, group defamation, especially when based on incitement of hate against race or ethnicity, is taboo.[146] Obviously, this reflects the catastrophe of World War II, never far from the minds of Germans. That lesson has now been incorporated into the objective ordering of values in Germany, subsumed within constitutional concepts like article 1 human dignity, as illustrated in the *Auschwitz Lie* case.[147] In the case, the Constitutional Court approved a prior restraint of a planned demonstration to publicize the demonstrators' belief that the Holocaust never occurred.[148] Despite the broad presumption favoring opinion rights, especially over public matters, as here, the Constitutional Court reasoned that the demonstration was based on the demonstrably false fact that the Holocaust never occurred.[149] False facts are without protection under German law.

Even if the communication was viewed as one of mixed fact and opinion, which ordinarily would be treated as presumptively protected opinion, the ban would still stand.[150] For then a balance must yet be struck with countervailing limitations. Applying the balance, opinions based on false facts receive little weight. By contrast, the law prohibiting group defamation and incitement of racial hatred, acting as a general law limitation on opinion rights, is a strong interest.[151] For Jewish people the Holocaust is inextricably part of their identity and personal dignity, the Constitutional Court reasoned. Respect for dignity, a fundamental principle of Germany, is a key guarantee that such persecution will not take place again. On such reasoning, the demonstration will produce group defamation, which outweighs the minimal communicative value at issue.[152] So the rights of groups can, in the right circumstance, outweigh individual rights. The recent rise of neo-Nazis groups and other extremists and their persecution of German minorities following the reunification of Germany would seem to fortify this conclusion. *Auschwitz Lie* thus vividly illustrates a distinct circumscription of German communicative freedoms, notwithstanding the flowering of free expression in recent years.

Soldiers Are Murderers I

Few cases have stirred modern passions as much as the recent set of *Soldiers Are Murderers* decisions, cases that reaped immediate and sharp criticism among the German public, necessitating a response by the full Constitutional Court in *Soldiers Are Murderers II* just one year after the rendering of the more cursory chamber opinion in *Soldiers Are Murderers I*.[153] Group defamation is again at the center of the controversy. All the notoriety involved attacks on the German army and militarism, a defamation by group association as compared to that of status in *Auschwitz Lie*.

The controversy at issue in *Soldiers Are Murderers I*, for example, concerned a protest of the 1991 Gulf War. Affixed to the car of the protestor, himself a famous conscientious objector from the draft, was a sticker that read, "Soldiers are Murderers." The *T* in the German word for soldier (*Soldaten*) was replaced with a cross. Below the sticker was a facsimile signature of Kurt Tucholsky, a reference to a famous playwright of the 1930s.[154] Another sticker depicted the famous photo by Robert Capa of a soldier during the 1936 Spanish Civil War shown being killed by a bullet at the point of impact with hands outstretched and weapon falling, with the caption, "Why?" A third sticker pronounced "Turn swords into plowshares."[155] The lower courts took the expression "murderer" literally, subjecting it to the criminal code, and interpreted "why?" and "soldiers" as directed at the German army, as compared to soldiers or war generally.[156] Based on this reasoning, the court ruled that the communication was proscribable as insulting and as hate inciting (*Volksverhetzung*).

Subjecting these findings to hard-look review, the Constitutional Court found that the communications simply did not objectively have those meanings. Rather, the communications were more logically interpreted as a general protest against war.[157] The use of "murderer" had a slang, idiomatic sense, not a technical criminal meaning; "why?" and "soldiers" were meant as a general protest against war, not as an attack on the military. The Constitutional Court thus remanded the case to the lower court to reperform the balancing of interests in view of the Court's instructions on the value of expression.

Despite what seems an easy case—to the Constitutional Court and to an American observer—the decision provoked a great outcry in Germany.[158] Perhaps this is because German civility norms have generally succeeded in shielding soldiers and governmental officials from sharp attack. Perhaps this is because the public recognizes what is apparent: German law in the 1990s empowers individualism more than before, and the change has occurred in a relatively short time, sneaking up somewhat on cat's feet to an unprepared public. The free individualism of German law has had the effect of encouraging a crude or rude tone to German public discourse, as in American law.

The theoretical underpinning for this enhanced emphasis on individualism flows from a recalibration of German constitutional norms. *Soldiers Are Murderers I* illustrates the doctrinal adjustment. The Constitutional Court defines communication freedoms as "in the interest of the right to personal development, with which communication is closely linked, as well as in the interest of the democratic process, for which it has constitutive meaning."[159] Since "the purpose of communication is to try to exert intellectual influence on the world—to effect the formation of opinion, and to convince [others]," one can say that to speak freely is essential to the human condition.[160] So conceived, communication can be linked integrally to the central values of article 1 human dignity and article 2 development of personality. Conceived as an essential part of human dignity, communication freedoms have a more solid theoretical ground than, for example, reliance on self-government. This builds a more solid base for expression, making it more difficult to limit. In this way, communication freedoms in the 1990s have been reconceived as truly among the most fundamental values of German society, a realization of the *Lüth* paradigm.[161]

In these respects, the development of modern German law parallels the movement in America, where the law has recently also emphasized the individual right to speak one's mind. In cases like *Hustler Magazine v. Falwell* or *R.A.V. v. St. Paul*, one might say free speech has almost become an end unto itself, pursued for the sake of the ideal of unfettered discourse, notwithstanding serious social and personal consequences that may ensue.[162] Under this regime, few limitations on public discourse will be permitted indeed, since to limit speech is to strike at a foundation of individuality and society.

Soldiers Are Murderers II

However well such thoughts might ring within academic circles, acceptance by the public is a different story. Far from being resolved by *Soldiers Are Murderers I*, the controversy arising from the Constitutional Court's protection of remarks that "soldiers are murderers" continued to fester and percolate throughout German society, resulting in serious and sustained criticism of the Constitutional Court.[163] Attempting to bring some closure to this open wound—more from a social perspective than a legal one—the Constitutional Court revisited these issues in *Soldiers Are Murderers II*.[164] This was an unprecedented gesture for the Court, coming on the heels of its earlier resolution of the controversy not more than one year before. Perhaps sensing its leadership role was on the line, the Constitutional Court attempted to quell the controversy, acting in a manner reminiscent of the Supreme Court in great American controversies, such as the *Brown v. Board of Education* desegregation dispute or the *Roe v. Wade* abortion controversy.[165]

Soldiers Are Murderers II was a consolidated appeal involving four cases of insult directed at the German army involving remarks that "soldiers are murderers" or "soldiers are potential murderers." In all four cases the ordinary courts found the speech sanctionable as criminal insult or slander and assessed money damages. The courts reasoned, in essence, that calling soldiers "murderers" stamped them as "criminals," thereby dehumanizing and denigrating them in the eyes of the public. This was a severe violation of their honor. The Constitutional Court split 5–3 over the disposition of three of the four cases, reflecting the division of opinion in the country, deciding only Case no. 2 by unanimous vote.[166]

In deciding to rehear the controversy, it thus seems clear that the Constitutional Court was more interested in addressing the German public and the judges of the ordinary courts than resolving the technical legal merits of the dispute, which, after all, it had already accomplished one year before. The main goal of the Constitutional Court was thus educational: to restate the fundamental tenants of free expression jurisprudence so that these lessons of German constitutionalism might best be imparted to society. This desire was certainly in keeping with the European belief that a purpose of law is to instruct. And the main lesson was that German citizens are free to speak their minds, even when these rights might conflict with protection of honor. Speech is increasingly favored over honor, a legacy of the 1990s. "Protected also is choice over the time and place of communication. A speaker possesses the right not only to publicize his opinion. He may also choose those circumstances which best afford the greatest dissemination or the strongest effect for his views."[167] In establishing such definitive speaker control over the form and circumstance of communication, the Constitutional Court deepened the scope of communication rights. The development is another move in the direction of American law, treating form and content as integrated aspects of communication.[168]

Expression must at times yield to the harms caused by defamation, the Constitutional Court noted. However, because excessive protection of personal honor can suffocate speech freedoms, the category of proscribable defamation must be narrowly construed.[169] To the extent the speech at issue involves an "essentially important question" of public discourse, even personal privacy interests may have to yield. Questions decisive for public discourse are presumptively protected.[170]

Shifting focus from principle to application, the Constitutional Court next considered the importance of the words or language actually used. "The precondition for every legal evaluation of a communication is . . . that its meaning be appropriately discerned. . . . Failure to understand properly a remark may lead to its suppression," which can chill assertion of expression rights. Thus, it is critical first to focus on the "meaning of the disputed remark."[171] Only by fairly understanding the content of speech, independent of its effects, can one determine its worth. Considered against these principles, the conclusions reached by the ordinary courts did not measure up. The deficiency in the ordinary courts' interpretations was that they assumed the remarks to be insulting without satisfactorily substantiating that conclusion. The Constitutional Court expanded the reasons for its conclusion.

First, the speakers made reference to all soldiers, not specific, identifiable ones nor even the defined set of soldiers who were members of the German army. The reference to the German army was just to make clear that the "statement all soldiers applied also to soldiers in the German army."[172] The context thus suggests that the statement "condemned soldiers and war generally." "Use of the word 'murderer' does not necessarily connote . . . its criminal connotation. . . . It is much more likely that what was meant was that killing during wartime is not an impersonal event but rather an act of man."[173] Thus, one cannot exclude an interpretation intending to show that the speaker meant to prick the conscience of soldiers so that they would assume personal responsibility for their actions and perhaps become conscientious objectors. In short, the Constitutional Court sensed that the remarks were meant more as a type of Brechtian theater—designed to produce a shock effect and thus focus attention on an important message—than as personal insults.

Second, the ordinary courts' conclusions that the statements were defamatory did not measure up to the prevailing definition of defamation. Defamation is sanctionable only when personal harm is the focus of the communication with any substantive content receding into the background, the definition set forth in *Stern–Strauss Interview*.[174] This definition is to be construed very narrowly, out of concern that loose interpretation will detrimentally chill exercise of expression rights.[175] The Constitutional Court chose to do this by tightening application of the definition. By contrast, the Supreme Court has accomplished the same end by narrowing the definition of defamation itself and then scrutinizing its application.[176] Despite the differing methodologies, the end result is the same: protecting expression through limiting its restriction to specifically enumerated, narrowly defined categories. Thus, the remarks are proscribable only "if they actually involved defamation."[177]

Tested against the standard of *Stern–Strauss Interview*, the Constitutional Court did not find the remarks to be defamatory. "The questions whether war and military service and their resulting killing of men is morally justifiable or not" is an important issue.[178] Indeed, "resistance to militarism and support of pacifism constitutes an essentially important question for public discourse for which a presumption of protection applies [Presumption Principle]."[179] Thus, the ordinary courts needed to consider whether these substantively valuable comments were pushed into the background by elements of defamation, as compared to the courts' approach of assuming that the statements were defamatory without independently proving their harm. Lacking persuasive proof of harm, the remarks could not be defamatory.

German law still provides for a concept of group defamation, as made clear in *Auschwitz Lie* or *Soldiers Are Murderers II*, in dramatic contrast to American law.[180] However, even under the concept of group defamation, the element of harm to group members must be at the fore.[181] This is likely to occur in two ways. One way is recognizable hate speech, consisting of denigration of characteristics like "ethnicity, race, or physical or mental attributes."[182] The denigration of Jewish people in *Auschwitz Lie* is an example of this. The second way is when statements denigrate specific people or associations of people.[183] In both cases, proof of harm is necessary, which was not evident in any of the cases at issue in *Soldiers Are Murderers II*. Beyond these two categories, it is more likely that any remark involves critical but protected commentary on a group's activities or social function.[184]

By tightening these definitions and demanding clear proof of harm caused by communication, the Constitutional Court is very much following the Supreme Court's lead in lending some precision to legal categories so that they might be applied discriminately. This should enhance protection of expression. Communication should be evaluated on its own terms—for whatever value is to be derived—independent of any harm it might cause. By separating communication from harm, each can be evaluated independently. By then applying the Constitutional Court's complete balancing regime, the relative merits and demerits of each can be compared to see which is weightier in the concrete circumstance.[185]

OFFENSIVE SPEECH

The idea of offensive speech is speech that causes offense to a listener. For speech to cause such offense, naturally, it involves some epithet, coarse or abusive language, or similar such crudity. For example, the prototypical case in American law is Paul Cohen's wearing of a jacket bearing the words "Fuck the Draft" in a public court room in 1971, the time of the Vietnam War.[186]

Now certainly there may be pleasure but no real merit in causing offense to others; it does not pay, in the long run, to be an annoyance. So the rationale for this type of speech does not lie wholly with the listener. Rather, protection of offensive speech tests the ability of a person to speak his or her mind, and also society's commitment to free speech. The social interest in offensive speech lies in allowing dissemination of unpopular ideas and words, challenging convention and imparting hard truths. Exposure to offensive speech also tests personal character. How a person responds is important. In America, the preferred response is not censorship but counterspeech—that is, speech to counter the disagreeable message, educating the speaker to behave better. If these measures fail, a person should develop a thick skin and walk away. Learning to get along with others in a diverse society is important, affording others their freedom, if not respect. As stated by Justice Kennedy, "To endure the speech of false ideas or offensive content and then to counter it is part of learning how to live in a pluralistic society, a society which insists upon open discourse towards the end of a tolerant citizenry."[187]

America

In American law, speech that merely causes offense to the listener may not be regulated by its content, leading to firm constitutional protection. This is a well-embedded principle of American communication law. In *Terminiello v. Chicago*, for example, the Supreme Court stated "a function of free speech under our system of government is to invite dispute. It may indeed best serve its high purpose when it induces a condition of unrest, creates dissatisfaction with conditions as they are, or even stirs people to anger."[188] Stated differently, the Supreme Court has a "longstanding refusal to allow damages to be awarded because the speech in question may have an adverse emotional impact on the audience."[189]

The leading case today for the proposition that offensive speech is protected is *Cohen v. California*, where the Supreme Court protected the crude war protest because the message, without more, merely provoked offense, and did not present any real "clear and present danger."[190] The proposition made manifestly clear in *Cohen* is that mere offense experienced by the listener is an insufficient reason on which to base regulation of speech.

In part this determination reflects the view that there is an inherent subjectiveness to the standard of offense: "One man's vulgarity is another's lyric."[191] Offensiveness, like outrageousness, is not susceptible to decision by a principled standard. Regulation of speech according to one's fancy would "cleanse public debate to the point where it is grammatically palatable to the most squeamish among us."[192] And in part this determination is based on the belief that free debate can best determine the course and quality of expression, not government or majoritarian control. Thus, the remedy for offensive speech is self-policing, like averting one's eyes or exiting the area of offense, not governmental control or "censorship."

> We are often "captives" outside the sanctuary of the home and subject to objectionable speech. . . . [The] ability of government, consonant with the Constitution, to shut off discourse solely to protect others from hearing it is, in other words, dependent upon a showing that substantial privacy interests are being invaded in an essentially intolerable manner. Any broader view of this authority would effectively empower a majority to silence dissidents simply as a matter of personal predilections.[193]

This effectively shifts the focus of regulation away from content (the offensiveness of the message) to issues of context (such as privacy, like one's home).

In the United States, offensive speech stands as a graphic reminder of the individuality at the root of American conceptions to freedom. Americans, through their individual expressions, control the tenor of discussion in the society, facilitating the building of democracy and culture.

Germany

German law on offensive speech has followed the progression of defamation law already discussed. Earlier regimes of expression allowed more control of the quality and tone of German speech, but the more recent trend approximates the freer tone of American law.

The earlier regime is characterized by *Deutschland–Magazin*, where a labor union press service distributed an article attacking the conservative *Deutschland–Magazin* as "a right-radical hate sheet" (*rechtsradikales Hetzblatt*), a form of nasty political epithet in post–World War II Germany.[194] Right-wing politics was the topic of controversy, as is so many of the early German cases. Confirming the judgments of the lower courts, the Constitutional Court ruled that the labor union was entitled to make the basic criticism, but that it had to express its charge in words less scurrilous than the ones chosen. The Court viewed the content of expression as different and separable from the particular form of expression.[195]

In *Deutschland–Magazin*, the Court did not find the curtailment of the speaker's rights to be a particularly severe measure. The speaker was only prohibited from using the phrase "right-radical hate sheet." That idea could easily be expressed in other language. Thus, it might be argued, the Court had not really prohibited communication of the idea so much as the form of that communication. Moreover, the sanction placed on the speaker—the prohibition on repeating the phrase—was thought to be minor.[196] Accordingly, no high-level review was merited. In this way, *Deutschland–Magazin* could be viewed as distinguishable from *Lüth*, where the injunction against communication of the speaker's idea was a severe limitation that merited searching review.

From an American perspective, the *Deutschland–Magazin* Court's restriction of the speaker's chosen communication would hardly be viewed as mild. Chosen words or expressions are fundamental aspects of speech in the American view, as much an integral part of the communication as its content. Thus, the German Constitutional Court's limitation of certain scurrilous epithets is a notable contrast with American law.[197] In the United States, control of the use or abuse of speech lies primarily with the people in the exercise of self-government. In Germany, by contrast, the Constitutional Court takes a more activist role in circumscribing the terms of public discourse around a more ascertainable line of propriety. Sharp and caustic speech is permissible, but not reckless or insulting language.[198] In this way, German law exhibits a stronger civility limitation than American. Responsibilities of citizenship weigh heavier, calling for a softer tone of language.

Yet as we observe from our discussion of defamation law, modern German law bestows somewhat more personal control over the tenor of discussion. Calling soldiers "murderers" is a good example. In that case, the Constitutional Court observed that even such offense was protected. "Protected also is choice over the time and place of communication. A speaker possesses the right not only to publicize his opinion. He may also choose those circumstances which best afford the greatest dissemination or the strongest effect for his views."[199] So treating form and content as integrated aspects of communication that are up to the speaker illustrates the freer tone of modern law.

HATE SPEECH

Hate speech is a particularly venal variety of offensive speech, as it targets another based on status, such as race, ethnicity, gender, sexual orientation, or creed, communicating hatred. Few nations protect such rancor. The nations of Europe and international conventions ban it. America may be the only land committed to freedom over these ideas.

America

By hate speech, Americans mean speech intended to express hate toward a person because of the person, usually because of the status of the person: his or her race, religion, ideological persuasion, gender, or sexual orientation. Hate speech of that sort is protected in America, in contrast to almost all, if not all, other countries in the world.

The leading case establishing protection of hate speech is *R.A.V. v. St. Paul*, a complicated case doctrinally and a harsh case factually.[200] Recall again that several teenagers fashioned a cross from a broken chair, placed it in the fenced-in yard of a black family that had recently moved into the neighborhood, and set it ablaze. Despite the gruesomeness of the act, singeing the conscience of the nation in its symbolic recall of the dark history of lynching, the Supreme Court found the actions legal as a matter of communication law because of the content discrimination present in the city ordinance used to sanction the acts, although the Supreme Court conceded the acts might be punishable as offenses under the criminal law, such as arson or trespass.[201] *R.A.V.* thus illustrates the near absolute commitment of the Court to the principle of free communication of ideas, notwithstanding the harm or pain caused by such expression. Such pain is, in the view of the Court, a burden to be borne in service to the idea of free expression. *R.A.V.* makes this dramatically clear in rejecting any new categorical exception from the First Amendment based on hate speech and in rejecting equality arguments on behalf of a person's status that would fortify such exception in opposition to the claims of free speech. A case like *R.A.V.* vividly demonstrates that free speech is the most fundamental organizing principle of American society today.

Based on *R.A.V.*, therefore, and on other cases, Americans are free to express hatred to one another, even on account of a person's race, religion, or gender as they are on most topics, including expression of offensive, outrageous, insulting, or disquieting speech.[202] In constitutionally protecting such hate speech, it is not that Americans are unsympathetic to the very real personal or social harm that might result from this expression, nor that they want to encourage people to be rude, crude, or hurtful to others. Rather, it is the deep American committment to free speech that dictates this outcome, and the accompanying view that messages of hate are better confronted openly in the free exchange of ideas rather than silenced through the force of law.[203] Ultimately, Americans trust people to make judgments about the use or abuse of speech; Americans trust people more than government. In this way, Americans rely on people and the political process to sort out the problems and consequences of speech, including its exaggerations, vilifications, and stirring of emotions. Unfortunately, the personal hurts caused by hate speech are an inevitable by-product of commitment to such unfettered discourse.

There is also an argument that hate speech reveals important truths about our world. We learn about the ugliness of speakers' messages or minds, thoughts grounded in ugly ideas such as racism, sexism, genocide, or ethnic cleansing. Unfortunately, our world, or part of it, is still ugly. The wars in Yugoslavia were a rude reminder of that. As with human nature, it is better to confront such hard truths than to repress them. Silencing hate speech dangerously misleads us from the fact that such ugliness exists. It is healthy to be reminded of the reality that the world is ugly. Only by recognizing evil can we face it and hope to change it. Thus, the real response to hate speech is to change the world.

Yet the world is hard to change. Ideas on speech may ring better in the classroom than in society. America has historically suffered its share of racism and discrimination. There is a deep irony in this. The United States is the most pluralistic country in the world. But not everyone has been assimilated in the "melting pot," the process by which all nationalities become American. Ethnic diversity also appears to have helped breed racism and discrimination.[204] In 1999 alone, a black man was dragged to his death behind a truck by two white supremacists; a gay man was tied to a post, like a crucifix, and left to die in the desert; and a neo-Nazi targeted, by shotgun, a Jewish community center.[205] Hatred cannot always be contained.

A companion case to *R.A.V.*, *Wisconsin v. Mitchell*, decided one year later, fleshed out the contours of the hate speech doctrine of *R.A.V.*, helping point the way toward a solution.[206] In *Mitchell*, the Supreme Court sustained a statute that enhanced criminal penalties for hate-inspired crimes. The Supreme Court justified this apparent discrepancy with a finding that the Wisconsin statute regulated only conduct, not speech, and thus the First Amendment was not implicated.[207] Viewing the cases of *R.A.V.* and *Mitchell* together, it is apparent more than ever that the Court is attempting to separate speech from conduct to the extent possible. Speech is presumptively protected because choices regarding expression have been largely left to individuals out of respect for human dignity, the pursuit of truth, or the concern that governments are too self-interested to regulate impartially. To be protected constitutionally, the act must possess communicative qualities, such as the burning of the cross in *R.A.V.* or a burning of a flag. In contrast, to the extent an act implicates little or no communicative value, there is little reason to shield it from government regulation. The government has a much stronger reason to regulate behavior when, like the arson or trespass in *R.A.V.*, or the assault and battery in *Mitchell*, the behavior is not primarily communicative.[208] Under *Mitchell*, the hate crimes of 1999, already mentioned, would be punishable. Separation of speech from conduct lies at the frontier of the Supreme Court's public discourse jurisprudence.

Germany

In Germany, hate speech is unconstitutional because of the harm to personality it represents. This is especially the case because Nazi Germany caused significant persecution based on personal status, especially that of being Jewish, disabled, homosexual, or gypsy. Human dignity arose as the barrier to protect against such personal denigration, as we have explored. Under modern German law, therefore, denigrating speech over race, ethnicity, gender, or physical appearance is outlawed.[209] At bottom, Germans do not completely trust people to make appropriate judgments about racial or other invective, a legacy of the Holocaust. More active monitoring of hate speech is therefore permissible than in the United States.

Cripple is the best case to illustrate the difference between the two laws over hate speech.[210] The case involved a published political satirization of a soldier who had recently been rendered a quadriplegic in an automobile accident. Despite his disability, he wanted yet to serve in the German army as a Czech translator. In a widely circulated Sunday paper, *Bild am Sonntag*, the soldier had asserted, "I don't know why the army declined my offer to serve: My head is still o.k."[211] A satirical magazine, *The Titanic*, poked fun at the soldier by featuring him in a regular column, "The Seven Most Embarrassing Personalities of the Month," complete with picture, alongside the designation "born murderer."[212] Text accompanying the picture stated that it was obscene to imagine that a quadriplegic would still want to serve in the army. "My head is still o.k., he says. . . . Soldiers are still able to act with impunity as potential murderers."[213]

The Constitutional Court found that the communication was intended as political satire and as an antimilitaristic statement.[214] In protecting these aspects of the communication, the Court displayed sensitivity to critical speech, noting that such is offensive and prone to suppression, which the Court must guard against.

While these aspects of the Constitutional Court's decision were speech protective, the Court's approval of a ban on use of the word "cripple" was speech restrictive. In response to the soldier's suit,

The Titanic's publisher had printed a reply in the magazine in which he stated that he found it obscene that the soldier, now a cripple, would yet want to serve in the military. "The fact that you, a cripple, . . . are determined to join . . . the German army, whose purpose it is to cripple or kill people we found obscene and named you as one of the seven most embarrassing personalities of March."[215] Use of the word "cripple" is demeaning, the Constitutional Court reasoned, because it connotes that a person is of lesser human worth. "Today, calling someone a 'cripple' is understood as a humiliation. It stamps someone as a person of lesser worth. . . . This is a severe violation of the complainant's personality rights. . . . [Banning the word] is not a burden on freedom of opinion."[216] As such, it is a formal insult punishable under the criminal code. *Cripple* teaches unmistakably that certain words are proscribable as a violation of fundamental human dignity.

While the strength of personality rights as a restraint on article 5 freedoms has diminished from its zenith in the 1970s, *Cripple* attests to the continuing strength of such rights. The German outcome contrasts dramatically with American law. Under American law, words themselves are almost always protected, notwithstanding their harm, because of the overriding value of speech, a principle made dramatically apparent in the recent battles over hate speech.[217] Indeed, American law over the last thirty years has sought to place almost no expression beyond free discourse, while concomitantly narrowing the range of any such exceptions.

As a matter of comparative law, the divergent German and American outcomes reveal differences in culture. In Germany, the integrity of the human person, as protected by article 1 human dignity and article 2 personality rights, is the ultimate legal value. One might say human dignity justifiably limits certain communication, such as degrading personal epithets, since such can be viewed as an attack on the inviolability of human personality. In comparison, in American law and American society, protection of the integrity of the human personality is less highly valued as a legal value. American's concern is more with individual and social freedoms, in which free speech plays a leading role. In turn, this reveals the tremendous amount of importance we place on free speech, a degree of freedom no other country reaches. We might say free speech is to us what human dignity is to the Germans.

NATIONAL SYMBOLS

A final topic of freedom of expression worth considering is treatment of national symbols, like a flag or national anthem. As the symbols of the nation, these icons represent the country and the polity it stands for. Citizens naturally identify with these images and the fundamental values they represent. Yet as symbolic expression of these ideas, national icons are susceptible to multiple interpretations as well. Perhaps the meaning of the symbol lies in the eyes of the beholder. In this way, a flag or national anthem becomes an object of comment or discussion. What role, if any, does the state have in controlling the content of this discussion? These are the questions we will explore in this final topic of free speech. Not surprisingly, this topic too affords further dramatic contrast and similarity between the two lands. Appropriately for comparative law, both countries offer cases involving essentially the same topic of denigration of national symbols at around the same time.

America

The American case is the famous *Texas v. Johnson*, where Gregory Johnson protested Reagan administration policies during the 1984 Republican Convention in Dallas, Texas.[218] After marching through city streets, chanting political slogans, and staging "die-ins" intended to dramatize the consequences of nuclear war, "Johnson unfurled . . . [an] American flag, doused it in kerosene, and set it on fire."[219] This brought Johnson afoul of a Texas statute that prohibited desecration of a venerated object. The question for resolution, thus, was how to treat the flag: as such a venerated object removed from ordinary discussion, or, instead, as an object of discourse, like any other, open to the meanings citizens give it.

The Supreme Court chose for open discussion: "If there is a bedrock principle underlying the First Amendment, it is that the government may not prohibit the expression of an idea simply because society finds the idea itself offensive or disagreeable."[220] And this idea applies as well to the flag. "The constitutionally guaranteed 'freedom to be intellectually . . . diverse or even contrary,' and the 'right to differ as to things that touch the heart of the existing order,' encompass the freedom to express publicly one's opinions about our flag, including those opinions which are defiant or contemptuous."[221] The government can no more compel desired conduct in respect of the flag than any other idea. "No official, high or petty, can prescribe what shall be orthodox in politics, nationalism, religion, or other matters of opinion or force citizens to confess by word or act their faith therein."[222] Thus, the flag, like any idea, cannot "go unquestioned in the marketplace of ideas."[223] Instead, the appropriate response is standard American doctrine: counter the offensive message with one's own view or tolerate the criticism. "We do not consecrate the flag by punishing its desecration, for in doing so we dilute the freedom that this cherished emblem represents."[224]

Germany

German law reaches the same result as American, although doctrinally it takes a different path. The key case is *Flag Desecration*, which concerned the sale of a satiric book of antimilitary prose and poetry, "Let Me Be in Peace" (*Lass mich bloss in Frieden*).[225] The controversy concerned the back cover of the book. The bottom half showed soldiers at attention saluting the German flag.[226] The top half depicted a man, with fly open, urinating. A urine trail was noticeable behind the flag. Putting the collage together, it looked like the man was urinating on the German flag. The lower courts found this to be a violation of the German criminal code, which made it an offense to desecrate the flag, as had the Texas legislature in *Texas v. Johnson.*[227]

Although the book cover contained obvious political opinion, the courts classified the expression as involving artistic not opinion rights.[228] Determination of the bounds of art thus became necessary, since artistic freedoms, like opinion freedoms, are essential to the free formation of ideas.[229] It was easy to characterize the book cover as art. The photo collage tangibly involved the artistic process, the essential standard laid down in *Mephisto.*[230] It did not lose its status as protected art because it was offensive or opinionated, since the government may not prescribe orthodoxy in art and since art can express opinion too.[231]

Finding that the book was art did not end the inquiry, despite the absolute language of article 5(3). Artistic freedoms can be limited by countervailing constitutional norms, the essential teaching of *Mephisto*. These countervailing constitutional interests can be individual or social: "An orderly human life in a community presupposes not only the mutual consideration of the citizens, but also a functioning state order, which is necessary to secure effective protection of basic rights in the first place."[232] The Constitutional Court went so far as to assert that the regulation of artistic expression is not limited to threats of a "clear and present danger." "Works of art that denigrate the constitutionally protected order cannot be regulated only when they directly threaten the existence of the state or constitution" (*wenn sie den Bestand des Staates oder der Verfassung unmittelbar gefährden*).[233] Rather, courts must balance artistic rights against the countervailing constitutional interests. This balance must involve a concrete working out of the values in context in an attempt to maximize both, again an application of the principle of concordance. The balancing of interests test applicable in artistic expression is essentially the same as that applicable to freedom of opinion cases.

The competing norm here was protection of the flag, derived somewhat freehandedly from the article 22 provision specifying that the flag must be red, black, and yellow. From this straightforward text, the Constitutional Court interpreted article 22 to presuppose "the right of the state to use state symbols to self-present itself" in order "to appeal to the state-feeling (*Staatsgefühl*) of citizens."[234] "As a free state, the Federal Republic is dependent on the identification of its citizens with the fundamental values symbolized by the flag. These protected values are present in the colors of the flag . . . which stand for the free democratic basic order."[235] As the flag serves an important symbol of the nation, its denigration might harm the authority of the state. Thus, Quint argues, "The countervailing interest recognized by the Court is the interest of the state in being free from attack on its basic principles and 'authority'; a freedom from a form of seditious libel that would injure the authority of the state and endanger 'internal peace.'"[236]

This interest in seditious libel contrasts with American law, where that interest is not accorded much weight unless a "clear and present" danger of violence is present. Seditious libel was not a factor in the two flag-burning cases, *Texas v. Johnson* and *United States v. Eichman*.[237] As compared to American law, German law accords more weight to values of stability and internal peace and grants the state more power to fight aggressively threats to its existence. Underlying this view is the important German concept of a "militant democracy," under which the state actively fights to preserve "the free democratic state order."[238] Germany's historical experiences are a major reason for these views.

Notwithstanding these interests, the "symbolic protection [of the flag] cannot be used to immunize the state from criticism," a conclusion mirroring that of *Texas v. Johnson*.[239] The collage appeared to be a protest against militarism. The content of the message was just "clothed" in the picture of a man urinating. Under German doctrine, the means (*Einkleidung*) of artistic expression are judged more leniently than the content (*Aussagen*) of the communication, because the means chosen are the very transformative elements that make it art.[240] The mistake of the lower court was to see insult in the urination rather than value in the protest. Accordingly, the Constitutional Court sent the case back to the lower courts with instructions to accord more weight to the artistic values in performing its balancing of interests. Like other cases of the 1990s, the *Flag Desecration* case illustrates the hard-look prong that a court may not choose an interpretation of a communication that leads to unconstitutionality without adequate substantiation of its reasoning.

Perhaps most notable to an American observer is that *Flag Desecration* presupposes that the state can protect itself against seditious libel. In more pathological periods, the protection of art might be turned against itself. For example, in a period of relative insecurity, attacks on state symbols may be perceived as attacks on the government or social order itself, leading to suppression of expression. Still, it is worth observing that the Constitutional Court sought to protect communication, a trend in keeping with the enhanced protection accorded article 5 freedoms in the 1990s, and one also very much in the spirit of American law.[241]

COMPARATIVE OBSERVATIONS

The communication laws of Germany and America developed similarly in its formative period after World War II. The two laws have much in common. Both view expression as essential to individual development, democratic self-government, and the formation of public opinion. Both accord wide scope to an individual's right to speak one's mind, protection of which does not depend on popularity or utility. Both countries centrally protect political, literary, artistic, and scientific speech.[242] The Courts of both countries consider communication freedoms to be fragile and, accordingly, scrutinize proposed restrictions and actively police the structure of public discourse to facilitate its exercise. These similarities are shared more than the differences between the two laws.

Notwithstanding these similarities, a closer look at the two laws reveals differences that are worth highlighting as a matter of comparative observation and as a way of gaining deeper insight into the quality of the two laws. First, American law is freer in its individualism and more zealous in its protection of expression. Over the last thirty years especially, the Supreme Court has sought to realize an ideal of unfettered discourse, freeing individuals to think as they like, speak as they like, and discourse freely, independent of government or community control. This is why American free speech can be viewed as the quintessential right of the American order, representing freedom itself. By contrast, German individual freedoms are more circumscribed, notwithstanding the recent pronounced emphasis on the right to say what one likes, whether "valuable or valueless, true or false, rational or irrational."[243] For example, in *R.A.V. v. St. Paul* the Supreme Court protected the right of white individuals to express hatred by placing a burning cross in the dead of night in the fenced-in yard of a black neighbor across the street.[244] In the *Auschwitz Lie* case, the Constitutional Court banned a demonstration intending to assert that the Holocaust never occurred.[245] Certainly one may doubt the wisdom of America's freedom, but comparatively speaking, American law empowers individuals to speak their minds more than German law.

Second, German civility norms of privacy and reputational interests are a stronger limiting influence on communication freedoms than American ones. This is the most important doctrinal difference between German and American law. For example, one can say "white son of a bitch, I'll kill you" in America, but one cannot call someone a "cripple" in Germany.[246] There is a difference over each country's valuation of hate speech or similar crude invective. Or one can parody a politically active preacher in America by describing his first sexual experience as occurring in an outhouse with his mother while drunk, but one cannot caricature a prominent politician in Germany as a sexually active pig cohabiting with justice.[247] Yet this last difference also points out a key similarity between the two laws. A key demarcation point in both societies is where communication interests intersect with recognized privacy interests. The working out of this tension determines the scope of public discourse. The difference, restated, is that German privacy and reputational interests exert stronger force than in American law, resulting in a concomitant limitation of public discourse. Perhaps the more interesting question is why the two laws differ in this respect. Partly, of course, the difference is textual: The German Basic Law expressly circumscribes communication freedoms and orders more highly personality rights, in comparison to the textually unbounded American First Amendment, which encounters no other express constitutional limitation. Yet this just focuses attention on the reasons for the deliberate ordering of values in Germany in comparison to America's value-neutral structure.

In Germany, this question goes back to the prioritization of human dignity and its corresponding right to free development of personality as the highest legal and cultural values. The silhouette of the German person is thus one of the integrity of personhood, including the right to shape one's character, a shaping to occur within the social community.[248] Obviously, this partly reflects the deep desire to protect the integrity of the human person, a lesson learned bitterly from the horrors of Nazism. It also reflects the influence of Kantian idealism and its emphasis on inner personal autonomy. It is worth pointing out, however, that Kantian autonomy is to unfold in a manner consistent with moral obligations, as compared to the American view of autonomy as seemingly the value itself. Under

Kant, passion is to be tamed by reason, an appeal to the head. In modern Germany, these ideas are rooted in the value-ordered Basic Law, which emphasizes positive and negative liberties, rights and responsibilities, as compared to the American Constitution's provision only of negative liberties and emphasis only on rights.

By contrast, American law has not developed a full set of personality rights. This lacuna has helped clear the way for the full assertion of speech freedoms. American free speech law has certainly encountered fewer obstacles to development as compared to German law. In America, the heart can come before the head; passion and emotion can be the communication as well as reason.

Another explanation for the comparatively free development of American law is the relative lack of cultural restraining norms. The United States is an extremely pluralistic society; Germany is more homogenous. The greater homogeneity of German society conveys a greater sense of social cohesion and shared sense of cultural norms. These civility limitations have led to a greater constraining influence on expression freedoms. For example, the sense of personal honor in Germany is still quite highly regarded. Thus, insulting or degrading speech is likely to be viewed more seriously as a personal affront, finding sanction in the law. In this way, cultural norms link rights to a greater sense of responsibility, braking the excesses of freedom. By contrast, in the United States the emphasis is more on people's free self-determination of the very norms that constitute society, free from almost any official constraint, a quest for which free speech has been indispensable. American free speech law, in fact, maps out the quest to be free: from convention, from order, and from control.

If American law can thus be characterized as tending to pursue freedom for its own sake, German law views freedom as realizable primarily through the social community and its value structure. Historically, the German state has been viewed as the corporate representative of community and its protector of basic values, as compared to the American propensity to rebell against authority. This difference over the idea of community helps explain how German group rights, such as those concerning group defamation or hate speech, are nurtured more for their ability to sustain community. In this way, there is a more amicable relation between freedom and authority in Germany.[249] In turn, this frees the German state to play a more active role in helping achieve a society in which rights can thrive. A notable example of this is the Constitutional Court's active support of institutional press freedoms in *Wallraff*, where the Court protected editorial confidentiality over individual expression.[250]

By contrast, American law posits no role for the state. Americans simply do not trust government. Significantly, this may be a carry over from the original rebellion from England, which yet imbues Americans with a sense of anti-authoritarianism, skepticism, and independence. Hence, in free speech law Americans discourage government from taking sides in a debate or making judgments about the use or abuse of speech. The core doctrine of content neutrality is a testament to Americans distrust of government. At bottom, Americans fear the dangers of the censor more than the dangers of managing speech at the margins, like hate speech, pornography, or commercial speech. Americans trust individuals, however imperfect, more than government. This helps explain, I think, why Americans protect an individuals' right to foment hate over governmental intervention on behalf of groups or communities.

From an individual's perspective, German law empowers a person with both rights and responsibilities. In communication freedoms, this view is most evident in the Constitutional Court's active valuation of expression to determine whether it makes a real contribution to the formation of public opinion and does not violate other community values, such as imperiling the state or intruding on another's privacy rights. In this way, the Constitutional Court judges speech by its content, pursuant to its value according to the objective order of values, as compared to the Supreme Court's quest for absolute content neutrality.[251] Stated otherwise, German expression is valued more for its ability to create and sustain community, in comparison to the American search for absolute individual freedom.[252] The contrasting treatment of group defamation, hate speech, and seditious libel evidences this.

A final difference worth observing is the countries' treatment of speech that threatens the social order. In America, expression on almost any topic is permitted, including insurgent or insurrectionist speech, short of incitement to violence.[253] Americans are comfortable with such robust freedom.

In Germany, by contrast, communication that might be threatening to the social order is monitored quite carefully and, where dangerous, is suppressed. The ban on dissemination of Nazi material is an example of this. Motivating this stance is, of course, the key concept of a "militant democracy," pursuant to which the government proactively defends the society against threats to its wellbeing. This background idea helps us better understand how Germany circumscribes seditious libel more carefully and also requires more overt loyalty, as in the obligations made part of the basic communication freedoms. Threats to social peace are also watched more closely, since they might create the conditions in which the social order would unravel, as was the experience under the Weimar republic. Restrictions on hate speech and group defamation are examples of this active monitoring of social harmony. These exceptions to what otherwise is a quite open and free concept of expression contrast significantly with American law. Yet they are much more in keeping with the more restrained laws of Germany's European neighbors and, for that matter, international standards. American speech, with its utter commitment to individual freedom, stands out as an aberration when viewed worldwide; this is not the case with German speech.

From these differences we can extrapolate some deeper cultural traits. In the United States free speech is the preeminent value. It is what links Americans to fellow citizens, the country, and nation as a whole. Through the critical exchange of public discourse, Americans speak out their hopes, fears, aspirations, emotions, and intentions. Through this process, importantly, Americans decide who they are as a people, what values they hold, and what ends are worth pursuing. In this way, American law is self-deterministic, individualistic, and absolutist in orientation. One might say that American law is radically individualist. American law represents freedom, near absolute freedom, freedom striving to transcend the social order.

Deciphering the cultural messages at the bottom of this exercise in individuality is revealing. The individualism rampant in free speech may reflect the individualism at the root of American culture and identity. From the pioneer days, to the nineteenth-century ideal of the self-made man, to the risk-taking entrepreneur of today, individuals are celebrated in the culture. The image of individualism helps fashion the type of people Americans are or aspire to be. As one of the country's foremost cultural symbols, the First Amendment also helps shape the kind of people we are.[254] There is reality to the image too. The underlying capitalistic economic order places people in the position of being largely responsible for their own fates. The need for survival in the marketplace has also fostered a spirit of individualism. The analogy between the marketplace of ideas and the marketplace is thus not so farfetched.

In Germany, by contrast, communication freedoms are important, but not the preeminent value that human dignity is. Carefully circumscribed by the variant values of human dignity, German law channels conduct along more distinct civility norms. In Germany more than in the United States, communication freedoms are exercised, or ought to be exercised, within the constraints of the social order. One ought to speak in a way cognizant of the impact of speech on others and society. A densely packed population and close proximity to neighbors makes this a prudent course. Individuals should attempt to be in accord with the sense of society. In this way, German law is more communal in approach.

These differences in treatment of speech may simply reflect the contrasting confidence, maybe even maturity, of the two societies. Never having truly faced undemocratic or totalitarian regimes and being relatively well acclimated to a multicultural, pluralistic society, the United States may simply exude more confidence in individuals' ability to perceive their own best interests and govern themselves.[255] The country is founded on this ideal. The current individualistic trend in Germany may likewise reflect the country's greater self-confidence along these lines.

Alternatively, American law may reflect the uncoupling of freedom from responsibility. Perhaps America needs a stronger rooting of its freedoms in a broader social construct in which one shares common goals with and common obligations to one's fellow citizens, as in the German Social State and *Rechtsstaat*. Perhaps America needs to define freedom less as a value onto itself and more as a value in relation to community. Such a fundamental reconception would obviously take a radical change in thinking.

Despite these differences, there is much to learn from the two laws, and much the two countries can learn from each other. For example, an important lesson to be learned from German law is the premise that threats to free expression can come from private as well as public sources. If free speech is truly the most prized freedom in America, it would make sense to guard against all threats to its exercise. Conversely, if one justifiably takes the position that expression freedoms are highly valued but also fragile, then the Constitutional Court might profitably transplant some of the techniques used by the Supreme Court to safeguard a vibrant system of free expression. Use of tools like strict scrutiny, categorical or weighted forms of balancing, and the overbreadth doctrine could help lend needed clarity and coherence to German law. These concepts might profitably transplant across cultures, albeit with some adjustments.

Still, most remarkable is the growing convergence of the two laws. The similar development of expression in two different legal cultures suggests something transcendent about the value of communication. We might say that communication rights are an essential part of a just and free society.

NOTES

1. Cohen v. California, 403 U.S. 15 (1971).
2. Masses Publishing Co. v. Patten, 244 F. 535, 540 (S.D.N.Y. 1917) (opinion by Judge Learned Hand).

3. GEOFFREY R. STONE, LOUIS M. SEIDMAN, CASS R. SUNSTEIN, & MARK V. TUSHNET, CONSTITUTIONAL LAW 1074 (3d ed. 1996).

4. *Id.*

5. Edward J. Eberle, *Roger Williams' Gift: Religious Freedom in America*, 4 ROGER WILLIAMS U. L. REV. 425, 432 (1999) (citations omitted).

6. "Congress shall make no law respecting an establishment of religion, or prohibiting the free exercise thereof; or abridging the freedom of speech, or of the press; or the right of the people peaceably to assemble, and to petition the Government for a redress of grievances." U.S. CONST. amend. 1.

7. Two measures were listed before the First Amendment in the original draft of a bill of rights, one dealing with Congressional representation and the other with Congressional pay, but these were not adopted, moving the First Amendment to the front of the bill. In 1992, finally, the measure concerning Congressional pay was adopted as the Twenty-Seventh Amendment.

8. Schenck v. United States, 249 U.S. 47 (1919); Abrams v. United States, 250 U.S. 616 (1919).

9. Gitlow v. New York, 268 U.S. 652 (1925).

10. As developed by the Supreme Court, public discourse entails discussion of all "ideas and opinions on matters of public interest and opinion," and not just government policies, actions, or actors. Hustler Magazine v. Falwell, 485 U.S. 46, 50–51 (1988). The concept of public discourse relates both to the building of culture and the functioning of a democracy. These ideas are developed more fully in Edward J. Eberle, *Hate Speech, Offensive Speech and Public Discourse in America*, 29 WAKE FOREST L. REV. 1135, 1179–81 (1994). Under German law, "public opinion" can be thought of as the "central structural element of modern democracy." Walter Schmitt Glaeser, *Die Meinungsfreiheit in der Rechtsprechung des Bundesverfassungsrerichts (1. Teil,)* 97 ARCHIV DES ÖFFENTLICHEN RECHTS 60, 107 (1972).

11. New York Times Co. v. Sullivan, 376 U.S. 254, 270 (1964).

12. Cantwell v. Connecticut, 310 U.S. 296, 301 (1940).

13. *Id.* at 309.

14. City of Ladue v. Gilleo, 512 U.S. 43 (1994).

15. *Id.* at 47.

16. *Id.* at 56.

17. Terminiello v. Chicago, 337 U.S. 1, 4 (1949).

18. West Va. State Bd. of Education v. Barnette, 319 U.S. 624, 642 (1943). Robert C. Post, *The Constitutional Concept of Public Discourse: Outrageous Opinion, Democratic Deliberaton, and Hustler Magazine v. Falwell*, 103 HARV. L. REV. 606, 630 (1990).

19. Cohen v. California, 403 U.S. 15, 24 (1971).

20. Cantwell v. Connecticut, 310 U.S. 296, 310 (1940).

21. "The censorial power is in the people over the Government, and not in the Government over the people." 3 ANNALS OF CONGRESS 934 (1794) (statement of James Madison).

22. *Cantwell*, 310 U.S. at 310.

23. Whitney v. California, 274 U.S. 357, 377 (1927) (Brandeis, J., concurring).

24. Texas v. Johnson, 491 U.S. 397 (1989).

25. 274 U.S. 357, 375–6 (1927) (Brandeis, J., concurring).

26. *Cantwell*, 310 U.S. at 310.

27. *Id.*

28. *Id.*

29. *Id.*

30. Cohen v. California, 403 U.S. 15, 24 (1971).

31. *Id.*

32. Post, *supra* note 18, at 638.

33. *Cohen*, 403 U.S. at 24.

34. Robert C. Post, *Racist Speech, Democracy and the First Amendment*, 32 WM. & MARY L. REV. 267, 279–82 (1991).

35. R.A.V. v. St. Paul, 505 U.S. 377 (1992).

36. Post, *supra* note 18, at 671.

37. For example, in R.A.V. v. St. Paul, 505 U.S. at 377, the Court rejected creation of an exception for hate speech. In Hustler Magazine v. Falwell, 485 U.S. 46 (1988), the Court rejected creation of an exception for intentional infliction of emotional distress.

38. 7 BVerfGE 198, 208 (1958), *citing* Palko v. Connecticut, 302 U.S. 319, 327 (1937), *translated in* DAVID P. CURRIE, THE CONSTITUTION OF THE FEDERAL REPUBLIC OF GERMANY 175 (1994). Wassermann observes that while both the individual and social components to speech are especially valued today, especially for their value in promoting truth and justice, this dual character of speech has roots that go back to the 1800s. KOMMENTAR ZUM GRUNDGESETZ FÜR DIE BUNDESREPUBLIK DEUTSCHLAND 415 (Rudolf Wassermann ed., 2d ed. 1989). From the standpoint of today, Kriele notes that expression promotes many values, including self-realization, truth, democracy, and a checking value. Martin Kriele, *Ehrenschutz und Meinungsfreiheit*, 30 NEUE JURISTISCHE WOCHENSCHRIFT [hereafter NJW] 1897 (1994). As in American law, German law is thus seeking to support expression on a multivalued foundation, as compared to reliance on any single root value. *See* Edward J. Eberle, *Practical Reason: The Commercial Speech Paradigm*, 42 CASE W. RES. L. REV. 411, 429–431 (1992) (a web of mutually reinforcing values provides a surer footing for expression freedoms). American and German law may thus be pursuing similar theoretical rationales.

39. 7 BVerfGE at 199–200.

40. *Id.*

41. Schmitt Glaeser, *supra* note 10, at 68–69.

42. Martin H. Redish, *Self-Realization, Democracy and Freedom of Expression: A Reply to Professor Baker*, 130 U. PA. L. REV. 678, 679–80 (1982); David A. J. Richards, *Free Speech and Obscenity Law: Toward a Moral Theory of the First Amendment*, 123 U. PA. L. REV. 45, 62 (1974).

43. Ronald Dworkin, *The Coming Battles Over Free Speech*, N.Y. REV. OF BOOKS, June 11, 1992, at 56–57; Richards, *supra* note 42, at 62–63.

44. C. EDWIN BAKER, HUMAN LIBERTY AND FREEDOM OF SPEECH 47–48 (1984); MARTIN H. REDISH, FREEDOM OF EXPRESSION: A CRITICAL ANALYSIS 11–13 (1984).

45. *Soldiers Are Murderers II*, 45 NJW 2943 (1994).

46. For example, see *id.*: Communication freedoms are "in the interest of the right to personal development, with which communication is closely

linked, as well as in the interest of the democratic process, for which it has constitutive meaning."

47. 7 BVerfGE 198, 208 (1958).

48. *Id.* at 210.

49. *See, e.g.*, ALEXANDER MEIKLEJOHN, POLITICAL FREEDOM 55–56 (1960) (Free speech "stands alone as the cornerstone of the structure of self-government. If that uniqueness were taken away, government by consent of the governed would have perished from the earth").

50. Palko v. Connecticut, 302 U.S. 319, 327 (1937), *as cited in Lüth*, 7 BVerfGE at 208. The Constitutional Court's patterning of expression on American roots was not coincidental.

51. *Lüth*, 7 BVerfGE at 208. Under the main German communication clause, Article 5(1) freedom of opinion, the key determinant is whether the communication contains opinion, not whether a communication is made, the key determinant under the American First Amendment. Classification as an opinion depends on whether the statement contains elements of taking a position, personal valuation or estimation. *NPD Europe*, 61 BVerfGE 1, 8 (1983); GRUNDGESETZ, KOMMENTAR [COMMENTARY] art. 5, p. 16 (Theodor Maunz, Günther Dürig, et al. ed. 1993) [HEREINAFTER MAUNZ–DÜRIG KOMMENTAR].

52. *See, e.g.*, New York Times Co. v. Sullivan, 376 U.S. 254 (1964); MEIKLEJOHN, *supra* note 49.

53. 12 BVerfGE 113 (1961).

54. *Id.* at 114–18.

55. *Id.* at 125.

56. *Id.* at 128–32. "An attack on the periodical's general reputation for veracity was a more powerful defense than denial of its particular allegations standing alone, and 'Der Spiegel' had opened itself up to such charges by its unreliable treatment of the facts in this case." CURRIE, *supra* note 38, at 190.

57. 12 BVerfGE at 130 ("Since the press has responsibility for contributing to the formation of public opinion, it must test for truth news and statements it publishes. . . . It is impermissible to lightly publish false news. . . . The truth may not consciously be distorted"). *Accord, Böll*, 54 BVerfGE 208, 219 (1980) (false quotations are not protected). *See also* MAUNZ–DÜRIG KOMMENTAR, *supra* note 52, at 52.

58. *See, e.g.*, Gertz v. Robert Welch, 418 U.S. 323, 339–40 (1974) (while "under the First Amendment there is no such thing as false idea . . . there is no constitutional value in false statements of fact"). A key difference in the two laws is that American law is more careful not to punish false statements, without more, when central speech values are at issue. *See, e.g.*, New York Times v. Sullivan, 376 U.S. 254 (1964) (speech protected despite false statements of fact). Letter from David Currie to Edward J. Eberle (Nov. 3, 1995). By contrast, German courts actively police the truth–falsity of statements. *See, e.g., Schmid–Spiegel*, 12 BVerfGE at 130.

59. A difference between the laws is, as Kommers notes, that German law "protects robust and caustic speech but not always reckless speech." DONALD P. KOMMERS, THE CONSTITUTIONAL JURISPRUDENCE OF THE FEDERAL

REPUBLIC OF GERMANY 381 (1989). For example, the use of false quotations in *Böll*, 54 BVerfGE at 219, could be considered reckless, and therefore unprotected.

60. *Compare* 54 BVerfGE at 208 ("For a free democratic state order [expression] is absolutely fundamental because it facilitates the ongoing intellectual exchange, the struggle [or battle] of opinions that is its life element") *with* Abrams v. United States, 250 U.S. 616, 6390 (1919) (Holmes, J., dissenting) ("The best test of truth is the power of the thought to get itself accepted in the competition of the market").

61. *Lüth*, 7 BVerfGE 198, 219 (1958).

62. *Soraya*, 34 BVerfGE 269 (1973).

63. The status of commercial speech as conventionally understood under American law—*see, e.g.*, Board of Trustees v. Fox, 492 U.S. 469, 473 (1989) (commercial speech is that which "proposes a commercial transaction")—is complicated under German law. Pure commercial speech in the sense of the proposal of an economic transaction or advertising has been held to be unprotected. *Chemist Advertising Case*, 53 BVerfGE 96 (1980). *See also Physician Advertising Case*, 71 BVerfGE 162 (1985) (prohibition on advertising upheld on grounds of need to protect public from undue influence and preserve public confidence in physicians). Thus, this form of German commercial speech can be regulated by the legislature through operation, essentially, of a deferential rational basis review test. However, to the extent commercial speech contains elements of opinion, it may receive protection under Article 5(1). *See, e.g.*, 71 BVerfGE at 175. *See, generally*, Schmitt Glaeser, *supra* note 10, at 72. Advertisements may also be protected as news under press freedom or under the citizens' general right to inform themselves. *See, e.g.*, 21 BVerfGE 271, 278–80 (1967) (invalidating prohibition on advertisement of foreign job opportunities on grounds it violates press freedoms and individual right to inform oneself from "generally available sources"). With these toeholds, it is quite possible German law will develop as American law has, resulting in general protection for commercial speech. Moreover, pure commercial advertising may receive constitutional protection under the article 12 occupational guarantees.

64. GG art. 139. For description of how this problem is treated in contemporary Germany, *see* Eric Stein, *History Against Free Speech: The New German Law Against the "'Auschwitz'—and Other—'Lies,'"* 85 MICH. L. REV. 277 (1986).

65. Marjorie Miller, *German Ban on Holocaust Denial Upheld; Justice: Rightists Sued Munich after a Speech Was Forbidden. But High Court Says the "Auschwitz Lie" Is Not Protected*, LOS ANGELES TIMES, Apr. 27, 1994, at A7.

66. *Auschwitz Lie*, 90 BVerfGE 241 (1994); *Cripple*, 86 BVerfGE 1 (1992).

67. *See Flag Desecration Case*, 81 BVerfGE 278 (1990) and *National Anthem Case*, 81 BVerfGE 1 (1990); *Horror Film Case*, 87 BVerfGE 209 (1992).

68. Peter E. Quint, *Free Speech and Private Law in German Constitutional Theory*, 48 MD. L. REV. 247, 249 (1989).

69. Skokie v. National Socialist Party of America, 373 N.E. 2d 21 (1978); Collins v. Smith, 578 F.2d 1197 (7th Cir.), *cert. denied* 439 U.S. 916 (1978)

(state may not prohibit demonstration of neo-Nazis seeking to publicize that Holocaust was fictional).

70. Amy Harmon, *Internet Sale of Nazi Books in Germany Assailed*, N.Y. TIMES, Aug. 9, 1999, at C12.

71. Alan Cowell, *German Court Begins Hearing Case of American Neo-Nazi*, N.Y. TIMES, May 10, 1996, at A5; *Danes Protest Against American Neo-Nazi*, N.Y. TIMES, Apr. 6, 1995, at A12.

72. Thomas Jefferson, Inaugural Address, *in* THE LIFE AND SELECTED WRITINGS OF THOMAS JEFFERSON 323 (ed. Adrienne Koch & William Peden) (New York, Modern Library, 1944).

73. Hugo L. Black, *The Bill of Rights*, 35 N.Y.U. L. REV. 865, 874 (1960).

74. Article 5 (Freedom of Expression) of the Basic Law provides,

(1) Every person shall have the right freely to express and disseminate his opinions in speech, writing, and pictures and to inform himself without hindrance from generally accessible sources. Freedom of the press and freedom of reporting by means of broadcasts and films shall be guaranteed. There shall be no censorship.

(2) These rights shall find their limits in the provisions of general laws, in provisions for the protection of young persons, and in the right to personal honor.

(3) Art and scholarship, research, and teaching shall be free. The freedom of teaching shall not release any person from allegiance to the constitution.

75. KOMMERS, *supra* note 59, at 366–67. These differences should be expected in provisions drafted in 1949 (article 5) as compared to 1791 (First Amendment).

76. GG art. 5(2). The general law limitation is a generally applicable neutral law that is not directed at expression. Thus, the law must further a legal interest independent and separable from expression itself; it cannot be directed at the content of the speech. Despite its similarity to the American concept of First Amendment content neutrality, the two are not the same. In German law, a "general law" can affect speech and yet be permissible so long as it applies "generally" and is not aimed at expression. The general civil code provision at issue in *Lüth* is an example of such a law. CURRIE, *supra* note 38, at 179. This concept of the "general law" arose in connection with interpretation of the Weimar Constitution, and is meant to counter the notion that the legislature can change speech protections at will. *See* Bodo Pieroth & Bernhard Schlink, GRUNDRECHTE STAATSRECHT II 161–63 (10th ed. 1994). The concern for protection of youth reflects the family and social interests that the young be able to develop with proper nurturing and care. It might be linked to article 6 family guarantees, including the right to bring up children. The limitation of personal honor seems attributable to Germany's aristocratic tradition, which places comparatively high value on one's good name and honor. The right to pursue freely art, research, and science reflects the influence of the 1849 Frankfurt Constitution. This provision, written by leading intellectuals, was designed to assure the autonomy of academic work and the German university. KOMMERS, *supra* note 59, at 426. Unlike art, research, and scientific freedoms, teaching is subject to the qualification that it "not release anybody from his allegiance to the constitution." GG art. 5(3).

77. Kommers observes that article 5(2) limitations on expression "invite [their] interpretation in light of other basic value decisions of the Constitution whose effect is often to confine the range or intensity of speech." KOMMERS, *supra* note 59, at 413.

78. Quint, *supra* note 68, at 250.

79. *Id.*

80. In the United States, the famous Holmes and Brandeis opinions of the period just after World War I have been enormously influential. *See, e.g.*, Schenck v. United States, 249 U.S. 47 (1919) (Holmes, J.); Abrams v. United States, 250 U.S. 616, 624, 630 (1919) (Holmes, J., dissenting); Whitney v. California, 274 U.S. 357, 372–80 (1927) (Brandeis, J., concurring). In addition, significant other progress was made during the period of the Hughes Court in the 1930s. *See, e.g.*, Hague v. Committee for Indus. Org., 307 U.S. 496 (1939); Near v. Minnesota, 283 U.S. 696 (1931). But the essential development of American law occurred after World War II in the Warren Court. *See, e.g.*, Brandenburg v. Ohio, 395 U.S. 444, 447 (1969) (per curiam); New York Times v. Sullivan, 376 U.S. 254 (1964); Roth v. United States, 354 U.S. 476 (1957). In Germany, only with the promulgation of the Basic Law was freedom of expression able to flower.

81. Gertz v. Robert Welch, Inc., 418 U.S. 323, 325–26 (1974).

82. In American history, there have been two great episodes of seditious libel testing the limits of speech protections in times of tension. The first was the controversy over the Sedition Act of 1798, which involved the Federalist administration of President John Adams attempting to silence its critics, including member of Congress, by jailing them. It took the election of President Thomas Jefferson to free these critics and the *New York Times* case to establish definitively the unconstitutionality of the act. The second period was the controversy, during World War I, over enforcement of the Espionage Act of 1917, as ventilated through cases like *Schenck, Abrams*, or *Debs*. The experience of these histories had a crucial influence on the Court's development of free speech theory, influencing a trend away from loosely stated rules calling for balancing and toward hard, categorical rules that remove significantly the element of discretion, as manifested in cases like *Brandenburg* or *New York Times*.

83. 376 U.S. at 254.

84. *Id.* at 279–80.

85. 395 U.S. 444, 447 (1969).

86. On false statements, *see Cantwell*, 310 U.S. 296, 310 (1940).

87. 388 U.S. 130 (1967).

88. *Whitney*, 274 U.S. 357, 357 (1927). *New York Times*, 376 U.S. at 273, *quoting* Crain v. Hurvey, 331 U.S. 367, 376 (1947). A public person is either a public official, which is pretty self-explanatory, or a public figure, which involves some element of the person achieving fame, notoriety, or special prominence. *Gertz*, 418 U.S. 323, 351 (1974). Under the many applications of the public-figure test, the Court has determined, for example, that a former college football coach, Curtis Publishing Co. v. Butts, 388 U.S. 130 (1967), and distinguished retired military officer, Associated Press v. Walker, 388 U.S. 130 (1967), were public figures, but that the former

wife of a tire magnate, Time Inc. v. Firestone, 424 U.S. 448 (1976), prominent local attorney, *Gertz*, private citizen accused of being a Soviet spy, Wolston v. Reader's Digest Ass'n., 443 U.S. 157 (1979), and scientist, Hutchinson v. Proxmire, 443 U.S. 111 (1979), were not public figures. Under the definition, most celebrities and famous members of society will be public figures.

89. *Schmid–Spiegel*, 12 BVerfGE 113 (1961).

90. For private persons, the rule of *Gertz v. Robert Welch, Inc.* applies, that "so long as they do not impose liability without fault, the States may define for themselves the appropriate standard of liability for . . . defamatory falsehood injurious to a private individual." States may allow recovery only for "actual injury," not "presumed or punitive damages." *Gertz*, 418 U.S. at 347, 349. These rules provide significant protection for reputational interests of private persons. At least in this way, personality interests also constrain American speech rights.

91. *Hustler*, 485 U.S. 46 (1988). *Strauss Political Satire*, 75 BVerfGE 369 (1987). The comparison of *Hustler* with the *Strauss Political Satire Case* is a popular topic in Germany. *See, e.g.*, Georgios Goundalakis, *Freiräume und Grenzen politischer Karikatur und Satire*, 13 NJW 810 (1995); Georg Nolte, *Falwell vs. Strauss. Die Rechtlichen Grenzen Politischer Satire in den USA und in der Bundesrepublik*, EUROPÄISCHE GRUNDRECHTE-ZEITSCHRIFT 253 (1988).

92. 485 U.S. at 56–57.

93. Eberle, *supra* note 10, at 1184.

94. 75 BVerfGE at 379.

95. *Id.* at 380. Technically, this was considered a criminal insult under StGB § 185.

96. *Falwell*, 485 U.S. at 55–56. *See* Cohen v. California, 403 U.S. 15, 24–25 (1971); Cantwell v. Connecticut, 310 U.S. 296, 310 (1940).

97. *Falwell*, 485 U.S. at 55.

98. *Id.*

99. *Cohen*, 403 U.S. at 25.

100. Post, *supra* note 18, at 630.

101. *Id.* at 632.

102. *Cohen*, 403 U.S. at 25.

103. Winters v. New York, 333 U.S. 507, 510 (1948).

104. 54 BVerfGE 208 (1980).

105. *Id.* at 217, *translated in* KOMMERS, *supra* note 59, at 419.

106. 501 U.S. 496 (1991).

107. *New York Times*, 376 U.S. 254, 270 (1964).

108. 30 BVerfGE 173 (1971). In *Mephisto*, the Constitutional Court split 3–3 in upholding an injunction against publication of a novel by Klaus Mann, the son of the great German writer Thomas Mann, on the grounds that the novel defamed the memory of a famous deceased actor. The central character of the novel was an actor named Hendrik Höfgen, whom Mann portrayed as having made his name by playing the devil in Goethe's Faust during the Nazi period. While other artists were persecuted, Höfgen "betrayed his own political convictions and cast off all ethical and humanitarian re-

straints to further his career by making a pact with . . . [those in] power in Nazi Germany." *Id.* at 174, *translated in* CURRIE, *supra* note 38, at 193.

109. *Soraya*, 34 BVerfGE 269 (1973); *Lebach*, 35 BVerfGE 202 (1973).

110. Quint, *supra* note 68, at 318.

111. 42 BVerfGE 143 (1976). The *Deutschland–Magazin* approach thus resulted in enhanced protection of rights. Paradoxically, this had mixed results for communication. On the one hand, the Court employed the variable standard of review to vindicate speech interests. On the other hand, the Court used the technique to enhance protection of other constitutional rights too, such as dignity and personality protections. When juxtaposed against communication interests, personality rights tended yet to prevail. *See, e.g., Böll*, 54 BVerfGE 208 (1980).

112. *Echternach*, 42 BVerfGE 167 (1976).

113. *Stern–Strauss Interview*, 82 BVerfGE 272 (1990); *Anti-Strauss Placard*, 82 BVerfGE 43 (1990) (Court invalidated libel judgment against protestors bearing placards stating "Strauss protects Fascists" and "Strauss, the Fascists' friend, protects Hoffmann, the Oktoberfestmurderer" because it was unfathomable that such simple statements could be viewed as defamation). Franz Josef Strauss was a very controversial politician in Germany who brought out the furies in people, who often savagely attacked him. Strauss often resorted to the courts to defend his "honor." *See, e.g., Judgment of Appellate Court of Hamm*, 1982 NJW 659 (Strauss depicted as sweating, stampeding bull, covered with red arrows, attacking a group of young people); *Judgment of Appellate Court of Munich*, 1971 NJW 844 (Strauss caricatured with limbs in form of swastika); *Judgment of Appellate Court of Hamm*, 1982 NJW 1656 (depicted as blood-soaked butcher, laughing as he sharpens a long knife); *Judgment of Munich Court* (VGH) 1984 NJW 1136 (depicted as big bad wolf in scene from Little Red Riding Hood); Georgios Goundalakis, *Freiräume und Grenzen politischer Karikatur und Satire*, 13 NJW 809 n. 4 (1995). By contrast, former Chancellor Helmut Kohl, himself subject to innumerable savage attacks, has never sought judicial relief to vindicate perceived slights of his honor. *Id.* at 816. Obviously, the granting of judicial relief encourages public figures to sue.

114. 81 BVerfGE 279 (1990) (flag); 81 BVerfGE 298 (1990) (anthem).

115. 82 BVerfGE at 272.

116. *Id.* at 273–74.

117. *Id.* at 273.

118. *Id.* at 273–74.

119. *Id.* at 274.

120. *Id.* at 275. The suit continued even though Strauss had died before its end, illustrating the high importance attached to personal dignity in Germany.

121. *Id.* at 280, *citing Lüth.*

122. *Id.*

123. *Id.*

124. *Id.* at 281.

125. *Id.*

126. *Mephisto*, 30 BVerfGE 173 (1971); *Deutschland–Magazin*, 42 BVerfGE 143 (1976).

127. Peter E. Quint, *The Comparative Law of Flag Desecration: The United States and the Federal Republic of Germany*, 15 HASTINGS INT'L. & COMP. L. REV. 613, 634–35 (1992).

128. Motor Vehicle Manufacturing Association v. State Farm Mutual Automobile Ins. Co., 463 U.S. 29, 43 (1983) (citations omitted):

The scope of review under the "arbitrary and capricious" standard is narrow and a court is not to substitute its judgment for that of the agency. Nevertheless, the agency must examine the relevant data and articulate a satisfactory explanation for its action including a "rational connection between the facts found and the choice made." In reviewing that explanation, we must "consider whether the decision was based on a consideration of the relevant factors and whether there has been a clear error of judgment." Normally, an agency rule would be arbitrary and capricious if the agency has relied on factors which Congress has not intended it to consider, entirely failed to consider an important aspect of the problem, offered an explanation for its decision that runs counter to the evidence before the agency, or is so implausible that it could not be ascribed to a difference in view or the product of agency expertise. The reviewing court should not attempt itself to make up for such deficiencies; we may not supply a reasoned basis for the agency's action that the agency itself has not given. We will, however, "uphold a decision of less than ideal clarity if the agency's path may reasonably be discerned."

129. Under conventional American doctrine, violations of individual rights trigger strict scrutiny, an inquiry requiring government to justify its regulation as "necessary to serve a compelling state interest . . . that is . . . narrowly drawn to achieve that end." Arkansas Writers' Project, Inc. v. Ragland, 481 U.S. 221, 231 (1987).

130. 82 BVerfGE 272, 281 (1990).

131. *Id.* ("The dimension of [article 5] protection depends, to be sure, on the purpose of the communication. Contributions to the dialogue of publicly important questions enjoy stronger protection than statements that only serve private interests").

132. *New York Times*, 376 U.S. 254, 270 (1964) ("We consider this case against the background of a profound national commitment to the principle that debate on public issues should be uninhibited, robust, and wide-open, and that it may well include vehement, caustic, and sometimes unpleasantly sharp attacks on government and public officials"). *Cantwell*, 310 U.S. 296, 310 (1940):

In the realm of religious faith, and in that of political belief, sharp differences arise. In both fields the tenants of one may seem the rankest error to his neighbor. To persuade others to his own point of view, the pleader, as we know, at times resorts to exaggeration, to vilification of men who have been, or are, prominent in church or state, and even to false statement. But the people of this nation have ordained in the light of history, that, in spite of the probability of excesses and abuses, these liberties are, in the long view, essential to enlightened opinion and right conduct on the part of the citizen of a democracy.

133. 82 BVerfGE at 282.

134. *Id.* at 277 ("To be sure, people who participate in public life increase the chance they will be objects of criticism. Those who render harsh judgments in the struggle for the formation of public opinion must be ready to accept sharp reactions"). This is the counterattack theory developed in

Schmid–Spiegel, reminiscent of the New York Times v. Sullivan "public figure" standard. Gertz v. Robert Welch, 418 U.S. 323 (1974).

135. 82 BVerfGE at 277.

136. *Id.* at 283.

137. *Id.* at 277.

138. *Id.* at 283–85.

139. *Id.* at 283. American libel law is ruled by the New York Times v. Sullivan, 376 U.S. 254, 280 (1964), actual malice standard ("that is, with knowledge that [the statement] was false or with reckless disregard of whether it was false or not").

140. 82 BVerfGE at 283–84. The indefiniteness of this standard is problematic for a system of law. Unfortunately, there has not yet been a further concretization of the standard. Letter from Dr. Bodo Pieroth to Edward J. Eberle (Aug. 26, 1995). In the recent case of *Böll Book Review,* NJW 1462 (1993), the Court applied the *Stern–Strauss Interview* standard and found that a critic defamed the reputation of the author Heinrich Böll in a book review of Böll's work that, among other things, called Böll "stone-dumb, clueless and talentless." To an American observer, this is somewhat of a surprising outcome, since the critique seems no more severe than standard fare in the American scheme. This would seem to illustrate the manipulability of the vacuous defamation standard, in contrast to the precise *New York Times* standard, 376 U.S. at 379–80.

141. 82 BVerfGE at 284.

142. *Id.* at 285.

143. *Id.*

144. It is fair to say that New York Times v. Sullivan overrules Beauharnais v. Illinois, 343 U.S. 250 (1952), on this point. In *Beauharnais* the Court affirmed the conviction under a group libel law of a speaker who demeaned black Americans. For arguments favoring group defamation approaches, see Charles R. Lawrence III, *If He Hollers Let Him Go: Regulating Racist Speech on Campus,* DUKE L. J. 431 (1990); Mari J. Matsuda, *Public Response to Racist Speech: Considering the Victim's Story,* 87 MICH. L. REV. 2320 (1989).

145. 505 U.S. 377 (1989) (state may not selectively proscribe racist fighting words); 578 F.2d 1197 (7th Cir.), *cert. denied* 439 U.S. 916 (1978) (state may not prohibit demonstration of neo-Nazis seeking to publicize that Holocaust was fictional). In this way, *Collins* and *Auschwitz Lie* illustrate the contrasting approach of the American and German Courts on this question.

146. *See* StGB §§ 130–31, discussed in Stein, *supra* note 64.

147. 90 BVerfGE 241 (1994).

148. German law allows prior restraint where planned events will likely lead, as perceived here, to criminal acts. *See* Federal Assembly Law [*Versammulungsgesetzes*; VersG] § 5, no. 4.

149. 90 BVerfGE at 249.

150. *Id.* at 248, *citing Bayer Dissident Stockholders,* 85 BVerfGE 1, 15 (1991).

151. 90 BVerfGE at 243.

152. *Id.* at 252–54.

153. *Soldiers Are Murderers I,* 45 NJW 2943 (1994); *Soldiers Are Murderers II,* 22 Europaische Grundrecht Zeitschrift [EuGRZ] 443 (1995).

154. In Germany, "Soldiers are Murderers" is a ready cultural reference to a famous 1931 work by Kurt Tucholsky, a relevant excerpt of which appears in *Soldiers Are Murderers II*.

155. 45 NJW at 2943.

156. *Id.* at 2944.

157. *Id.* at 2943–44.

158. *See, e.g.*, Gerhard Herdegen, Kommentar to "Soldaten sind Mörder," *id.* at 2933.

159. 45 NJW at 2943.

160. *Denial of Responsibility for World War II*, 90 BVerfGE 1, 14 (1994).

161. These thoughts are echoed in the Court's now common ringing defense of the individual right to speak one's mind: "The right to freedom of opinion guarantees everyone the right to assert freely their opinion: Everyone has the right to say what she thinks, even when she does not provide or cannot provide any verifiable reasons for her view." "Even sharp and extreme criticism does not lose protection. Value judgments are protected, regardless of whether they are 'valuable' or 'worthless,' 'true' or 'false,' 'emotional' or 'rational.'" 45 NJW at 2943. This trend of explicit linkage of communication to personality rights is deliberate. It is a reaction against tying expression too exclusively to political speech, which might have the effect of limiting speech rights. Thus, article 5 has a certain ethical quality as an end in itself, paralleling the development in American law. MAUNZ–DÜRIG KOMMENTAR, *supra* note 51, at 18.

162. Eberle, *supra* note 10, at 1185–86.

163. *See, e.g.*, Stephen Kinzer, *An Old Stab at Soldiers Opens Battle in Germany*, N.Y. TIMES, Jan. 15, 1996, at A5, *citing, e.g.*, former Chancellor Helmut Kohl ("We cannot and must not stand by while our soldiers are placed on the same level with criminals") and Kurt Biedenkopf, then governor of Saxony ("It is outrageous that soldiers who take the risks of serving in our army should be called murderers. [My] sons . . . have served in the army. . . . I feel personally insulted by this decision").

164. 22 EuGRZ 443 (1995).

165. Brown v. Board of Education, 347 U.S. 483 (1954) (Brown I), *confirmed in* Brown v. Board of Education, 349 U.S. 294 (1955) (Brown II), *reconfirmed in* Cooper v. Aaron, 358 U.S. 1 (1958); Roe v. Wade, 410 U.S. 113 (1973), *confirmed and reversed in part in* Planned Parenthood of Southeastern Pennsylvania v. Casey, 505 U.S. 833 (1992).

166. 22 EuGRZ at 443, 456. Only Judge Haas wrote a dissenting opinion, in which she decried the Court's use of intensive scrutiny, preferring that the Court defer more to the ordinary courts. She also believed that soldiers, including their honor, merited protection from the legal system instead of scorn. *Id.* at 457–58. Her views thus seemed in accord with a fair portion of the German public.

167. *Id.* at 550.

168. *See, e.g.*, Cohen v. California, 403 U.S. 15, 26 (1971).

169. 22 EuGRZ at 451.

170. *Id.*

171. *Id.*

172. *Id.*

173. *Id.*
174. *Id.* at 454.
175. *Id.*
176. New York Times v. Sullivan, 376 U.S. 254 (1964), is the leading case.
177. 22 EuGRZ at 454.
178. *Id.*
179. *Id.*
180. *Auschwitz Lie*, 90 BVerfGE 24 (1990), discussed later in text.
181. *Id.*
182. *Id.*
183. 22 EuGRZ at 454.
184. *Id.*
185. *Id.* at 456.
186. Cohen v. California, 403 U.S. 15 (1971).
187. Lee v. Weisman, 505 U.S. 577, 590 (1992).
188. 337 U.S. 1, 4 (1949).
189. Hustler Magazine v. Falwell, 485 U.S. 46, 55 (1988).
190. 403 U.S. at 15.
191. *Id.* at 25.
192. *Id.*
193. *Id.* at 21 (citation omitted).
194. 42 BVerfGE 143, 144 (1976). The term "right-radical hate sheet" has clear historical overtones, dredging up memories of the Nazi hunting and persecution of victims. This appears to be the basis on which the Court viewed this phrase as particularly ill-chosen. Quint, *supra* note 68, at 319 n. 222.
195. 42 BVerfGE at 149–50. ("Restrictions on opinion freedoms which are exclusively limited to the form of expression are less severe limitations." "Generally—if not always—formulations of thoughts may be changed without difficulty without harming the idea sought to be communicated").
196. *Id.* at 151; Quint, *supra* note 68, at 321.
197. *See, e.g.,* Cohen v. California, 403 U.S. 15, 26 (1971):

Much linguistic expression serves a dual communicative function; it conveys not only ideas capable of relatively precise, detached explication, but otherwise inexpressible emotions as well. In fact, words are often chosen as much for their emotive as their cognitive force. We cannot sanction the view that the Constitution, while solicitous of the cognitive content of individual speech, has little or no regard for that emotive function which, practically speaking, may often be the more important element of the overall message sought to be communicated.

The Supreme Court even scrutinizes expressive conduct to make sure that "the government interest is unrelated to the suppression of free expression." Texas v. Johnson, 491 U.S. 397, 407 (1989) (citations omitted) (qualifying more lenient standard of United States v. O'Brien, 391 U.S. 367 [1968]).
198. The Constitutional Court similarly excised a particular use of "cripple" in the *Cripple Case*, 86 BVerfGE 1 (1992).

199. *Soldiers Are Murderers II*, 22 Eu GRZ 443, 550 (1995).

200. 505 U.S. 377 (1992).

201. *Id.* at 379–80.

202. *See, e.g.*, Collins v. Smith, 578 F.2d 1197 (7th Cir.), *cert. denied* 439 U.S. 916 (1978) (state may not prohibit demonstration of neo-Nazis seeking to publicize that Holocaust was fictional).

203. Eberle, *supra* note 10, at 1205.

204. Charles Lewis Nier III, *Racial Hatred: A Comparative Analysis of the Hate Crime Laws of the United States and Germany*, 13 DICKINSON J. INT'L. L. 241, 263 (1995).

205. Kimberly Ann Orlandi, *The First Amendment—A Protection of Free Speech*, R. I. JEWISH HERALD, Sep. 2, 1999, at 1.

206. 508 U.S. 476 (1993).

207. *Id.* at 487.

208. Eberle, *supra* note 10, at 1193–94. In *Mitchell*, several young black men and boys were discussing a scene from the movie *Mississippi Burning*, which they had just seen. The scene depicted a white man beating a young black boy who was praying. Upon seeing a white boy across the street, the group of black people rushed at the white boy and beat him severely.

209. StGB art. 130–31.

210. 86 BVerfGE 1 (1992).

211. *Id.* at 3.

212. The designation "born murderer" was a biting pun. One of the other personalities featured that month as "embarrassing personalities" was listed with her maiden name, which in German is "born" (*geb*). The then German president, Richard von Weizsacker, also was listed as "born citizen." Thus, the term "born murderer" was satire directed at this common usage. *Id.* at 2.

213. The reference to soldiers as murderers came from an earlier speech by the publisher in which he asserted that every soldier is a potential murderer. The German army prepares people to be murderers. The speech attracted a lot of attention, resulting in the speaker being sanctioned. *Id.* at 3–4.

214. *Id.* at 11–12. The mistake of the lower court was to interpret the usage "murderer" in a literal sense, applying the criminal code. The magazine was itself devoted to satire, the Court reasoned. Thus, readers knew what to expect.

215. *Id.* at 4.

216. *Id.* at 13. Use of the term was not even justifiable in the context of describing the horrors of war. To some, use of the word "cripple" conjures memories of the Hitler era, since the disabled, viewed as "inferior" stock, were often victims of Nazi persecution.

217. *Compare* Wisconsin v. Mitchell, 508 U. S. 476 (1993) (may constitutionally punish hate-inspired conduct) *with* R.A.V. v. St. Paul, 505 U.S. 377 (1992) (hate-inspired fighting words not beyond first protection). For strong arguments favoring excision of hate speech, *see* Lawrence, *supra* note 144; Matsuda, *supra* note 144.

218. 491 U.S. 397 (1989).

219. *Id.* at 399.

220. *Id.* at 414.

221. *Id.* (citations omitted).

222. West Virginia Board of Education v. Barnette, 319 U.S. 624, 642 (1943).

223. *Johnson*, 491 U.S. at 418.

224. *Id.* at 420. A companion case to *Texas v. Johnson*, United States v. Eichman, 496 U.S. 310 (1990), fared no better, as the Court struck down a Congressional statute prohibiting flag desecration because of its content bias in prescribing desired treatment of the flag.

225. 81 BVerfGE 278 (1990).

226. *Id.* at 280.

227. StGB § 90a declares,

(1) Whoever publicly, in an assembly or through the distribution of publications . . .

1. insults or maliciously casts into contempt the Federal Republic of Germany or one of its states or its constitutional order, or

2. defames the colors, the flag, the coat of arms or the anthem of the Federal Republic or one of its states, will be punished by imprisonment of up to three years or by a fine. (*Translated in* Quint, *supra* note 127, at 628 n. 86).

228. 81 BVerfGE at 291.

229. *Id.* Theoretically, it should make a difference whether artistic or opinion freedoms are at issue, since art is textually unbounded in comparison to the textual circumscription of opinion. In practice, however, the Constitutional Court has implied limitations on artistic freedoms. Thus, in reality there is no practical difference between artistic and opinion freedoms.

230. *Id.* at 292. In *Mephisto*, the Constitutional Court set down the definitive definition of art. "The essential characteristic of artistic activity is the artist's free and creative shaping of impressions, experiences and events for direct display through a specific language of shapes. All artistic activity is a mix of conscious and unconscious events that is not rationally orderable. Intuition, fantasy and artistic understanding all effect artistic creations, such creations are primarily not informational but rather an immediately direct expression of the individual personality of the artist." *Mephisto*, 30 BVerfGE 173, 188–89, *translated in* KOMMERS, *supra* note 59, at 427.

231. 81 BVerfGE at 292, *translated in* Quint, *supra* note 127, at 631.

232. 81 BVerfGE at 292.

233. *Id.*

234. *Id.* at 293.

235. *Id.*

236. Quint, *supra* note 127, at 632. "Criminal code section 90a(1)(1) therefore seems to be quite frankly a seditions libel statute of the type fundamentally rejected in the United States under the principles of New York Times v. Sullivan." *Id.* n. 113.

237. 491 U.S. 397 (1989); 496 U.S. 310 (1990).

238. Quint, *supra* note 127, at 633. "Thus protection of the flag forms one of the bulwarks . . . against subversion of the state." *Id.* at 634.

239. 81 BVerfGE at 294.

240. Quint, *supra* note 68, at 295.

241. A companion case, *National Anthem Case*, 81 BVerfGE 298 (1990), reached essentially the same conclusions as *Flag Desecration*. The case involved a published satirization of the German national anthem.

242. Donald P. Kommers, *The Jurisprudence of Free Speech in the United States and the Federal Republic of Germany*, 53 S. CAL. L. REV. 657, 692 (1980).

243. *Denial of Responsibility for World War II*, 90 BVerfGE 1, 15 (1994); *Soldiers Are Murderers*, 45 NJW 2943, 2943 (1994).

244. 505 U.S. 377 (1989) (may not selectively proscribe fighting words).

245. 90 BVerfGE 241 (1994).

246. Gooding v. Wilson, 405 U.S. 518 (1972) (Georgia law at issue overbroad and therefore unconstitutional); *Cripple*, 86 BVerfGE 1 (1992).

247. Hustler Magazine v. Falwell, 485 U.S. 46 (1988); *Strauss Political Satire Case*, 75 BVerfGE 369 (1987).

248. Kommers, *supra* note 242, at 675.

249. *Id.* at 694.

250. *Wallraff*, 66 BVerfGE 116 (1984). In this case, an investigative reporter worked clandestinely for a tabloid in order to obtain information as to its workings and then published his results, reflecting negatively on the tabloid.

251. Kommers notes, "The Supreme Court demands a legal posture of neutrality toward all political ideas uttered in the public forum; the Federal Constitutional Court envisions a polity capable of legally defending those fundamental political values and principles of the Basic Law." Kommers, *supra* note 242, at 693.

252. An example is Germany's proscription of group defamation and hate speech out of a desire to curb discord in society. *See, e.g., Cripple*, 86 BVerfGE 1 (1992).

253. *Brandenburg*, 395 U.S. 444 (1969).

254. STEVEN H. SHIFFRIN, THE FIRST AMENDMENT, DEMOCRACY, AND ROMANCE 87 (1990).

255. Obviously, this is more an ideal than reality. Events such as the bombing in Oklahoma City on April 19, 1995 or the April 20, 1999, student killings of students at Columbine high school in Colorado (both timed around Hitler's birthday), or the August 1999 targeted shootings of Jews in a Los Angeles Jewish community center by an American neo-Nazi might give one pause about the viability of such faith. Nevertheless, "the constitutional right of free expression . . . put[s] the decision as to what views shall be voiced largely into the hands of each of us, in the hope that use of such freedom will ultimately produce a more capable citizenry and more perfect polity and in the belief that no other approach would comport with the premise of individual dignity and choice upon which our political system rests." Cohen v. California, 403 U.S. 15, 24 (1971).

8

Comparative Observations

Having evaluated human dignity, personality and privacy, and freedom of expression in German and American constitutional law, the similarities and differences in the countries' constitutional vision, doctrine, and technique become evident. Through our exercise of comparison we have gained important insight into the nature of human personality as conceived within a constitutional setting, both as personality is developed within a specific culture and as it reflects on the human condition, transcending national borders. We have also obtained a portrait of the two societies, revealing alternative visions of the construction of freedom and its relationship to community.

We have examined in some detail the specific traits of human personality identified and preferred in the two countries. Now we are in a position to put these together to form a human composite. We have also uncovered some of the interests valued by each social order, especially as asserted in limitation to claims of freedom. From this we discern a pattern to the makeup of each society. This last chapter, accordingly, gathers the observations uncovered through our comparative survey and forms a portrait of human personality and its relation to society. Certainly, this portrait is tentative, dependent on the limited nature of this survey. Three aims guide our inquiry. First, we want to derive a silhouette of human personality. Second, we want to obtain a portrait of the legal cultures of the two societies. Third, drawing upon these inquiries, we want to see how we might fashion a vision of human personality and freedom suitable for the twenty-first century.

SILHOUETTE OF HUMAN PERSONALITY

There is much the two laws have in common. Both developed formatively in the period after World War II, evidencing the emerging phenomenon of human rights, particularly in Western legal culture.[1] Both accord broad freedom to individuals to shape their destiny while balancing individual aspiration against the demands of maintaining social order. Both laws rely on an activist Court to shape these freedoms against the clutches of majoritarian control.

There is also much similarity in the idea of human freedom as manifested concretely in specific human rights. The content of these rights has much in common as well, at least in a general sense. In the survey undertaken here, we have seen how the countries value human personality and privacy, human autonomy and self-determination, and freedom of expression as essential ingredients to the human condition as that state is envisioned at the beginning of the twenty-first century. The resonance of these human attributes in two cultures suggests something fundamental about them. We might call them, tentatively, essential to modern man and woman, reflective and constitutive of their identity, at least as envisioned within these Western cultures. Other attributes might also be identified. The idea of human rights comprises other freedoms than the specific ones examined here. In a broader survey we would have observed further resonance, again in a general way, between the two societies, in freedoms of conscience, equality, and certain rights to fair treatment and fair hearing. In this sense, the concept of human rights itself is an essential attribute of the two countries.

As we look more carefully at the nature of these freedoms in the two cultures, we observe both similarity and difference in their conception. The freedoms that most closely approximate one another, of the ones surveyed, are freedom of expression, autonomy rights, and its subset of abortion law. This convergence in the idea of freedom reveals something basic about the human condition, especially as it relates to society. First, the high valuation of expression is attributable, in part, to its role in furthering the functioning of democracy and the political participation on which it depends. Freedom of expression is indispensably constitutive to the functioning of democracy. Not surprisingly, both Germany and the United States rely on this aspect of expression to support their democratic orders. In this way, free speech and democracy go hand in hand. Expression too is an indispensable attribute of human dignity, valued as an intrinsic part of human personality. Thus, broad and deep rights of freedom of expression reaffirm the centrality of human dignity in rich and varied ways.[2] In a sense, exercise of communication freedoms circumscribes significant dimensions of a person's personality. Both countries conceive of expression along these individual and social dimensions, forming an important resonance between them.

With the search for meaning in life in the twentieth century, it is appropriate that both laws accord wide latitude to citizens to pursue their destinies over a core of essential matters. This is the main aim of the respective autonomy laws. Such facilitation of personal control over life is another important common thread between the two countries. Especially revealing here is the growing convergence in practical terms in abortion laws, a particularly knotty problem that requires a careful balance between liberty and community. Also especially congruent are matters central to personal existence and identity, such as a range of sexual and reproductive matters, including ones over procreation, conception, and certain sexual identity, and ones that go to the very termination of life itself, whether as abortion or suicide. Man and woman determine crucial ingredients of their existence.

Of course, the specific construction of human rights in the two countries differs as well as converges, and these differences, upon closer examination, seem as great as the similarities. The main differences in the quality of human rights include the range of freedom of action, which is broad in Germany but more narrow in America; the creation and nourishment of an interior sphere in German law, which is mainly absent in American law; the absolute commitment to human dignity in Germany, radiating throughout the legal order; and the absolutist quality of American free speech law in comparison to its vibrant yet more restrained counterpart in Germany. These last two differences reveal how we might characterize the difference between the two as a German Constitution of dignity and an American Constitution of liberty, these being the architectonic values of each order.

In Chapter 4 we examined how the German focus on interiority seems especially indicative of the historical German yearning for spiritual freedom. But we might also envision it as a consequence of the overriding concern for human well-being, fortifying inner as well as outer freedom. Of these rights that differ in conception, freedom of action may well be the most surprising. A broad concept of freedom of action would seem most appropriate to a Constitution of liberty, as in America. But instead it is part of the German order, demonstrating how dignity also bestows liberty and action, and how liberty can have a more restrained interpretation under the American Constitution. The future of American liberty, especially as to whether it might serve a more emancipatory role, would appear to be a burning issue at some point in the twenty-first century. If so, the meaning of the Ninth Amendment, as a final preserve of freedom, will become crucial.

As a human composite, we can see that both social orders vest man and woman with basic freedoms to master essential conditions of their fate, and to take the measures necessary to realize human capacity. The areas of greatest overlap in our survey comprise, in a sense, a core of central personality traits for man and woman as we enter the twenty-first century. By way of summation, this central core includes dignity and its particular radiation of self-worth, self-determination, self-realization, and self-respect. No realization of human capacity would be possible without these necessary ingredients. The core further comprises freedom of expression in all its magnitude, including freedom of thought, belief, emotion, and opinion; free choice over matters central to personal existence and identity, including especially a range of sexual and reproductive matters; and a certain freedom of action to pursue directly one's chosen vision in life. As we frame this portrait of modern man and woman, we can see that it is a constitutional vision, reflecting constitutionalism as a dominant influence in shaping human personality in our age and in our Western culture.

LEGAL CULTURES

Notwithstanding this core of convergence between the two countries, a closer look at the two laws reveals differences as well as similarities, and these differences seem as pronounced as the similarities. These differences are worth noting, in the spirit of comparison, because they bring out, in bold relief, the underlying cultural traits of the countries. At bottom, this inquiry reveals two paths to freedom and its relation to community, which is now our focus.

First and foremost, the countries contrast over the nature of their constitutional vision as set out in the text of the basic charter and as amplified by the two high Courts. The German vision, set out with reasonable clarity, reflecting the systematization of German legal science, centers around the human person as a "spiritual–moral" individual, and his or her dignity, including especially his or her ability to realize human capacity and satisfaction. Human values are thus the focal point of the legal order. The idea of human rights reflects this dignitarian flavor as well, consistent again with the concept of a Constitution of dignity. We can thus see that the aim of German law is to vindicate human dignity.

By comparison, the American constitutional vision is simpler, if not sketchier. The American focus is preeminently on outlining the limits of government, reflecting the original American republican revolution, and securing a basis for the pursuit of liberty and happiness. Americans are skeptical about government. Accordingly, they trust people more than government to promote personal welfare. In keeping with this defensive focus, the American charter does not set forth a comprehensive vision of how to pursue liberty or happiness, unlike the core of values enumerated in the German Constitution of dignity. Pursuit and realization of values is left mainly to individual discretion, as compared to circumscription of that choice along dignitarian parameters in the German scheme. The American focus on limitation of government, thus, is more consistent with a Constitution of liberty. Accordingly, personal choice, liberty, and individualism seem most appropriate.

Second, individualism and personal choice also follow from the American view of the Constitution, which limits official but not private action. In fact, the contrasting influence of the Constitutions in private law reveals a fundamentally different view concerning the distinction between public and private law and the impact of a constitution on society. In the United States the assumption is that there is a clear conceptual difference between the public and private realm of society. Private actors are free to act beyond the influence of the Constitution, their conduct shaped primarily only by the standards of statutory or common law. Only public actions must adhere to the Constitution, together with those private parties acting on behalf of government under the state action doctrine. Thus, the operative question in America for determining the reach of the Constitution is who is acting: State action is a prerequisite to application of the Constitution. These doctrines, in turn, illuminate another perspective on the pervasive American concern of limiting the reach of state authority in order to preserve private liberty.

In Germany, by contrast, there is no absolute separation between the public and private spheres. Under German doctrine, the status of a person, whether public or private, is not as relevant, in contrast to American law. Rather, the operative question under German law is whether the basic right is being curtailed. Private and social forces can threaten rights just as severely, if not more so, than state actions. Accordingly, the Basic Law applies, at least in-directly, to safeguard rights against impairment by private forces as well. There is an affinity between German doctrine and the views of the American legal realists.[3] The German view rests on the assumption underlying the Basic Law that certain basic values are so fundamental that they should apply throughout society as part of its governing principles.

The countries' contrasting value structures may also be attributable in part to the differing complexion of the populations. The United States is extremely heterogenous; Germany, by contrast, is relatively homogenous, although Germany is increasingly becoming more pluralistic. It stands to reason that the more homogenous the population, the greater possibility there is for consensus. Since America is so pluralistic, it is difficult for the population to agree on core values. Hence, it makes sense to leave value choices to individuals.

However, America's white population at the time of the Constitution's framing (the group then in control, to the unfortunate exclusion of people of color) was, like Germany's, relatively homogenous. Thus, the difference in the value structures of each country's population may influence the Courts' approach to interpretation of the basic charter more than any original intent. The difference in population complexion would seem to be a significant factor over the last fifty years, the formative period of the two laws. In the United States, the Supreme Court has fashioned broad spheres of personal freedom in this period. Perhaps the Supreme Court has so acted in order to fashion circuit breakers within the diverse society. Consciously or not, the Supreme Court may have kept this aspect of the Constitution "in tune with the times."[4]

Third, enumeration of rights and responsibilities in the two legal orders follows from these contrasting visions. The German constitutional value order, grounded in the underlying philosophic thought of Kant, reflects a careful calibration of rights and responsibilities, interpreted by the Constitutional Court as an "objective value-order," one that must apply generally in society, affecting all legal relationships. Since human dignity is the apex of this value structure, it naturally radiates throughout the legal system, in public and private law. An essential part of human dignity is basic rights and corresponding obligations.

While basic rights are mainly defensive or subjective in function, connoting a personal sphere of liberty, only rarely is such subjective liberty a matter of complete discretion. Instead, personal liberty is subject to limitation by the constitutional order, textually secured through express reservation or by necessary implication.[5] In this sense, rights are limited by obligations to others, as made manifest through the law. Yet limitations of liberty are themselves not a matter of parliamentarian discretion or social control. Rather, liberty may be restrained only upon justification pursuant to the value order.[6] In this sense, dignitarian morality acts as the "higher law" of German constitutionalism.[7] One important role of the Constitutional Court is to control application of this idea of higher law.

German rights also contain an objective or positive dimension, obligating government to effectuate their command. Human dignity makes decisive claims to official action along these lines. Notable examples of this include the Constitutional Court's implication of a zone of privacy to protect individuals from a prying public in the context of fabricated, sensationalistic reporting in *Soraya*, or accurate but negative reporting in *Lebach*. That these dignitarian radiations trumped even freedom of expression claims illustrates the strength of the constitutional vision of dignity. Further, the Court's implication of a positive duty to protect fetal life against even the dignitarian rights of women to determine their fate, in the *Abortion* cases, is another notable example of the far-reaching claim to governmental action that can result from such objectivism.

By contrast, Americans share the concept of negative liberties with the Germans, but do not have a corresponding principle of positive rights or duties. Thus, Americans have little claim to governmental action, even over matters of human dignity.[8] In fact, we might see the "purely negative freedom of American constitutionalism" as inhibiting the "full liberation of the human personality" and the "full realization of human freedom," especially when contrasted with the German model.[9] American rights, like privacy, are instead mainly spheres of personal autonomy. Unlike German negative liberties, rights are not coupled with responsibilities, either through textual reservation or by implication, except what may be reasonably ferreted out of the legal system itself. Not surprisingly, lacking the context of an underlying philosophic base, American rights have more of an absolutist quality to them; there are few textual or background restraints on individual freedom. Again, we can see how this leads to a Constitution of liberty.

Fourth, the contrasting visions of the two laws have dramatic consequences for the concepts of human dignity, personality, and privacy in the two laws. German autonomy concepts are reasonably well thought out, constituting an integrated whole, reflecting again the classification and comprehensiveness of German legal science. There is an inner dimension, focusing on the "moral–spiritual" essence of a human being, and there is an outer dimension, reflecting a person's activity in the world. Both dimensions, of course, radiate from the same source of human dignity.

American autonomy law, by contrast, mainly reflects a search for personal identity and self-realization. These themes fit uneasily into an inner–outer dichotomy. Personal decision making over topics like procreation, contraception, or child rearing certainly partakes of self-realization in relation to the world, but also bespeaks inner identity. These American rights mainly reflect personal autonomy pursuant to the negative concept of liberties.

A closer review of the specific enumeration of American and German personality rights illuminates these points. German personality law reflects the broad themes of German law: human dignity and its cognates, including valuation of life as an end in itself, worth and equal worth, and freedom to act within the constraints of the value order. This accounts for some of the sharpest differences with American law. Foremost among these is the focus on the interior component of human personality, an emanation of the inner striving for freedom. Through its jurisprudence, the Constitutional Court has attempted to capture and preserve the essence of human personhood and personality, and safeguard it amidst the challenges of modern society. Hence, the Constitutional Court seeks to identify and fortify an inner space, "in which to develop freely and self-responsibly . . . personalities . . . [into] which [people] can retreat, barring all entrance to the outer world, in which one can enjoy tranquility and a right to solitude."[10] The *Census* cases, by limiting official use of personal information on account of human autonomy, show how such nurturing of human personhood can make a difference with respect to modern social and economic developments.[11] This aspect of German law seems particularly well suited to the challenges of the information age.

While the *Census* cases are the most dramatic illustrations of this strand of interiority, the Constitutional Court has carved out related emanations of human personality in limitation of political and social forces and in service of the inner person. Most notable here is the right to control personal information, crystallized into a general right of informational self-determination. Intimate information reflects human personality, according to the Constitutional Court, being an ingredient to conception of personhood from inside and outside perspectives. Accordingly, the person participating in this aspect of "life-formation" should have a measure of control over these matters. Based on this reasoning, the Constitutional Court has extended degrees of protection over personal data, honor and rights to one's good name, portrayal of self, image, and spoken word.[12]

These doctrines are simply not part of American constitutional law. This may be because the textual support in the U.S. Constitution is scant as compared to that in the German Basic Law. It may be because Americans lack the certitude of a vision corresponding to the German focus on the centrality of personality. Perhaps this explains the Supreme Court's more cautious approach as compared to the Constitutional Court. It may also be because American society is a very public society, with great emphasis on participation in politics, culture, and the society. Such participation is vital to the functioning of the democracy and the community, but such public focus may also have diverted energy from development of a vital private sphere.

The Supreme Court's cautiousness may also be out of regard for states' sovereignty, the value underlying federalism. Most American substantive due process cases involve a second-guessing of state actions, which the Supreme Court ordinarily is hesitant to do.[13] In fact, the Supreme Court has embarked upon another venture to limit federal power in favor of state sovereignty.[14] By contrast, in Germany, a different federal state, personality cases mainly involve federal law.[15] Hence, any second-guessing is with respect to a coordinate branch of government. On such a level field, the full steering effect of the Constitutional Court can be exercised, perhaps without the inhibition of the Supreme Court. Still, with the integrated German court system, many German cases involve the Constitutional Court's second-guessing of the ordinary courts, which the Constitutional Court too is hesitant to do. Thus, at bottom, the two Courts are cautious for different reasons, attributable to the different federal structures.

The difference in constitutional doctrine may also be because American private law, unlike German law, did not develop privacy concepts comprehensively, and thus, unlike German constitutional law, American constitutional law had no ready base to stand on.[16] Lacking grounding in personality, other values, most notably free speech, can be exercised in the United States without the braking influence of dignitarian concerns. Moreover, American private law does not connect to constitutional law in the more seamless way that it does in Germany. For example, the norms of the constitutional value order seep into German private law, especially through the general clauses of the Civil Code. And article 2 personality and article 5 communication freedoms are textually limited by provisions of the legal order. Thus, there are better opportunities for cross-fertilization between German constitutional and private law.

Even in the area where there is the greatest overlap between the two autonomy laws—issues relating to identity, self-determination, and autonomy—these differences are evident. German law is grounded in the philosophy of human capacity and dignity, "factors constitutive for individual self-discovery and self-understanding."[17] These desires yield, even, a "striving toward unity of psyche and body."[18] American autonomy decisions, such as those over contraception or procreation, by contrast, are grounded in privacy rights and self-realization, not dignity and its elevated cognates, like human inviolability. American rights thus do not couple freedom with a concomitant concern for well-being, in comparison to the Germans.

These differences in the concept of personality reflect differences in the two legal cultures. The German vision reflects careful ordering of the characteristics of human personhood, especially those called upon in social intercourse, to facilitate well-being. Freedom to develop human capacity is sought, indeed encouraged, to the maximum extent compatible with the freedom of everybody else. Thus, moral obligation and respect for others requires that freedom be exercised within the bounds of community. In this view, freedom can truly exist only with provision for well-being, mutual toleration, and respect. It is in this sense that the "human person is an autonomous being developing freely within the social community."[19] He or she is not "isolated and self-regarding," but "related to and bound by the community."[20] Thus, individual self-determination is offset by responsibility, civility, and participation.

By contrast, American law places tremendous faith in individuals' ability to choose and realize choice. The root value in the United States is personal liberty more than any moral concept like dignity. Choosing one's fortune is integral to the American system of self-government with respect to politics, culture, and personal life. In this sense, freedom is more complete than in Germany, unbounded by any value constraining liberty except those that people themselves determine.

Most emblematic of this somewhat absolutist quality of American freedom is, of course, commitment to free speech. More than any other freedom in America, free speech receives the most favor; the United States accords especially elevated status to free speech. Free speech is integral to the spirit of the people and the shaping of American culture. For these reasons, we can say free speech is to Americans what human dignity is to Germans.

There are several explanations for this. One is cultural pluralism. With such vibrant pluralism over ethnicity, religion, and opinion, free speech forms one of the main common denominators in America. Free speech is a presumptive zone of freedom where all Americans can put aside or air differences and speak openly to or about one another. Uninhibited discussion is indispensable to the formation of democracy and culture, and this is especially the case in the United States.

A second explanation is, in fact, American democracy. American democracy was formed on the radical idea, 200 years ago, that the people, not a parliament or monarch, are the governors. Since through democratic self-government people rule, it makes especial sense that they receive as much information as possible to facilitate sound decision making. Moreover, participation by as many people as possible, which free speech facilitates, is crucial to success of the democracy as well. It is not healthy for any society to have outsiders. A final explanation, by no means meant to be exhaustive, is that free speech follows naturally from the pursuit of liberty. Freedom to think and speak freely is an essence of liberty itself.

In contrast to the absolutist quality of American speech, we observe that German communication freedoms are more constrained. The main constraint is dignity, the root value of the social order. Dignitarian interests can limit expression, as in rights to reputation, honor, and personality. Dignity is the glue between rights-protective and rights-restrictive interpretations, even over the idea of freedom of expression.

Viewed in this light, we have a different perspective on the German Constitution of dignity as compared to the American Constitution of liberty. The German vision of constitutional democracy serves as an alternative strategy to organize society, one reflecting the benefits, perhaps, of added perspective and experience. There are obvious indigenous influences that led to the erection and makeup of the German constitutional value order, especially to empower and guide personal decision making. Kantian philosophy, Christian natural law, and nineteenth-century German legal science are decisive theoretical influences. The German experience with anarchy during the Weimar Republic and of dehumanization during the Nazi period, including severe limitation of human personality and capacity and even annihilation of life itself, are crucial histories. The erection and makeup of the German value order may, in fact, reflect a desire to channel human behavior out of fear that evil might arise (again) from unchained human passion. These concerns might also help explain how and why Germany attempts to constrain excessive individualism.

Alternatively, however, German constitutionalism might reflect the added wisdom of comparative experiences. For example, much would seem to have been learned from the lessons of more unrestrained majoritarianism, as in France or even England, and its tendency to limit human capacity.[21] Other lessons might be learned from more legally unbounded liberty, as in America, and its tendency to encourage excessive passion or unleash unbridled social or economic power that might overshadow personal dignity. Against these histories and experiences, emphasis on the inviolability of human personhood becomes a final check against power, official or private, that might operate arbitrarily. That is an important contribution to public philosophy.

The contrasting constitutional visions might explain the different stances of the two constitutional Courts. Both Courts are countermajoritarian institutions, asserting the values of the constitutional order against the excesses of majoritarian rule. As a matter of comparative law, this is itself notable: It is worth recognizing that outside American borders the Supreme Court is not the only activist judiciary. Yet the Constitutional Court is aggressively activist in a way that the Supreme Court is not. The Constitutional Court actively sets out to realize in society the values of the Basic Law, attempting to coordinate constitutional text with social reality. The wholesale rewrite of legislation in the *Census* cases and the *Abortion* cases attests to this. The Constitutional Court thus acts somewhat more like the Supreme Court did in the first third of the twentieth century under the substantive due process regime, censoring governmental actions, where necessary, for reasonableness. The Constitutional Court is a prime force to further the vision of dignity and guide its application in society.

By contrast, the Supreme Court today mainly rules when it must to enforce a limitation of government. One major exception to the Supreme Court's preferred caution, of course, is its recent decision in *Bush v. Gore*, which settled the 2000 presidential election.[22] Yet it is hard to imagine the Supreme Court creating claims to governmental action to protect constitutional values, as the Constitutional Court did in implying a right to protection of life in the *Abortion* cases or in facilitating redress of privacy and personality claims in *Mephisto, Soraya,* or *Lebach.* In this way, the Basic Law, as interpreted by the Constitutional Court, acts like a blueprint for society, whereas the American Constitution is more like an outline of government.

The approaches of the two Courts mirror their different missions. The German Constitutional Court places a premium on the text of the Basic Law, its structure and purpose, and its applicability to current social and economic conditions. The Constitutional Court carefully examines principles and postulates that underlie general, open-ended textual provisions, such as the rule of law, the Social State Principle, and, of course, the capacious concept of "human dignity." The Constitutional Court's excavation of a deeper meaning to the Basic Law, trying to capture the spirit as well as the letter of the basic charter, imbues its interpretive stance with a certain dynamism. In some cases, most notably *Soraya,* the Constitutional Court even openly acknowledged that it would employ its perceived notions of justice to rectify wrongs in the written law.[23]

By comparison, the Supreme Court focuses on text, Framers' intent, and precedent as a general interpretive strategy. The Supreme Court is ordinarily uncomfortable trying to excavate a deeper meaning to open-ended rights provisions (such as due process), preferring to stick to the letter of the text or, if necessary, history or tradition to ground capacious language. And the Supreme Court eschews using extratextual sources such as natural law. These interpretive techniques reflect its desire to adhere to a stable rule of law founded on a defensible basis; to interpret, but not announce law.[24]

The Constitutional Court actively attempts to maintain the essence of constitutional concepts while keeping constitutional text "in tune with the times."[25] Recall, for example, the Constitutional Court's attempts to preserve the principle of human dignity amidst a changing world in the *Census* cases, in relation to changing computer technology, or the *Transsexual* cases, in relation to evolving medical and moral developments. By contrast, the Supreme Court generally makes adjustments to changing social and economic conditions only gradually, and often amidst great anguish and controversy.[26] American constitutionalism thus seems tied to the past in a way that German law is not. In these ways, the Constitutional Court is forward in focus, whereas the Supreme Court looks backward.[27]

From these differences in constitutional vision, technique, and doctrine, we can extrapolate deeper differences in legal culture. The German prioritization of human dignity raises moral autonomy to the forefront of society; it is the higher law of German constitutionalism. Thus, persons have expansive freedom to act and to develop human ability, but that freedom is coupled with a concern for well-being, including solidifying the inner realm of personality. Moral autonomy, moreover, is not a one-way street; it involves responsibility too, including to others that one must recognize, even if through enforcement of the moral order. Accordingly, freedom is to unfold within the social community, which can both empower and limit human activity, depending on resolution of the conflict between individual and social claims.[28] Rights are thus exercised within a framework of duties and responsibilities, mediated ultimately by the Constitutional Court's interpretation of this higher law.

In American law, by contrast, the focus is on freedom to pursue one's vision of liberty or happiness, unbounded by a strong sense of legally constructed moral order. Americans thus tend to exercise rights without corresponding legally proscribed duties or responsibilities. Beyond the sanction of the law, people might recognize duties or responsibilities out of a sense of self-restraint or obligation. Naturally, American rights are more individualistic and absolutist in orientation.

HUMAN PERSONALITY IN THE TWENTY-FIRST CENTURY

As we now enter the twenty-first century, new phenomena will test us and our conceptions of human liberty and human satisfaction. We will learn even more about the state of the human condition. Experience has a way of putting ideas to the acid test.

Certainly it is not possible to frame any comprehensive vision of human personality now, for the future, or for the present twenty-first century that might suit the coming age. Truth, especially about humankind, is elusive and difficult to fathom. Often we work in the shadows, without complete knowledge, trying to achieve understanding by tracing patterns or outlines, not the thing itself. To an extent, that has been the approach of this book: deciphering human personality through the traits and characteristics registered in the legal culture. And that inquiry has revealed much about certain essences of human personhood. Human dignity, self-determination, freedom, and control over life, as tested through crises over time and through the social order, would appear to be certain verities of human life, at least as we have seen it over the last half of the twentieth century.

How these essential traits of human personhood will affect or be affected in the twenty-first century is, of course, hard to say. We can only venture a guess. Much will depend on the challenges that the twenty-first century presents. Most of these we do not know. But the outlines of some of them are evident.

As we begin this century it is clear that there is an ongoing significant and pervasive technological revolution that affects all major aspects of society. Commerce, medicine, privacy, and politics are just some of the areas affected. One part of this revolution is information. The computer has facilitated access to information of unprecedented scope, variety, and dimension. And through the computer, information is accessible at any time in instantaneous fashion. With information so readily available, there is always the possibility of abuse or manipulation: the specter of Big Brother. Another part of the revolution is technological innovation itself. Medical research, for example, now examines the mysteries of life, breaking its essence into DNA and other basic elements. Already we have seen the effects of this research. Gene technology, cloning, artificial insemination, and the ability to prolong life are central challenges to the meaning of human life and existence.

Another challenge we face is the global economy. Ruled by Wall Street and the search for the bottom line, governments, societies, and people are increasingly subject to the rules of the marketplace. The ability to move capital across borders instantaneously through the click of a computer mouse has meant that there is no escaping the judgments of investors. The dictates of efficiency, wealth creation, and productivity promote a uniform code of conduct across national borders as cultures and patterns of life reorder along these lines for economic survival. It is even entering American politics. Democratic presidential candidate Bill Bradley lamented in October 1999 that "the new global economy just doesn't care about the 6:30 dinner. It doesn't care that you don't know how to use a computer. The global economy isn't worrying about you at all."[29] In Germany, the cherished social welfare state seems at risk.

A final trend, already evident, is the movement toward interdependent global solutions to increasingly global problems. Crime, environmental ills, corruption, drugs, and performance of capital markets are some examples of problems that defy national solutions, requiring international assistance. Increasingly, cooperation among nations is necessary. This may lead to enhanced regionalization, as in the European Union, or it may lead to deeper structures of international governance, as in the United Nations or the World Trade Organization. Or it may lead to unanticipated government structures, organizations, or movements of people. The securing of any such new structures on the basis of human liberty and welfare will be an acute challenge.

To meet these challenges and others not yet within our ken, much will be required of us. Particularly, we will need to draw upon the reservoir of human potential that lies at the root of human being. Reliance on certain fundamentals of human personhood thus seems especially desirable. Distilling the essence of what we have learned in our study, it seems reasonable to recognize as indispensable human traits human dignity, self-determination, freedom of expression, and development of human capacity, including over inner freedom. A few words about these traits and their relevance to the twenty-first century seems in order as we anticipate the future.

Human dignity is essential to maintain a focus on human values as the central concern of society. As we rely ever more on machines and technology, as seems predictable, it is important more than ever not to lose focus on the centrality of human being. Commitment to human dignity seems the best way to assure that people will be valued intrinsically for who they are, not for what they do. In a world of technology, it is especially important that people not be depersonalized and treated as objects or means to an end. Likewise, with the demands of the global economy inducing conformity, especially its propensity to channel human behavior along prescribed routes, it is essential that people are valued as worthy beings per se, quite apart from what they produce. Emphasis of the inviolability of human personhood is a final, ultimate check against the constraining influence of these powers. German law, especially, has shown how human values can be brought to the fore in society through commitment to human dignity.

With the information revolution showing every sign of continuing unabated, and with other ongoing important technological, social, and economic changes afoot, access to and control over information seems paramount. Thus, freedom of expression is especially vital. As citizens of the twenty-first century, we need as much information as we can process in order to better understand our world, our lives, and our future. Vibrant speech freedoms are necessary to the building and securing of democracy and the social order. Deliberation is essential to the formulation of sound public policies. We also need information and freedom to think and deliberate over ourselves as we fashion the course of our lives, achieving personal control. The sanctuary of the mind, finally, provides needed respite from the challenges of the world. Freedom of thought, ideas, and expression are crucial traits that will be called upon significantly in the future.

Human creativity will also be at a premium as we anticipate the future. Human rights that encourage development of human capacity are, therefore, very important. In our survey of German and American law we have seen two paths to development of human capacity. German law proactively sets out to nourish the well-being of individuals, bestowing significant autonomy but helping to channel such freedom in ways that promote personal growth and fulfillment. American law focuses on privacy—the right to be let alone—not well-being, leaving choices that affect human welfare to individuals as part of their autonomy. The relative merits and demerits of each position have been extensively cataloged in Chapters 4, 5, and 6. The law of each country has demonstrated how each path works.

German law demonstrates how the law can actively facilitate human capacity, and this has merit. Yet the innovativeness at the root of American society is a testament to the success of the American emphasis on freedom and individuality. In the United States, emphasizing freedom has unleashed significant human capacity and creativity. Thus, we might identify facilitation of human capacity as the essential trait, leaving the manner in which that is done to cultural choice. A premium is likely to be placed on issues central to personal identity and existence.

Given the evident challenges of the twenty-first century, such as technology and globalization, it is crucial that people have time for leisure, personal development, and nurture. We all need a certain distance and refuge from the demands of society. Hence, creation and maintenance of a private zone, presumptively inaccessible accept on permission, where a person can concentrate on inner freedom and nourishing of the soul, seems essential. Here German law has taken the lead, demonstrating how a person can remain faithful to the soul amidst the challenges of modern life.

One aspect of inner freedom that is likely to come to the fore is control over personal information. With the computerization of the world, information of endless variety and quantity is available, including information personal to people. Possession of detailed personal information carries a serious threat of abuse, including coercion and manipulation of human autonomy. The more that is known about a person, the easier the person is to control. In this way, control of information is itself control. To safeguard the inviolability of human personhood, personal control over intimate information thus seems essential as a matter of personal autonomy. Here too, German law, with its development of informational self-determination, shows the way by which human autonomy can be safeguarded amidst severe technological change.

Certainly, there are other traits indispensable to the human condition that will be called upon to solve central problems of the twenty-first century. I have only offered a preliminary sketch. The task of conceptualizing human personality to meet the challenges of the future in ways compatible with human freedom and welfare is an urgent one for us all.

CONCLUSION

Through examination of these contrasting constitutional visions, we discover alternative conceptions of humanity, personality, and community, as outlined in public law, conceptions that can be enriching, ennobling, or both. Perhaps this is the central purpose of comparative law: we learn, by looking at others, important truths about ourselves, truths that can then be reevaluated or reaffirmed. Certainly, there is much to learn about the two laws, and much the two laws can learn from each other. For example, the *Census* cases demonstrate a sensible way to preserve the inviolability of personhood and human freedom amidst dramatic technological change. American law might profitably develop similar rights of informational self-determination, a logical evolution of First Amendment law. In addition, if Americans want to pursue a more coherent vision of community, the German method of coupling rights with duties, individually and socially, points the way toward introducing communal values into the social order. Through attempting to secure human dignity for all, we would perhaps be less preoccupied in securing our own claims. In this way, we might escape our obsession with "rights talk" and learn to appreciate the value of human solidarity.

Conversely, if dignitarian rights are justifiably viewed as indispensable to German law, then the Constitutional Court might profitably transplant certain of the techniques employed by the Supreme Court to preserve fundamental rights. For example, importation of strict scrutiny analysis would lend a degree of clarity and precision to German rights analysis. To a degree, this already has occurred, evidencing the transplantation of concepts across cultures, albeit with some adjustment.[30] Perhaps pursuit of a mutual cultural influence is not so far off after all. Perhaps therein lies a path to greater understanding and, ultimately, satisfaction.

NOTES

1. In Germany, personality rights, for example, have a long lineage in the private law. However, the modern cases, starting with *Elfes*, mark the essential development. In the United States, cases like Meyers v. Nebraska, 262 U.S. 390 (1923), or Skinner v. Oklahoma, 316 U.S. 535 (1942), might be thought of as originating an emphasis on autonomy. But Griswold v. Connecticut, 381 U.S. 479 (1965), is the essential case for this development of American law. The pattern is similar for the evolution of other rights.

2. William J. Brennan, Jr., *The Constitution of the United States: Contemporary Ratification*, 19 U. C. DAVIS L. REV. 2, 12 (1985) (lecture presented at Georgetown University Law Center on Oct. 12, 1985).

3. Peter E. Quint, *Free Speech and Private Law in German Constitutional Theory*, 48 MD. L. REV. 247, 340–41 (1989) noting, for example, Cohen, *The Basis of Contract*, 46 HARV. L. REV. 553 (1933); Hale, *Force and the State: A Comparison of "Political" and "Economic" Compulsion*, 35 COLUM. L. REV. 149 (1935). *Note also* the influence of the German "free law" school on American legal realists. Herget & Wallace, *The German Free Law Movement as the Source of American Legal Realism*, 73 VA. L. REV. 399 (1987).

4. *Griswold*, 381 U.S. at 522 (Black, J., dissenting).

5. *See, e.g.*, GG art. 2 and 5.

6. In all cases, the essence of the right must be preserved. GG art. 19(2).

7. By higher law I mean all actions must be judged for conformity with dignity as the dispositive norm of the Basic Law's value order. Note, for example, the contrasting effect of human dignity in *Elfes* (rights enhancing) and *Mephisto* (rights constrictive).

8. On occasion, dignitarian interests can make a claim for government action. *See, e.g.*, Goldberg v. Kelly, 397 U.S. 254 (1970) (dignity can make a claim to procedural due process protections).

9. Donald P. Kommers, *Comments on Part I, in* GERMANY AND ITS BASIC LAW: PAST, PRESENT AND FUTURE—A GERMAN–AMERICAN SYMPOSIUM 66–67 (Paul Kirchhof & Donald P. Kommers, eds., 1993).

10. *Microcensus*, 27 BVerfGE 1, 6 (1969).

11. *Lebach*, and its concern for rehabilitation of a felon, evidences this too.

12. *See, e.g., Census Act*, 65 BVerfGE 1 (1984); *Mephisto*, 30 BVerfGE 173 (1971); *Soraya*, 34 BVerfGE 269 (1973); *Lebach*, 35 BVerfGE 202 (1973); *Böll*, 54 BVerfGE 208 (1980).

13. Note, for example, Justice Harlan's famous formulation: "Judicial self-restraint . . . will be achieved in this area, as in other constitutional areas, only by continual insistence upon respect for the teachings of history, solid recognition of the basic values that underlie our society, and wise appreciation of the great roles that the doctrines of federalism and separation of powers have played in establishing and preserving American freedoms." *Griswold*, 381 U.S. 479, 501 (1965) (Harlan, J., concurring).

14. In history, the Supreme Court has often tried to effectuate a regime of dual federal–state sovereignty. *See, e.g.*, United States v. E. C. Knight, 156 U.S. 1 (1895). Usually, the Court's efforts on behalf of states' rights have failed, being unworkable in practice. It is thus surprising that the Court has decided to pursue this path again. *See, e.g.*, United States v. Lopez, 514 U.S. 549 (1995).

15. The German federalist structure differs from the American system. The German federal government contains most legislative powers, including all those exercised in the United States. In addition, the German federal government has the power over private law, such as contract, tort, or criminal law, areas traditionally left to the American states. Some powers are exclusively federal; others are shared with the *Länder*. By contrast, federal legislation, interestingly, is mainly carried out by the *Länder*. DAVID P. CURRIE, THE CONSTITUTION OF THE FEDERAL REPUBLIC OF GERMANY 34 (1994). For a description of the nuances of German federalism, *see id.* at 33–101; DONALD P. KOMMERS, THE CONSTITUTIONAL JURISPRUDENCE OF THE FEDERAL REPUBLIC OF GERMANY 69–120 (1989).

16. Despite strong arguments for a law based on the notion of an "inviolate personality"—*see, e.g.*, Samuel D. Warren & Louis D. Brandeis, *The Right to Privacy*, 4 HARV. L. REV., 193, 205–07 (1890); Roscoe Pound, *The Interests of Personality*, 28 HARV. L. REV. 343, 445 (1915)—which may have mirrored the German law, American personality law never fully developed. These matters are discussed in Chapter 4. Moreover, since the rise of First Amendment law, signaled most dramatically by New York Times v. Sullivan, 376 U.S. 254 (1964), interests of personality, especially honor and reputation, have been eclipsed by free speech interests.

17. *Right to Heritage I*, 79 BVerfGE 256, 264 (1989).

18. *Transsexual*, 49 BVerfGE 286, 299 (1978).

19. *Mephisto*, 30 BVerfGE 173, 193 (1971).

20. *Life Imprisonment Case*, 45 BVerfGE 187, 227 (1977).

21. The French Revolution was a pivotal event for Germany and Europe generally. Under the influence of the philosophy of Rousseau, the leaders of the Revolution tried to ascertain the true common good of the political community. Hence, liberty lies with the people as a whole, unrestrained by notions of fundamental rights. This led to significant abuses and horrors. Since the Puritan Revolution of 1642, England has been ruled by Parliament. With the Glorious Revolution of 1689, the monarchy was

restored, but on the terms of Parliament. Thus, the rule of Parliament, representing the will of the people, is supreme, unbounded by a written, strong guarantee of fundamental rights. Even in England today there has not been, until just recently, a strong, enforceable set of rights inherent in people. *See, e.g.*, The Sunday Times v. United Kingdom 2 EHRR 245 (1979–80) (European Court of Human Rights finding U.K. in violation of European Convention on Human Rights for prior restraint on press reports concerning thalidomide disaster); Attorney General v. Guardian Newspapers (*Spycatcher*), 3 ALL ER 316, 343 (1987) (upholding prior restraint on publication of book, *Spycatcher*, which discussed memoirs of former officer of British Secret Service, MI5). The book at issue, known as *Spycatcher*, revealed intimate secrets of British intelligence. The book was widely available outside England, but not in England. Ironically, rights in Britian to a certain extent rely on enforcement through the outside, such as the European Court of Human Rights, as in *Spycatcher*, or like institutions, such as the Court of Justice of the European Community. *See, e.g.*, European Community Commission v. UK 1982 Eur. Comm. Rep. 2601, CCM Common Mkt. Rep. Dec. #8853 (application of principle of comparative worth, equal pay for equal work of men and women). Rights enforcement will now become more effective. In October 2000 England took a forceful step toward adoption of a written guarantee of basic rights by enacting the Human Rights Act, which incorporates the European Convention on Human Rights.

22. 531 U.S. 98 (Dec. 12, 2000).

23. *See also Elfes*, 6 BVerfGE 32, 41 (1957).

24. *See, e.g.*, Bowers v. Hardwick, 478 U.S. 186, 194–95 (1986). Ironically, in recent states' rights cases the Supreme Court openly employs structural reasoning, excavating a deeper meaning to the Constitution. *See, e.g.*, Printz v. United States, 521 U.S. 898 (1997).

25. *Griswold*, 381 U.S. 479, 522 (1965) (Black, J., dissenting).

26. *See, e.g.*, Brown v. Board of Education, 347 U.S. 483 (1954) (signaling end of separate but equal doctrine); West Coast Hotel Co. v. Parrish, 300 U.S. 379 (1937) (signalling demise of *Lochner* substantive due process).

27. *Compare*, for example, *Transsexuality*, 49 BVerfGE 286 (1978) (rooting sexual identity to sense of well-being) *with Bowers v. Hardwick*, 478 U.S. 186 (looking to history and tradition to limit sexual self-determination).

28. *Compare*, for example, *Mephisto*, 30 BVerfGE 173 (1971) (human dignity may constrain free expression) *with Transsexuality*, 49 BVerfGE 286 (1978) (human dignity empowers sexual self-identity).

29. James Dao, *Bradley Wants More Spending to Ease Stresses on Families*, N.Y. TIMES, Oct. 8, 1999, at A24.

30. *Right to Heritage II*, 90 BVerfGE 263, 271 (1994) (applying heightened intensive scrutiny).

Selected Provisions of the Constitution of the United States

We the People of the United States, in Order to form a more perfect Union, establish Justice, insure domestic Tranquility, provide for the common defence, promote the general Welfare, and secure the Blessings of Liberty to ourselves and our Posterity, do ordain and establish this Constitution for the United States of America.

AMENDMENT I [1791]

Congress shall make no law respecting an establishment of religion, or prohibiting the free exercise thereof; or abridging the freedom of speech, or of the press; or the right of the people peaceably to assemble, and to petition the Government for a redress of grievances.

AMENDMENT III [1791]

No Soldier shall, in time of peace be quartered in any house, without the consent of the Owner, nor in time of war, but in a manner to be prescribed by law.

AMENDMENT IV [1791]

The right of the people to be secure in their persons, houses, papers, and effects, against unreasonable searches and seizures, shall not be violated, and no Warrants shall issue, but upon probable cause, supported by Oath or affirmation, and particularly describing the place to be searched, and the persons or things to be seized.

AMENDMENT V [1791]

No person shall be held to answer for a capital, or otherwise infamous crime, unless on a presentment or indictment of a Grand Jury, except in cases arising in the land or naval forces, or in the Militia, when in actual service in time of War or public danger; nor shall any person be subject for the same offense to be twice put in jeopardy of life or limb; nor shall be compelled in any criminal case to be a witness against himself, nor be deprived of life, liberty, or property, without due process of law; nor shall private property be taken for public use, without just compensation.

AMENDMENT VIII [1791]

Excessive bail shall not be required, nor excessive fines imposed, nor cruel and unusual punishments inflicted.

AMENDMENT IX [1791]

The enumeration in the Constitution, of certain rights, shall not be construed to deny or disparage others retained by the people.

AMENDMENT XIII [1865]

Section 1. Neither slavery nor involuntary servitude, except as a punishment for crime whereof the party shall have been duly convicted, shall exist within the United States, or any place subject to their jurisdiction.

Section 2. Congress shall have power to enforce this article by appropriate legislation.

AMENDMENT XIV [1868]

Section 1. All persons born or naturalized in the United States, and subject to the jurisdiction thereof, are citizens of the United States and of the State wherein they reside. No State shall make or enforce any law which shall abridge the privileges or immunities of citizens of the United States; nor shall any State deprive any person of life, liberty, or property, without due process of law; nor deny to any person within its jurisdiction the equal protection of the laws.

Section 5. The Congress shall have power to enforce, by appropriate legislation, the provisions of this article.

AMENDMENT XV [1870]

Section 1. The right of citizens of the United States to vote shall not be denied or abridged by the United States or by any State on account of race, color, or previous condition of servitude.

Section 2. The Congress shall have power to enforce this article by appropriate legislation.

Appendix B

Selected Provisions of the Basic Law for the Federal Republic of Germany of May 23, 1949

PREAMBLE

Conscious of their responsibility before God and man,

Inspired by the determination to promote world peace as an equal partner in a united Europe, the German people, in the exercise of their constituent power, have adopted this Basic Law.

Germans in the Länder of Baden-Württemberg, Bavaria, Berlin, Brandenburg, Bremen, Hamburg, Hesse, Lower Saxony, Mecklenburg-Western Pomerania, North Rhine-Westphalia, Rhineland-Palatinate, Saarland, Saxony, Saxony-Anhalt, Schleswig-Holstein and Thuringia have achieved the unity and freedom of Germany in free self-determination. This Basic Law thus applies to the entire German people.

I. BASIC RIGHTS

Article 1 [Human dignity]

(1) Human dignity shall be inviolable. To respect and protect it shall be the duty of all state authority.

(2) The German people therefore acknowledge inviolable and inalienable human rights as the basis of every community, of peace and of justice in the world.

(3) The following basic rights shall bind the legislature, the executive, and the judiciary as directly applicable law.

Article 2 [Personal freedoms]

(1) Every person shall have the right to free development of his personality insofar as he does not violate the rights of others or offend against the constitutional order or the moral law.

(2) Every person shall have the right to life and physical integrity. Freedom of the person shall be inviolable. These rights may be interfered with only pursuant to a law.

Article 3 [Equality before the law]

(1) All persons shall be equal before the law.

(2) Men and women shall have equal rights. The state shall promote the actual implementation of equal rights for women and men and take steps to eliminate disadvantages that now exist.

(3) No person shall be favored or disfavored because of sex, parentage, race, language, homeland and origin, faith, or religious or political opinions. No person shall be disfavored because of disability.

Article 4 [Freedom of faith, conscience, and creed]

(1) Freedom of faith and of conscience, and freedom to profess a religious or philosophical creed [*Weltanschauung*], shall be inviolable.

(2) The undisturbed practice of religion shall be guaranteed.

(3) No person shall be compelled against his conscience to render military service involving the use of arms. Details shall be regulated by a federal law.

Article 5 [Freedom of expression]

(1) Every person shall have the right freely to express and disseminate his opinions in speech, writing, and pictures and to inform himself without hindrance from generally accessible sources. Freedom of the press and freedom of reporting by means of broadcasts and films shall be guaranteed. There shall be no censorship.

(2) These rights shall find their limits in the provisions of general laws, in provisions for the protection of young persons, and in the right to personal honor.

(3) Art and scholarship, research, and teaching shall be free. The freedom of teaching shall not release any person from allegiance to the constitution.

Article 6 [Marriage and the family; children born outside of marriage]

(1) Marriage and the family shall enjoy the special protection of the state.

(2) The care and upbringing of children is the natural right of parents and a duty primarily incumbent upon them. The state shall watch over them in the performance of this duty.

(3) Children may be separated from their families against the will of their parents or guardians only pursuant to a law, and only if the parents or guardians fail in their duties or the children are otherwise in danger of serious neglect.

(4) Every mother shall be entitled to the protection and care of the community.

(5) Children born outside of marriage shall be provided by legislation with the same opportunities for physical and mental development and for their position in society as are enjoyed by those born within marriage.

Article 7 [School education]

(1) The entire school system shall be under the supervision of the state.

(2) Parents and guardians shall have the right to decide whether children shall receive religious instruction.

(3) Religious instruction shall form part of the regular curriculum in state schools, with the exception of non-denominational schools. Without prejudice to the state's right of supervision, religious instruction shall be given in accordance with the tenets of the religious community concerned. Teachers may not be obliged against their will to give religious instruction.

Article 8 [Freedom of assembly]

(1) All Germans shall have the right to assemble peacefully and unarmed without prior notification or permission.

(2) In the case of outdoor assemblies, this right may be restricted by or pursuant to a law.

Article 9 [Freedom of association]

(1) All Germans shall have the right to form corporations and other associations.

(2) Associations whose aims or activities contravene the criminal laws, or that are directed against the constitutional order or the concept of international understanding, shall be prohibited.

(3) The right to form associations to safeguard and improve working and economic conditions shall be guaranteed to every individual and to every occupation or profession. Agreements that restrict or seek to impair this right shall be null and void; measures directed to this end shall be unlawful. Measures taken pursuant to Article 12a, to paragraphs (2) and (3) of Article 35, to paragraph (4) of Article 87a, or to Article 91 may not be directed against industrial disputes engaged in by associations within the meaning of the first sentence of this paragraph in order to safeguard and improve working and economic conditions.

Article 10 [Privacy of correspondence, posts and telecommunications]

(1) The privacy of correspondence, posts and telecommunications shall be inviolable.

(2) Restrictions may be ordered only pursuant to a law. If the restriction serves to protect the free democratic basic order or the existence or security of the Federation or of a Land, the law may provide that the person affected shall not be informed of the restriction and that recourse to the courts shall be replaced by a review of the case by agencies and auxiliary agencies appointed by the legislature.

Article 11 [Freedom of movement]

(1) All Germans shall have the right to move freely throughout the federal territory.

(2) This right may be restricted only by or pursuant to a law, and only in cases in which the absence of adequate means of support would result in a particular burden for the community, or in which such restriction is necessary to avert an imminent danger to the existence or the free democratic basic order of the Federation or of a Land, to combat the danger of an epidemic, to respond to a grave accidents or natural disaster, to protect young persons from serious neglect, or to prevent crime.

Article 12 [Occupational freedom, prohibition of forced labor]

(1) All Germans shall have the right freely to choose their occupation or profession, their place of work, and their place of train-

ing. The practice of an occupation or profession may be regulated by or pursuant to a law.

(2) No person may be required to perform work of a particular kind except within the framework of a traditional duty of community service that applies generally and equally to all.

(3) Forced labor may be imposed only on persons deprived of their liberty by the judgment of a court.

Article 13 [Inviolability of the home]

(1) The home is inviolable.

(2) Searches may be authorized only by a judge or, when time is of the essence, by other authorities designated by the laws, and may be carried out only in the manner therein prescribed.

(7) Interferences and restrictions shall otherwise only be permissible to avert a danger to the public or to the life of an individual, or, pursuant to a law, to confront an acute danger to public safety and order, in particular to relieve a housing shortage, to combat the danger of an epidemic, or to protect young persons at risk.

Article 14 [Property, inheritance, expropriation]

(1) Property and the right of inheritance shall be guaranteed. Their content and limits shall be defined by the laws.

(2) Property entails obligations. Its use shall also serve the public good.

(3) Expropriation shall only be permissible for the public good. It may only be ordered by or pursuant to a law that determines the nature and extent of compensation. Such compensation shall be determined by establishing an equitable balance between the public interest and the interests of those affected. In case of dispute respecting the amount of compensation, recourse may be had to the ordinary courts.

Article 15 [Socialization]

Land, natural resources, and means of production may for the purpose of socialization be transferred to public ownership or other forms of public enterprise by a law that determines the nature and extent of compensation. With respect to such compensation the third and fourth sentences of paragraph (3) of Article 14 shall apply mutatis mutandis.

Article 17 [Right of petition]

Every person shall have the right individually or jointly with others to address written requests or complaints to competent authorities and to the legislature.

Article 17a [Restriction of certain basic rights by laws respecting defense and alternative service]

(1) Laws respecting military and alternative service may provide that the basic right of members of the Armed Forces and of alternative service freely to express and disseminate their opinions in speech, writing, and pictures (first clause of paragraph (1) of Article 5), the basic right of assembly (Article 8), and the right of petition (Article 17) insofar as it permits the submission of requests or complaints jointly with others, be restricted during their period of military or alternative service.

(2) Laws respecting defense, including protection of the civilian population, may provide for restriction of the basic rights of freedom of movement (Article 11) and inviolability of the home (Article 13).

Article 18 [Forfeiture of basic rights]

Whoever abuses the freedom of expression, in particular the freedom of the press (paragraph (1) of Article 5), the freedom of teaching (paragraph (3) of Article 5), the freedom of assembly (Article 8), the freedom of association (Article 9), the privacy of correspondence, posts and telecommunications (Article 10), the rights of property (Article 14), or the right of asylum (Article 16a) in order to combat the free democratic basic order shall forfeit these basic rights. This forfeiture and its extent shall be declared by the Federal Constitutional Court.

Article 19 [Restriction of basic rights]

(1) Insofar as, under this Basic Law, a basic right may be restricted by or pursuant to a law, such law must apply generally and not merely to a single case. In addition, the law must specify the basic right affected and the Article in which it appears.

(2) In no case may the essence of a basic right be affected.

(3) The basic rights shall also apply to domestic artificial persons to the extent that the nature of such rights permits.

(4) Should any person's rights be violated by public authority, he may have recourse to the courts. If no other jurisdiction has been

established, recourse shall be to the ordinary courts. The second sentence of paragraph (2) of Article 10 shall not be affected by this paragraph.

II. THE FEDERATION AND THE LÄNDER

Article 20 [Basic institutional principles; defense of the constitutional order]

(1) The Federal Republic of Germany is a democratic and social federal state.

(2) All state authority is derived from the people. It shall be exercised by the people through elections and other votes and through specific legislative, executive, and judicial bodies.

(3) The legislature shall be bound by the constitutional order, the executive and the judiciary by law and justice.

(4) All Germans shall have the right to resist any person seeking to abolish this constitutional order, if no other remedy is available.

Article 21 [Political parties]

(1) Political parties shall participate in the formation of the political will of the people. They may be freely established. Their internal organization must conform to democratic principles. They must publicly account for their assets and for the sources and use of their funds.

(2) Parties that, by reason of their aims or the behavior of their adherents, seek to undermine or abolish the free democratic basic order or to endanger the existence of the Federal Republic of Germany shall be unconstitutional. The Federal Constitutional Court shall rule on the question of unconstitutionality.

(3) Details shall be regulated by federal laws.

Article 22 [The flag]

The federal flag shall be black, red and gold.

Article 79 [Amendment of the Basic Law]

(1) This Basic Law can be amended only by a law expressly amending or supplementing its text. In the case of an international treaty respecting a peace settlement, the preparation of a peace settlement, or the phasing out of an occupation regime, or designed to promote the defense of the Federal Republic, it shall be sufficient,

for the purpose of making clear that the provisions of this Basic Law do not preclude the conclusion and entry into force of the treaty, to add language to the Basic Law that merely makes this clarification.

(2) Any such law shall be carried by two thirds of the Members of the Bundestag and two thirds of the votes of the Bundesrat.

(3) Amendments to this Basic Law affecting the division of the Federation into Länder, their participation on principle in the legislative process, or the principles laid down in Articles 1 and 20 shall be inadmissible.

NOTE

As amended up to July 16, 1998. Translation by Christian Tomuschat (Berlin) and David Currie (Chicago). Published by the Press and Information Office of the Federal Republic of Germany. Translations of the Basic Law used in this book mainly rely on this translation.

Selected Bibliography

BADURA, PETER. *Generalprävention und Würde des Menschen*, 19 JURISTEN-
ZEITUNG 337 (1964).

BAKER, C. EDWIN. HUMAN LIBERTY AND FREEDOM OF SPEECH (1984).

BICKEL, ALEXANDER. THE LEAST DANGEROUS BRANCH (1962).

Black, Hugo L. *The Bill of Rights*, 35 N.Y. U. L. REV. 865 (1960).

Bloustein, Edward J. *Privacy as an Aspect of Human Dignity: An Answer
to Dean Prosser*, 39 N.Y. U. L. REV. 962 (1964).

BORK, ROBERT. THE TEMPTATION OF AMERICA (1990).

Brandeis, Louis D., & Samuel D. Warren. *The Right to Privacy*, 4 HARV. L.
REV. 193 (1890).

Brennan, William J., Jr. *The Constitution of the United States: Contemporary Ratification*, 19 U. C. DAVIS L. REV. 2 (1985).

Brugger, Winfried. Der moderne Verfassungsstaat. Rechtsvergleichunge
Bemerkungen aus Sicht der amerikanischen und der deutschen
Verfassung (1999) (on file with author).

Brugger, Winfried. *Legal Interpretation, Schools of Jurisprudence, and
Anthropology: Some Remarks from a German Point of View*, 42 AM.
J. COMP. L. 395 (1994).

CURRIE, DAVID P. THE CONSTITUTION OF THE FEDERAL REPUBLIC OF GERMANY
(1994).

Degenhart, Christoph. *Das allgemeine Persönlichkeitsrecht*, 5 JURISTISCHE
SCHULUNG 361 (1992).

Eberle, Edward J. *Roger Williams' Gift: Religious Freedom in America*, 4 ROGER WILLIAMS U. L. REV. 425 (1999).

Eberle, Edward J. *Human Dignity, Privacy, and Personality in German and American Constitutional Law*, 1997 UTAH L. REV. 963.

Eberle, Edward J. *Public Discourse in Contemporary Germany*, 1997 CASE W. RES. L. REV. 797.

Eberle, Edward J. *Hate Speech, Offensive Speech, and Public Discourse in America*, 29 WAKE FOREST L. REV. 1135 (1994).

Ewald, William. *Comparative Jurisprudence (1): What Was It Like to Try a Rat?* 143 U. PA. L. REV. 1889 (1995).

Favoreu, Louis. *The Constitutional Council and Parliament in France*, in CONSTITUTIONAL REVIEW AND LEGISLATION: AN INTERNATIONAL COMPARISON 81 (C. Landfried ed., 1988).

Fletcher, George P. *Human Dignity as a Constitutional Value*, 1984 U. W. ONTARIO L. REV. 171.

Glaeser, Walter Schmitt. *Die Meinungsfreiheit in der Rechtsprechung des Bundesverfassungsrerichts (1. Teil)*, 97 ARCHIV DES ÖFFENTLICHEN RECHTS 60 (1972).

GLENDON, MARY ANN. ABORTION AND DIVORCE IN WESTERN LAW (1987).

GLENDON, MARY ANN. RIGHTS TALK: THE IMPOVERISHMENT OF POLITICAL DISCOURSE (1991).

Goundalakis, Georgios. *Freiräume und Grenzen politischer Karikatur und Satire*, 13 NEUE JURISTISCHE WOCHENSCHRIFT 809 (1995).

Grimm, Dieter. *Die Meinungsfreiheit in der Rechtsprechung des Bundesverfassungsrericht*, 48 NEUE JURISTISCHE WOCHENSCHRIFT 1697 (1995).

Herdegen, Gerhard. *Kommentar zum "Soldaten sind Mörder,"* 45 NEUE JURISTISCHE WOCHENSCHRIFT 2933 (1994).

Jefferson, Thomas. *Inaugural Address, in* THE LIFE AND SELECTED WRITINGS OF THOMAS JEFFERSON 323 (Adrienne Koch & William Peden, eds. 1944).

KANT, IMMANUEL. FOUNDATIONS OF THE METAPHYSICS OF MORALS (L. W. Beck trans., 2d ed. 1959).

KIRCHHOF, PAUL, & DONALD P. KOMMERS, eds. GERMANY AND ITS BASIC LAW: PAST, PRESENT AND FUTURE—A GERMAN–AMERICAN SYMPOSIUM (1993).

KOMMENTAR ZUM GRUNDGESETZ FÜR DIE BUNDESREPUBLIK DEUTCHLAND (Rudolf Wasserman ed., 2d ed. 1989).

KOMMERS, DONALD P. THE CONSTITUTIONAL JURISPRUDENCE OF THE FEDERAL REPUBLIC OF GERMANY (1989).

Kommers, Donald P. *The Constitutional Law of Abortion in Germany: Should Americans Pay Attention?* 10 J. CONTEMP. HEALTH L. & POL'Y. 1 (1994).

Kommers, Donald P. *The Jurisprudence of Free Speech in the United States and the Federal Republic of Germany*, 53 S. CAL. L. REV. 657 (1980).

Krause, Harry D. *The Right to Privacy in Germany—Pointers for American Legislation?* 1965 DUKE L. J. 481.

Kriele, Martin. *Ehrenschutz und Meinungsfreiheit*, 30 NEUE JURISTISCHE WOCHENSCHRIFT 1897 (1994).

Lawrence, Charles R., III. *If He Hollers Let Him Go: Regulating Racist Speech on Campus*, 1990 DUKE L. J. 431.

MADISON, JAMES, ALEXANDER HAMILTON, & JOHN JAY. THE FEDERALIST PAPERS (Isaac Krammick ed., Penguin Books 1987) (1788).

Matsuda, Mari J. *Public Response to Racist Speech: Considering the Victim's Story*, 87 MICH. L. REV. 2320 (1989).

MEIKLEJOHN, ALEXANDER. POLITICAL FREEDOM (1960).

Mintz, Jonathan B. *The Remains of Privacy's Disclosure Tort: An Exploration of the Private Domain*, 55 MD. L. REV. 425 (1996).

Neuman, Gerald L. *Casey in the Mirror: Abortion, Abuse and the Right to Protection in the United States and Germany*, 43 AM. J. COMP. L. 273 (1995).

Pieroth, Bodo. *An Essay on an Export from the United States: Constitutional Doctrine and Ideas*, 9 ST. LOUIS U. PUB. L. REV. 311 (1990).

PIEROTH, BODO, & BERNHARD SCHLINK. GRUNDRECHTE STAATSRECHT II (10th ed. 1994).

Post, Robert C. *The Constitutional Concept of Public Discourse: Outrageous Opinion, Democratic Deliberation, and Hustler Magazine v. Falwell*, 103 HARV. L. REV. 606 (1990).

Post, Robert C. *Racist Speech, Democracy and the First Amendment*, 32 WM. & MARY L. REV. 267 (1991).

Pound, Roscoe. *The Interests of Personality*, 28 HARV. L. REV. 343 (1915).

Quint, Peter E. *The Comparative Law of Flag Desecration: The United States and the Federal Republic of Germany*, 15 HASTINGS INT'L. AND COMP. L. REV. 613 (1992).

Quint, Peter E. *Free Speech and Private Law in German Constitutional Theory*, 48 MD. L. REV. 247 (1989).

REDISH, MARTIN H. FREEDOM OF EXPRESSION: A CRITICAL ANALYSIS (1984).

Schlink, Bernhard. *German Constitutional Culture in Transition*, 14 CARDOZO L. REV. 711 (1993).

Schwartz, Paul. *The Computer in German and American Constitutional Law: Towards an American Right of Informational Self-Determination*, 37 AM. J. COMP. L. 675 (1989).

Stein, Eric. *History Against Free Speech: The New German Law Against the "'Auschwitz'—And Other— 'Lies,'"* 85 MICH. L. REV. 277 (1986).

STONE, GEOFFREY R., LOUIS M. SEIDMAN, CASS R. SUNSTEIN, & MARK V. TUSHNET. CONSTITUTIONAL LAW (3d ed. 1996).

Zimmerman, Reinhard. *An Introduction to German Legal Culture, in* INTRODUCTION TO GERMAN LAW 1 (Werner F. Ebke & Matthew W. Finkin, eds. 1996).

Index

ABOUT THE AUTHOR

Edward J. Eberle is Professor of Law at Roger Williams University School of Law, Bristol, RI, and Series Editor of Praeger's Issues in Comparative Public Law.